Computer-Mediated Communication

Human-to-Human Communication Across the Internet

Susan B. Barnes
Rochester Institute of Technology

Boston   New York   San Francisco
Mexico City   Montreal   Toronto   London   Madrid   Munich   Paris
Hong Kong   Singapore   Tokyo   Cape Town   Sydney

Executive Editor: Karon Bowers
Vice President, Editor-in-Chief: Karen Hanson
Editorial Assistant: Jennifer Trebby
Marketing Manager: *Mandee Eckersley*
Production Assistant: Marissa Falco
Electronic Composition: Publishers' Design and Production Services, Inc.
Composition and Prepress Buyer: Linda Cox
Manufacturing Buyer: JoAnne Sweeney
Cover Administrator: Kristina Mose-Libon

For related titles and support materials, visit our online catalog at www.ablongman.com

Library of Congress Cataloging-in-Publication Data

Barnes, Susan B.
    Computer-mediated communication: human to human communication across the Internet / Susan B. Barnes.
    p. cm.
    Includes bibliographical references and index.
    ISBN 0-205-32145-3 (pbk.)
    1. Internet—Social aspects. 2. Telematics. 3. Communication and technology. I. Title.
HM851 .B37 2002
303.48'33—dc21

                                                                    2002019462

Printed in the United States of America

10 9 8 7 6 5 4 3 2 1   RRD-IN   07 06 05 04 03 02

CONTENTS

PREFACE

Introduction

At the present time, an estimated 153.84 million Americans or more operate computers.* Young children grow up using computers at home and in school. Teenagers play online games and exchange instant messages with their friends. Students and teachers create their own personal Web pages. Organizations depend on electronic mail as a primary communication medium and electronic shopping is on the rise. From work to play, computer-mediated communication (CMC) is an important aspect of our daily lives.

Most students entering college are experienced computer users. They have used computers to write papers and research reports. In the book *Extra Life: Coming of Age in Cyberspace*, journalist David S. Bennahum explored his personal experiences growing up with computers. He first used computers to play games and, in school, he learned networking skills. Bennahum describes the computer room in his high school as follows:

> The computer room in a primitive sense was a forerunner of the Internet. When we were logged in each of our accounts appeared as homes that together made a town. And it was up to us to run the place, to be good citizens (pp. 122–123).

Early studies of the Internet described it as a "virtual community" in which people shared experiences and expertise. A recent Internet study showed that a growing number of Americans are using their computers as a communication medium. Internet communication has introduced profound social changes because it alters the ways in which people communicate with each other. Today, people use the Internet to seek health information, find new jobs, do online stock trading, and download music. Besides seeking information, people build and maintain social relationships through the Internet. E-mail allows parents to keep in touch with their children away at college. Students socialize on the Internet by exchanging instant messages with their friends, playing online games, and talking to people in chat rooms. On a larger level, the Internet could help citizens build a new society because it brings people together in a "global village."

The first step in the process of global citizenship is learning how to use CMC as an effective method for human communication. Behind all Internet communication is people, which is why this book primarily utilizes an interpersonal and human communication approach to the study of CMC. However, as computer technology advances, it will become increasingly difficult to distinguish between communicating with a person and communicating with a software program, because intelligent agent programs are being written to simulate human conversational styles. To prepare students for the present and future use of CMC, this book also includes sections on approaches to human–computer interaction (HCI).

*Source: Nau, Inc./Nielsen Rating Service, November 2000

Presently, CMC and HCI are blending together. Human-centered computer design is based on human behavior and interpersonal communication. For example, the original design of the graphical user interface was based on human styles of learning. As interface design evolves, it is incorporating conversational exchanges written by programmers and agent software. Moreover, voice recognition software enables users to speak rather than type messages into a computer. Computer interaction is increasingly becoming closer to a human conversation. Human-centered approaches to computing already influence the ways in which people interact with their computers. For instance, Reeves and Nass (1996) have observed that people treat computers as other people rather than as machines. As a result, understanding CMC involves examining how people interact both with their communication tools and each other.

In contrast to mass media, which delivers information and entertainment into the home, the Internet extends the space of individual and cultural activities. The Internet both reinforces and extends social networks because it interconnects individuals in a global dialog. Today's student is truly a citizen of the Internet age. However, being a good citizen also requires understanding technology terms, concepts, and social issues related to global communication. Beginning with electronic mail and progressing to the global village, this book will explain Internet terms and introduce you to theories associated with CMC in the communication discipline. Additionally, we will explore some social issues and challenges facing global citizens.

Computer-Mediated Communication: Human to Human Communication Across the Internet has the following four major sections: Part I: Overview of Computer-Mediated Communication (CMC), Part II: Interacting through CMC, Part III: CMC and Group Communication, and Part IV: CMC and Society. Each section was written to further develop your understanding of how CMC is used in contemporary society and to provide you with different ways of thinking about how CMC is used to build interpersonal relationships, develop group communication, and support public communication both locally and globally. There is also a Web site available at: www.ablongman.com/barnes.

REFERENCES

Bennahum, D. S. (1998). *Extra life: Coming of age in cyberspace*. New York: Basic Books.

Howard, P., Raine, L., & Jones, S. (2000, Oct. 2). *The Internet in everyday life: The first decade of a diffusing technology* [Online] 33 pp. Available: http://www.pewinternet.org (May 29, 2001).

Reeves, B., & Nass, C. (1996). *The media equation: How people treat computers, television, and new media like real people and places*. Stanford, CA: CSLI Publications, Cambridge University Press.

Statistical Abstract of the U.S.: No. 282 (Feb., 1998). U.S. National Center for Educational Statistics: Internet Access in public schools brief February, 1998.

ACKNOWLEDGEMENTS

Many people have contributed to the creation of this book. Over the years, I have collected hundreds of e-mail messages and student observations about their Internet use. All of these people deserve recognition. However, their privacy also needs to be respected. Names and identifying information have been removed from examples of private e-mail and discussion groups. In some cases, the examples are composites of several different messages. When material is used from public academic lists, authors are properly cited for their ideas.

Computer-mediated communication is a new topic that has been introduced into communication departments. My own understanding of the topic has been greatly influenced by the work of Gerald M. Phillips. Phillips's astute observations about online culture have shaped my understanding about how people communicate through the Internet. His concepts are incorporated throughout this book, and I hope his ideas inspire current Internet users as much as they have stimulated me.

Several grants help to support this research. A grant from Fordham's Donald A. Mc-Gannon Center enabled me to research the topics of cookies, intelligent agents, and software robots. James Capo, the program director, deserves recognition for his support of this project. Additionally, Everett Parker needs to be acknowledged for his work with me on community networks. Fordham Deans Nancy Bush and Robert Himmelberg also provided support through Ames grants, which funded my research assistants, whom I would like to thank, especially Grace Ekanem and Ge Jin (Jingle).

Personal thanks go to Nancy Phillips, Wendy Snetsinger, Marie Radford, Robert Rubyan, Frank Dance, and Lance Strate, for providing support and examples for this book. Members of the Media Ecology Discussion List and Media Ecology Association also provided provocative discussions about the nature of CMC and the Internet, especially Gary Gumpert and Susan Drucker. Additionally, I need to thank my husband Roger Berger for his understanding and support during the writing of this book.

Special thanks to my editor Karon Bowers who was very supportive throughout this project. Developing a book on a new topic is always difficult, and this book would not have been completed without her continuing guidance and encouragement. Jennifer Trebby, Marissa Falco, and the editorial and production staff at Allyn & Bacon also need to be acknowledged for their help on this project.

No textbook is ever written without the guidance of outside reviewers. The following reviewers contributed to this project:

Dudley D. Cahn, SUNY at New Paltz;
Lynne Kelly, University of Hartford;
Judith Yaross Lee, Ohio University;
Tony Lentz, Penn State University; and
Timothy Rumbough, Bloomsburg University;
Craig Scott, University of Texas-Austin; and
Leonard Shedletsky, University of Southern Maine.

PART I

Overview of Computer-Mediated Communication

Computer-mediated communication (CMC) has evolved from text-based interaction to using streaming video as a method of interpersonal communication. As technology develops, the concept of CMC continually expands. Although the technology changes, interactivity remains a key reason why Internet communication supports interpersonal communication. Behind all Internet communication is people communicating with others, either directly or through software design. Internet interactivity occurs as interpersonal interactivity, informational interactivity, and human–computer interaction (HCI).

Today, information interactivity transpires through the Web, which adds a graphical interface to the Internet. The Web combines elements of informational interactivity with interpersonal interactivity because increasingly older CMC genres such as chat and discussion groups are being integrated into Web sites. HCI is the way people interact with their computers, and it is based on human communication and behavior patterns. Programmers design interfaces to be conversational. Moreover, computers are such a new technology that people often react to computers in the same way they react to other people. With the introduction of intelligent-agent software and voice recognition programs, computer interaction is becoming even closer to human conversation. In the future, it will become increasingly difficult to distinguish between interpersonal interactivity and HCI on the Internet.

Part I, "Overview of Computer-Mediated Communication," provides a foundational description of CMC research and its characteristics. Both early and contemporary research approaches are covered to provide a foundation for thinking about CMC and its relationship to communication principles. Another aspect of computer-based communication is the way people interact with their computers. HCI concepts are discussed in Chapter 3. The fastest-growing area of the Internet, the World Wide Web, is covered in Chapter 4. In addition to accessing information, people are increasingly using the Web as a method of interpersonal communication. Part I explains all three types of Internet interactivity: interpersonal, HCI, and informational.

1 Introduction to Computer-Mediated Communication

Chapter Overview

It is difficult to imagine living in a world without the Internet. Over the past thirty years, the Internet has changed the way people work, learn, play, and communicate. Computer-mediated communication (CMC) has evolved from text-based interaction to graphical virtual environments. Although the technology keeps advancing, conversation styles used on the Internet today are based on earlier text-based interactions. For instance, language conventions used in multi-user dungeon (MUD) games and Internet relay chat (IRC) are now used by teenagers who share instant messages. To fully understand the nature of CMC, students need to explore past and present online genres, while keeping an eye out for future developments.

Since the introduction of the Internet, computer-mediated communication has developed a variety of genres. These include electronic mail, discussion groups, chat, MUDs, instant messenger (IM), and the World Wide Web (Web). Today, these genres keep expanding with the integration of computers and wireless technologies. This chapter introduces students to

- Definition of CMC
- Informatics and conferencing
- Different CMC genres
- The relationship between CMC and mass media
- Interpersonal mediated communication
- Early research theories about CMC

Computer-Mediated Communication

From older CMC genres, newer ones emerge. For instance, IRC has been incorporated into Web-based chat. Instead of logging on and typing information to join an Internet channel, people now click on a button with the mouse. Although the tools are different, the process of chatting with others remains the same. Similarly, discussion lists have been incorporated into Web design. Web sites, such as that of the *New York Times*, include areas for reader discussions. Many of you are already familiar with the ways in which the Web has incorporated a variety of CMC capabilities.

CMC Definition

Most students come to college with CMC experience, such as using electronic mail (e-mail), chat, or instant messenger. Originally, **computer-mediated communication** was defined as a form of electronic written communication. However, as networking tools advanced, the category of CMC expanded to include new software developments, such as instant messenger and the Web. Today, the term *computer-mediated communication* (CMC) is used to refer to a wide range of technologies that facilitate both human communication and the interactive sharing of information through computer networks, including e-mail, discussion groups, newsgroups, chat, instant messages, and Web pages.

The driving force behind current changes in communication technologies is the **Internet**. The Internet is generally defined as a "network of networks" because it consists of many smaller computer networks that are interconnected to each other. Individuals exchange messages and share information through the Internet in a variety of ways. For example, people send e-mail messages, engage in real-time conversations through chat, participate in discussion lists, play games, and send instant messages to their friends. Each of these Internet genres creates its own unique social environment. (Figure 1.1). For instance, instant messages and chat are used for fun and recreation; in contrast, discussion lists are used to talk about serious business, political, and academic topics.

Informatics and Conferencing

CMC can be divided into the two major categories of **informatics** and **conferencing**. Informatics involves using the computer as an information manager and a system for the electronic storage and retrieval of digital data. The Web, for instance, falls into this category. The type of digital information distributed through informatics includes simple text, sound files, graphics, and movies. Advanced computer interfaces add visual elements and sophisticated computer graphics to information exchanges. As a result, visual communication is now playing a larger role in CMC interaction. At present, informatics is used in educational, organizational, recreational, and commercial contexts.

In contrast to informatics, conferencing occurs when the computer is used to connect people. For instance, computers support communication among students, between students and teachers, among employees, between family members, and between producers and consumers of products or services. Much of this communication occurs through the exchange of electronic mail. Additionally, programs such as discussion lists, bulletin board systems (BBS), and newsgroups support conferencing. Online groups are generally organized to discuss a specific topic of interest. People from around the world can read and post messages to electronic discussion groups and engage in a global conversation. CMC genres such as MUDs, chat, and instant messenger also foster social discourse and interaction. Although CMC can be used for both informatics and conferencing, electronic mail is the most popular Internet genre.

CMC Genres

Electronic mail or e-mail was an unexpected outcome of early networking systems. It originally developed during the government-sponsored Advanced Research Projects Agency

FIGURE 1.1   Internet Genres

Type of Genre	*Description*
Simple E-mail exchange	Similar to a phone call, two people exchange messages.
Mailing list/ discussion group	A consistent multiple-user interaction that occurs over a long period of time. Core group members may remain the same as others join and leave the list. Over time, members can begin to bond as they share a sense of communal space.
Bulletin boards/ forums/newsgroups	A more complicated social interaction with an increased sense of space.
Real-time chat/IRC chat	Conversations are more fluid and overlapping because they occur in close to real time. A sense of being in the same room with other people is created. The "room" metaphor makes it easier to perceive a sense of space.
Instant messenger	Short conversations that occur in close to real time. IMs are often exchanged between people who know each other through face-to-face situations, such as family members and friends.
Multiplayer games/ MUDs/MOOs	The use of characters and the structure of these games fosters complex group dynamics and adds a stronger element of fantasy to online interactions.
Web pages	In contrast to the other genres that are text-only interactions, Web pages add pictures, graphics, sounds, and movies to the Internet experience. Many Web pages are designed to present rather than exchange information. However, discussion and chat features can be incorporated into page designs.

Network (ARPANET) experiment in the early 1970s. Prior to the development of the ARPANET, **packet switching** and the establishment of communication protocols made possible computer-based communication. Packet switching enables messages to be transmitted as discrete packets of information and sent over any available route through the network. When all of the packets arrive at their destination, they are reassembled as a complete message. With the invention of the ARPANET and packet switching, people could send messages to remote computers and share computing resources.

Although the sharing of resources was a goal of the ARPANET creators, to their surprise the most popular feature of the system was e-mail. Computer researchers began to distribute working papers and brief communications through the network. These messages could be distributed widely and rapidly to all sites connected to the system. With the aid of networking, computer scientists quickly formed an electronic research community. Graduate students could apprentice to professors who could offer fascinating problems and develop their skills no matter where they were physically located. Colleagues could work together based on shared interests, and physical proximity was no longer a requirement for friendships to develop. This online sharing of information and personal expertise contributed to the rapid development of computer technology in the United States. In the 1980s, increased computing power combined with the decrease in cost of personal computers made computers available to more people.

Today, over 50 percent of American households have personal computers (PC).[1] Many of these machines have modems that connect to telephone lines. Adding a modem to a personal computer transforms the PC into an *interpersonal computer*, a computer that facilitates human-to-human communication. People are now using their computers as a medium of communication to contact business associates, friends, and relatives. The following section is an overview of CMC genres, with examples of message exchanges.

Electronic Mail (E-mail)

As previously stated, **electronic mail** or **e-mail** is the most popular method of CMC. E-mail allows for one-to-one or one-to-many communication. As a result, it can be used for both human and mass communication. For example, two people can share their intimate thoughts through e-mail, or it can be used to send thousands of the same advertising messages (spam) to different people around the world. Simply stated, e-mail is used for interpersonal, small group, and mass communication (Figure 1.2).

But e-mail is no longer tied to personal computers. Advances in wireless communication enable people to access their e-mail from remote locations with portable devices. Additionally, **embedded computing**, the placement of computer chips into all types of devices, is becoming more widespread. Soon people will have ubiquitous access to their e-mail accounts because computer chips are being placed in cell phones, cars, and handheld gadgets.

Discussion Lists

Discussion list is a term commonly used to refer to **asynchronous communication**, or communication that allows participants to read messages at different times. Three common types of discussion groups are listservs, Web forums, and newsgroups. To create a listserv discussion group, someone must set up a discussion list on a networked host computer. This requires disk space to store messages and software to send and receive messages to and from list members. Host computers are usually large mainframe or minicomputers. These machines act as a clearinghouse for sending and receiving information.

Lists are either **moderated** or **unmoderated**. In moderated communication, the moderator, usually the owner of the list, reserves the right to make all decisions about the posting of messages. In highly moderated lists, the moderator will read all of the incoming messages before they are distributed to list members. However, this type of intensive monitoring is rarely necessary and it can be extremely time-consuming. As a result, most lists

[1]Source: NTIA and ESA, U.S. Department of Commerce, using U.S. Bureau of the Census *Current Population Survey* supplements.

FIGURE 1.2   Basic E-mail Message

```
Date:      February 12, 2003
From:      wizkid@hotmail.com
To:        barnes@mailservice.rit.edu
CC:
Subject:   Missed Class

Dear Professor Barnes,

I'm sorry that I missed class today. Last night, I came down with the
flu and I'm still not feeling well. I'll bring you a letter from
health services and get the class notes from another student.

See you in class on Thursday.

John
```

tend to be unmoderated. When messages are sent to unmoderated lists, they are automatically distributed to all group members.

Because of the widespread use of the Web, some sites incorporate discussion areas into their designs. The *New York Times* site, mentioned earlier in this chapter, is an example. E-mail messages are sent to the *Times*, messages are placed on the site, and both journalists and readers can interact with each other and share opinions about news topics.

Newsgroups

Newsgroup messages are stored on a news server where people post messages just like placing a message on a bulletin board. People do not need to subscribe to the newsgroup to read messages. Anyone with access to a newsreader can read and respond to posts. Newsgroups exchange messages in a format similar to that of a bulletin board, through direct information "feeds" between participating computer sites. According to information posted to the newsgroup news.lists, there are more than 58,402 different sites that send and receive newsgroups, more than 10,696 different newsgroups worldwide, and more than 20 million different users. Many universities and online service providers support newsreader software. (Figure 1.3).

Chat Rooms

Chat rooms are places where people meet online. Live **chat** is an interactive feature of computer networks because it occurs in almost-real time. Chat is exchanged between two

---

FIGURE 1.3   Newsgroup Example

```
Tues, 21 Jan 1997   12:52:25    alt.Internet    Thread 6 of 37
Lines 17      Re: Cyberporn     43 Responses
```

bobb@springnet.com Bob Brown at Spring Industries,Inc. News server
Anonymous wrote:

```
: Let's face it, he was just doing his job. Magazines see big
: profits in reporting the seedy side of cyberspace and
: corporations want to own it. How best to do it but to incite
: the Washington crowd into regulations that force out all small
: providers allowing the large ones to step in and offer fully
: censored connection for only twice the price??
```

Hey, maybe this journalist will turn out to be the Lee Iacocca
of journalism! You remember Lee, the car salesman turned Ford
exec who successfully lobbied the Nixon administration to scrap
regulations requiring life-saving passive restraints in
automobiles, only to turn around and promote his Chrysler
products for including airbags a couple of decades later. Yeah,
he was just doin' his job. We should respect that. <Smirk>

Composite message from a newsgroup discussion about pornography on the Internet.

sweethearts, or, according to Fox (1995), "it can be party-like: a roomful of people talking at once, the mingled messages reading like a script. Everybody types what they want to say and their words are immediately printed on everybody else's screen" (p. 6). Many online services make chat rooms available to their subscribers. Some people meet in the same chat room at the same time on a given day. Others move from room to room looking for interesting conversations (Figure 1.4).

Instant Messenger

A popular new trend in CMC is a feature called **instant messenger** (IM). This feature enables people who are logged onto their computers to exchange short messages in **synchronous communication**, or real time, with their friends. For example, the America Online Service allows users to create "buddy lists." When an AOL member connects to the Internet, the AOL software will identify the buddies on their list who are also online. Buddy list members can then start exchanging messages with each other. Instant messenger brings together at the same time individuals who are physically separated.

Embedded computing and wireless communication now extend instant messages beyond computers. For instance, people can now receive instant messages on their cell

---

FIGURE 1.4   Chat Example

```
<Smurfy-2> AAAAAAAAAAAAAAAAAAAAAAH, THERE
+IT GOES AGAIN!!!
<Smurgy-2> *sob* is anybody out there. . . . . .
+. . *Waaaauuuggghhhh***
<mischief> What's wrong, smurf?
<Smurfy-2> there's too many net splits that flood
+my screen
<michief> Well, as long as your personal life's
+in order . . .
<Smurfy-2> it syas all these /whois's on people
+I've never heard of . . .It logs me out and back
+on . . . My screen floods . . .
<Smurfy-2> *sob*
<michief> There, tthere smurfette.
* Smurfy-2 grabs mischeif and starts sobbing on
+his shoulder *sob*
<frank) mischief is a girl
<Smurfy-2> oops
```

Source: Herz,1995, p. 137

phones. At home or walking down the street, we can share short instant messages with our friends.

MUDs, MOOs, and Collaborative Virtual Environments

MUDs (multi-user dungeon or dimension) are online games. They use software programs that accept multiple player connections over the network. The software gives each player access to a shared database of "rooms," "exits," and objects. Players navigate the database from "inside" one of the rooms, and they see only the objects located in the particular room that they are in. Players move from room to room through the exits that connect the rooms. MUDs can be viewed as a type of **virtual reality**, or an electronically represented "place" that can be visited. The **interface** to the database is generally text based, and all commands are typed into a keyboard. Feedback is most often displayed as text on the computer screen.

There are two basic types of MUDs, adventure and social. MUDs originally started as adventure games in which players gained levels based on their success in killing computer-controlled creatures and solving puzzles. These combat-oriented games feature complex interactions between players and the computer-maintained environment. Players simultaneously connected to the MUD can talk with each other in synchronous time (Figure 1.5). As MUDs progressed, they developed into social gatherings with the ability to cre-

---

FIGURE 1.5   MUD Interaction. MUD players can interact with other players and objects. The following is an adventure game MUD interaction with a cursed or possessed object.

```
You see a shiny sword.
>Get sword
You try to pick up the sword and are surprised as it flies out of your
hands.
The sword of Damocles is hanging above you. It suddenly falls straight
down at you.
You are massacred into small fragments by the Sword of Damocles!!!
You die.
You have a strange feeling.
You hear an eerie laugh from the sword.
You see the corpse of Dalmer the lowly serf, and a word.
>Get all from corpse
Your hands pass right through the corpse. You're a ghost you schmuck!
```

Source: Shah & Romine, 1995, *Playing MUDs on the Internet*, p. 208.

ate software objects. In social MUDs, people build a new world together, rather than engage in combat.

MOOs (MUDs—object oriented) add additional objects to the database, such as rooms, exits, "things," and notes. MOOs support an embedded programming language that enables players to describe types of behavior for the objects they create. MOOs facilitate the creation of virtual reality objects that enable the user to experience different types of environments and locations. For example, users enter *LambdaMoo* through a coat closet and then exit the closet to enter the "living room." *LambdaMoo* is not a physical environment, rather, it is created through the exchange of written messages. Players interact in a perceptual space.

With the introduction of the Web, online games have added visual features that enable users to express themselves in new ways. For example, a program called the *Palace* mixes chat and MUD features together. Users are represented by visual **avatars** (an embodiment or bodily manifestation), and conversations are displayed in cartoon-like bubbles above the avatar. The term was first applied to CMC by Neil Stephenson in his science fiction novel *Snow Crash*. As computer graphic technology improves, avatars are being designed to enable users to visually express human characteristics and emotions. Avatars are used in **collaborative virtual environments** (CVEs) to represent individuals and game players. Collaborative virtual environments are three-dimensional, computer-generated virtual worlds used in games, such as *Quake* and *Doom*. Players are physically separated and come together in the visual world represented through the network.

The World Wide Web

The fastest-growing part of the Internet is the **World Wide Web,** an interconnected assortment of Internet computer servers that conform to the same network interface protocols. Because all of these systems use the same protocols, Web-based information can be read on any type of computer. The basic unit of a Web site is a page. Individual Web pages are linked together to create an entire Web site. The **home page** is the first document that users encounter when they visit a site. Home pages introduce the user to the site, inform users about the purpose of the site, state what type of information can be found on the site, and provide links to other relevant documents. Web sites run the gamut from corporate sites to personal ones (Figure 1.6).

Increasingly, the Web is being utilized as a medium of interpersonal communication. For example, **Weblogs** are a new form of personal journalism in which an individual takes on the role of columnist, reporter, analyst, and publisher to share information through the Web. Individuals use Weblogs as a form of personal expression. Adding guest lists and e-mail addresses to these sites provides methods of feedback and interaction. Similarly, **Web**

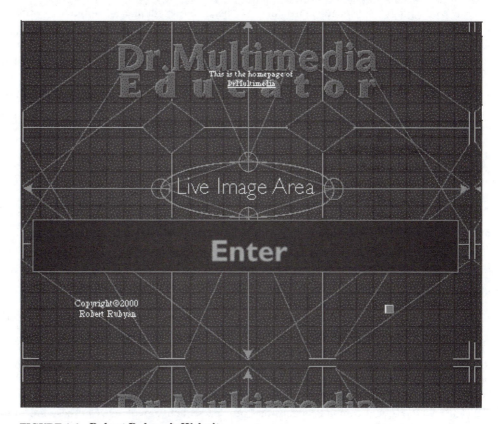

FIGURE 1.6   Robert Rubyan's Web site

© 1999, 2000, 2001, 2002 by Robert Rubyan. Used by permission.

rings connect personal home pages together into Web communities. These communities are usually organized around a topic of interest. Members of these communities often read each others sites and comment on them.

Although the Web is most often used as an informatics system to store and access information, many sites incorporate discussion and feedback features that enable Web users to respond to Web content and discuss topics of interest. As a result, many Web sites combine informatics and conferencing features.

CMC as Media Environments

CMC creates media environments by enabling people to communicate with each other. When talking about CMC, a distinction needs to be made between using computers as a technology and using them as a tool. When people use computers to perform tasks such as word processing or database retrieval, they are using them as tools. In contrast, when people are communicating with other people through a computer network, they are using the computer as a medium of communication. According to Postman (1985), while "a technology . . . is merely a machine," it "becomes a medium as it employs a symbolic code, as it finds its place in a particular social setting" (p. 86). Thus, "a medium is the social and intellectual environment a machine creates" (p. 86). When people engage in CMC, they use computers to connect to a network of other people to exchange information and ideas. This new intellectual and social environment is often called **cyberspace**, which will be discussed in the next chapter. Once an isolating productivity tool, networked computers now support the acquisition, creation, and exchange of communication between individuals, groups, and organizations. These online interactions create media environments.

CMC and Communication Models

Early communication media models focused on the one-way *delivery* of messages, rather than the interaction between people. For example, ancient Greek ideas about rhetoric and persuasion described communication as the process of effectively sending a message to a listener. In ancient times, rhetoric was a verbal activity in which a speaker attempted to persuade an audience. Aristotle identified three aspects of the persuasion process: ethos (the source), pathos (audience emotion), and logos (the message). With the introduction of electronic media, rhetorical ideas have now been applied to the analysis of mass media messages, CMC, and Web sites.

Presently, rhetorical concepts are also being used to develop computer-related technologies. **Captology** (computers as persuasive technologies) is the study of the design, analysis, and theory of persuasive computing, which is using computers to change people's attitudes and behavior. According to Fogg (1999), "captology focuses on the planned persuasive effects of computer technologies" (p. 27). These include virtual environments designed to motivate responsible drinking, CD-ROMs developed to persuade kids to eat better foods, and computer games that provide seductive experiences. These are software programs created by individuals and organizations to persuade people to alter their attitudes and behavior.

Persuasive technologies are written by programmers to seduce computer users in three basic steps. First, *enticement* grabs the user's attention and makes a promise. Second, a *relationship* is developed between the user and the program by fulfilling part of the promise and making more promises. Finally, *fulfillment* occurs when the program fulfills the promise in a memorable way. According to Khaslavsky and Shedroff (1999), an example of persuasive technology is the game *Tetris*, which gained a loyal following and followers who showed an emotional attachment to the software.

In both human and computer communication, the rhetorical process is often visualized as a linear process (Figure 1.7). Similarly, government officials and industry professionals frequently describe the Internet as linear communication. For instance, the idea of delivering information to individuals and schools through the Internet is a linear view. But, in contrast to delivering information in a single direction, the Internet is an interactive medium that supports two-way communication and feedback. **Feedback** is a process that enables communicators to regulate the flow of messages. For instance, feedback provides information to the sender about how a message is received. Feedback was added to the Shannon–Weaver model of communication, which uses the following five components to describe the communication process: *information source, transmitter, channel, receiver*, and *destination* (Figure 1.8). In human communication, feedback enables senders and receivers of messages to interactively check to see if a message has been properly understood.

Interactivity is a central feature of human communication because face-to-face communication is a two-way flow of messages. In contrast to linear models, circular models allow senders and receivers to exchange positions in the communication process. These models more clearly represent reciprocal two-way interactions. Additionally, human communication is **transactional**, because understanding the meaning of messages depends on the assumptions and foreknowledge of the receiver and the context in which the communication occurs. Communicators need to share *common fields of experience*. Schramm developed a communication model that introduced the concept of fields of experience as an essential factor in determining whether a message would be received at the destination in the way the sender intended. Without common fields of experience, such as language, common backgrounds, a common culture, and so forth, messages cannot be understood. Fields of experience significantly expand linear models of communication because they add understanding to message delivery.

FIGURE 1.7 Linear Model. A traditional linear model of communication is based on Aristotle's rhetorical concepts about public speakers creating messages to be delivered to audiences. Today, these ideas are being applied to the design of computer-related technologies such as captology.

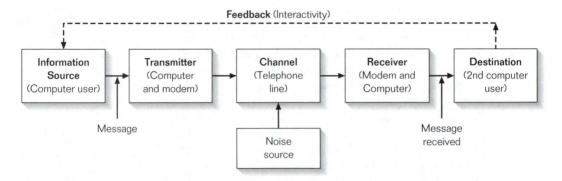

FIGURE 1-8   Linear Model with Feedback Applied to E-Mail Exchange. Mechanical models of communication introduced the idea that senders use communication channels to send messages to receivers. Feedback was later added to this model to determine whether messages had been properly received. The model was first applied to telephone communication and can easily describe the sending and receiving of e-mail messages.

Shared experience is an idea that is central to CMC because participants are often geographically dispersed. For successful CMC to occur, correspondents must work to establish commonality. When people come together from around the world, their social, personal, and linguistic experiences are very different, and these differences can interfere with proper message reception. As a result, online correspondents may have to spend more time establishing a shared experience than people talking in face-to-face situations (Figure 1.9).

Computers as a Communication Device

The idea of using computers as a communication medium was first introduced by J. C. R. Licklider and Robert Taylor. In 1968, Licklider and Taylor published an article titled "The Computer as a Communication Device." This paper provided conceptual ideas for the development of the Internet. As director of the Defense Department's Office of Information Technology, Taylor funded the ARPANET, which developed into the Internet. Several new key ideas were introduced by Licklider and Taylor. First, they realized that telecommunication networks were more than sending and receiving information from one point to another. Communicators are active participants and they play a central role in the communication process. Second, communication is a mutually reinforcing process, which involves creativity. Third, the digital computer is a flexible, interactive medium that can be used to support cooperative human communication. Finally, they introduced the idea of common frameworks, or **mental models**, to computer-based communication. They describe the role of mental models in a project meeting as follows:

> Many of the primary data the participants bring to the meeting are in undigested and uncorrelated form. To each participant, his own collections of data are interesting and important

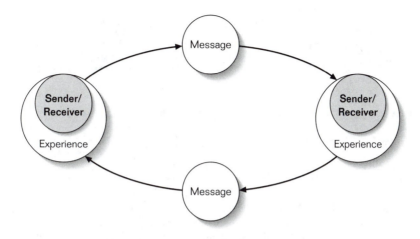

FIGURE 1.9 Circular Model with Fields of Experience. Circular models more accurately describe the two-way human communication process in which senders and receivers exchange positions. Additionally, an individuals fields of experience will influence whether the message is received as the sender intended because experience influences our understanding of messages.

in and of themselves. And they are more than files of facts and recurring reports. Thus, each individual's data are reflected in his [her] mental model. Getting his [her] colleagues to incorporate his [her] data into their models is the essence of the communications task (Licklider & Taylor, 1968, p. 23).

New communication systems need to allow individuals to communicate their individual mental models to others (Figure 1.10). Mental models are the models that people have of themselves, others, the environment, and objects, with which they interact. An individual's mental models are developed through experience, communication, and instruction. Mental models develop through conscious information processing and are built from personal interpretations of existing knowledge. For example, people create mental images of the people they correspond with through e-mail. We imagine what others look like when we haven't met them face-to-face by creating mental models.

CMC, Human, and Mass Communication

Today, the Internet enables people to communicate with each other, and it supports mediated human communication. According to Ong (1982), "In real human communication, the sender has to be not only in the sender position but also in the receiver position before he or she can send anything. . . . Human communication is never one-way. Always, it not only calls for response but is shaped in its very form and content by anticipated response"

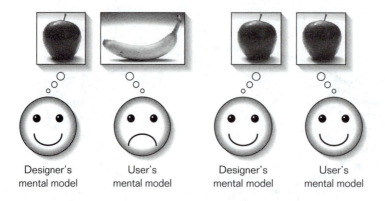

| Designer's | User's | Designer's | User's |
| mental model | mental model | mental model | mental model |

FIGURE 1.10   Mental Models. Mental models, such as a spreadsheet and home page, are incorporated into CMC and computer interface to design to make it easier for people to operate computers and conceptualized Internet interactions. They are successful when the designer and user conceptualize the same image or model.

(p. 176). In face-to-face communication, the voice is the channel for the symbolic environment of speech that is used to create spoken language. When using CMC, the computer network becomes the symbolic environment in which human communication occurs.

Used as a communication medium, the Internet supports one-to-one (e-mail), one-to-many (Web pages), many-to-one (surfing the Web for information), and many-to-many exchanges of messages (discussion lists and conferences). Consequently, the Internet can be used to carry both mass and human communication, and it is a hybrid mixture of both. The hybrid nature of the Internet makes it a difficult medium to study precisely because it incorporates aspects of both human and mass communication.

Traditionally, the communication discipline has been separated into the two distinct areas: human communication and mass communication. Each of these has its own separate theoretical backgrounds, research perspectives, and literature foundations, and so students have often regarded these as two different areas of communication studies. Now, the Internet brings them together. Before the Internet, breaking communication studies into human or mass communication was fairly easy. Communication that occurred in a face-to-face setting (interpersonal, small group, organizational, public speaking) fell into the category of human communication. In contrast, communication that was mediated (television, radio, newspapers, magazines, books) could be categorized as mass communication. For some reason, many textbooks describing human and mass communication neglected to discuss the telephone. Like the Internet, the telephone does not neatly fit into a category because it is a medium that can be used to support human communication that does not require a face-to-face setting.

Interpersonal Mediated Communication

A notable book that bridges the gap between human and mass communication is Gumpert and Cathcart's (1986) *Inter media: Interpersonal Communication in a Media World*. These authors describe **interpersonal mediated communication** as "any person-to-person interaction where a medium has been interposed to transcend the limitations of time and space" (p. 30). Media that support interpersonal mediated communication include telephones, letters, CB radios, e-mail, answering machines, and videocassettes.

Additionally, Cathcart and Gumpert (1986) describe how a medium can shape an interpersonal relationship. "For example, a handwritten or typed letter can facilitate a personal relationship over distance, but the time it takes to transport the message along with the lack of immediate feedback alters the quality and quantity of information shared" (p. 30). Messages must be written in a language and sent to another location, which takes time. The alphabet is the primary symbol system used in letter correspondence, and feedback is slower. Letter writing is a form of interpersonal mediated communication that generally occurs between two people. There are many reasons for writing letters, including staying connected with friends and family, sharing personal experiences, applying for a job, and developing a new friend (pen pals). Many of these motivations for writing letters can be applied to e-mail correspondence.

In addition to using media to maintain interpersonal relationships, researchers have observed that people can develop interpersonal relationships with media content and television performers. For example, in 1956 an article appeared in the *Journal of Psychiatry* that explored the ways in which media and media performers create the illusion of interpersonal relationships. The authors, Horton and Wohl, called this phenomenon **para-social relationships**. Para-social relationships are the seeming face-to-face relationships that develop between spectator and performer through radio, television, and the movies. These authors contend that there is "an implicit agreement between the performer and viewer that they will pretend the relationship is not mediated—that it will be carried on as though it were a face-to face-encounter" (p. 185). Thus, people can believe that they develop an interpersonal relationship with technology.

Similarly, Meyrowitz (1985) in *No Sense of Place* describes television's encroachment upon physical places such as our living rooms, dens, and bedrooms. He argues that the unidirectional mass medium of television offers the illusion of face-to-face interaction with performers and political figures. As a result, television has the psychological impact of a face-to-face encounter. Meyrowitz refers to the relationship between the audience and television performer as a **para-social interaction**, because the television set is a mediated form of communication. Despite the fact television is mediated;

> . . . viewers come to feel they "know" the people they "meet" on television in the same way they know their friends and associates. In fact, many viewers begin to believe that they know and understand a performer better than all the other viewers do. Paradoxically, the para-social performer is able to establish "intimacy with millions" (Meyrowitz, 1985, p. 119).

Meyrowitz contends that establishing the "feeling" of having an interpersonal relationship with a television performer is making *media friends*. Used as a medium of communication, the computer is different from the television set. In contrast to making media friends through the unidirectional messages transmitted through television, computer networks enable people to interact with each other one-on-one or in small groups. Making media friends through a computer network is actually establishing a connection with another individual—a real person, not a performer. These early research studies about television can provide some insight into how people currently relate to their computers, which will be discussed further in Chapter 3. The next section describes early CMC research.

Early CMC Research

During the 1950s, computers were introduced into business settings. Studies of office automation began to appear in the early 1960s. For instance, Engelbart (1963) explored how knowledge workers could use computer technology to support small group decision making. In 1978, sociologist Starr Roxanne Hiltz and computer scientist Murray Turoff wrote their pioneering book called *The Network Nation: Human Communication via Computer*. This book explored the business use of e-mail. Early studies of CMC examined the role of computer networks in organizational settings. Hiltz and Turoff (1978) state:

> The beginning user of a computer-mediated written form of communication is usually most conscious that all the kinds of cues [visual information, facial expression, eye contact, body movement, psychophysiological responses] are *missing*, and has an initial tendency to try to ascertain some of these cues by supplementing the written channel with a visit or a telephone call. As the user becomes more practiced, however, there is the development of skill peculiar to this medium and the recognition that it has many potential advantages (p. 81).

Pioneering CMC researchers argued that the elimination of visual and verbal information and direct feedback from interpersonal correspondence would make computers a "cold" medium in which people would not build emotional attachments. They believed that the plain-text characteristic of e-mail would make it difficult for people to understand situations and communicate with each other. This view became known as the **cues-filtered-out** perspective. *Cues filtered out* is an umbrella term used to describe the view that CMC has low social presence because it removes prominent social cues found in face-to-face exchanges. Lack of social cues can produce antisocial or impersonal behavior in online interactions. Additionally, the lack of social presence and context cues can lead to an increase in uninhibited behavior patterns, such as **flaming**.

In contrast to this early research, Rice and Love (1987) discovered that a percentage of CMC contains **socioemotional content**. Rice and Love define socioemotional content "as interactions that show solidarity, tension relief, agreement, antagonism, tension, and disagreement" (p. 91). People use CMC to share interpersonal information. As a result, later research, such as Baym's (2000) study about online soap opera communities, explores the ways in which people build interpersonal relationships through the Internet.

Hyperpersonal CMC

Although CMC correspondents are physically separated, interpersonal relationships do develop through the Internet. In some instances, levels of affection and emotion that develop through CMC relationships can equal or surpass face-to-face relationships. Walther (1996) calls this phenomenon *hyperpersonal communication*. **Hyperpersonal CMC** occurs when CMC "is more socially desirable than we tend to experience in parallel FtF [Face-to-Face] interaction" (p. 17) (Figure 1.11).

Walther (1996) suggests that four different, but related, elements influence hyperpersonal CMC. These include the *receiver*, the *sender*, *asynchronous channels* of communication, and *feedback*, topics previously discussed in this chapter. Sometimes, CMC message receivers will inflate their perceptions or mental models about online partners. The lack of shared face-to-face social cues often makes CMC recipients exaggerate subtle social and personality cues exchanged through messages. As a result, receivers of CMC messages will create stereotypical and idealized impressions of others. These idealized interpretations of others contribute to hyperpersonal communication.

Additionally, senders of CMC messages can engage in **selective self-presentation**. With the elimination of physical appearance and vocal attributes, CMC enables computer users to reflect, edit, and select the information and cues transmitted to receivers. As a result, CMC communicators can carefully craft how they present themselves. Selective self-presentation works better in asynchronous CMC because one has time to prepare and reflect before sending a message. In contrast, synchronous CMC requires an immediate reply from participants, making it more difficult to edit and refine messages.

When communication does not require people to participate at the same time (asynchronous), individuals can correspond at time internals that are convenient. For example,

---

FIGURE 1.11 Hyperpersonal Communication.

In some cases, CMC relationships can be more satisfying than face-to-face ones. Consider the following message:

```
[An] aspect of CMC which I have discovered is that I can make
friends. The medium, however, has forced me to re-define what I mean
by a "friend," since I have never seen any of the people with whom I
can share my professional and personal concerns. By virtue of the
medium's anonymity, CMC becomes rather like a confessional. I sit
alone in my den, compose my messages, and send them out to people who
"hear" what I say and then give me advice or cut me down or share
their own thoughts. One friend I have, a prominent writer and scholar,
has been kind enough to listen to my concerns about the future of
university teaching and the fears and worries a young professor who is
striving for tenure has to face. The benefit of having such a friend
off my own campus has been enormous. . . . This quality of anonymity
in friendship, however, is a totally new experience. I find myself
trying to picture what each of these people looks like, what the sound
of their voice might be. . . . While gaining the benefit of their
words, their thoughts and advice, I lose that subliminal interaction
so important to friendship. On the other hand, were it not for CMC I
might not know these people at all.
```

Source: Loughlin, 1993, p. 4

e-mail eliminates the need for telephone tag and corresponding with a person at a particular time. Communicators can concentrate on the social and task dimensions of communication because time spent on one does not take time away from the other. Consequently, some researchers have suggested that the asynchronous nature of CMC makes it a better method of communication than face-to-face interaction because message construction is more intentional.

Feedback is an important element in CMC, and the lack of social cues can intensify its significance in the communication exchange. Without feedback, CMC ends because senders and receivers need to have behavioral confirmation in the communication process. Moreover, media with restricted communication channels can idealize a receiver's interpretation of a message. CMC can produce an intensified feedback loop because selectively sent and selectively perceived messages are often understood as positive feedback. According to Walther (1996):

> Off-line, we respond to others based largely on our expectations despite what their actual behavior may present. At the same time, when disconfirming social data are less available and what does occur is selectively sent and selectively perceived, the reciprocal process of behavioral confirmation may be more likely (p. 28).

Lack of social cues combined with the interactive exchange of messages can lead to positive impression formation. Feedback, which occurs through interactive message exchange, is a central characteristic of hyperpersonal CMC.

Interactivity

An unique feature of Internet communication is interactivity. Computer-based communication technologies support interactivity among users or between users and information. According to Rafaeli (1988), interactivity and social interaction relate to a spiral metaphor of communication. Most communication students are familiar with Dance's (1967) classic helical model of communication (Figure 1.12). It shows that human communication is both circular and progressive. According to Dance (1967), communication continuously turns "back upon itself . . . affected by its own past conformations" (p. 297). This description applies to CMC because it is through the exchange and progression of messages that interpersonal relationships develop.

In addition to being a feature of human communication, interactivity can also be a defining characteristic of media, for instance, two-way cable systems, telephone systems, e-mail, and interactive video games. Rafaeli and Sudweeks (1998) state, "interactivity is associated with those message qualities which invite people and make people gravitate to groups on the net" (p. 173). Thus, interactivity is an important aspect of CMC because it supports message interest and involvement (Figure 1.13).

However, different CMC genres support different degrees of interactivity. Fully interactive media enable senders and receivers to exchange positions, and many CMC genres support full interactivity. For example, discussion lists are interactive conversations among group participants. In contrast to an individual e-mail message, discussion list messages are organized around topics or **threads**. A thread is a chain of interrelated messages that respond to each other. Additionally, interactivity plays a central role in online social

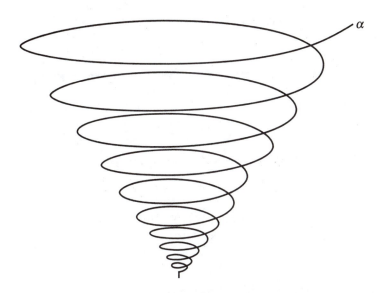

FIGURE 1.12   Dance's Helical-Spiral Model. Dance's helical-spiral model adds the ideas of time and process to a model of communication. This is particularly relevant to CMC correspondence because Internet relationships build over time and through the process of regularly exchanging e-mail, instant messages, and chat.

© 2002 by Frank E.X. Dance, used by permission.

dynamics and group communication. People must exchange messages for a group to remain active and interesting. E-mail, discussion lists, instant messenger, and chat fall into the category **interpersonal interactivity**—two-way correspondence between people in which senders and receivers can exchange positions and develop ongoing relationships.

Beyond person-to-person CMC, the characteristic of interactivity also applies to new media, such as CD-ROMs and the Web, because they provide opportunities for audiences to interact with media content, participate in the process of content creation, and send messages to content creators. In contrast to passive media consumption, such as watching television, new media support the active participation of audience members. However, interacting with content is different from interacting directly with other people in that interacting with people is generally more active and engaging. An exception to this rule is persuasive technology, which is designed to capture and maintain a user's attention. Generally, interacting with information is limited by the fact that all information must be programmed into the software or Web site. In contrast, people can provide an unlimited amount of data. **Informational interactivity** is designed to acquire, navigate, and locate information. This includes clicking on Web page links, filling out online forms, and searching for topics of information. Another type of interactivity involves interacting with software, **human–computer interaction** (HCI), which refers to the ways in which users interact with computer hardware and software, including the mouse, keyboards, graphical interfaces, and voice recognition.

New media incorporate interactive features that enable people to access information and media content, such as online newspapers, shopping services, library information,

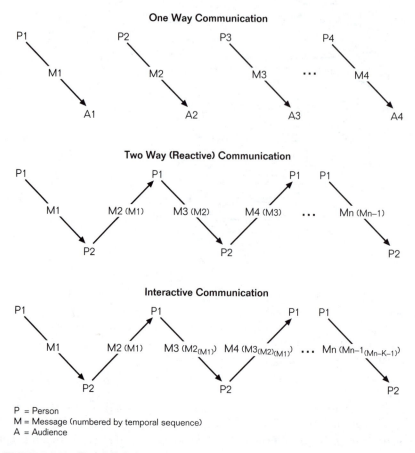

One Way Communication

Two Way (Reactive) Communication

Interactive Communication

P = Person
M = Message (numbered by temporal sequence)
A = Audience

FIGURE 1.13   Rafaleli & Sudweek's One Way, Two Way, and Interactive Models of Communication. These models illustrate the progression from sending a one way message to an audience to interactively exchanging numerous messages between people across the Internet.

© 1998 American Association for Artificial Intelligence. Interactivity on the Nets, Sheizaf Rafalei & Fay Sudweeks, *Network & Netplay*, pp. 173–189.

music files, and video on demand. Designers and programmers create interactive features to help people find information and navigate Internet resources. In contrast, the interactive nature of an online discussion group depends on the participants and the exchanges taking place between and among group members. Activities of individuals rather than programming features establish the interactive dynamics of e-mail versus Web pages. Although all CMC genres are interactive, interactivity occurs in three different ways—interpersonal interactivity, informational interactivity, and human–computer interaction.

Summary

Unlike other mass media, such as newspapers, magazines, television, and radio, that support the mass distribution of messages (one-to-many) and personal media, including the telephone and letter writing, which foster interpersonal correspondence (one-to-one), the Internet can be used to distribute messages in any number of directions. CMC describes computer applications that enable people to communicate with each other through computer networks. There are many different CMC genres, including e-mail, discussion groups, chat, instant messenger, and the Web. Present and future developments in embedded and wireless technologies are moving access to these genres off the desktop and onto portable devices.

CMC is used for a variety of purposes, including information seeking (informatics), small group discussion, and interpersonal correspondence (conferencing). A key characteristic of CMC is interactivity, which includes interpersonal interactivity, information interactivity, and human–computer interaction. Rhetorical concepts have been applied to the study of Internet interpersonal correspondence and the development of persuasive technology. Captology examines the ways in which computers are used to change people's attitudes and behavior. At present, Internet communication brings together elements of both human and mass communication. The Internet is often used as a medium to support interpersonal mediated communication by transcending the limitations of time and space in interpersonal correspondence.

Early CMC researchers argued that the *cues filtered out* in Internet communication would lead to low social presence and antisocial behavior. In contrast, Rice and Love discovered that people add *socioemotional cues* to their online messages. Moreover, Walter's research revealed that people using CMC develop *hyperpersonal relationships* in which CMC can be more socially desirable than face-to-face experiences. Although the Internet is a new medium, many different CMC genres have already emerged, each with its own unique characteristics and behavioral patterns. The various ways in which people use CMC will be discussed in the following chapters. But first we will examine the characteristics of the Internet that influence human communication.

TERMS

ARPANET (Advanced Research Projects Agency Computer Network), first operational in 1969, was the first large-scale interconnected mainframe computer network; it became the foundation for today's Internet.

Asynchronous communication allows people to communicate at different times. Internet asynchronous communication includes e-mail, discussion lists, Web sites, and newsgroups.

Avatar refers to the icons, pictures, or drawings that players use to represent themselves in online environments, such as the *Palace*.

Captology is the study of the design, analysis, and theory of persuasive computing, which uses computers to change people's attitudes and behavior.

Chat is computer users engaging in online dialog with other users from around the world by typing messages back and forth to each other. Most chat occurs within "rooms" that are sponsored at various locations on the global network.

Collaborative virtual environments are three-dimensional, computer-generated virtual worlds in which indiviuals are represented by visual avatars.

Computer-based communication and **computer-mediated communication** are terms that describe popular applications of the network, including electronic mail, electronic bulletin boards, electronic conferencing.

Conferencing occurs when the computer is used to connect people together. For example, computers are used to support communication among and between students, teachers, employees, and family members.

Cues filtered out is an umbrella term that has been used to describe research that argues that computers have low social presence and consequently deprive participants of prominent social cues. Without these social cues, the discourse is left in a social vacuum.

Cyberspace is the physical, conceptual, and perceptual space created by computer networks. It has become a term that is used to encompass all aspects of computer-mediated communication, ranging from the interpersonal exchange of electronic mail to the mass distribution of messages through the World Wide Web.

Discussion lists enable small groups of people to exchange e-mail messages among themselves.

Electronic mail or **e-mail** is an Internet tool for transmitting textual messages and documents. E-mail is asynchronous and users have mailboxes that receive and store messages.

Embedded computing is the placement of computer chips into all types of devices, such as portable digital assistants, cars, and cell phones.

Feedback is a mechanism between the source and receiver of a message that is used to regulate the flow of communication.

Flaming is the exchange of rude or hostile messages between online participants.

Home Pages are the first introductory page of a Web site, which contains links to other pages. In interface design, the home page is often represented as a house icon. Clicking on the icon will bring the user back to the home page.

Human–computer interaction (HCI) refers to the ways in which users interact with computer hardware and software, including the mouse, keyboards, graphical interfaces, and voice recognition.

Hyperpersonal CMC occurs when CMC is more socially desirable than parallel face-to-face experiences.

Informatics is using the computer as an information manager and a system for the electronic storage and retrieval of digital data.

Informational Interactivity s programmed into software and is designed to acquire, navigate, and locate information, including clicking on Web page links, filling out online forms, and searching for topics of information.

Instant messenger is a feature that enables people who are logged onto their computers at the same time to exchange short messages with each other.

Interface is the point at which users interact with their computers. Interface technology includes the graphical interface, the mouse, and keyboard.

Internet is a "network of networks"that consists of many smaller computer networks that are interconnected to each other to form a large global computer network.

Interpersonal interactivity is two-way correspondence with people. Senders and receivers can exchange positions and develop ongoing relationships. E-mail, discussion lists, and chat would fall into this category.

Interpersonal mediated communication is person-to-person communication in which a medium, such as a telephone, letter, e-mail, or answering machine, is being used to transcend the limitations of time and space.

Mental models are the models that people have of themselves, others, the environment, and objects, which they interact with. An individual's mental models are developed through experience, communication, and instruction.

Moderated lists are discussion lists in which the moderator, usually the owner of the list, reserves the right to make all decisions about the posting of messages. In some cases, the moderator will read all of the incoming messages before they are distributed to list members.

MOOs (multi-user domain—object oriented) MOO software adds additional programming features to MUDs.

MUDs (multi-user domain or multi-user dungeons) are online games in which players are involved in fantasy adventures that they create together as the game progresses.

Newsgroups are message areas that are defined by subject. Newsgroups were originally part of the Usenet networking system.

Packet-switching is a technique of breaking messages down into smaller information packets that are easier to send across the Internet. When all the packages arrive at their destination, they are reassembled in the correct sequence.

Para-social interaction is the illusion of an interpersonal relationship that develops between the audience and television performer.

Para-social relationships are the seeming face-to-face relationships that develop between spectator and performer through radio, television, and the movies.

Selective self-presentation occurs in CMC because the elimination of physical appearance and vocal attributes enables CMC users to reflect, edit, and select the information and cues transmitted to receivers.

Sociomotional content is online interactions that display feelings of solidarity, tension relief, agreement, antagonism, tension, and disagreement.

Synchronous communication occurs at the same time. Internet synchronous communication includes chat, MUDs, and instant messenger.

Threads are a series of postings to a particular message area or discussion group that are interconnected and linked together. Threads start with an initial message followed by all of the various comments made in reply to the initial post.

Transactional is a view about communication that argues that understanding the meaning of messages depends on the assumptions and foreknowledge of the receiver and the context in which the communication occurs.

Unmoderated lists automatically distribute messages to all group members.

Virtual reality is a term that is used to refer to a wide range of computer-based communication technologies that enable people to visualize, manipulate, and interact with people, computers, and digital data.

Weblogs are a new form of personal journalism in which an individual takes on the role of columnist, reporter, analyst, and publisher to share information through the Web.

Web rings have emerged to provide a method for linking together common Web-based interests. Sites are banded together into linked circles that enable people to find them more quickly and easily.

World Wide Web (WWW or Web) is a hypertext-based multimedia information and resource system designed for use with the Internet.

E X E R C I S E S

1. Explain how the characteristic of interactivity supports human communication through the Internet.

2. Compare exchanges through e-mail to conversations in a chat room or instant messenger. What are the similarities and differences? How does time (synchronous/asynchronous) influence the style of conversation?

3. Describe your own personal experiences communicating in the various different Internet genres. Are there any that you have not experienced? Try to find out more information about the unfamiliar genres.

4. Examine the illustrations of the various genres described in this chapter and/or find your own examples. What do these examples tell you about how language is used on the Internet? How is it similar or different from traditional written language?

5. Select one of the communication models described in this chapter and use it to explain a communication exchange between two people across the Internet.

W E B   S I T E S

First Monday (online journal). http://www.firstmonday.dk
Journal of Computer-Mediated Communication (online journal). http://www.ascusc.org/jcmc/
Persuasive Technology. http://www-ped.stanford.edu/captology/

B I B L I O G R A P H Y

Abbate, J. (1999). *Inventing the Internet*. Cambridge, MA: The MIT Press.
Barnes, S., & Greller, L. M. (1994, April). Computer-mediated communication in the organization. *Communication Education, 43* (2), 129–142.
Baym, N. K. (2000). *Tune in, log on: Soaps, fandom, and online community*. Thousand Oaks, CA: Sage Publications, Inc.
Benford, S., Greenhalgh, C., Rodden, T., & Pycock, J. (2001). To what extent is cyberspace really a space? Collaborative virtual environments. *Communications of the ACM, 44* (7), 79–85.
Beniger, J. R. (1987, June). Personalization of mass media and the growth of pseudo-community. *Communication Research, 14* (3), 352–371.
Bukatman, S. (1993). *Terminal identity*. Durham, NC: Duke University Press.
Cathcart, R., & Gumpert, G. (1986). The person-computer interaction: A unique source. In G. Gumpert & R. Cathcart (Eds.), *Inter media: Interpersonal Communication in a media world* (pp. 323–332. New York: Oxford University Press.
Dance, F. (1967). *Human communication theory*. New York: Holt, Rinehart & Winston.
Dougherty, D., & Koman, R. (1994). *The Mosaic handbook*. Sebastopol, CA: O'Reilly & Associates.

Engelbart, D. E. (1963). A conceptual framework for the augmentation of man's intellect. In Paul W. Howerton & David C. Weeks (Eds.), *Vistas in information handling, Vol. I* (pp. 1–29). Washington, DC: Spartan Books.

Fogg, B. J. (1999). Persuasive technologies. *Communications of the ACM, 42* (5), 26–29.

Fox, D. (1995). *Love bytes: The online dating handbook.* Core Madera, CA: Waite Group Press.

Gibson, W. (1984). *Neuromancer.* New York: Ace Books.

Gumpert, G., & Cathcart, R. (1986). *Inter media: Interpersonal communication in a media world* (3rd ed.). New York: Oxford University Press.

Hiltz S. R., & Turoff, M. (1978). *The network nation: Human communication via computer.* Reading, MA: Addison-Wesley Publishing Company, Inc.

Horton, D., & Wohl, R. R. (1956/1986). Mass communication and para-social interaction: Observation on intimacy at a distance. In G. Gumpert & R. Cathcart (Eds.), *Inter media: Interpersonal communication in a media world* (3rd ed., pp. 185–206). New York: Oxford University Press.

Khaslavsky, J., & Shedroff, N. (1999). Understanding the seductive experience. *Communications of the ACM, 42* (5), 45–49.

Licklider, J. C. R., & Taylor, R. (1968, April). The computer as a communication device. *Science and Technology* [Online], 41 pp. Available: http://gatekeeper.dec.com/pub/DEC/SRC/research-reports/abstracts/scr-rr-061.html (July 10, 2001).

Loughlin, T. W. (1993, January). Virtual relationships: The solitary world of cmc. *Interpersonal Computing and Technology: An Electronic Journal for the 21st Century, 1* (1). [Online], 7 pp. http://jan.ucc.edu/~ipct-j/(March 20, 2002).

Innis, H. A. (1951). *The bias of communication.* Canada: University of Toronto Press.

McQuail, D., & Windahl, S. (1993). *Communication models for the study of mass communication* (2nd ed.) New York: Longman.

McLuhan, M., & Fiore, Q. (1967). *The medium is the massage.* New York: Bantam Books.

Mitchell, W. J. (1995). *City of bits: Space, place, and the infobahn.* Cambridge, MA: The MIT Press.

Meyrowitz, J. (1985). *No sense of place.* New York: Oxford University Press.

Ong, W. J. (1982). *Orality and literacy: The technologizing of the word.* London: Methuen.

Postman, N. (1985). *Amusing ourselves to death.* New York: Penguin Books.

Rafaeli, S. (1988). Interactivity: From new media to communication. In Hawkins, R. P., Wiemann, J. M., & Pingree, S., Eds., *Advancing communication science: Merging mass and interpersonal processes.* Beverly Hills, CA: Sage Publications.

Rafaeli, S., & Sudweeks, F. (1998). Networked interactivity. In F. Sudweeks, M. McLaughlin, & S. Rafaeli (Eds.), *Network and netplay: Virtual groups on the Internet* (pp.173–189). Cambridge, MA: The MIT Press.

Rice, R. E., & Love, G. (1987). Electronic emotion: Socioemotional content in a compuer-mediated communication network. *Communication Research, 14* (1), 85–108.

Shah, R., & Romine, J. (1995). *Playing MUDs on the Internet.* New York: John Wiley & Sons.

Sproull, L., & Kiesler, S. (1991, September). Computers, networks and work. *Scientific American,* 116–123.

Stephenson, N. (1992). *Snow crash.* New York: Bantam Books.

Stone, A. R. (1995). *The war of desire and technology at the close of the mechanical age.* Cambridge, MA: The MIT Press.

Strate, L. (1995). Experiencing cybertime: Computing as activity and event. *Interpersonal Computing & Technology: An Electronic Journal for the 21st Century, 3* (2), [Online], 78–91. http://jan.ucc.nau.edu/~ipct-j (March 28, 2002).

Walther, J. B. (1996, February). Computer-mediated communication: Impersonal, interpersonal, and hyperpersonal interaction. *Communication Research, 23* (1) 3–43.

Characteristics of Computer-Mediated Communication

Chapter Overview

Can you imagine accessing your computer through your eyeglasses and surfing the Web as you walk down the street? Placing chips into eyewear is just one of the many new computer devices currently under development. Instead of using desktop computers, computer chips are being embedded in clothing, eyeglasses, portable digital assistants, cell phones, and automobiles. These devices, combined with wireless technologies, allow us to access e-mail and instant messages any place, any time. Anywhere and everywhere, we will be ubiquitously connected to the global network.

Computer networks collapse time and space by enabling people to quickly communicate over vast distances. All types of data can be digitized and distributed through the network. These physical characteristics of the Internet influence the ways in which people communicate with each other because we can now easily connect with people around the world. Internet characteristics influence how messages are exchanged and understood. This chapter introduces the following topics:

- Internet characteristics
- Analog versus digital media
- Cyberspace and cybertime
- CMC characteristics that foster fantasy and play
- CMC and frame theory
- Playfulness and flow theory

Internet Characteristics

Computer networks enable people to quickly distribute messages around the world, which extends the reach of human communication. No other medium can collapse both time and space. Additionally, computers have the ability to store and retrieve digital information exchanged during the communication process. As a result, the Internet enables people to store, retrieve, and share information instantly on a worldwide level. McLuhan's vision of a global village is now fulfilled: " 'Time' has ceased, 'space' has vanished. We now live in a global village" (McLuhan & Fiore, 1967, p. 63). Both television and computer networks have contributed to the formation of a global communication network that broadcasts news about people living around the world. For instance, Americans watch news stories about the Middle East crisis and Singaporians see floods in Pennsylvania.

Analog Versus Digital Media

In contrast to broadcast television, the Internet transmits information in a digital format. Analog and digital are two ways in which messages are formatted to be transmitted through different media. **Analog media** formats correspond to some feature or characteristic of the object they represent. For instance, electronic formats for reproducing music or images use electrical impulses. These impulses modulate the current, which directly coincides with the sound or image being recorded. In contrast, **digital media** store and distribute information by transforming it into a binary mathematical code of 1s and 0s, or on-off signals. Once converted into a binary code, information can be transmitted electronically through computer networks. All types of information, including numbers, text, graphics, images, video, and sound, can be turned into a binary code. Unlike analog formats, digital formats of 1s and 0s are arbitrary, having no correspondence to what they represent.

Information converted into a digital format can be used by a variety of computer-based systems. For example, text and images turned into binary code can be used in Web design, desktop publishing, and multimedia presentations. Similarly, digital text-based messages can be read on everything from a personal computer to a cell phone. Information stored in digital formats can be used in a variety of ways on different types of devices.

Nicholas Negroponte, the Director of the MIT Media Lab, describes the difference between analog and digital media as the difference between atoms and bits. Atoms make up physical media, such as books, audiotapes, and videocassettes. It is more difficult to get atoms into the hands of people than it is to distribute bits of information over a network. To get books from the printing plant to readers, the books have to be physically shipped on trucks and sent to stores. In contrast, when books are distributed in a digital format, they can be sent directly from the source of information to the reader through a computer network. Digital books are much easier to transport from one place to another, and it takes less time to move them around the world.

Gradually, mass media are becoming digital and are converging. **Media convergence** is the integration of all types of mediated communications into an electronic, digital format, an integration propelled by the widespread use of computers and networking systems. Convergence integrates mass media, including television, books, newspapers, and magazines, with interpersonal communication. Convergence paves the way for the development of multimedia products that mix text, data, graphics, and video together for distribution through digital networks. Individuals can use digital video editing tools to create their own multimedia Web sites.

Negroponte also argues that we are moving toward a universal, fiber-optic, high-speed communication network that can carry hundreds of channels of video programming and information. The shift from broadcast television to fiber-optic systems makes the air waves (or ether) available for new types of communication services, including cell phones, portable digital assistants (PDAs), and wireless Web devices. Broadcast communication technologies that now use the air waves to transmit signals will shift underground and distribute information through wires. In contrast, telephone technologies that now travel through wires will move into the air waves. This change is called the **Negroponte flip**. Negroponte views digital media as similar to traditional analog media methods for delivering information to large audiences. But a feature that makes digital media different from analog media is interactivity, discussed in the previous chapter. Interactivity enables individuals to use these technologies to communicate with other people. In contrast to mass media, interactivity supports interpersonal communication. For example, the Web provides opportunities for people to interact with media content, create personal Web sites, participate in Web discussions, and exchange messages with content providers. In contrast to passive media, such as television, digital media support active viewer participation. The Internet has been described as a feedback mechanism because it enables people to interactively exchange messages.

Digitalization

Interactivity and digitalization are two media characteristics of the Internet. The alphabet was one of the first symbol systems to be converted into a digital format. Letters of the alphabet were transformed into binary numbers that could be read by computers. This conversion, known as the **American Standard Characters for Information Interchange** or **ASCII**, is a universal standard that can be understood by all types of computer systems. It encodes the English alphabet and numerals into a sequence of seven digital bits, or a line of seven binary digits. Because e-mail is text based, it is a simple application to set up on computer systems; it is also the most popular application. Although ASCII can be understood across computer systems, it has limitations. ASCII is limited to 128 English characters because that is how many different sequences of seven 1s and 0s can be used. The code does allow for upper- and lowercase characters, but it does not support currency symbols or the Chinese, Japanese, Hebrew, or Arabic alphabets.

As computer technology developed, all types of symbol systems, from text to video, became digitized. According to Pavlik (1998), **digitalization** "refers to the process of storing any information or communication in computer-readable format of 1s and 0s, or digits" (p. 375). New technologies, such as streaming digital audio and video, transform the Internet into a full multimedia system. Online services such as American Online allow their members to send and receive digital photographs and create their own home pages with text, graphics, and sound files. Any type of data stored in a digital format can be sent through the Internet.

Time and Space

Digitalization enables computer networks to bridge time and space. According to Innis (1951), a communication medium creates a bias that emphasizes the idea of space or time: "A medium of communication has an important influence on the dissemination of knowledge over space and time and it becomes necessary to study its characteristics in order to appraise its influence in its cultural setting" (p. 33). When a new major communication technology is introduced into a culture that shifts the bias from time to space, this new technology could have profound cultural consequences. By focusing on how a technology alters people's perception of time and space, communication researchers can begin to understand how a new technology might influence social situations.

Prior to the invention of the telegraph, the metaphor of geography or transportation was used to describe communication systems. Information could be moved only as fast as a train could travel, which was about thirty-five miles per hour. According to Carey (1988), "the movement of goods and the movement of information were seen as essentially identical processes and both were described by the common noun 'communication' " (p. 15). At the center of communication was the concept of controlling the movement of signals or messages over a distance. Through the ages, humans have wanted to increase the speed and efficiency of messages traveling through space.

After the invention of the telegraph, the transportation metaphor no longer applied to information because space was removed as a constraint from the spread of news and events. Postman (1992) says that eliminating the barrier of space in information flows contributed to the following social changes: state lines were erased, information was no longer bound by a physical context, and information was turned into a commodity that could be bought and sold.

During the twentieth century, many new communication technologies emerged that further eliminated space constraints, including the telephone, radio, television, and the Internet. These technologies have become a global communication network that instantaneously distributes messages around the world. In the 1960s, McLuhan (1964) coined the term **global village** to illustrate how electric media abolish both space and time. He stated, "[Through] electricity, we everywhere resume person-to-person relations as if on the smallest village scale" (p. 225). McLuhan used the concept of a village to illustrate how television, radio, and telephone technologies enable local messages to be shared on a global level.

Computer networks alter our ideas of both time and space. Sproull and Kiesler's (1991) research on networked organizations suggests that "the networked organization differs from the conventional workplace with respect to both time and space" (p. 116). Because e-mail messages are sent and received in asynchronous time to different locations (the same office or geographically across the world), e-mail creates a communication context that has no shared physical space or shared sense of time. William J. Mitchell (1995) describes this process as follows:

> The keyboard is my cafe. Each morning I turn to some nearby machine—my modest personal computer at home, a more powerful workstation in one of the offices or laboratories that I frequent, or a laptop in a hotel room—to log into electronic mail. I click on an icon to open an "inbox" filled with messages from around the world—replies to technical questions, queries for me to answer, drafts of papers, submissions of student work, appointments, travel and meeting arrangements, bits of business, greetings, reminders, chitchat, gossip, complaints, tips, jokes, flirtation. I type replies immediately, then drop them into an "outbox," from which they are forwarded automatically to the appropriate destinations (p. 7).

According to Bukatman (1993), "The computer has, along with television, altered the social and psychological experiences of space and time in an unprecedented and unexpected manner" (p. 104). When computers are networked, sharing the same scrolling text on multiple screens creates a new space for people to communicate and share information.

Cyberspace

The new perception of space created by computer networks is often called *cyberspace*. Gibson (1984) created the word *cyberspace* in his science fiction novel *Neuromancer* to describe futuristic computer networks. His characters enter a virtual world of data using neurological computer interfaces that directly connect computers to the human nervous system. He assembled the word as an "act of pop poetics" to describe today's computer culture. "Cyber" comes from the term **cybernetics**, created by Norbert Weiner—derived from the Greek word *Kubernetes* or "steersman"—to describe the science of feedback and control. Cybernetics was first applied to machine systems; later it was expanded to include human social systems. In Gibson's novels, the term *cyberspace* refers to the idea of people steering through a matrix of digital data.

Although Gibson writes about an imagined future, his inspiration for the term *cyberspace* came from watching kids playing video arcade games. In an interview, he described these games as "a feedback loop with photons coming off the screens into the kids' eyes, neurons moving through their bodies, and electrons moving through the video game. These kids clearly *believed* in the space games projected" (McCaffery, 1992, p. 272). Gibson observed that video game and computer users appear "to develop a belief that there's some kind of *actual space* behind the screen, someplace you can't see but you know is there" (p. 272). It is a "nonspace," a hyperdimensional realm that we enter through technology.

Today, *cyberspace* is used synonymously with other words such as *cyberia, dataspace*, the *digital domain*, the *electronic realm, information space, virtual reality, computer networking*, and the *Internet*. Used as a collective term, Strate (1999) defines cyberspace as "*the diverse experiences of space associated with computing and related technologies*" (original emphasis, p. 383). Because *cyberspace* is used in many different ways, Strate argues that different levels of cyberspace need to be identified. He divides cyberspace into three different levels, called *zero order, first order*, and *second order* (Figure 2.1).

Cybermedia Space		
Aesthetic space	Information or dataspace	Interactive or relational space
Physical Space	**Conceptual Space**	**Perceptual Space**
Paraspace or Nonspace	**Spacetime**	

FIGURE 2.1   Strate's The Orders of Cyberspace

© 1999 Lance Strate, *Western Journal of Communication*, The Western States Communication Association. Used by permission.

Physical and Perceptual Space

Strate (1999) applies a building metaphor to the construction of cyberspace: "The sense of space generated through our experience of computing may in fact be entirely constructed and imaginary" (p. 389). The *zero order* of cyberspace is the basement or foundation upon which cyberspace is built. It is the awareness that cyberspace is different from other types of spaces. The *first order* of cyberspace is the next level of building blocks that create cyberspace. These include physical space, conceptual space, and perceptual space. The computer exists in actual space, and interface design uses perspective to create the perceptual illusion of space on the computer screen. Combined with the conception of space created by social interaction, these building blocks create the *second order* of cyberspace, or synthesis. Our understanding of cyberspace is an amalgamation of the aesthetic space created by the computer's interface, the information space established by the network, and the social space experienced through human interaction. Simply stated, cyberspace is the imaginary construction of space that is built by combining technological and interpersonal interactions.

Telepresence

Most communication researchers (Dery, 1993; Stone, 1995) write about conceptual cyberspace or the sense of space created by the mind when people interact with computers and engage in CMC. The experience of presence created by CMC and computer-based communication systems is called **telepresence**. In virtual reality environments, telepresence allows human operators to remotely control robots. For instance, a person controls a robot arm to fix a space ship. In an office environment, telepresence is created when people participate in a videoconferencing session. Experiencing the presence of others over distances is a form of telepresence.

Social Space

Telepresence is a term often associated with technology. In contrast, the perception of social space through computer networks is based on interpersonal communication. Social space is very important in CMC and in the formation of interpersonal relationships. As complex technologies increasingly mediate communication, they enable people to communicate with each other in cyberspace instead of real space. Cathcart and Gumpert (1986) argue that for a "mediated exchange to work as interpersonal communication, there must be tacit agreement that the participants will proceed as though they are communicating face to face" (p. 325). Similarly, Stone (1991) has observed that people who converse in electronic space act as if they are meeting in a physical public space. Online participants often behave as if they are in a real and not a virtual place. As a result, "there exists the pervasive recognition that a new and decentered spatiality has arisen that exists parallel to, but outside of, the geographic topography of experiential reality" (Bukatman, 1993, p. 105). Although cyberspace does not exist in a physical sense, people believe and behave as if it is an actual place. This perception of space can make the experience of electronic space feel as if it is a "real" experience. However, people can become confused about the public nature of the Internet.

Private Versus Public Space

Newsgroups are considered "public" spaces on the Internet because anyone with access to a Usenet feed can read the messages. In contrast, discussion lists can be either public or private. People have to take the extra step of joining or subscribing to a discussion list. Some discussion groups are open and make themselves available for anyone to join, while others are private and by invitation only. The nature of conversation can change if people perceive themselves to be speaking in a public forum rather than a private conversation. Moreover, the process of joining a group has a different implied social contract than reading messages posted to a public bulletin board. As a result, discussion list participants will share personal information.

There are thousands of different discussion groups on the Internet talking about subjects ranging from Apple Computers to zoology. However, people can get confused about whether the exchange of messages occurs in a public or private space. This happens for two major reasons. First, in most groups a small number of people post the majority of the messages. This creates the illusion that the group is much smaller and more intimate than it actually is. For example, Seabrook (1997) observed that active participation on Usenet consisted of only 2–4 percent of the population. In most online groups, only about 10 percent of the membership actively contribute to the conversation; most of the participants **lurk** and do not participate in the discussion. In another example, a group with 350 members, over 50 percent of the 24,633 messages shared over two years were sent by 10 people (see Barnes, 2001). In online group discussion, the small number of actual group participants creates the impression of a small group rather than a large crowd. Because people perceive the group to be small, they often reveal personal information. A second reason people think the Internet is a private space is the personal nature of online conversations. For example, many books about CMC describe intimate conversations, including *Virtual Spaces: Sex and the Cyber Citizen, Love Online: A Practical Guide to Digital Dating,* and *War of the Worlds.* Cybersex has also been a topic featured on HBO and *Dateline NBC.*

In contrast, e-mail messages are not private because they can be read by system administrators or recovered from hard drives after they have been deleted. For example, the *Star Report* revealed that Monica Lewinsky's deleted e-mail messages had been recovered from her home and office computers. A good rule of thumb is to consider e-mail to be a postcard. Do not write anything in an e-mail message that you would not want other people to read. Additionally, e-mail messages can be saved or forwarded to other people who are not group members, and e-mail can be distributed without our knowledge. Moreover, messages posted to Web-based discussion lists are available to anyone with access to the Web. Some discussion groups, particularly support-oriented groups, try to maintain some privacy standards because these groups are set up to enable people to share their intimate feelings.

When joining any discussion or chat group, you should be aware of the private versus public nature of the group. Introductory welcome messages will often provide some information about this. For example, some academic discussion groups will provide a welcome statement that provides specific instructions on how to cite messages distributed through the list. The moderators of some academic lists view electronic messages as a form of publishing and want the authors of e-mail messages to receive proper citations. In contrast, support groups often want their conversations to remain private. Not everyone has the same impression of the private versus public nature of cyberspace.

Cybertime

Besides cyberspace, cybertime is also a characteristic of CMC that needs to be considered. Strate (1996) identifies three aspects of cybertime. The first aspect is the computer's time-telling functions, such as its internal clock that records the time a file is saved and the amount of time required to execute a command. Second, the computer is a representational medium that communicates a sense of symbolic, fictional, or dramatic time. Finally, each computer user has his or her own subjective sense of time. For example, when people play computer games they often become so involved with the games that they do not realize how much time they are spending on the computer.

Computers both display time and communicate a sense of time. The sense of time created by participating in computer-generated virtual worlds is called *virtual time*. Computer-generated 3-D graphics can communicate the illusion of reality along with time. Time concepts include timelines, game time, narrative time, and dramatic time. Three-dimensional space adds to the notion of time because users have the sensation of moving in time through cyberspace.

Scholars have recognized the influence computers have had on our concepts of time. For instance, Bertman (1998) argues that today we live life at warp speed, like the crew depicted on the TV series *Star Trek*. Technologies, such as the Internet, which operate at the speed of light have changed the fundamental nature of our lives in three ways. First, warp speeds disengage people from their past because traditions become irrelevant. Second, warp speeds send us moving toward the future. The promise of new technologies, such as advanced interfaces and high-speed multimedia networks, blinds us to the present. Finally, ignoring the past and focusing on the future isolates us in the present. People are frantically rushing through time without enjoying the immediate moment.

Synchronous and Asynchronous CMC

Messages exchanged through the Internet are either synchronous (at the same time) or asynchronous (at different times). Chat and instant messenger are synchronous forms of CMC. In contrast, e-mail, newsgroups, and discussion lists are asynchronous. For example, if you send an e-mail message to a discussion group, each member of the group will only receive the message after individually logging on to an Internet Service Provider (ISP) and downloading the message with a mail application such as Pegasus Mail, Eudora, or Hotmail. You can send the message in the morning and it can take minutes, hours, or days for everyone to receive it. The time delay between when you sent the message and when others receive it is a defining characteristic of asynchronous CMC. However, Strate (1995) contends, "although the e-mail messages we receive were composed at some point in the past, there is a tendency to experience them as if they were being communicated in the present" (p. 80). As a result, Internet communication can blur the distinctions between past, present, and future.

In contrast to asynchronous communication, synchronous Internet correspondence occurs in close-to-real time. As you type words on your keyboard, others logged into the conversation receive the message almost instantaneously. The speed with which your typing appears on the screens of others depends on the quality of the hardware and the Internet connection. Quite often, participants can see each other's sentences at the same time they are being typed. Examples of synchronous Internet communication include chat rooms, Internet relay chat (IRC), instant messenger, and multi-user domain (MUD) environments.

Characteristics of CMC

CMC allows people to bridge time and space to develop interpersonal relationships through both synchronous and asynchronous communication. As a result, conditions of attendance no longer require face-to-face physical presence. Instead, individuals can virtually present themselves to others. However, the text-based presentation of self encourages others to use their imagination to fill in missing pieces of information, such as physical appearance and tone of voice. Characteristics of the Internet lead to the use of fantasy and play in CMC because participants receive limited amounts of information about other people. Socially constructed concepts of time and space add fantasy elements to our understanding of Internet messages.

Conditions of Attendance

Both cybertime and cyberspace alter the conditions of attendance required for CMC because CMC creates a socially produced concept of space that does not require physical presence. People can communicate anywhere there is a computer and telephone line. As a result, the use of computer networks significantly alters our relationship to space in the communication process. In contrast to traditional concepts of interpersonal communication that require face-to-face participation, online communication enables individuals to form friendships and conduct business without ever meeting in person. As with the telephone, geographic proximity is not a requirement for Internet communication. Although the Internet makes it easy to communicate across distances, text-based messages do not include a full range of visual and verbal information.

Fantasy

Because face-to-face information is missing in CMC, communicators need to add elements of fantasy and play to the communication process. Increasingly, our daily interactions have shifted away from interpersonal interactions toward mediated ones. According to Meyrowitz (1985), mass media have the ability to "offer the illusion of face-to-face interaction with performers and political figures" (p. 119). Relationships that develop through mass media between actors and viewers are based on fantasy. According to Horton and Wohl (1956), "para-social relations provide a framework within which much may be added by fantasy" (p. 186).

In para-social relationships, fantasy compensates for the lack of reciprocity. Performers do not respond to audience members. Para-social television relationships are characterized as one-sided, nondialectical, controlled by the performer, and not open to mutual development. Despite these limitations, the television character offers a continuing relationship for the viewer that can be incorporated into daily life. Over time, the viewer comes to believe that he or she "knows" the media personality more intimately than other people. Sometimes, para-social relationships replace real ones because the time pressures of modern life make it difficult to maintain face-to-face relationships and contacts. Unlike para-social relationships that form with television characters, Internet relationships are two-sided, dialectical, and open to mutual development.

As with para-social relationships, fantasy is a central characteristic of understanding messages exchanged through CMC. Fantasy is important because it is used to compensate for the lack of visual and aural information. Each participant creates an image of himself or herself and an image of the *other*. For example, Reid (1991) states, "Users of IRC treat the medium as frontier world, a virtual reality of virtual freedom, in which participants feel free to act out their fantasies, to challenge social norms, and exercise aspects of their personality that would under normal interactive circumstances be inhibited" (p. 12). Fantasy is an element in everything from exchanging e-mail messages to playing online games.

Finding creative ways to write and to present yourself through text-only correspondence is central to successful CMC relationship building. Creative writing will evoke imaginative images in the minds of others. Fantasy in CMC has both positive and negative aspects. In online adventure games, the co-creation of fantasy images constructed by players makes the game interesting and fun to play. Conversely, fantasy can lead to false projections because it is difficult to see all personality aspects of online friends. Without the mundane reality check of daily face-to-face encounters, it is easy to project images of perfection on to our online relationships. This is especially true for romantic partners. Romantic interests in cyberspace are often built on fantasy rather than reality (see Booth & Jung, 1996). Consequently, romantic connections established through CMC need to be verified through other media before a face-to-face encounter occurs (Figure 2.2).

FIGURE 2.2   Stages for Transforming a CMC Relationship into a F2F One

---

When transforming a relationship from CMC interactions to face-to-face encounters, people usually go through the following stages:

Stage 1: Computer-mediated exchange of messages.

Stage 2: Read Online Profiles and arrange to meet at regular times.

Stage 3: Check personal or business Web sites to verify the identity of the person.

Stage 4: Exchange photographs.

Stage 5: Talk on the telephone.

Stage 6: Arrange to meet in person.*

Stage 7: Continue the relationship on a face-to-face basis, end the relationship, or continue to meet only on the Internet. (In a face-to-face meeting physical attraction comes into play, which can influence whether people continue to see each other. However, some relationships that work online do not translate into face-to-face friendships.)

---

* It is best to arrange to meet an online friend for the first time in a public location. If the encounter does not go well, each of you can go home alone.

Adapted from Barnes, 2001.

Play and IRC

In IRC, the fantasy aspect of CMC becomes strikingly playful. For example, researchers have observed that IRC interaction can resemble the real-life play genres of charades, a masked ball, having a party, and putting on a show. Players can mask their actual identities and create an online personality, while their true identity remains anonymous. Anonymity is a characteristic of CMC that enables people to behave and play in ways they would never do in face-to-face contexts, such as engage in hate speech, as described in Chapter 12.

Play theory is one way to examine IRC exchanges. For example, researchers have studied the work of Gregory Bateson and applied it to CMC. Bateson (1972) formulated a theory about language, play, and fantasy in human interaction inspired by watching monkeys in the San Francisco Zoo:

> What I encountered at the zoo was a phenomenon well-known to everybody: I saw two young monkeys *playing*, i.e., engaged in an interactive sequence of which the unit actions or signals were similar to but not the same as those of combat. It was evident, even to the human observer, that the sequence as a whole was not combat, and evident to the human observer that to the participant monkeys this was "not combat."
>
> Now, this phenomenon, play, could only occur if the participant organisms were capable of some degree of metacommunication, i.e., of exchanging signals which would carry the message "this is play" (p. 179).

This observation led Bateson to conclude that play may be an important step in the evolution of language. Today, play is performing a similar role in the development of electronic language. People are extremely creative about the ways in which they use the computer keyboard to invent linguistic and graphic forms of playful expression (see Chapter 5). Both established and newly invented emoticons, such as the smiley face :), help to foster a sense of *digital play* in computer-mediated exchanges.

Generally, play is considered an activity that is set apart in time and space from ordinary life. Computer-mediated genres create perceptual spaces that insulate online players from real-world activities and set them apart from day-to-day events. According to Danet, Rudenberg-Wright, and Rosenbaum-Tamari (1998), digital play shares the following characteristics with real-life play: It is voluntary, intensely absorbing, done for its own sake, and more or less rule-governed.

Play is often associated with games. Games are played by following rules and fall into two general categories, finite and infinite. Philosopher James Carse (1986) describes these categories as follows: "A finite game is played for the purpose of winning, an infinite game for the purpose of continuing the play" (p. 3). When playing finite games, we know that someone has won a game when all of the other players agree on the winner. Sometimes, players seek the approval of spectators or referees. A difference between finite and infinite games is the ways in which rules are defined. The rules in finite games are externally defined; in contrast, the rules in infinite games are internally defined. When playing infinite games, players often make up the rules as the game progresses, and the rules can change during the course of play.

IRC has been used to play finite games, such as *Jeopardy* (Figure 2.3). However, online play generally tends to fall into the second category. Chat, MUDs, MOOs, and other online role-playing activities support the creation of infinite games. (Figure 2.4). For ex-

---

FIGURE 2.3   IRC *Jeopardy*: An Example of a Finite Game Played on the Internet

---

Alexbot imitates Alex Trebek from the popular television show Jeopardy. IRC Jeopardy runs twenty-four hours a day, seven days a week, and never stops. Alexbot is constantly playing the game and interacting with human players. The following is an excerpt:

```
<alexbot> Welcome to Jeopardy! A new game is be
+ginning now.
<alexbot> Categories for this game are:
<alexbot> Third_Reich Alaska Name_That_Tune_2
+Guys_Named_Al TV_Occupations Shakespeare_Char-
+acter
<ZeEd> [I hate] you alex
<alexbot> zeed: keep it clean, this is a family
+game! Otherwise I will have to call the bouncers.
<alexbot> Please wait while preparing the next
+Guys_Named_Al question . . .
<alexbot> Current category: Guys_Named_Al. Ques-
+tion Value: 200.
<alexbot> Question 16 of 30: he's married to Kim
+Basinger:
<ZeEd> aLeXz baldwin
<alexbot> zeed: That is CORRECT! You win 200.
+Your total is 1400.
<alexbot> Please wait while preparing the next
+Guys_Named_Al question . . .
```

Source: Herz, 1995, pp. 121–122.

ample, a study done by researchers from the Hebrew University of Jerusalem analyzed an infinite chat game started by a systems operator named Thunder. Thunder first sent out messages announcing a series of new IRC channel names, including +bagelnosh and +hsonlegab (bagelnosh spelled backwards), before settling on the name +Weed. The topic for the channel was described as follows: sssssssssssssss hmmm where's all that smoke from? +Weed. As participants joined the channel, they engaged in a role-playing game of smoking marijuana. The symbolic play combined the concepts of childlike pretend play with skillful IRC performance as participants used linguistic and graphic cues to simulate the acts of inhaling and exhaling the smoke.

```
Line 204 <Rikitiki> *inhales deeply*
Line 214 <Rikitiki> *exhales slowly*
Line 291 <Thunder> *exhales* sssssssssssssssss
```

(Danet et al., 1998, p. 62.)

As the conversation progressed, participants developed clearer ways of expressing themselves with limited keyboard symbols. Patricia Wallace (1999) also describes the role play observed in this chat session:

> The rules that governed this IRC performance were conceptually similar to those that control the preschoolers' role-play games, though obviously far more complex. This role play required enormous creativity to maintain the illusion, but the strictures were there. Any one joining the channel was expected to pretend to be stoned, and use all the creativity they could muster to do it (p. 42).

These playful aspects of chat can also be used to present formalized performances. For example, an English filmmaker named Stuart Harris formed a virtual acting troupe to perform an IRC version of Shakespeare's *Hamlet*, called *Hamnet*. It was first performed in December 1993 and repeated in February 1994 with Ian Taylor, a member of the Royal Shakespeare Company, playing the title role. Actors involved in the production came from around the world, including London, Tel Aviv, Slovenia, Oslo, and various cities in the United States. Each performance was presented in real time with live performers and audience members. However, the second *Hamnet* performance also included a bot (short for robot) that accidentally killed Hamlet in the middle of the production. The cast hammed up their lines by combining Shakespeare's poetry and plots with IRC jargon, acronyms, clever puns, and references to popular culture. Online actors used textual and typographic art to add to the performance qualities. For example, the famous line "To be or not to be" was written in speedwriting as "2b or not 2b."

Harris directed the production by creating an eighty-line script for performers to type. When people joined the Hamnet Channel, they were asked if they wanted to be a performer or an audience member. The available parts were listed with the number of lines to be per-

---

FIGURE 2.4   MUDs and IRC Communities Are Examples of Infinite Games

---

The following is a sample exchange between players:

```
<Wizard> Come, brave Knight! Let me cast a spell of
protection on you. . . . . Ooops - wrong spell! You don't mind
being green for a while- do you???
<Prince> Lioness: please don't eat him...
<Storm> *shivers from the looks of lioness*
<Knight> Wizard: Not at all.
<Bel_letre> *hahahah*
<Lioness> Very well, your excellency. *Looks frustrated*
<Knight> Wizard: as long as I can protect thou ass, I'd be
utter grateful! :-)
<Bel_letre> *Plays a merry melody*
```

Source: Reid, 1991, p. 13–14.

formed. Each performer was privately sent his or her lines with a number showing where the line fit into the play. Lines were entered in numeric sequence, for example, the actor with line 24 waited until line 23 appeared. After rehearsing how to use the IRC commands properly, the performance commenced before a restless audience.

Only two of the lines in Harris's version of *Hamnet* are from the original play. The remaining lines include IRC jargon, acronyms, and speedwriting. Danet, Wachenhauser, Bechar-Israeli, Cividalli and Rosenbaum-Tamari (1995) compared lines from the original *Hamlet* to lines in *Hamnet*:

> . . . line from the original is:
>
>> QUEEN GERTRUDE Hamlet, thou hast thy father much offended (*Hamlet*, Act III, Scene 4: 9).
>
> Instead of merely quoting it intact, Harris exploits it to allow for a pair of adjacent near-homonyms, with comic effect:
>
>> ```
>> <Prompter> Psst! Thou hast they father much offended. . [47]
>> <Queen> Oh, right. . . . Yr dad's pissed at u [48]
>> ```
>
> (p. 12)

Online play can collapse for a variety of reasons. For example, the first attempt to perform the Internet production of *Hamnet* ended abruptly when a lightning bolt cut the power to the director's Internet access provider. But the performance was resumed after the producers logged back onto the Internet via a different connection route. Digital play can also stop when participants become offended or disturbed by what is happening in the game. Moreover, catastrophic real-world events, such as earthquakes, hurricanes, or war, will stop play activities because game participants will use the Internet to distribute the late-breaking news. For example, earthquake information has been distributed through the Internet when telephone lines were unavailable.

Digital Play in Group Discussion

As with chat, there is a playful aspect to discussion groups. For example, Kuehn (1993) applied play theory to an analysis of an online bulletin board group. He describes two different types of communication play associated with CMC. *Participatory play* occurs when participants can alter their interactions to achieve communication goals. The interactive nature of CMC supports participatory play. The second type of play, *elite dominated communication play*, exists only by making media content choices and is primarily a passive activity. For example, people select television programs to watch or they access information from the Web. This is similar to information interactivity, which was described in the previous chapter.

Kuehn (1993) states that there are two different types of participatory play choices occurring in CMC: (1) the decision to participate in a CMC genre and (2) the unique characteristics of the Internet that provide cues for communication play. The decision to join a bulletin board service (BBS), discussion group, or newsgroup could be considered a desire to engage in a form of communication play. Due to a lack of visual information in CMC, keyboard symbols are a unique CMC characteristic used in communication play. Communication play is the transformation of a serious situation into a play situation. Goffman (1974) classified the following behavior patterns as play: jokes, dramas, sports contests, games, simulations, and role playing. In CMC, playful exchanges include jokes, irony, and keyboard symbols suggesting play behavior (Figure 2.5).

CMC and Frame Theory

Digital play can be understood by identifying the different psychological frames used during online exchanges. According to Bateson (1972), *psychological frames* are similar to picture frames because they tell the viewer that he or she "is not to use the same sort of thinking in interpreting the picture that he [or she] might use in interpreting the wallpaper" (p. 187). Simply stated, frames show the context in which messages should be understood. By understanding the social situations in which communication occurs, people can compare the social landscape (background) to particular people, events, and behaviors (figures). As a result, frames can provide important pieces of social information, and they contribute to **metacommunication**, communication about the communication process.

Researchers have applied Goffman's frame analysis, a method for organizing experience, to the study of CMC. According to Goffman (1974), when individuals attend to a situation, they need to ask the following question: "What is it that's going on here?" (p. 8). Each individual will experience an event differently. For instance, opposing rooters at a basketball game will not experience the same game the same way. A goal of Goffman's (1974) approach is to isolate some general frameworks of social understanding for making sense out of events "and to analyze the special vulnerabilities to which these frames of reference

---

FIGURE 2.5 Content Cues That Indicate Play

In his analysis of BBS services and play communication, Kuehn identified the following as indicators of shifts into play:

1. Textual manipulations signifying jokes, irony, witticism, and sarcasm.

   Example: `I larned eferythang I knou in hai skool.`

2. Conventional text emphasis symbols that were used to convey conversation tone and nonverbal communication. Included were underlinings, exclamations, misspellings for slang purposes, capitalizations for emphasis.

   Example: `Whatsamatta, you a friggin' GROWNUP or sumpthin'?!`

3. Unconventional symbolic representations of nonverbal communication. These could be unique combinations of keyboard symbols to give readers a view of the author's facial expressions, verbal pauses "<hmm>," and possibly gestures.

   Example: `hmm . . . I didn't know that a System 36 used Ms-Dos 3-3 :-)`

Adapted from Kuehn, 1993

are subject" (p. 10). The term *frame* in this context refers to the basic principles of social organization and an individual's subjective involvement in the organization of experience. This is not social organization, but the ways in which individuals organize events in their minds.

Five different types of play frames can be found in the IRC game of smoking a joint, previously described (Figure 2.6). The first two are the real frame and the unreal frame, or the difference between physical reality and the fantasy elements of CMC. The third is identified as "let's play IRC," and it is a play frame that has the characteristics of reduced accountability and a willingness to reveal information. Besides hiding an individual's identity, the anonymous nature of CMC can lead to increased personal disclosure. However, self-disclosure in chat does not have clearly defined rules of behavior because the participants' motivations for revealing personal information are often unclear. For example, people will be serious, playful, and sometimes deceitful when they self-disclose, and it is difficult to know which is which. The fourth play frame is "let's have a party." In this frame, players flirt and play word games with each other. On a larger level, the motivation to play is driven by the idea of having fun. In the final frame, "let's pretend," rules begin to be established for the mastering of the verbal simulation of smoking pot. Participants compete with each other for the most skillful use of language and graphic representations. By organizing the CMC experience into different frames, we can better understand the online communication process and the role of play in text-only exchanges.

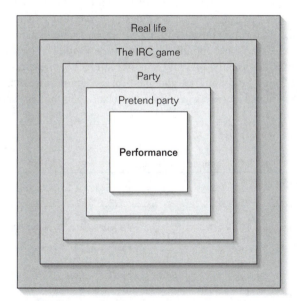

FIGURE 2.6   Five Nested Frames Used to Analyze an IRC Party

Source: © 1998 American Association for Artificial Intelligence. "Hmmm . . . Where's that Smoke coming From? Writing, Play and Performance on Internet relay Chat," Brenda Danet, Lucia Ruedenberg, Yehudit Rosenbaum-Tamari, *Network & Netplay*, pp. 41–76.

Play and Flow Theory

Play creates an enjoyable experience for online correspondents, which is an important aspect of **flow theory**. Webster, Trevino, and Ryan (1993) have applied flow theory to the study of CMC. Flow theory argues that flow experiences are enjoyable experiences in which we feel in control of our actions and a deep sense of enjoyment (Csikszentmihalyi, 1990). It is a subjective psychological experience that portrays CMC as being playful and exploratory. The flow state is characterized by four dimensions: control, attention focus, curiosity, and intrinsic interest. Webster et al. applied these factors to CMC in the following way:

a) the user perceives a sense of control over the computer interaction
b) the user perceives that his or her attention is focused on the interaction
c) the user's curiosity is aroused during the interaction
d) the user finds the interaction intrinsically interesting (p. 413).

These four dimensions are both interdependent and connected. For instance, curiosity and intrinsic interest can be combined into one dimension called *cognitive enjoyment* (Figure 2.7). People must have an intrinsic interest in computers to use them, and exchanging e-mail messages involves curiosity and imagination because missing information must be conceived. There is a relationship between flow and increased e-mail communication. The more involved a user is in the interaction, the more enjoyable the experience. Flow encourages exploratory behavior, such as seeking information from the Web or participating in a MUD world. In work environments, a positive subjective flow experience should be an important reason for performing an activity. However, overinvolvement with CMC can interfere with work tasks because employees spend time sending e-mail or playing games instead of working. Additionally, playful computer interactions may take longer to complete than less playful ones. Studying flow and playfulness requires researchers to both observe computer users and interview users to better understand their feelings about CMC.

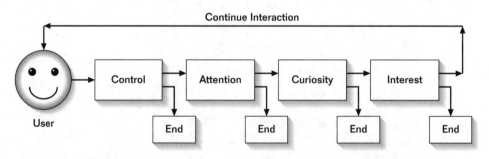

FIGURE 2.7   Flow Graphic. The flow state is characterized by four dimensions: control, attention focus, curiosity, and intrinsic interest. It is an enjoyable experience and CMC users must remain interested and curious about the communication exchange for interaction to continue.

Summary

Digital communication can be instantly sent around the world. As a result, the Internet alters our concepts of time and space. Cyberspace is a complex mix of physical, perceptual, and conceptual notions of space. Together, these concepts of space create the illusion of a social space that exists during CMC correspondence. CMC social space is considered both public and private, depending on the nature of the group and the type of information being exchanged. Similarly, the Internet alters our concepts of time. People can correspond in synchronous and asynchronous time depending on which CMC genre they use.

Internet characteristics of time and space influence the ways in which people socially interact with each other. The elimination of physical presence in CMC correspondence makes fantasy a characteristic of CMC because fantasy compensates for missing information. Realizing that play is a central element of CMC, researches have used Goffman's frame theory as a method to analyze different aspects of online play. Play makes the CMC experience enjoyable, which is a central element of flow theory. Consequently, flow theory has been applied to the analysis of CMC to better understand how people use control, attention, focus, curiosity and interest in Internet communication.

EXERCISES

1. Select an aspect of cyberspace (physical, perceptual, social, etc.) and describe your personal experiences with this type of mediated space. How do you understand the concept of space when using a computer network?

2. The dimension of space often overshadows the idea of time in CMC. Observe yourself working on a computer and describe your personal experiences with cybertime. For example, do you work with a clock displayed on your screen? Are you aware of how much time you spend on the computer? Do you sort your files by date and time? Do you get impatient when the computer does not execute commands instantly? How else do you experience cybertime?

3. Observe a chat discussion. Can you find examples of playful encounters? How important is the characteristic of play in encouraging interaction between participants? Do playful people appear to be more popular in the group? Why or why not?

4. Observe a chat group or online discussion and place the correspondence into different contextual frames.

5. Interview several people about their e-mail experiences using the criteria of flow theory. Ask the following questions:

   a. Do you perceive yourself in control of your computer and the messages you send through e-mail?
   b. How much time do you spend exchanging e-mail with other people?
   c. Do you find e-mail interesting and do you enjoy exchanging e-mail messages?

   Write up the responses in terms of flow theory.

T E R M S

Analog media formats correspond to features or characteristics of the object they represent. For instance, electronic formats for reproducing sound or images use electrical impulses that correspond to the original sound or image.

American Standard Characters for Information Interchange or *ASCII* is a universal standard for English alphabet characters that can be understood by all types of computer systems.

Cybernetics is the science of feedback and control, discussed in the previous chapter. It was first used by Norbert Weiner originally to describe machines and was later expanded to include human social systems.

Digital media store and distribute information by transforming it into a binary mathematical code of 1s and 0s, or on-off signals. Once converted into a binary format, information can be transmitted electronically through computer networks.

Digitalization refers to the process of converting information into the computer-readable format of 1s and 0s to be transmitted through computer networks.

Emoticons are smiley faces and other ASCII character designs that add clarity, expressiveness, emotions, and aesthetic elements to Internet communication.

Flow theory argues that flow experiences are enjoyable experiences, in which people feel in control of their actions and a deep sense of enjoyment. The flow state is characterized by four dimensions: control, attention, focus, curiosity, and intrinsic interest.

Global village is a term coined by Marshall McLuhan to illustrate how electric media abolish both space and time.

Lurk is a term used to describe people who read discussion list and online messages, but who do not respond or engage in conversation.

Media convergence is the integration of all types of mediated communications into an electronic, digital format propelled by the widespread use of computers and networking systems.

Metacommunication is communication about communication itself.

Negroponte flip is the idea that broadcast communication technologies that use the air waves to transmit signals will shift underground and distribute information through wires. Conversely, telephone technologies that now travel through wires will move into the air waves.

Telepresence is the experience of presence created when using a communication medium, such as a telephone, computer network, or teleconferencing system.

W E B S I T E S

Electropolis by Elizabeth Reid. http://www.aluluei.com
Journal of Computer-Mediated Communication. http://www.ascusc.org/jcmc

B I B L I O G R A P H Y

Agre, P. (1998). The Internet and public discourse. *First Monday, 3* (3) [Online], 10 pp. Available at http://www.firstmonday.dk/issues/issue3_3/agre/. Downloaded April, 14, 2000.

Barnes, S. B. (2001). *Online connections: Internet interpersonal relationships*. Cresskill, NJ: Hampton Press.

Bateson, G. (1972). *Steps to an ecology of mind*. New York: Ballantine Books.

Bertman, S. (1998). *Hyperculture: The human cost of speed*. Westport, CT: Praeger.

Booth, R., & Jung, M. (1996). *Romancing the net*. Rocklin, CA: Prima Publishing.

Bukatman, S. (1993). *Terminal identity*. Durham, NC: Duke University Press.

Carey, J. W. (1988). *Communication as culture*. New York: Routledge.

Carse, J. P. (1986). *Finite and infinite games: A vision of life as play and possibility*. New York: The Free Press.

Cassidy, M. F. (2001, March). Cyberspace meets domestic space: Personal computers, women's work, and the gendered territories of the family home. *Critical Studies in Media Communication, 18*, (1), 44–65.

Cathcart, R., & Gumpert, G. (1986). The person-computer interaction: A unique source. In G. Gumpert & R. Cathcart (Eds.), *Inter media: Interpersonal communication in a media world*, (pp. 323–332). New York: Oxford University Press.

Csikszentmihalyi, M. (1990). *Flow: The psychology of optimal experience*. New York: Harper and Row.

Danet, B., Rudenberg, L., & Rosenbaum-Tamari, Y. (1998). Hmmm . . . Where's that smoke coming from? Writing, play and performance on internet relay chat. In F. Sudweeks, M. McLaughlin, & S. Rafaeli (Eds.), *Network & netplay*. Menlo Park, CA: AAAI Press/The MIT Press.

Danet, B., Wachenhauser, T., Bechar-Israeli, H., Cividalli, A., & Rosenbaum-Tamari, Y. (1995). Curtain time :@/00 GMT: Experiments with virtual theater on Internet relay chat. *Journal of Computer Mediated Communication*, Vol. 1, Issue 2, (Online) 55pp. Available: http://www.ascusc.org/jcmc/vol1/issue2/contents.html (Downloaded March 28, 2002).

Dery, M. (1993). *Flame wars: The discourse of cyberculture*. Durham, N.C.: Duke University Press.

Gibson, W. (1984). *Neuromancer*. New York: Ace Books.

Goffman, E. (1974). *Frame analysis: An essay on the organization of experience*. New York: Harper and Row.

Herz, J. C. (1995). *Surfing on the Internet*. Boston: Little, Brown and Company.

Horton, D., & Wohl, R. R. (1956/1986). Mass communication and para-social interaction: Observation on intimacy at a distance. In G. Gumpert & R. Cathcart (Eds.), *Inter media: Interpersonal communication in a media world* (3rd ed., pp. 185–206). New York: Oxford University Press.

Innis, H. A. (1951). *The bias of communication*. Toronto: University of Toronto Press.

Kuehn, S. (1993). Communication innovation on a BBS: A content analysis. *Interpersonal Computing and Technology, 1* (2) [Online], 12 pp. Available: http://www.helsinki.fi/science/optek/1993/n2kuehn.txt. Downloaded April 21, 2001.

McCaffery, L. (1992). *Storming the reality studio: A casebook of cyberpunk and postmodern fiction*. Durham, NC: Duke University Press.

McLuhan, M. (1964). *Understanding media*. New York: Signet Books.

McLuhan, M., & Fiore, Q. (1967). *The medium is the massage*. New York: Simon & Schuster.

Meyrowitz, J. (1985). *No sense of place*. New York: Oxford University Press.

Mitchell, W. J. (1995). *City of bits: Space, place, and the infobahn*. Cambridge, MA: The MIT Press.

Negroponte, N. (1995). *Being digital*. New York: Random House.

Odzer, C. (1997). *Virtual spaces: Sex and the cyber citizen*. New York: Berkeley Books.

Pavlik, J. V. (1998). *New media technology: Cultural and commercial perspectives* (2nd ed.). Boston: Allyn & Bacon.

Phleagar, P. (1995). *Love online: A practical guide to online dating*. Reading, MA: Addison-Wesley Publishing Company.

Postman, N. (1992). *Technopoly: The surrender of culture to technology*. New York: Alfred A. Knopf.

Reid, E. M. (1991). *Electropolis: Communication and community on Internet relay chat* [Online], 40 pp. Available: http://www.ee.mu.oz.au/papers/emr/electropolis.html. Downloaded May 15, 1997.

Salvador, T. (1996, October). A matter of good practice. *Interpersonal Computing and Technology, 4* (3–4) [Online], 41–48. Available: http://jan.ucc.nau.edw/~ipct-j (Downloaded March 28, 2002).

Seabrook, J. (1997). *Deeper: My two-year odyssey in cyberspace*. New York: Simon & Schuster.

Slouka, M. (1995). *War of the worlds*. New York: Basic Books.

Sproull, L., & Kiesler, S. (1991). *Connections: New ways of working in the networked organization.* Cambridge, MA: The MIT Press.

Stone, A. R. (1991). Will the real body please stand up?: Boundary stories about virtual cultures. In M. Benedikt (Ed.), *Cyberspace: First steps* (pp. 81–118). Cambridge, MA: The MIT Press.

Stone, A. R. (1995). *The war of desire and technology at the close of the mechanical age.* Cambridge, MA: The MIT Press.

Strate, L. (1995). Experiencing cybertime: Computing as activity and event. *Interpersonal Computing & Technology: An Electronic Journal for the 21st Century, 3* (2), [Online], 78–91. Available: http://jan.ucc.nau.edu/~ipct-j (Downloaded March 28, 2002).

Strate, L. (1996). Cybertime. In L. Strate, R. Jacobson, & S. Gibson (Eds.), *Communication and Cyberspace* (pp. 351–377). Cresskill, NJ: Hampton Press.

Strate, L. (1999, Summer). The varieties of cyberspace: Problems in definition and delimitation. *Western Journal of Communication, 63* (3), 382–412.

Wallace, P. (1999). *The psychology of the Internet.* New York: Cambridge University Press.

Webster, J., Trevino, L. K., & Ryan, L. (1993). The dimensionality and correlates of flow inhuman-computer interactions. *Computers in Human Behavior, 9,* 411–426.

3 Human–Computer Interaction (HCI)

Chapter Overview

New ways of interacting with computers blur the boundaries between CMC and human–computer interaction (HCI) because voice recognition and human behavior patterns are incorporated into interface design. All levels of interactivity occur through the computer's interface. For instance, informational interactivity is communication between Web page creators and users. This type of interactivity occurs through Web and interface design. Many Web pages are designed to support CMC genres, such as online games, chat, and discussion groups. In addition to providing access to information, HCI is integral to both informatics and conferencing activities on the Internet. People must feel comfortable sitting in front of a computer and interacting with it before they can engage in information seeking and Internet correspondence.

The theory and practice of HCI is based on human conversation and behavior. Programmers write conversational messages to communicate with users. As interface technology advances, voice recognition and intelligent agents are being incorporated into interface design. Intelligent agents converse with users through programmed conversational patterns. These simulated conversations are very realistic, and users are not always aware that they are conversing with a program, not a person. The following HCI concepts are presented to provide an understanding of how people interact with their computers:

- A historical overview about the development of HCI
- HCI terminology
- Learning theory and interface design
- Future trends in computer interface design, including voice recognition, social interfaces, and intelligent agent software
- The computer as source (CAS) model versus the computer as medium (CAM) model for examining the ways in which people interact with computers

As computer technology becomes more sophisticated, new methods for interacting with computers are emerging. Traditionally, CMC refers to people using computer networks to communicate with other people. With the introduction of the Web, it has become more difficult to separate CMC and human–computer interactions (HCI) because Web design includes elements from both CMC and HCI. Web designers incorporate e-mail, discussion areas, and other CMC genres into Web pages. Interface researchers use the term **human–computer–human interaction** (HCHI) to describe human interaction with technology that moves beyond the individual computer and into network communication. In contrast, communication scholars use the term CMC.

HCI and HCHI software programs incorporate features that resemble human communication because interface designers write messages that are conversational. Examples include: "Do you want to save this file?" and "You've got mail." Although interface design is not a direct form of interpersonal communication, people do create the messages being communicated to users. So, human communication is an aspect of the design process. At present, programmers are developing new ways for people to interact with their computers that are more conversational. Voice recognition and intelligent agent software transform written interface interaction into verbal exchanges. People can now talk to their computers to execute commands, and computer software can verbally respond.

Development of Human–Computer Interaction

An **interface** is a contact point between a person and a technology. For example, the doorknob is the interface for a door. Similarly, the computer's screen, keyboard, and mouse are the contact points between a person using the computer (user) and the machine. Sutcliffe (1989) describes the **computer interface** as the part of the system that the user sees, hears, and communicates with. Early electronic computers used punch cards and teletype machines as an interface. Information was fed into the machines through punched cards, and information came out of the computer on the teletype machine. This first method of computer interaction was called **batch processing**. Batch processing, the first generation of interfaces, was using punch card technology to input data to be calculated into a computer. But this method was very slow. People would supply punch card instructions and wait hours or days until their cards were processed.

After World War II, many new methods for computer interaction were developed through military projects. For example, the Whirlwind and SAGE projects introduced the use of light pens and display screens as computer interfaces. In 1960, J. C. R. Licklider, an MIT psychology professor, wrote a paper that described *human–computer symbiosis*, the idea that people should be able to think and interact with a computer at the same time. Building on Licklider's idea, Ivan Sutherland created the first interactive computer, called *Sketchpad*.

Sutherland was an MIT graduate student of J. C. R. Licklider and Claude Shannon, the originator of the famous Shannon–Weaver model of communication. *Sketchpad* used a graphical style of interaction that enabled a computer to quickly respond to a user's actions by immediately updating drawings displayed on a screen. Completed in 1962, *Sketchpad*, the first system ever built for interactive computer graphics, was a technological milestone. It demonstrated that computers could be used for something other than data processing. As a result, *Sketchpad* is considered the historical starting point for computer graphics and was an important step in the development of **interactive computing**.

The concept of interactive computing, directly interacting with a computer in real time, was further developed by Douglas C. Engelbart at the Stanford Research Institute in

California. Engelbart's goal was to develop interactive computer systems that would match computational capabilities with human capabilities (Figure 3.1). He wanted to design a new category of computer applications for augmenting human thinking. Using electronic computers, Engelbart envisioned a future in which individuals and small groups would be able to perceive, think, reason, analyze, and communicate with each other. Engelbart and his team designed a series of interactive computer tools, which included the first mouse. These tools became the foundation for the future development of hypertext, computer-supported cooperative work (CSCW), the graphical user interface (GUI), electronic mail, videoconferencing, and the Web. The technologies pioneered by Sutherland and Engelbart helped to transform computers from batch-processing data calculators into interactive communication devices that immediately responded to human commands.

Human–Computer Interaction (HCI)

Human–computer interaction (HCI) is the way in which people interact with computers, including the interface, keyboard, mouse, and other input and output devices. HCI brings many disciplines together, including psychology, sociology, ergonomics, education, computer science, software engineering, and artificial intelligence. It deals with human factors associated with computer interfaces, such as levels of knowledge, work environment, productivity, and satisfaction. As computer-based digital technologies become available to more people, there is a need to make them easy to access and use. This is the role of the interface.

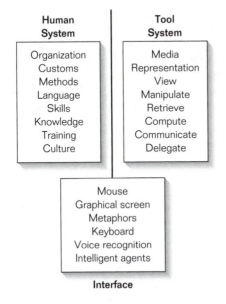

FIGURE 3.1 Interface System. The Interface is the point of contact between the computer and the user. The original model for human–computer interaction was developed by Douglas C. Engelbart. Contemporary interface designs are based on human behavior and conversation.

Desktop Metaphor

One way to make interfaces easier to use, is to apply a visual metaphor to the design. A metaphor is a figure of speech in which one thing is spoken about in terms of something else. Stated another way, it is a comparison between things that are dissimilar. For example, if you compare an Apple Powerbook to a Gateway laptop, you are making a literal comparison between similar things because both are computers. In contrast, if you say that a computer is like a thinking mind, then you are creating a metaphor. Like a linguistic metaphor, a visual one points to a resemblance to something else. For instance, the **desktop metaphor** used in many computer interface designs makes a comparison between objects found in an office and computer commands.

The desktop metaphor was originally created at Xerox Palo Alto Research Center (PARC). The PARC designers realized that it would be easier for office workers to operate a computer if the interface resembled objects from a normal working environment. Consequently, they adopted the idea of the computer screen as a desktop. The desktop metaphor was later used by Apple Computer for its Macintosh series of computers. Similarly, Microsoft adopted the desktop metaphor for its Windows operating system environment. The desktop metaphor is an electronic representation of familiar office objects (Figure 3.2). The computer screen displays small pictures or icons that represent file folders, file cabinets, and a trash can or recycling bin. Objects displayed on the "desktop" are directly manipulated with a mouse. Today, most computer users work with a desktop interface such as Windows or Macintosh when they use their computers.

Direct Manipulation

At present, there are two major types of computer interfaces—**command line** and **graphical user**. The first generation of interface design required people to input information through punched cards. The second generation, command line interfaces, introduced interactivity into interface design by having people type text-based commands on a keyboard. The third generation, called *graphical interfaces*, introduced the feature of **direct manipulation**. Direct manipulation interfaces are a more naturalistic style of interaction because

FIGURE 3.2   Desktop Metaphor. The most popular metaphor in interface design is the desktop. The metaphor was originally used to make it easier for office workers to use computers. By using familiar office concepts, people could easily conceptualize computer functions.

they add visual communication to the process of operating a computer. Users point and click on icons rather than type textual commands. According to Shneiderman (1987), direct manipulation replaces "complex command language syntax [with] direct manipulation of the object of interest" (p. 180). Direct manipulation provides immediate visual feedback during computer operations by enabling users to manipulate objects displayed on a screen. This graphical approach to interface design, which often takes the form of the desktop metaphor, works on several different levels of representation. These levels are based on cognitive learning theory.

Human–Computer Interaction and Cognitive Theory

In the 1950s, psychologists, linguists, philosophers, and anthropologists joined forces to explore symbolic activities and understand how people construct meaning from the world. Their efforts started the **cognitive revolution**, and researchers began to explore different ways in which the mind works to acquire knowledge. For example, Bruner's (1966) research on child development revealed that children go through three different learning stages in which they use three different mentalities, identified as *enactive, iconic*, and *symbolic*. In the enactive stage, children learn through action and interacting with the world. The second stage, iconic, is heavily dependent on visual information and the ability to understand abstract images. Finally, in the symbolic stage, children learn words and language. According to Bruner, people use these three different mentalities to acquire knowledge and construct meaning about the world in which they live.

Before the cognitive revolution, it was generally believed that language was the only communication system used to acquire knowledge about the world. But today, researchers argue that people use many different intelligences and symbol systems to understand their environment. Inspired by cognitive research, Alan Kay and his team at Xerox PARC began to experiment with developing computer languages that could be understood by children. Kay applied Bruner's learning theory research to interface design and invented an interface model called "Doing with Images Makes Symbols" (Figure 3.3). Children would first interact with the computer by using a mouse to select visual icons on the screen. Afterwards they could move to a symbolic level of programming.

Graphical interfaces use three different levels of representation (enactive, iconic, and symbolic). A mouse is used as a form of enactive representation to actively navigate and manipulate text and icons displayed on a computer screen. Visual icons and windows are incorporated into the design as a level of iconic representation. For the third level of symbolic representation, the Xerox researchers created an object-oriented programming language called *Smalltalk*. Kay's first two levels of representation, the icons and mouse, were later applied to graphical interfaces developed by Apple Computer and Microsoft.

Graphical User Interfaces

Early personal computers, such as the Apple II and IBM PC, used command-line interfaces. The shift from command-line to graphical user interfaces developed as the computer's dis-

---

FIGURE 3.3   Doing with Images Makes Symbols

Alan Kay developed an interface design model, "Doing with Images Makes Symbols," that was inspired by theories of human cognitive learning and behavior.

DOING with	mouse	enactive	Know where you are, manipulate
IMAGES makes	icons, windows	iconic	recognize, compare, configure, concrete
SYMBOLS	Smalltalk [computer language]	symbolic	tie together long chains or reasoning, abstract

---

Source: Used by permission from Alan Kay.

play screen replaced teletype printers as user interfaces. As display screens replaced print-ers, computer designers began to use *windows* as a technique to present groups of infor-mation to the user. Information presented in windows could be presented in the form of text, numbers, graphics, and icons. The introduction of icons into computer screen design later developed into graphical user interface technology. Ichbiah and Knepper (1991) describe graphical user interfaces (GUI) as follows:

> A method of displaying text and graphics on a computer screen using pictures and images formed by patterns of dots. A text interface, in contrast, displays information with only num-bers, letters, and punctuation symbols. GUIs are thought to help make a computer easier and more pleasant to use. The Apple Macintosh computer has a built-in GUI. Microsoft Win-dows is software that puts a GUI on top of text-based DOS on IBM PCs and compatibles (p. 276).

Today, the graphical Web has replaced command-line or text-based interfaces as a method for engaging in CMC and accessing information from the Internet. In graphical user interface design, a visual object is first selected on the computer screen with a mouse. The user then chooses an action from a list of command menus to make the object do something. For example, the user can select an icon of a document with the mouse, and then go to the command menu and choose "open." The document will then open and appear on the com-puter screen.

The Macintosh, first introduced in 1984, was the first computer to be marketed with a graphical interface. Levy (1994) says that graphical interfaces were a key factor in mak-ing computers accessible to ordinary people: "Before 1984 the concept of ordinary human beings participating in digital worlds belonged to the arcane realm of data processing and science fiction. After Macintosh, these digital worlds began to weave themselves into the fabric of everyday life" (p. 8). According to Levy, introducing people to user-friendly graphical interfaces altered our perceptions about computing because graphical interfaces enabled average people to operate computers. Similarly, graphical Web browsers make it easier for people to use the Internet.

After the popularity of the Macintosh, Microsoft developed its own graphical interface, called *Windows*. In contrast to Kay's idea of developing graphical interfaces to enable children to learn how to program computers, Macintosh and Windows interfaces were developed to make operating a computer easier or **user-friendly**. According to Heckel (1984), user-friendly software is software that communicates well with the user. By representing computer operations primarily on iconic and enactive levels, people do not have to learn or remember complicated programming commands when operating their computers.

Replacing written computer commands and syntax with visual icons adds a level of **visual communication** to computer interaction. Visual communication is the way in which individuals interpret and create visual messages. The visual icons used in graphical interfaces make operating a computer so much easier that graphical interfaces have been developed for many different types of digital devices, including the Internet, portable digital assistants, and Web TV, and their widespread use has made them a standard feature for personal computing, portable digital devices, and Internet access. As computers and digital devices are used by more people, older designs are adapted and new ones are developed for greater accessibility and ease of use. Some of these new designs incorporate voice recognition and intelligent agents. As a result, the next generation of interfaces will incorporate more human communication characteristics.

Voice Recognition Software

Most people prefer speaking to writing. Currently, technology exists to enable people to interact with their computer through natural-language voice commands. **Natural-language programs** enable users to speak in a normal conversational pattern into a computer to execute commands. These programs also allow users to dictate text. **Speech recognition** is the ability of a computer to understand spoken instructions. However, speech recognition is not an exact science. Users must first spend time training the program to learn the patterns of the speaker. Additionally, like-sounding words in the same sentence can create a problem for the speech software because there may not be enough context for the program to puzzle out the meaning. Programs such as IBM's *Via Voice Gold* and Dragon System's *Naturally Speaking Preferred* enable users to combine voice-driven commands with mouse and keyboard commands.

Voice recognition interfaces are currently being applied to a new information service called **voice portals**. Voice portals combine the interactivity of the Internet with the simplicity and availability of telephone services. Services are accessed through cell phones and are designed for people who need information when they are away from their computers. Services include providing information about traffic, restaurant locations, hotel reservations, airline schedules, and stock quotes. Another type of voice recognition interface is Sprint's voice-activated dialing for cellular-phone users. Sprint's cellular phones can store a series of voice-activated numbers in memory that users can easily trigger. In the future, voice recognition may become the preferred method of computer interaction.

The Social Interface

Another emerging trend in interface design is the **social interface**. A social interface incorporates intelligent agent programs to create a method of interaction that more closely resembles human conversations. The development of social interfaces is based on the work of Stanford researchers Byron Reeves and Clifford Nass, who argue that *media equal real life*. Reeves and Nass conducted a series of experiments to demonstrate that people use their knowledge about people to make judgments about computers. Consequently, people react to computers the way they react to other people (Figure 3.4).

Microsoft developed the first commercial social interface, called *Microsoft Bob*, based on the work of Reeves and Nass. *Microsoft Bob* was an attempt to develop an interface that more closely resembled real-world situations with face-to-face interactions. Moreover, it was the first commercial attempt to shift the interface paradigm away from graphical approaches toward social ones. Instead of interacting with visual icons, users would interact with the Friends of Bob. Leonard (1997) describes the interface as follows:

> The friends of Bob include fourteen "personal guides," each of which has a different personality. . . . The guides express their personalities through pithy one-liners and brief animated movement—when surprised, Rover [a cartoon dog] may utter a phrase like "Land Sakes!" and waggle his ears.
>
> The guides offer a series of choices for navigational tools, but Bob includes no manual. It is the personal guides or nothing (although for those who absolutely can't abide neurotic "gryphons" or importuning animals, one guide takes the form of a no-nonsense wall-mounted speaker (p. 74).

Microsoft Bob introduced conversational interactions into interface design. However, the program was a commercial failure because users did not like the "personalities" of the characters. Despite *Bob's* failure in the marketplace, social interfaces continue to develop as intelligent agent software is integrated into interface design. Rather than manipulate visual icons, this new approach enables users to delegate tasks to personalized software agents. Maes (1994) describes agents in the following way: "We have modeled an interface

---

FIGURE 3.4   Reeves and Nass Social Rules and Computers. Reeves and Nass discovered that people react to computers in the same way that they react to other people. In experiments, when a computer is substitued for a person, the following rules about praise and criticism apply:

Rule 1: People will think they performed a task better when they are flattered by a computer.

Rule 2: People will like the computer more when they are flattered by it.

Rule 3: Whether praise is appropriate or not will have no impact on what people think about the computer that has praised them.

Rule 4: People will like the compuer more and believe that the computer is better when it praises them rather than when it criticizes them.

Source: Adapted from Reeves and Nass, 1996.

agent after the metaphor of a personal assistant" (p. 40). Agents are designed to talk to people in a conversational style that is similar to CMC.

However, Shneiderman (1997) is troubled by the term *intelligent* in software design because of its obvious reference to humans. He states, "The metaphors and terminology we choose can shape the thoughts of everyone from researchers and designers to members of Congress and the press" (pp. 97–98). As a result, designers have a responsibility to select the best metaphor possible for the technology they create. At present, the metaphor of an intelligent agent is being applied to software programs that converse with users through natural language. Increasingly, the metaphors and tools associated with HCI and CMC relate to human characteristics.

Intelligent Agents

Although the introduction of graphical interfaces made computers easier to use, the current generation of graphical interfaces is becoming complex and difficult for users to operate. This can occur because it is hard for people to remember the meanings of numerous icons displayed on the screen. One solution to this visual complexity problem is to integrate intelligent agent software into interface design. **Intelligent agents** are generally defined as software that helps people by acting on their behalf to locate information or solve problems. They serve a mediating role between people and software programs. Software agents are designed to deal with two practical programming concerns: helping (1) to simplify the complexities of computing and (2) to overcome the limitations of current graphical user interface designs.

At times, the sequence of commands input into a graphical interface can become a series of tedious steps. Direct manipulation makes users spell out and input each action for the computer to explicitly execute. Many of these steps can be automated with the aid of agent technology. For example, Web browser agents keep track of the Web sites a user visits and customizes the user's view of the Web. Personal shopping assistants help users find desired items quickly without having to surf through pages of merchandise. Once the shopper's preferences are learned, the agent will arrange items appropriately. Agents automate computer interaction.

Mailer Daemons and Bots

One of the early software programs used to automate repetitive computer tasks was the daemon. Originally, daemon software programs were developed to help perform digital housework. For example, mailer daemons deal with a host of mailing problems, including returning messages sent to nonexistent addresses. These programs were written to handle time-consuming routine computer tasks. According to Leonard (1997), daemon programs later evolved into a more sophisticated program called a *bot.* "Bot" stands for "software robot." According to Leonard (1997):

A bot is a software version of a mechanical robot. Like a mechanical robot, it is guided by algorithmic rules of behavior—*if this happens, do that; if that happens, do this.* But instead of clanking around a laboratory room bumping into walls, software robots are programs that maneuver through cyberspace, bouncing off of communication protocols and operating systems (p. 7).

Bots come in a variety of forms. For example, programs that carry on conversations are called *chatterbots*. The first computer program to have a conversation with a person was the chatterbot program called *ELIZA*. Alexbot, who runs the IRC *Jeopardy* game, is another example of a chatterbot. This bot did such a good job of mimicking Alex Trebek that Trebek threatened to sue. As a result, the bot is now called RobBot. IRC *Jeopardy* runs twenty-four hours a day, seven days a week, and never stops. RobBot is constantly playing the game and interacting with human players.

However, not all bots are playful. Some bots can become disruptive and annoying. As a result, many IRC channels do not allow bots because it is difficult to tell a malicious bot from a benign one. For example, Quittner (1995) wrote an article about a bot that was using his online identity. He first became aware of the software impostor when a mailer daemon sent back a bounced e-mail message to his account that he did not write. After receiving the strange e-mail message, Quittner decided to track down the person who was responsible. But the impersonator turned out to be a software bot. It was a program written by a hacker who Quittner had been interviewing for a book he was writing. After confronting the hacker, the bot disappeared from the network.

Bots are written for both fun and mischief. However, some researchers are concerned that the development of bots could have negative consequences for the online environment. A major concern about bots is what happens after they are let loose on the Internet, because once bots are placed on the network, they are out of the direct control of their programmers. Bots are designed to autonomously complete tasks without the aid of a human operator. Leonard (1997) describes the problem as follows:

> Each technological advance paves the way for new pitfalls, each reaction breeds its own counter-reaction. If there is a technological problem, someone somewhere in the massively parallel-processed Net will come up with a solution, and that solution will fast be adopted by others. If bad bots run amok, good bots will appear to counteract them or the system as a whole will be redesigned to quash their delinquent outbursts.
>
> There is no end to the cycle. There is no ultimate solution to the problems engendered by bots and humans in the wild Net. The system as a whole is in a constant fretful balance, a state of uneasy stability, a perpetually evolving standoff (p. 26).

Bots introduce autonomous behavior and simulated conversation into CMC. As computer software becomes more conversational, people will increasingly be interacting with software programs rather than human beings. Communication researchers examining CMC will have to factor this new type of interaction into their research efforts.

Characteristics of Agents

Agents are autonomous. This means that agents have control over their own actions. As a result, agents introduce the concept of **indirect management** into HCI. Indirect management allows users to give general guidelines to agents, who then execute commands. The agent metaphor is one of a personal assistant who collaborates with the user. Indirect manipulation occurs when a user activates agent technology to perform an indirect task for them, such as filtering and forwarding e-mail, searching for information, and helping to arrange a travel itinerary.

Agents are goal driven. Programming scripts predefine their actions and define goals. Agents are also driven by rules that define goals. Some agent programs are designed to change their goals over time. Other types of agents can be designed to sense changes in their environment and respond to these changes. For instance, an agent programmed to respond to an environment is instructed to do *y* when *x* occurs. As autonomous programs, agents can continue to work after the user has left his or her computer. For example, agents can be programmed to search overnight for information on the Internet and present the findings to the user in the morning.

In multiagent systems, agents interact and communicate with other agents. Some can learn or change their behavior based on previous experiences. Although agent technology has been around for a number of years, the use of agents is still in its early stage of development. With the explosion of information on the Internet and the increased complexity of graphical interfaces, agents are being developed to make access to information and computer interaction easier.

Agents and Interfaces

Negroponte (1997) uses the metaphor of a butler to describe the role of agents in HCI. The success of interface agent design depends on anthropomorphism. **Anthropomorphism** is the attribution of human characteristics to a computer. The goal of interface agent design is to create a lifelike computer character that can converse and visually react to the user.

According to Riecken (1994): "The basic idea of agent research is to develop software systems which engage and help all types of end users" (p. 20). Goodman (1994) describes agents in action:

> While you're busy doing something else, your electronic agent connects to a flight reservation service, locates flights that meet your time schedule, books the reservation (even paying for the tickets with your credit card), and sends you an e-mail message with confirmation data. Even that e-mail message has agentlike powers, because the note will ask you if you want to insert the flight data into the calendar that is kept in your personal communicator. A tap of the Yes button makes that happen (p. 125).

Agents can search through databases to locate information on specific topics. Once information is obtained, agentlike processes can also create customized newspapers and assemble articles that relate to specific industries and interests. Maes states: "I hope agents will make people feel more comfortable dealing with the overload of information, more in control. Confident agents are working on their behalf, are reliable, and never become tired; they are always looking to help the user" (cited in Berkun, 1995, p. 11).

For people to feel comfortable with agents, they must be able to communicate easily with them. Cohen and Levesque (1997) argue that there must be a common language shared between agents and users to facilitate the communication process. As the technology of interface design shifts from the desktop to agents, it will become necessary for communication students to examine both the ways in which people communicate with each other through computers and also how people communicate with the software. Instead of invoking commands by clicking on icons with a mouse, people will talk to their computers.

Software designers deliberately try to use a conversational style in their software because people's expectations about HCI are often based on what they expect from human-to-human interaction. Written messages play an important role in both HCI and CMC; however, people do not always realize that some of the e-mail messages they receive are sent to them by a software program. For instance, students will reply to messages sent to them by mail programs that return e-mail messages. Distinguishing between messages generated by a software agent (HCI) and messages written by a human being (CMC) is becoming more difficult. As interface agents become a common method of computer interaction, these new interface designs in which software talks to people blur the boundaries between HCI and CMC.

Chatterbots

Computer scientists working on natural-language programs use the Turing test as a measure of how realistic their programs are when they converse with people. The test is designed to determine whether a program can imitate a human being in typed, written conversation. Judges sit in one room and a person and computer are placed in a different room. The judges ask questions of both the human and a computer and try to determine which questions are being answered by the computer and which ones are answered by the human. If the computer deceives the judges, it is said to have passed a Turing test. Chatterbots have passed the Turing test.

The *ELIZA* program, created by Joseph Weizenbaum and one of the first natural-language programs created, is categorized as a chatterbot. **Chatterbots** are designed to carry on a conversation with a person. *ELIZA* was programmed to parody a Rogerian psychologist, who mirrors a patient's comments. For instance, if a patient mentions a topic, the psychologist will repeat it back to the patient. By quoting part of a user's sentence and changing simple pronouns, the program gave the impression that it was human. *ELIZA* became part of computer folklore because it was reported that Weizenbaum's secretary asked him to leave the room when she conversed with the program. *ELIZA* was also an early example of Reeves and Nass's view that people anthropomorphize computer technology. In fact, Weizenbaum was so concerned about people's attachment to the *ELIZA* program that he became an outspoken critic of artificial intelligence.

A program that has successfully passed the Turing test on numerous occasions is *Julia*, a MUD-based bot. *Julia* interacts with other users in a MUD environment as if she were another player. *Julia* clearly blurs the boundaries between software and human interactions; people often do not realize that she is a program. For instance, it took one young man several weeks to realize that *Julia* was a software program. *Julia* keeps track of various MUD statistics about room locations and can answer questions about locations and players. *Julia* understands who she is and the fact that she is situated in a MUD world. Her conversational style is natural and she has been programmed to appear "human." *Julia* describes herself in a variety of ways and sometimes appears coy (Figure 3.5).

The coyness comes from the fact that traditionally MUDs were occupied by male players, and female players often received many advances. After spending years in male-dominated MUDs, *Julia's* programming code deals in large part with detecting and deflecting male passes. The tendency of people to anthropomorphize also makes *Julia* appear to be human. Even experienced MUD players who know that *Julia* is a software program often express an emotional reaction to her that is generally reserved for biological entities, such as people and pets. *Julia* elicits surprisingly emotional reactions from her conversational partners.

At the present time, computer programs do not have artificial intelligence and machines cannot think. Although computers can recognize words, they do not understand language. Software programs can only mimic human conversation within limited contexts. Alexbot, or RobBot, is a perfect example of how this works because the task performed by the bot is restricted to the game of *Jeopardy*. Similarly, *Julia* exists in a limited software environment. When written for MUDs and IRC, bots are created for fun and they liven up social spaces on the Internet. In contrast, social interfaces incorporate bots to make using a computer easier and less complex.

FIGURE 3.5   A Conversation with the Intelligent Agent Julia. This software program mimics human conversation so well that people do not always realize that they are conversing with a program, not a person. Intelligent agents add human conversational styles to human–computer interaction.

```
You say, "julia, how old are you?"
Julia says, " I am 21 years old."
You say, "julia describe yourself"
Julia whispers, "I'm 5'1" tall, weigh 123 lbs, with close-cropped
frizzy blond hair and dark brown eyes."
You say, "julia, what color are your eyes?"
Julia whispers, "I have dark brown eyes, Lenny."
[ . . .]
You say, "julia, what sex are you?"
Julia says, "Can't you tell?"
You say, " julia what sex are you>"
Julia says, " Don't you know?"
You say, " julia, what sex are you?"
Julia says, " I'm female."
```

Source: Foner, 1999, p. 331.

Computers as Social Actors (CAS) Model

As computer interfaces integrate intelligent agent software, people will be communicating with computers that are more conversational. The research of Moon and Nass (1996) and Reeves and Nass (1996) indicates that people project personality traits onto computers. These personality traits appear psychologically real to users. As a result, people often consider computers to be an independent social actor or source of information. Sundar and Nass (2000) set up an experiment to test the **computer as source (CAS) model** against the **computer as medium (CAM) model**.

Considering the computer to be a medium for distributing information is consistent with traditional mass communication research. For instance, **media effects research**, the study of the affect of mass media messages on audiences, examines messages and their characteristics. The medium itself is not a factor in this type of analysis. Similarly, the CAM model is based on the concept that a computer is a medium between the user and the programmer. When people reply to program messages displayed on their computer screens, they are indirectly dealing with a person (the programmer or Web designer), rather than a machine. In terms of communication theory, the programmer is seen as the source of information. Users respond to messages that programmers create.

In contrast to this view, Sundar and Nass (2000) discovered that people respond to computers as an independent source of information. The CAS model argues that users do not think beyond the machine to the programmer. Instead, they consider the computer to be the source of information. Moreover, users respond socially to computers. Studies examining the social response to computers reveal that users' social expectations about computers and their response to the machine are based on social rules that apply to human behavior.

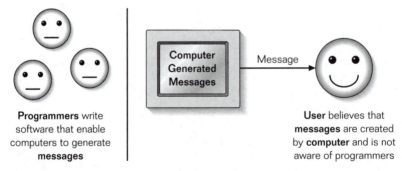

Programmers write software that enable computers to generate **messages**

Computer Generated Messages

Message

User believes that **messages** are created by **computer** and is not aware of programmers

FIGURE 3.6   Computer as Source (CAS) Model. In traditional communication models, messages are created and sent by individuals and people working in organizations, not the technology transmitting the message. According to this view, software messages would be created and sent by programmers, and programmers are the source of information. In contrast, computer users perceive computer messages to be created by the computer and the computer is the source of information. Most computer users are unaware of the programmers that write the software to generate messages

For example, "A computer that praises itself or criticizes other computers is . . . perceived to be less friendly than a computer that praises other computers or criticizes itself" (Sundar & Nass, 2000, p. 3). The common explanation for this behavior toward computers is the fact that individuals are socially unaware that they should behave any differently. Because computers are a new technology, people apply human social rules to them because they do not know what else to do.

Sundar and Nass make a sharp distinction between CMC and HCI interaction. With CMC, users know that they are interacting with other people. In contrast, HCI is perceived as interaction with a computer. CMC clearly uses the computer as a medium to deliver messages. In HCI, the computer is both the source of information and the medium for distributing the message, and people tend to forget about the role of the programmer (Figure 3.6). As a result, the computer is viewed as a social actor in the communication exchange.

Summary

Human–computer interface design can be divided into the following four categories: batch processing, command line, graphical user, and social interface. Cognitive theory was used in the development of graphical user interfaces that enable users to directly manipulate visual objects on a computer screen. Current developments in interface design are adding speech recognition and intelligent agents. The addition of intelligent agents to interface design shifts the design paradigm from direct manipulation to indirect manipulation because agents perform autonomous actions.

The computer as medium (CAM) model views the computer as a medium between the programmer and user. When people interact with programs or Web pages, they are indirectly interacting with the programmer or designer. This view is consistent with traditional communication theory. In contrast, the computer as source (CAS) model introduces a new approach to examining the relationship between people and technology. In contrast to viewing the programmers, people, or organizations as the source of information, this model considers the computer to be the source of information. The model is based on the idea that people anthropomorphize their relationship with their computers. As a result, computer users perceive computers to be the source of information rather than the medium that delivers information.

TERMS

Anthropomorphism is attributing human characteristics to a computer.

Batch processing is using punch card technology to input data into a computer to be calculated.

Chatterbots are bots that can talk and are designed to carry on a conversation with a person.

Cognitive revolution refers to a movement started in the 1950s by psychologists, linguists, philosophers, and anthropologists to explore symbolic activities and understand how people construct meaning from the world.

Command-line interfaces that use text-based interaction on which users have to type commands into a keyboard.

The computer as medium (CAM) model is based on the concept that a computer is a medium between the user and the programmer. When people reply to program messages displayed on their computer screen, they are dealing with a person (the programmer or Web designer) rather than a machine.

The computers as source (CAS) model argues that people respond to computers as an independent source of information. Users do not think beyond the machine to the programmer; instead, they consider the computer to be the source of information.

Computer interfaces are the part of the system that the user sees, hears, and communicates with.

Desktop metaphors use an electronic visual representation of familiar office objects, such as file folders, file cabinets and a trash can or recycling bin, to make it easier to operate a computer. Macintosh and Windows use the desktop metaphor.

Direct manipulation provides immediate visual feedback during computer operations by enabling users to manipulate objects displayed on a screen.

Graphical user interface is a method of displaying information and executing computer commands using pictures displayed on the computer screen and a hand-held device called a mouse.

Human–computer interaction (HCI) is the way in which people interact with computers, including the interface, keyboard, mouse, and other input and output devices.

Human–computer–human interaction (HCHI) describes human interaction with technology that moves past interacting with an individual computer and into network communication.

Indirect management allows users to give general guidelines to agents, who then execute commands.

Intelligent agents are generally defined as software that helps people by acting on their behalf to locate information or solve problems.

Interactive computing is directly interacting with a computer in real time using a keyboard, mouse, light pen, or other input device.

Interfaces are contact points between a person and a technology.

Media effects research examines messages distributed through the media and their impact on audiences.

Natural-language programs enable users to speak into a computer in a normal conversational pattern.

Social interface is a new approach to interface design that incorporates intelligent agent technology to create a method of computer interaction that more closely resembles human conversation.

Speech recognition is the ability of a computer to understand spoken instructions.

User-friendly is a term that describes computer systems that are easier or friendlier to use. For instance, the Macintosh is described as user-friendly because it has a graphical interface.

Visual communication is the way in which individuals interpret and create visual messages.

Voice portals combine the interactivity of the Internet with the simplicity and availability of telephone services. Internet services are accessed through cell phones and they are designed for people who need information when they are away from their computers, including information about traffic reports, restaurant locations, hotel reservations, airline schedules, and stock quotes.

EXERCISES

1. Conversational interfaces blur the boundaries between CMC and human–computer interaction. Discuss whether or not people should be made aware of the fact they are interacting with software rather than an actual person. How and when should they be made aware of the difference?

2. In addition to software and interface design, Web sites also use visual metaphors to help users navigate through information. What types of metaphors can be used in Web design to help people access information through the Internet?

3. Discuss the advantages and disadvantages of comparing computers to human minds. What does this comparison tell us about human relationships to technology? What other metaphors might be better?

4. Try to identify ways in which the use of language has changed as the result of computer technology. For instance, how is the @ sign now used?

5. According to Reeves and Nass, people attribute human characteristics to computers. Do you agree or disagree with this idea? Why or why not? Observe your own behavior with computers. Can you describe any personal examples of anthropomorphism?

6. What do you think: Is the computer a medium or a source of information? Explain your position.

BIBLIOGRAPHY

Barnes, S. B. (1997). Douglas Carl Engelbart: Developing the underlying concepts for contemporary computing. *IEEE Annals of the History of Computing, 19* (3), 16–26.

Berkun, S. (1995, April). Agent of change. *Wired,* 116–117.

Bradshaw, J. M. (1997). *Software agents.* Menlo Park, CA: AAAI Press/MIT Press.

Bruner, J. S. (1966). *Toward a theory of instruction.* Cambridge, MA: Harvard University Press.

Cleary, S. (2000, September 18). Speak and you shall receive. *The Wall Street Journal Interactive Edition.*

Cohen, P. R., & Levesque, H. J. (1997). Communicative actions for artificial agents. In J. M. Bradshaw (Ed.), *Software agents* (pp. 419–436). Menlo Park, CA: AAAI Press/MIT Press.

Engelbart, D. C. (1963). A conceptual framework for the augmentation of man's intellect. In P. W. Howerton & David C. Weeks (Eds.), *Vistas in information handling, Vol. I,* (pp. 1–29). Washington, DC: Spartan Books.

Foner, L. N. (1999). Are we having fun yet? Using social agents in social domains. In K. Dautenhahn, (Ed.), *Human cognition and social agent theory* (pp. 323–348). Amsterdam: John Benjamins Publishing Company.

Gardner, H. (1983). *Frames of mind: The theories of multiple intelligences.* New York: Basic Books.

Gardner, H. (1999). *Intelligence reframed: Multiple intelligences for the 21st Century.* New York: Basic Books.

Goodman, D. (1994). *Living at light speed.* New York: Random House.

Heckel, P. (1984). *The elements of friendly software design.* New York: Warner Books.

Herz, J. C. (1995). *Surfing the internet: A nethead's adventures on-line.* New York: Little, Brown & Company.

Ichbiah, D. & Knepper, S. L. (1991). *The making of Microsoft: How Bill Gates and his team created the world's most successful software company.* Rocklin, CA: Prima Publishing.

Johnson, R. R. (1998). *User-centered techology.* Albany: State Univerity of New York Press.

Kay, A. C. (1977, September). Microelectronics and the personal computer. *Scientific American*, pp. 231–244.

Kay, A. C. (1987). *Doing with images makes symbols: Communicating with computers.* Stanford, CA: University Video Communications [videotape].

Kay, A. C. (1990). User interface: A personal view. In Brenda Laurel (Ed.), *The art of human–computer interface design* (pp. 191–207). Reading, MA: Addison-Wesley Publishing Company.

Laurel, B. (1993). *Computers as theatre.* Reading, MA: Addison-Wesley Publishing Company.

Laurel, B. (Ed.). (1990). *The art of human–computer interface design.* Reading: Addison-Wesley Publishing Company.

Leonard, A. (1997). *Bots: The origin of a new species.* San Francisco, CA: HardWired.

Levy, S. (1994). *Insanely great: The life and times of Macintosh, the computer that changed everything.* New York: Viking.

Maes, P. (1994, July). Agents that reduce work and information overload. *Communications of the ACM, 37* (7), 18–21.

Moon, Y., & Nass, C. (1996, December). How "real" are computer personalities? Psychological responses to personality types in human–computer interaction. *Communication Research, 23* (6), 651–674.

Negroponte, N. (1997). Agents: From direct manipulation to delegation. In J. M. Bradshaw, ed., *Software agents,* pp. 57–66. Menlo Park, CA: AAAI Press/The MIT Press.

Negroponte, N. (1995). *Being digital.* New York: Alfred A. Knopf.

Norman, D. A. (1988). *The psychology of everyday things.* New York: Basic Books.

Papert, S. (1980). *Mindstorms.* New York: Basic Books.

Papert, S. (1996). *The connected family.* Marietta, GA: Longstreet Press.

Quittner, J. (1995, April). Autonata no grata. *Wired,* 119–122, 172–173.

Reeves, B., & Nass, C. (1996). *The media equation: How people treat computers, television, and new media like real people and places.* Stanford, CA: CSLI Publications, Cambridge University Press.

Renk, J. M., Branch, R. C., & Chang, E. (1994). Visual information strategies in mental model development. *Selected Readings from the 25th Annual Conference of the International Visual Literacy Association,* pp. 81–91.

Riecken, D. (1994, July). Intelligent agents. *Communications of the ACM, 37* (7), 18–21.

Shneiderman, Ben. (1987). *Designing the user interface: Strategies for effective human–computer interaction.* Reading, MA: Addison-Wesley Publishing Company.

Schneiderman, B. (1997). Direct manipulaiton versus agents: Paths to predictable, controllable, and comprehensible interfaces. In J. M. Bradshaw (Ed.), *Software agents* (pp. 97–108). Menlo Park, CA: AAAI Press/MIT Press.

Sculley, John. (1987). *Odyssey.* New York: Harper & Row, Publishers.

Sundar, S. S., & Nass, C. (2000, December). Source orientation in human–computer interaction: Programmer, networker, or independent social actor? *Communication Research* [Online], 17 pp. ProQuest, Record Number 339204133 [July 9, 2001]

Sutcliffe, Alistair. (1989). *Human–computer interface design.* New York: Springer-Verlag.

4 The Web

Chapter Overview

The fastest growing area of the Internet is the World Wide Web. Web sites are created by individuals, organizations, government agencies, and corporations. Although some scholars consider the Web to be a form of mass communication, increasingly the Web is being utilized for interpersonal communication. For instance, Weblogs are a form of individual journalism and Web rings connect individual Web sites together into Web communities (see Chapter 11). Moreover, media corporations use the Web to build audience communities, and commercial businesses utilize the Web to engage consumers in online transactions.

Web technologies have advanced to include streaming audio and video, and individuals use these technologies to communicate with friends and family. For instance, Webcams are set up in hospitals to broadcast images of newborn babies to relatives. So, in addition to distributing information, the interactive nature of the Web also supports interpersonal communication. Topics covered in this chapter include

- A short history of the Web
- Web characteristics, including hypertext and browsers
- A discussion of interaction and transaction
- The relationship between mass media and the Web
- Types of Web sites
- Strategies for evaluating Web site information
- A uses and gratifications approach to Web usage

Today, it is difficult to imagine American culture without the Web, but the Web has only existed for a little over ten years. In 1990, Tim Berners-Lee originally developed the software protocols for the World Wide Web while he was working at CERN, the European high-energy physics laboratory in Geneva, Switzerland. Initially, the Web was designed to be an electronic library for physicists. Berners-Lee was trying to make it easier for scientists to share research information through the Internet. By placing information into a universal file format that could be read by any computer system, scientists around the world could easily share data resources. In March 1991, Berners-Lee released the World Wide Web software to a limited number of people working at CERN. The original software was a text-based system, and it quickly spread throughout the physics community. The following August, the software was made available on the Internet, and it quickly spread around the world. With the introduction of graphical Web browsers, use of the Web exploded (Figure 4.1). Today, Berners-Lee runs the World Wide Web Consortium to help direct the future development of the technology that he first invented.

Web Characteristics

The Web introduces a number of new characteristics to CMC. These include hypertext, graphical interface technology, and transactional exchanges. Web sites combine both informational and interpersonal interactivity to enable individuals, organizations, and corporations to communicate with each other more easily.

Hypertext

Interactivity is a key feature of Web pages. The majority of Web interactivity is informational because users select the type of content that they want to view. Informational interactivity on the Web is created through *hypertext*, which connects pages together. Ted Nelson coined the term **hypertext** in 1965 to describe nonsequential reading and writing. Hypertext adds interactive features to texts because it enables readers to jump from one piece of information to the next. Nelson envisioned the creation of a large, computerized *docuverse* that would electronically interconnect the world of literature in ways we are unable to connect printed texts. For instance, reference material cited in one text would be directly connected to the original source materials. Readers would be able to interactively move between texts and explore the electronic docuverse created by computer networks (Figure 4.2).

FIGURE 4.1   Early Rapid Growth of the Web

Year	# of Host Sites
1993	623
1994	11,576
1995	23,000
1996	1,000,000
1997	1,500,000
1998	3,500,000
1999	4,000,000
2000	8,000,000
2001	26,000,000+

Sources: Hoffman, Novak, & Chatterjee, 1995; Adamic & Huberman, 2001.

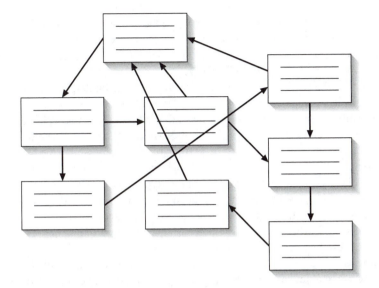

FIGURE 4.2 Illustration of Hypertext Links. Hypertext links connect various pieces of data together, which allows users to jump from one link to another. Links can be arranged in a linear sequence or they can be scatttered across the Internet.

The nonlinear structure of hypertext documents is based on association, rather than a fixed order. With hypertext, information is placed in multiple layers with links to references and examples. In Web sites, a hierarchy of information is created to fit the need of the site. More important information is on the top, or at the beginning of the site. Hypertext documents are linked together from one to another no matter where the documents are geographically located. Berners-Lee created hypertext as a text-based navigational system that would allow users to move freely among many different documents located around the world.

A central concept associated with the Web is the idea of a link. **Internal links** connect pages within a Web site. **External links** connect pages from different Web sites. Links are indicated by underlined words, phrases, visual icons, and audio clips. When the computer's arrow cursor goes over a link, its icon will change to a pointing finger. Information on a single Web page can also be linked to **anchors**. Anchor points make navigating a Web page easier. Instead of breaking documents up over a number of Web pages, some Web designers will keep an entire document on one long scrolling page with linked anchor points. Today, hypertext links are used in a wide range of multimedia documents, including CD-ROMs, interactive fiction, online encyclopedias, and Web pages.

Graphical Browsers

One of the early sites to adopt Web technology was the National Center for Supercomputing Applications (NCSA) at the University of Illinois. Marc Andreessen, a member of the

NCSA computing staff, understood the potential of the Web and began developing a graphical interface for the text-based Web software. As described in the previous chapter, *graphical interfaces* enable computer users to interact with visual icons instead of text-based commands when they operate their computers.

At the time Andreessen discovered the Web, he was an undergraduate at the University of Illinois at Urbana-Champaign (UIUC). He had a part-time job at NCSA building tools for scientific visualization. Andreessen started working on Mosaic, a graphical interface for the Web, to be used as a scientific tool. However, he soon realized that the project would be much larger than he expected. Eric Bina joined Andreessen in the Mosaic project, and together they finished Mosaic, the first Web browser. A **browser** is a program that interprets and displays documents formatted in the **hypertext markup language** (HTML). HTML provides codes used to format Web documents. Individual codes define the hierarchy and nature of the various components of the document and specify hypertext links. For example, <TITLE>Introduction to Computer-Mediated Communication</TITLE> would show the title of a Web page (Figure 4.3).

Andreessen soon left academic life to start his own company called Netscape. At Netscape, he wrote a new browser called Netscape Navigator. The popularity of Netscape and the widespread use of the Web encouraged people at Microsoft to develop a rival product called Internet Explorer. Visually friendly browsers have contributed to the increased use of the Internet because they allow people to easily access information by clicking on words and visual icons.

Navigation and Nontext Features

Graphical browsers add many nontext features to Internet interaction, including icons, logos, maps, photographs, sounds, and video files. Every software program designed to work with a graphical interface introduces new visual elements into human–computer interaction. According to Bolter (1991), "every sophisticated program presents its user with a new vocabulary of data elements that have their own visual expression. These elements become topical units that the user combines to construct meaningful texts" (p. 54). For instance, browsers add visual toolbars to help users navigate the Web (Figure 4.4).

Web pages include the visual features of arrows, buttons, and scroll bars, which enable users to navigate Web documents. For example, an arrow pointing to the right moves

---

FIGURE 4.3   Sample of HTML

```
<HTML> [All pages begin with this tag]
<HEAD> [This tag contains header information, for example, page title]
<TITLE>Computer-Mediated Communication</TITLE>
</HEAD>
</HTML> [This tag ends the HTML document]
```

FIGURE 4.4 The Netscape Browser

Source: © 1999 Netscape Communication Corporation. Used with permission. Netscape Communications has not authorized, sponsored, endorsed, or approved this publication and is not responsible for its content.

one page forward, and an arrow pointing to the left moves backward. Other navigation features include the title tag, title of the page, links, navigation icons, site maps, and internal search engines. **Search engines** are software tools that help users to locate information and content placed on the Web. These include Yahoo!, Alta Vista, and Hotbot. At present, search engines are text based and they find information through keyword searches. Most search engines use some of the words in the title tag of a Web page as keywords for indexing sites.

Every Web page must have a short and descriptive name. Depending on the browser, the title will either appear in the title bar of the window or at the top of the screen. Besides describing the page, the title is used in indexes and bookmarks. For instance, search engines will pick up the title of the site as its default description. Titles should describe the site, for example the CMC Textbook Site, The Antique Clock Company, or Jane Smith's Personal Web site.

As previously discussed, hypertext links are the "hot spots," iconic buttons, or link anchors that connect related pieces of information. For example, links are often created between a term and information that will further explain the term. Similarly, anchors are used for text navigation because they will take readers to different sections of a text. Links can connect to information located on a single site or they can connect to remote sites located on the Internet.

Site maps and indexes help users navigate an individual site. An index or site map will provide a quick overview of the site. An index is an alphabetical listing of the major components of a Web site. In contrast, site maps present a visual representation of the site. These maps are often linked to the sections of the site that they represent. Site maps, navigational icons, and links are all nontextual features incorporated into Web pages. Browsers add nontextual visual elements to the process of searching the Web to make locating information easier.

Web Addresses

Every Web page has its own unique address. **URL** stands for uniform resource locator and it is the address of the Web page. URLs contain information about where the file is located on the Internet. The following is an example:

```
http://www.fordham.edu/communication/welcome.html
protocol//server name (also includes domain name)/path/file name
```

Http:// stands for **hypertext transfer protocol**. It is a communication protocol that Web browsers understand and permits them to move from Web page to Web page around the Internet. The next part of the Web address is the name of the server. Some companies have their own servers, or people can pay a fee to have their site placed on the server of an Internet provider. For example, America Online (AOL) allows its members to place Web sites on the AOL server.

The **domain name** identifies the type of organization operating the Internet server. The five generic domains are gov, edu, com, net, and org (Figure 4.5). Domain names can also be based on physical locations; for example, country codes are included in some Web addresses. Two-letter country codes are based on the International Standards Organization Codes for the representation of names and countries. Examples of country codes include us for the United States, fr for France, jp for japan, and ca for Canada. Domain names are registered, and it is estimated that over 10 million domain names have already been taken (Sandvig, 2000).

As the popularity of the Web grew, corporations began to realize that domain names could be a valuable property. As a result, a number of corporations began purchasing names. For example, Proctor and Gamble purchased many of their prized brand names, such as clearasil.com and charmin.com. They also acquired generic names like babydiapers.com and cough.com. In some cases, the fee for registering a name has been inflated by third-party brokers who set prices for names. Enterprising individuals have purchased domain names with the hope of cashing in by selling the name. For instance, Mark Hogarth, a research fellow at Cambridge University, registered the domain names of 129 living authors and set up a site called writerdomains.com. He was intending to sell the names back to the writers for a percentage of their gross annual sales. Writer Jeanette Winterson (2000) sued Hogarth and won her name back in court. She then posted the decision on a Web site located at http://www.jeanettewinterson.com. Actors have also been targets for this type of Internet name scam. For instance, Julia Roberts had to go to court to win her name back on the Web.

Web Sites and CMC

Like books, magazines, and newspapers, many Web sites are designed to distribute media content to mass audiences. As a result, the Web is considered a mass medium. However, in addition to distributing mass information, some Web sites also incorporate CMC features. For example, Web sites often post user e-mail messages, provide discussion areas, incorporate chat software, and enable users to connect to MUD worlds. Information sites often add CMC features to make the site more interactive. For example, discussion areas add reader interaction to newspaper sites.

Frequently, online newspapers will provide discussion areas to enable readers to interact with the newspaper and other readers. In traditionally printed newspapers, only published letters to the editors are shared with readers. In contrast, online newspapers include ongoing discussion topics as a regular feature of their sites. Readers can exchange messages

---

FIGURE 4.5 Internet Domain Names

Original Domain Names	Example
com (commercial)	http://www.yahoo.com
edu (educational)	http://www.fordham.edu
gov (government)	http://www.whitehouse.gov
mil (military)	http://www.army.mil
net (network)	http://www.att.net

New Domain Names	Example of Use
int (international organizations)	[A new designation for for organizations established by international treaties.]
biz (businesses)	http://www.Netware.biz
name (individuals)	http://www.sue_barnes.name
pro (professionals)	http://www.DrRobertSmith.pro
museum (museums)	http://www.Whitney.museum
coop (business cooperatives)	http://www.AppleCBS.coop
aero (aviation)	http://www.southeastairlines.aero

Note: In addition to domain names, there are also country codes (United States = us, France = fr, Japan = jp).

with journalists, the newspaper staff, and each other. This type of interpersonal interactivity is not possible with traditionally printed mass media.

Intercasting

As discussed in Chapter 2, mass media are all converging into a single global medium. A driving force behind convergence is the widespread use of the Internet and the Web. New intercast technologies are developing to enable television technologies to receive both television programs and Internet connections. The term **intercasting** reflects this change by combining the idea of the Internet with the concept of broadcasting. Streaming video technologies, on the other hand, add television features to the Web.

Webcasting, or using small cameras to capture and transmit images through the Internet, is another way to broadcast images. Individuals can purchase inexpensive cameras and connect them to their personal computers. Webcasting is used for everything from capturing images of college campus activities to sharing images of newborn children through services made available to parents. Relatives and friends can reply to the image by typing messages that appear like a chat transcript on the computer screen.

Individuals can use Web cameras to experiment with creating their own Web programs that are transmitted across the Internet. For instance, a Block Island businessman set up a Webcam to capture images of the Block Island ferry. The purpose of the site is to raise the island's profile. In business, Web cameras are also used by organizations for teleconferencing because they enable Internet communication to include visual as well as verbal information. Cues that were filtered out in text-only correspondence can now be included in Webcasts.

Webcams support the development of personal broadcasting. **Personal broadcasting** is created by individuals using inexpensive video cameras, computer hardware, and software. These images are transmitted across the Internet. O'Sullivan (1999) describes two ways in which personal broadcasting is different from network broadcasting: First, personal broadcasting is created by private individuals instead of media corporations; second, the programming content of personal broadcasting is personal rather than commercially oriented. This new form of broadcasting is another example of how people are using the Web as an interpersonal medium.

Interaction and Transaction

As discussed in the first chapter, interactivity is a central feature of CMC and Web interaction. Many commercial Web sites use the interactive nature of CMC to conduct transactions with consumers. **Transaction features** are tools that allow a user to enter into a financial arrangement with a person or company through a Web site. Transaction features include purchasing products, online banking, using a credit card on the Internet, and filling out an online form. Frequently, organizations collect information about the people visiting their site through the forms they fill out or by placing a cookie on a user's hard drive.

Cookies are small data files stored on an individual's computer by a Web browser. Although programmers argue that cookies are harmless, computer magazines report that cookies have been used to retrieve e-mail addresses, real names, and Web activities. This information can later be fed into other types of database systems to build consumer profiles. When cookies were first introduced, computer users were often unaware that the cookies were being placed on their computers. However, software browsers now let users know when a cookie is being stored on their machines.

Business transactions are growing on the Web. *Interactive Week* estimates that Internet consumer sales is a $44.4 billion dollar business. Many companies are turning to Internet marketing because it supports the current trend toward one-to-one marketing, which attempts to build more direct relationships between companies and consumers. This type of marketing uses a highly personalized approach by creating individualized messages directed toward specific customers. Software tools, such as cookies, enable companies to address individual people directly when they visit a company's site through the ability of cookies to customize the user's interface. For example, when I log on to Amazon.com, a welcome message appears that says, "Welcome Sue Barnes."

Mass Media and the Web

In contemporary culture, mass communication has replaced interpersonal communication as a method for establishing social concepts and behaviors. According to Beniger (1987), "The most important innovation in communication technology since writing for the development of modern society has been the emergence of mass media and a gradual shift from interpersonal to mass communication as the basis of societal control" (p. 352). Although mass communication is an economical way to distribute messages to large audiences, face-to-face communication in intimate groups is more effective for influencing attitudes and behavior. Companies try to create mass messages that convey the impression of interpersonal communication. New technologies enable organizations to target and personalize mass messages. For instance, specialized magazines, targeted mailing lists, neighborhood-edition newspapers, and talk radio all make mass messages appear more interpersonal.

Technologies such as lithographic reproduction, photography and high-speed printing, transatlantic telegraphic news reporting, illustrated daily newspapers, mass mailing (direct marketing), mass-circulation magazines, radio, and television have been shaping the attitudes and behavior of people. Beniger (1987) states: "Although intimate group relations remained important, increased attention to mass media ultimately came—because the individual's time and energy were limited—at the expense of interpersonal communication" (p. 353). Publishers, editors, and others who were interested in attracting large audiences knew the limitations of their medium compared to more intimate means of interpersonal communication. For example, long after the invention of the typewriter, Sears, Roebuck and Co. continued to send handwritten letters to their customers because they appeared more "personal." Today, the Publishers Clearinghouse Sweepstakes uses computer technology to print individual names on millions of promotional letters to individualize its messages.

Messages targeted toward specific individuals imply intimacy. Efforts to personalize mass communication by obscuring the size of the audience receiving the message have blurred the distinctions between interpersonal and mass communication. This trend has been accelerated with the introduction of computer technology because database marketing and customized printing can individually address direct-mail letters. These messages appear to be written to individuals rather than large groups. Similarly, cookies enable Web sites to welcome individual users by name. Beniger (1987) says, "Gradually each of us has become enmeshed in superficially interpersonal relations that confuse personal with mass messages and increasingly include interactions with machines that write, speak, and even "think" with success steadily approaching that of humans" (p. 354). Beniger describes this transformation of traditional community into impersonal association as **pseudo-community**. Pseudo-community is created when centralized communicators distribute personalized mass messages. For example, unsolisicited telephone calls from telemarketers are often difficult to distinguish from a legitimate personal call.

Researchers today are concerned about the ways in which computers are used to personalize messages both on- and offline. Cookies enable computer servers to both store and retrieve information about a user. It is a tool that allows shopping applications, such as Amazon.com, to save user preferences and then use this information to customize messages displayed on its Web site. Customer information can also be collected and used to generate e-mail messages. On a larger scale, computer software can be used to build consumer profiles that identify individual consumers with specific products and buying habits. This information can then be used in a variety of ways for marketing purposes. For instance, Amazon will recommend books to people based on products they have previously purchased.

Advertising and the Web

Originally, the Internet was established as a research network and advertising was discouraged. However, with the development of the Web, the network has increasingly become more commercialized. One of the earliest forms of Web advertising was the **banner ad**. They first appeared in 1994 on HotWired's Web site, the online presence of *Wired Magazine*. Banner ads, advertising logos and billboard-style ads placed on Web pages, are purchased by advertisers and help to provide revenue for the site. Many commercial sites sell Web advertising space to finance their operation. As Web software has evolved, banners have gone from static visual representations to animated graphics. Most banners provide links to another site that will provide further information about the product or service being advertised.

The rates paid for banner advertising is often based on **click-through rates**, the percentage of users who click through a banner and to go to the advertiser's site. Rates are calculated by dividing the number of people who see the banner by the number of people who actually click on it. For instance, if 500 people see a banner and only 5 click on it to visit the advertiser's site, the click-through rate is 1 percent. The higher the click-through rate, the more money a site can charge for advertising space. When animation is added to a banner, the click-through percentage increases.

Advertisers are also attracted to CMC genres. For example, banners are often found at Web-based chat rooms. Finding chat on the Web requires users to go to a specific site before entering a chat session. Advertising banners and logos can be placed on these sites. Topic-centered chat and discussion groups are attractive to advertisers because they can reach specific types of audiences. Similarly, people who set-up a Yahoo discussion group or a HotMail e-mail account will receive numerous advertising messages in exchange for these free services. The Web enables marketers to identify groups with specific interests and direct messages toward individuals and group members.

Newspapers and the Web

Banner advertising is frequently found on sites created by traditional newspapers and magazines. Similar to print media, online newspapers sell advertising space to support themselves. Many traditional print-based newspapers have created online counterparts. For example, *USA Today* and the *New York Times* have Web sites. Newspaper presence on the Web is designed to create a favorable image for the paper and to increase readership. Much of the news content distributed on these sites is the same as in the printed publication. However, some online versions of newspapers add Web-only features to attract the interest of Internet users, for instance the *Cybertimes* online.

Television and the Web

After the introduction of the Web, the television industry began to explore ways of converging television and Internet technology to create interactive TV. For instance, cable modems bring Internet access to home computers and television sets. Microsoft's WebTV provides a set-top box to connect television to the Web, and a number of cable providers are now including Internet connections as part of their service.

Broadcast and cable television networks also use the Web. Generally, broadcasters use the Web as a promotional tool to support their regularly broadcast programs. Some programs, such as *Dateline NBC*, ask viewers to vote on issues and set up live chat sessions with guests featured on the program. In 1996, the National Broadcasting Company (NBC) and Microsoft Corporation teamed up to create MSNBC, a combined Internet and television company. MSNBC runs 24/7 cable news broadcasts complemented by its Web site, which provides in-depth coverage of topics and issues presented on the television programs.

A number of Web sites have also been developed to provide additional information about televised stories. For example, sports fans can find information and sports news, and soap opera fans can look up plot lines and information about their favorite characters. Television sites also allow viewers to check program listings and news updates. In general, the Web can supplement television news coverage and entertainment programming by providing more detailed information about issues, events, and television personalities.

The Web also provides an opportunity for television stations to transfer their brand names to online news content sites. For instance, the Cable News Network (CNN) has successfully transferred its brand name to CNN Interactive (http://www.cnn.com) to provide an online news service. In addition to written articles, the site contains video and audio clips of current events. Moreover, CNN is developing an historical archive of news items that can be accessed through the Internet.

Radio and the Web

Similar to television sites, radio station Web sites expand on information provided in broadcast news and programs. For example, WNYC, a New York City public radio station, provides information about its program schedule, news stories, and on-air personalities (http://www.wnyc.org). During news reports, the station will frequently tell listeners to visit its Web site to receive additional story information. Moreover, the station's Web site promotes local concerts and free events.

With the development of **streaming audio** software programs, such as Real Audio or Media Player, local radio stations are also broadcasting through the Internet. Broadcasting through the Web eliminates the high costs of licensing and bypasses government regulations. Web radio sites attract new listeners and reach a global rather than local audience. For example, foreign students can connect to the Internet to listen to radio stations from their home country. Similarly, Fordham students and graduates can log on to http://www.wfuv.org to listen to the public radio station located on the Fordham campus. Producers of syndicated radio shows also make their programs available through the Internet. For instance, the music from the *Hearts of Space* Web site (http://www.hos.com) allows people to listen to their various programs and download program lists.

Types of Web Sites

Web sites are created by individuals, companies, organizations, and governments, and consequently, sites are developed for a variety of purposes. Alexander and Tate (1999) have identified six different types of Web sites, including advocacy, business, informational, news, entertainment, and personal. Identifying types of Web sites provides a context for understanding the messages being communicated (Figure 4.6).

Advocacy Web Sites

The primary purpose of advocacy sites is to influence public opinion and encourage activism. Advocacy sites are created to influence the legislative process, influence voters, promote a cause, and increase membership in an organization. During elections, candidates use the Web as a medium to both distribute information and encourage people to participate in the campaign process (see Chapter 14). Organizations such as the American Cancer Society and the National Multiple Sclerosis Society use the Web to distribute information and gain public support for medical research. Additionally, the National Multiple Sclerosis Web site (http://www.nmss.org) frequently hosts live Internet programs that are broadcast through the Web. During live broadcasts, listeners can e-mail questions to the panelists, who respond in real time. Recordings of the live programs are saved and made available through the site. In addition to broadcasting programs, the site also acts as an archive for viewing and disseminating medical information.

Business Web Sites

There are a variety of business Web sites that are designed to sell or promote products and services. These sites include online catalogs, corporate Web sites, and electronic malls. Used as a commercial medium, the Web can provide benefits to both companies and con-

---

FIGURE 4.6   Types of Web sites

Type	Purpose	URL Address
Advocacy	To influence public opinion, To promote a cause	Frequently ends in .org
Business	To promote a product or service	Frequently ends in .com
Informational	To provide factual information	Variety of endings, especially .edu and .org
News	To provide information about local, regional, national, or international news	Frequently ends in .com
Personal	To fulfill a variety of reasons for an individual	Variety of endings, especially .com and .edu
Entertainment	To provide enjoyment.	Variety of endings

Source: From Marie L. Radford, Susan B. Barnes, and Linda R. Barr, *Web Research Selecting, Evaluating, and Citing*, Copyright 2002. Reprinted by permission of Allyn & Bacon.

sumers. Companies can use the Web as an online catalog to enable people to order products. Web sites provide detailed information about products and services and enable consumers to comparison shop. Additionally, business sites can help consumers find and order products from local distributors. For both companies and consumers, the Web can help bring transactions to a conclusion.

Informational Web Sites

A wide variety of information—census data, train schedules, immigration information—is available on the Web. People can search the U.S. Census database or look up the train schedule for the Orient Express running between Singapore and Thailand. Individuals, lawyers, educators, and historians can access the United States Immigration and Naturalization Web site (http://www.ins.gov) for a wealth of information. In addition to enabling people to download forms, the site also provides historical information about immigration to the United States along with government-sponsored research on immigrants.

Many universities have Web sites that provide information to students about course descriptions, schedules, and campus events. Some provide server space for students to post their own personal Web pages. Students sometimes create informational Web sites to present information about their favorite hobby or fan information, concert schedules, biographies, and reviews of their favorite recording artist or celebrity. Individuals, educational institutions, organizations, governments, and commercial businesses all place information on the Web.

News Web Sites

Newspaper, radio, and television sites are designed to distribute news content, providing current information about local, regional, national, or international events or concentrating on specific topics, such as technology news, stock market reports, and entertainment news. The Web sites created by news organizations with a non-Web counterpart duplicate media content; for instance, key news stories from New York's *Newsday* will be posted on its Web site. News sites often provide discussion areas for readers to exchange comments and ideas with each other. Additionally, the *New York Times's* site enables readers to order previously published articles for a small fee.

In addition to news distributed by traditional news sources, news on the Web can be created by individuals, for instance, the *Drudge Report*. Matt Drudge, a former network employee, began posting network gossip on the Internet, an activity that evolved into the *Drudge Report*, a publication that occasionally distributes misleading and incorrect information. The *Drudge Report* does not follow the traditional newspaper model for checking and rechecking sources of information. As more individuals use the Web as a personal medium, checking the credibility of information becomes extremely important.

Entertainment Web Sites

Entertainment sites cover a range of recreational activities, including movie listings, sound clips, games, chat rooms, fanzines, and jokes. Games are an integral part of CMC. Versions of the shows *Jeopardy* and *Wheel of Fortune* have been developed for the Web. Players compete to be placed on a daily Web list of "Top Ten Players." Games can be played individually or with other people connected to the Internet.

Web sites devoted to television programs, such as *The X-Files* and *Late Night with David Letterman* are popular on the Web. Beyond providing information about these programs, the Web also enables fans to communicate with each other. Chat rooms, newsgroups, and Webzines allow fans to discuss characters and plot lines. These sites are especially popular with soap opera fans, who originally developed a strong presence on the text-based Internet. Today, Sony Entertainment operates a site called *Soap City* that provides story lines, cast information, weekly updates, fan chat areas, and live-chat forums with soap opera actors. Sports sites, such as *ESPN Sports Zone*, are also popular entertainment sites for sports fans.

A unique type of entertainment site is a **parody site**, a site that makes fun of another Web site. For example, whitehouse.net is a parody of whitehouse.gov, the official White House Web site. At times the two sites visually look alike, but the parody site presents humorous articles and links. Similarly, a number of parody sites have been created to make fun of the *Drudge Report*, including www.drudge.com.

Personal Web Sites

Personal Web pages represent the Web at its most basic and eclectic level. Personal home pages enable individuals to create their own content and distribute it globally. In contrast to e-mail, discussion groups, and chat, the Web enables individuals to use graphics, sounds, photographs, and video clips to present themselves through the Internet. Pictures displayed on personal Web pages generally include self-portraits, pictures of family and friends, humorous pictures, and images of pets. As a medium of expression, personal Web pages include autobiographies, resume information, e-zines (electronic magazines), opinion essays, portfolio samples, and student projects (Figure 4.7). Including e-mail address and guest books on personal Web pages provides a way for the owner of the page to receive feedback and response from people who visit the site.

Evaluating Web Sites

As stated in the preceding section, checking the accuracy of Web information is very important. Many students use the Web as a source of information for project and research reports, and information interactivity on the Web is one aspect of CMC. Web sites are created by such a variety of individuals and organizations that evaluating Web information is an important skill that students must learn. Librarians and teachers have identified five basic criteria for evaluating Web content: accuracy, authority, objectivity, coverage, and currency.

Accuracy

Newspapers, magazines, and television news programs check and edit their content before it is published or televised. Professional journalists are taught to check their facts. However,

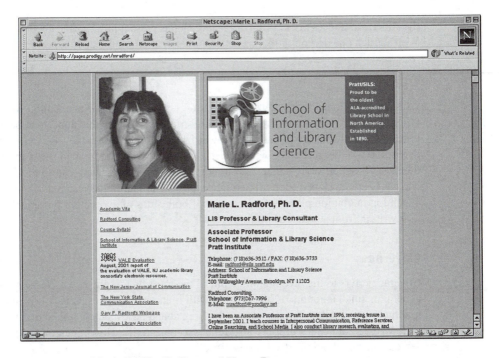

FIGURE 4.7   Marie Radford's Personal Home Page

© 2002 Marie Radford. Used by permission.

news sites are only one Web category; other types of sites may not check for accuracy. As a result, users must check the facts they find on the Web. Misspelled words and grammatical mistakes indicate that a site may have not been checked properly before it was placed on the Web. If you are using information found on the Web in a school project or report, try to verify the information with another source. Look for bibliographies and ways to support the facts you find online. Sometimes you may need to go to your college library to look up facts published in books.

Authority

The second criterion for in evaluating Web content is to determine the authority of the source of the information. Identify the author who wrote the information and the organization sponsoring the site. Is the information presented as a fact or opinion? Almost anyone can place a page on the Web; savvy students learn to quickly identify legitimate sites and authors. Look on the site to see if the organization describes itself, and look for biographical information about the author. The reputation of the organization and author will help you determine whether the site presents expert facts or promotional material. For example, both the American Cancer Society and drug store chains present information about cancer on the Web. Which one do you think is a better authority on the subject of cancer?

Objectivity

Examining the objectivity of the information is a key factor in evaluating Web content. Often, commercial interests present Web information in a way that appears to be objective, but commercial sites are often biased toward a particular product they are trying to sell. To determine whether a site is objective, first look at the Web address to see if the ending of the site is .com or .org or .edu. A commercial ending should alert you to the fact that the site has been developed for commercial purposes and therefore has a bias. Another way to check for an opinion piece is to determine if both sides of a topic are presented. Is the author writing from a balanced point of view?

Coverage

Coverage refers to the breadth and depth of the information presented. Some sites present general or small amounts of information with links to other sites. Check how much information is contained on the site you are looking at and how much is linked to other sources. The coverage of a story or topic also relates to objectivity. How much information is presented and are all points of view described?

Currency

Currency is the timeliness of the information. For example, The *New York Times* and CNN Web sites are updated on a daily basis. Some Web sites, however, have not been updated in a year or two and others have been totally abandoned. Look at the information on the bottom of the page to see when the information was placed on the Web and how often it is revised. Current events sites need to be updated on a daily basis. On the other hand, information about classical subjects, such as Ancient Greece, does not need to be revised that often, but check to make sure that someone is maintaining the site properly.

Uses and Gratification Models for Evaluating Web Usage

In addition to evaluating Web information, researchers also investigate why people use the Web. For example, the Pew Internet and American Life Project reported that close to 30 million Americans download music files from the Internet, thus entertainment is a primary motivation for Web usage. Consequently, new-media researchers view Web behavior as similar to traditional mass media audience behavior. Audience members have their own varied reasons for selecting messages to pay attention to, and they often select content to match their own tastes, ideas, and informational needs. **Uses and gratification research** argues that media use offers rewards expected by audience members. These rewards are considered to be psychological effects valued by viewers. Audience members expect media use to gratify a psychological need, and they evaluate the medium based on the perceived gratification they receive from using it.

The model describes the following pattern: Social and psychological needs generate expectations about the media, which lead to the selection of and exposure to the media; exposure to the media results in need gratification and/or other, unintended consequences. The model perceives audience members as active information seekers. According to Kaye (1998), "New media technologies allow users more features with which to manipulate their media choices thus increasing satisfaction, expectations and media use gratifications" (p. 27). Motivations for watching television have been well researched. These include entertainment or diversion, personal relationship, personal identity, monitoring current events and issues, accomplishing tasks, and information seeking. Media use in this model refers to selecting and paying attention to media content. One's attitude about the medium, the gratification being sought, and the gratifications received follow a casual chain (Figure 4.8).

Kaye's (1998) study on Web usage uncovered six motivational categories: entertainment, social interaction, passing time, escape, information, and Web site preference. The strongest motivation for Web use is entertainment followed by social interaction and then as a way to pass time. Respondents accessed the Web to interact with friends and family and did not use it to escape feelings of loneliness, a motivation for watching television. Self-enhancement is also a motive for Web usage. Kaye states, "Web users who access sites for entertainment, escapist, social, or information needs exhibit greater Web affinity than users who just want to pass the time or go straight to a specific home site" (p. 35). Additionally, the amount of time people spend on the Web is positively associated with Web use motivations.

In a different study, Tewksbury and Althaus (2000) applied a uses and gratifications model to Web use to see if people who are anxious about computer use are less likely to believe the Web will meet their informational needs. The study revealed that "gratifications tend to be associated with specific and predictable patterns of Web site visitation" (p. 133). Experienced Web users believe that they receive a high degree of satisfaction from its use.

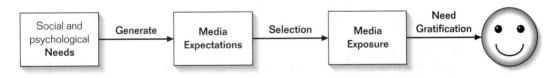

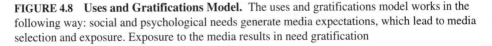

FIGURE 4.8   Uses and Gratifications Model. The uses and gratifications model works in the following way: social and psychological needs generate media expectations, which lead to media selection and exposure. Exposure to the media results in need gratification

Reasons for site use corresponded with the gratifications obtained. For example, entertainment gratification was positively related to arts and sports sites. Similarly, issues and events gratifications were positively associated with news, sports, and political sites. Web users seeking entertainment and information are satisfied with their use of Web sites that provide information. These two studies illustrate how uses and gratification models can be used to explore Web behavior.

Summary

The fastest-growing segment of the Internet is the World Wide Web (WWW). Two important characteristics of the Web are hypertext and graphical technologies. Hypertext enables pages to be linked together, and graphical technologies add multimedia features to the Internet. The Web supports both informational and interpersonal interactivity. By combining these media organizations can interactively communicate with their viewers and advertisers can collect consumer data to personalize their messages. Web sites can be divided into the six major categories of advocacy, business, informational, news, entertainment, and personal, all of which need to be critically evaluated.

Individuals create Web pages to present online resumes and promote topics of interest. Nonprofit organizations develop Web sites to advocate for social change and increase group membership. Government agencies set up sites to disseminate information and enable citizens to download forms instead of visiting government offices. Media corporations are exploring how to use the Web as an interactive medium to distribute content, provide programming information, and encourage audience participation. Advertisers use the Web to create personalized messages targeted toward specific types of consumers. Researchers who are interested in why people use the Web have applied uses and gratifications research to Web analysis. According to Kaye's study (1998), the strongest motivations for Web use are entertainment followed by social interaction and passing time.

W E B   R E S O U R C E S

Introduction to HTML: werbach.com/barebones/
iVillage Personal Home Page Tutorial: auth.ivillage.com/images/homepages/tutorial.html
Home Pages Beginners Help: boards2.ivillage.com/messages/get/phbeg46.html
MSNBC: www.msnbc.com
CNN: www.cnn.com
The New York Times: www.nytimes.com
Webcam World: www.Webcamworld.com
Developing Critical Skills for the Web: www.capecod.net/schrockguide/eval.htm
milton.mse.jhu.edu:8001/research/education/net.html
www.vuw.ac.nz/~agsmith/evaln/evaln.htm
lib.nmsu.edu/instruction/evalcrit.html
euphrates.wpunj.edu/faculty/wagnerk

TERMS

Anchors are linked points on the same Web page.

Banner ads are advertisements placed on Web sites. They frequently appear as a long, horizontal box at the top of a Web page.

Browsers are programs that interpret and display documents that are formatted in the Hypertext Markup Language (HTML).

Click-through rates are a way to calculate the price of Web banner advertising by determining the percentage of users who click through a banner ad to go to the advertiser's site.

Cookies are mechanisms that enable computer servers to both store and retrieve information about a user.

Domain names identify the type of organization operating the Internet server. The five generic domains are gov, edu, com, net, and org.

External links connect pages from different websites together and links are indicated by underlined words, phrases, visual icons, and audio clips.

Hypertext is nonsequential reading and writing. Information is linked together rather than presented in a linear way, which creates informational interactivity.

Hypertext markup language (HTML) provides codes that are used to format hypertext documents. Individual codes define the hierarchy and nature of the various components of the document as well as specify hypertext links.

Hypertext transfer protocol (HTTP) is a communication protocol Web browsers understand that enables users to move from Web page to Web page around the Internet.

Intercasting is a term that refers to the combination of the Internet and television broadcasting.

Internal links connect pages together within a Web site.

Parody Web sites are satires of another site on the Web, such as www.whitehouse.net, which pokes fun at the official White House Web site.

Personal broadcasting is created by individuals using inexpensive video cameras and computer hardware and software to transmit images across the Internet.

Pseudo-community is the transformation of traditional community relationships into impersonal associations.

Search engines are software tools that enable Web users to locate information and content placed on the World Wide Web.

Streaming audio (or video) is a compressed, digital system for sending multimedia information across the Internet in real time.

Transaction features are tools that allow a user to enter into a financial transaction with a person or company sponsoring a Web site, including purchasing products, filling out an online form, online banking, and using a credit card on the Internet.

URL stands for Uniform Resource Locator and it is the address of the Web page.

Uses and gratifications is a research method that contents audience members expect media use to gratify a psychological need, and audience members evaluate the media based on the perceived gratification they receive from using it.

Webcasting is using small cameras to capture and transmit images through the Internet.

EXERCISES

1. Find different sites on the Web that fit into the six Web site categories. Describe the purpose of each site.

2. *Designing a personal Web page project.* Creating a personal Web page is a two-step process. First, you must decide what type of information should be included on your page and then you need to put the data into an HTML format. Many software programs are available to automatically add the HTML code to a design. Moreover, Web pages can also be created with a simple word processing program and a basic knowledge of HTML programming. (An introduction to these skills is available at http://werbach.com/barebones/ and other sites on the Web.)

3. *Evaluating Web sites project.* Select a topic to research on the Web, such as cyberspace or computer-mediated communication. Type the topic into your favorite search engine. Then use the five criteria described in this chapter to evaluate at least two of the sites located by the search engine.

4. Search for the same topic using different search engines. Compare and evaluate the results. Which search engine located the most relevant information?

BIBLIOGRAPHY

Abbate, J. (1999). *Inventing the Internet.* Cambridge, MA: The MIT Press.

Adamic, L. A., & Huberman, B.A. (2001). The Web's hidden order. *Communications of the ACM, 44* (9), 55–59.

Alexander, J. E., & Tate, M. A. (1999). *Web wisdom.* Mahwah, NJ: Lawrence Earlbaum Associates.

Beniger, J. R. (1987, June). Personalization of mass media and the growth of pseudo-community. *Communication Research, 14* (3), 352–371.

Berners-Lee, T. (1999). *Weaving the Web.* San Francisco: Harper Collins.

Bolter, J. D. (1991). *Writing space: The computer, hypertext, and the history of writing.* Hillsdale, NJ: Lawrence Erlbaum Associates.

Delany, P., & Landow, G. P. (1991). *Hypermedia and literary studies.* Cambridge, MA: The MIT Press.

Galkin, W. S. (1997, January). Your clickstream is showing: Privacy of online consumer information. *Computer Law Observer, 22.* Available: http://www.lawcircle.com/issue22.html

Graziano, M., & Rainie, L. *The music downloading deluge.* Pew Internet & American Life Project. [Online], 8pp. Available: http://www.pewinternet.org [April 24, 2001].

Guglielmo, C. (1997, December 8). No sacred trust: Personal data up for grabs. *Inter@ctive Week*, pp. 72–74.

Hoffman, D. L., Novak, T. P. & Chatterjee, P. (1995). Commercial scenarios fo the Web: Opportunities and challenges. *Journal for Computer Mediated Communication, 1* (3) (pp. 25) (Online) Available: http://www.ascusc.org/jcml/vol1/issue3/hoffman.html (Downloaded March 28, 2002).

Howell, G. T. (1992). *Building hypermedia applications.* New York: McGraw-Hill.

Kaye, B. K. (1998). Uses and gratifications of the World Wide Web: From couch potato to Web potato. *The New Jersey Journal of Communication, 6* (1), 21–40.

O'Sullivan, P. B. (1999). "Personal broadcasting": Theoretical implications of the Web [Online], 12 pp. Paper presented at the International Communication Association Conference, San Francisco, May, 1999. Available: http://www.ilstu.edu/~posull/PersBroad.htm. (August 19, 2001).

Radford, M., Barnes, S., & Barr, L. (2002) *A student's guide for evaluating Web sites.* Boston: Allyn & Bacon/Longman.

Sandvig, C. (2000). Understanding a domain name policy gone wrong. *The CPSR Newsletter, 18*, (3). Available: http://www.cpsr.org/publicaiotns/newsletters/issues/2000/Summer2000/sandvig.html

Schultz, H. (2000). *The elements of electronic communication*. Boston: Allyn & Bacon.

Staten, J. (1996, March 13). Netscape tricks raise security concerns. *MacWeek*. Available: http://www.zdnet.com/macweek/mw_1001/gw_net_tricks.html

Stefik, M. (1996). *Internet dreams: Archetypes, myths, and metaphors*. Cambridge, MA: The MIT Press.

Tewksbury, D., & Althaus, S. L. (2000, Spring). An examination of motivations for using the World Wide Web. *Communication Research Reports, 17*, (2), 127–138.

Winterson, J. (2000, October). He stole my name. *Brill's Content*, 90–93.

PART II

Interacting Through CMC

Language is the primary way in which people communicate with each other. Internet characteristics alter the ways in which people use language. In electronic writing, graphic markers or emoticons are added to compensate for the lack of visual information. As discussed in Chapter 1, the development of computer-based messages has been analyzed from a rhetorical point of view. This section discusses electronic language and how CMC users alter written correspondence to communicate more effectively.

People present themselves to others in CMC primarily through written correspondence. With carefully crafted language and the use of programming commands, they can create online personalities. Many people report that they have developed relationships through CMC. As Internet relationships develop, their breadth and depth increase. Eventually, many correspondents want to expand their use of communication channels beyond the Internet to include telephone calls and eventually a face-to-face meeting.

This second section explores the ways people use electronic language to communicate with others and develop relationships. After describing language use, the section moves on to discuss the ways in which individuals present themselves to others and build relationships. Internet relationship building involves sharing common experiences, having feelings of security and satisfaction, understanding the other, and reciprocal correspondence. Using the Internet to develop interpersonal relationships is the theme of this section.

CHAPTER

5   Language and the Internet

Chapter Overview

Language is central to human communication. Internet communication primarily occurs in the form of written language. As previously stated, Internet characteristics influence the ways in which people use language and understand messages. Internet correspondence uses language in new and unique ways. People mix elements of oral speaking into online writing to compensate for missing visual and aural cues. Similarly, they add emoticons to convey moods and indicate ironic comments. In real-time online environments, such as chat and instant messenger, acronyms are frequently mixed in with words to speed up typed responses to messages.

Styles of online discourse often follow patterns established in face-to-face and mediated interaction. For example, gender patterns observed in face-to-face communication can be found in Internet conversations. Additionally, the Web introduces television-like visual elements into CMC. Rhetorical approaches are being applied to Web analysis to examine the persuasive visual and verbal elements in Web-based messages. This chapter discusses the following topics on how people use electronic language and rhetorical methods to analyze messages:

- Orality and literacy
- Features of electronic language, including acronyms and graphic accents
- Figurative language and metaphor
- The use of speech-act theory in CMC and HCI
- Gendered discourse in CMC
- Rhetoric and the Internet
- Welch's rhetorical approach to the Web

Many Internet genres narrow the channels of interpersonal communication from visual and verbal information (including language content, vocalizations, facial expression, eye contact, and body movement) to text-only interaction. These genres include e-mail, discussion lists, newsgroups, discussion lists, chat, IRC, and instant messenger. Because online communication is still developing as a method of human communication, each of these genres has its unique way of using language. For example, spelling tends to be better in discussion lists because people take more time to compose their thoughts. In contrast, spelling is less important in chat and instant messenger because these genres are filled with acronyms to speed up response time.

Orality and Literacy

Electronic writing mixes elements of orality and literacy together. Because CMC provides limited sensory channels of information, participants often play with language to show emotional cues and create the impression that they are speaking to each other rather than writing. For instance, examine the following phrase: "Uhm . . . that's an interesting idea." By typing in paralinguistic sounds and indicating pauses, the writer is attempting to depict spoken language. According to Lee (1996), the use of specialized language and jargon helps to define online communities, and "new members embrace the lingo as signs of belonging" (p. 287). In every type of computer-mediated environment, the use of capital letters stands for SHOUTING. Ellipses are used in a similar way to represent a pause in vocal communication

CMC combines the permanence of a written text with the spontaneity of spoken conversation. The interactive nature of CMC supports the use of multiple voices that resemble a group discussion. In contrast to the printed page, which encourages a linear and single point of view, electronic discourse supports overlapping points-of-view that are written by many authors. Consequently, electronic texts more closely resemble a conversation rather than a written article.

Oral Versus Written Cultures

Scholars such as Ong (1982), McLuhan (1964), and Havelock (1963) have explored the differences between cultures that are primarily oral and ones that are written. Oral culture is based on practical experience, memory, and performance skills. Moreover, people who live in oral cultures perceive the world as immediate and concrete because communication occurs in face-to-face settings. Face-to-face correspondence is filled with nonverbal sensory information, such as tone of voice, physical context, and gestures. According to Ong (1982), "Spoken words are always modifications of a total situation which is more than verbal. They never occur alone, in a context simply of words" (p. 101). In contrast, printed words do stand alone. Extratextual context is missing and writers must create the context and define situations. The lack of contextual cues makes writing a more formal activity than oral conversations. In contrast to traditional writing, Internet users tend to incorporate the informality of oral conversation in their online writing styles.

The Internet can most easily be used as a method of distributing and transferring text-based documents. The term *electronic mail* creates an analogy between using the Internet and letter writing. But, most e-mail is less formal than traditional written correspondence. According to Lee (1996), e-mail is a junction between orality and literacy because it can be used to exchange both formal text and informal dialog.

Informal e-mail messages are similar to the verbal messages that people leave on answering machines, the language is often spontaneous, short, and imprecise. Similarly, informal e-mail messages tend to have typos and grammatical errors. Here is an example: `"OK, OK, i got the point. . . it aint workin' for u now."` The author of this message is playing with capitalization and improper grammar to try and capture a sense of spoken language. Other symbolic alterations that transform the written word into an informal spoken style include abbreviating words to respond faster to messages—you (u), female (f), male (m), and location (loc)—and the use of acronyms as a symbolic shortcut: CU (see you later), IMHO (in my humble opinion), and ROTFL (rolling on floor laughing).

The mixing of oral features into written text alters the symbolic form of written language and plays with the use of letters and words. For example, a prevalent form of online expression is to add extra letters and exaggerate the punctuation: NNNNNNNNNOOOOOOOOO!!!!!!!!! Playing with written language adds more feeling and begins to create a context for the remark. As a result, Lee (1996) states, "E-mail merges the literate emphasis on sight with the breezy informality of talk, with its many variations of sound" (p. 287). Informal e-mail messages are more spontaneous and off-the-cuff. Conversely, formal messages tend to follow the traditional process of writing a printed letter or memo. In formal messages, authors take the time to reflect about the content of the message, they edit the document, and they check for spelling errors before the message is sent through the network. Consequently, formal messages maintain a traditional use of language. In contrast, informal messages play with new symbolic structures that compensate for the lack of face-to-face visual and emotional cues. Writing in a style that uses exaggerated punctuation and playful language creates an impression of orality.

Ong (1982) states, "the electronic transformation of verbal expression has both deepened the commitment of the word to space initiated by writing and intensified by print and has brought consciousness to a new age of secondary orality" (p. 135). The telephone, television, radio, and various forms of electronic technology have introduced **secondary orality**. Secondary orality is more deliberate and self-conscious than primary orality because it is based on the use of writing and print, which are essential for the manufacture, operation, and utilization of the technologies that support secondary orality. For example, television news programs are scripted and read by newscasters from teleprompters. A second feature of secondary orality is its tendency to support the formation of groups.

> Like primary orality, secondary orality has generated a strong group sense, for listening to spoken words forms hearers into a group, a true audience, just as reading written or printed texts turn individuals in on themselves. But secondary orality generates a sense for groups immeasurably larger than those of primary oral culture (Ong, 1982, p. 136).

An example of how secondary orality forms groups is fan culture. Jenkins's (1992) research on fan culture describes how fans use texts from television programs to form subcultural communities: "For most fans, meaning production is not a solitary and private process but rather a social network of an organized fan culture" (p. 75). Computer networks have intensified fan communication because they enable fans to compare notes, develop elaborate theories, and collaborate with each other. Fans view fictional characters and their actions as both "real" and "constructed." Characters are understood as "real" people with personal histories that can be explored and also as fictional constructions that are controlled by writers and producers. This double interpretation of the text combines theory and criticism because competing interpretations and evaluations of common texts are proposed, debated, and negotiated by fans. Moreover, fans speculate about the nature of the mass media and their relationship to it. Fans express their interpretations of media texts in a variety of ways. For example, they write stories and desktop-published newsletters, post electronic magazines (zines) on the Internet, create songs, and produce home videos about their favorite programs.

Baym (1995a) researched an online fan group called rec.arts.tv.soaps (r.a.t.s.), a recreational discussion list of daytime soap operas. She contends that "over the course of nearly a decade the thousands of people who have participated in r.a.t.s. have created a dynamic and rich community filled with social nuance and emotion" (p. 138). As previously stated, group membership is often based on learning the paralinguistic cues used by group members, such as acronyms for soap opera programs and characters. In CMC, **paralanguage** is the visual appearance of written language, which includes punctuation, spelling, grammar, keyboard characters, and the use of spaces between words.

Acronyms

Acronyms are popular paralingusitic cues. Online participants often incorporate acronyms into their messages to speed up their response time (Figure 5.1). Traditionally, an acronym is a word formed from the initial letters or portions of letters belonging to a group of words. For example, the word *radar* is an acronym for *radio detecting and ranging*. Similarly, the online community called the *WELL* stands for *Whole Earth 'Lectronic Link*. But the use of acronyms in chat does not follow the traditional acronym definition. Instead of spelling new words from groups of words, first letters are used as a shorthand for phrases. For instance, BRB stands for Be Right Back and face-to-face is written as F2F.

The replacement of full words by letters and symbols creates a new style of speedwriting. Speedwriting is frequently used in synchronous CMC genres. For instance, chat participants need to become familiar with a variety of acronyms to understand online conversations. People will spontaneously invent new acronyms and forms of speedwriting during their online exchanges.

In some chat environments, such as CompuServe's CB (Citizen's Band), emotional cues will be shown as markers placed between the less-than and greater-than keyboard symbols. For example, <g> signifies grin and <s> stands for smile. An emerging trend in online conversation is to place emotional markers before and after sentences to compensate for the lack of face-to-face expression; for example, <happy> I just got a new dog! </happy>. This convention mimics HTML tags. In addition to written emotional cues, graphic accents are also used to enhance written messages.

Graphic Accents

Many computer systems used for CMC support only a low-end ASCII character set. As a result, Internet users are limited to American upper- and lowercase letters, numerals, punctuation symbols, and commonly used mathematical symbols (such as, $, %, +, =, etc.). The most common forms of **graphic accents** (also called **emoticons**) are smiley faces. The first smiley face was used around 1980, when Carnegie Mellon University student Scott Fahlman invented the first smiley using ASCII symbols. Since that time, numerous variations on the smiley face have been designed (Figure 5.2).

Graphic accents (GAs) is a term that refers "generically to emotional, artistic, and directional devices" (Witmer & Katzman, 1998, p. 5). According to Katzman (1994), propo-

FIGURE 5.1   Internet Acronyms

AAMOF	As a Matter of Fact
AFAIK	As Far As I Know
B/C	Because
BAC	By Any Chance
BCNU	Be Seeing You
BK	Because
BRB	Be Right Back
BTW	By The Way
CMIIW	Correct Me If I'm Wrong
CUL	See You Later
CU L8R	See You Later
CYA	See You
EOD	End Of Discussion
EOT	End of Thread
FDROTFL	Falling Down Rolling On The floor Laughing
FITB	Fill In The Blank
FOTCL	Falling Off the Chair Laughing
FWIW	For What It's Worth
FYI	For Your Information
GIWIST	Gee I Wish I'd Said That
IAC	In Any Case
IMCO	In My Considered Opinion
IMHO	In My Humble Opinion
IOW	In Other Words
KISS	Keep It Simple Stupid
LOL	Laughing Out Loud
MORF	Male Or Female
NRN	No Reply Necessary
OIC	OH!, I See
OTOH	On The Other Hand
PLS	Please
PMJI	Pardon My Jumping In
POV	Point Of View
ROFL	Rolling on Floor Laughing
RSN	Real Soon Now
RTFM	Read The Freaking Manual
SITD	Still In The Dark
THX	Thanks
TIA	Thanks In Advance
TTBOMK	To The Best Of My Knowledge
TTFN	Ta Ta For Now
TTYL	Talk To You Later
TYVM	Thank You Very Much
WYSIWYG	What You See Is What You Get

FIGURE 5.2   Emoticons. Most Internet users are familiar with emoticons, especially the familiar smiley face. However, when Japanese users encountered these symbols, they became confused and developed their own set of symbols that more closely mirror the Japanese culture.

U.S. and European Emoticons		Japanese Emotions	
: -)	Regular smile	(^_^)	Regular smile
: - | |	Anger	(^o^;>)	Excuse me
: -))	Very happy	(^o^)	Happy

Source: Adapted from Pollack 1996, August 12.

nents of graphic accents argue that they add clarity to expression and a quality of folk vernacular to online discourse; in contrast, critics contend that pictorial Internet slang fosters linguistic laziness and ignorance. In a study examining GAs and gender, Witmer and Katzman (1998) discovered that neither men nor women used graphic accents very often. However, "the computer users who do include GAs in their discourse tend to be women" (p. 9). Additionally, graphic accents often alter the meaning of messages that could otherwise be interpreted as angry or hostile. For instance, the GA ;-) indicates irony to clarify online comments. Graphic accents are commonly found in chat correspondence that uses a playful tone of voice.

GAs have the potential to add expressiveness, emotions, and aesthetics to Internet communication. Despite the limitations of ASCII keyboard characters, people have used these symbols to create unique and artistic messages. For example, @--->--- or @}-`-,-`-- are symbols for roses that are often exchanged in a romance chat room. Kozar (1996) examined the playful re-creation of Chinese New Year "cards" by Chinese students through the Internet. She used the word *re-creation* to refer to the recycling of traditional Chinese motifs and to signify the practice of incorporating festive symbols from other cultures into electronic greeting cards. It is a common practice for online friends to exchange greeting cards that are designed in ASCII art. For example, Christmas, Valentine's Day, and Halloween images are often e-mailed to friends and family members (Figure 5.3). Some people who receive electronic greetings alter them and remail them to others. As a result, the anonymous artist who designed the original card could become the recipient of his or her own reauthored creation. Kozar (1996) says that although Internet copyright and intellectual property rights are subjects of current debates, ASCII artists don't have a problem with the rewriting of their work and that it "has been suggested that people post their creations on public sites precisely because they want them to be used and circulated" (p. 19). Designing ASCII art requires the ability to select and place the appropriate ASCII characters to define the larger design and fill in the space (Figure 5.4). The use of GAs and ASCII art adds to the playful quality of CMC correspondence.

Humor and Linguistic Characteristics

Humor beyond the use of playful ASCII characters is an important element in online correspondence. Humor serves at least four social functions in discussion groups: self-presentation,

FIGURE 5.3   Halloween Greeting Card Circulated Anonymously through the Internet

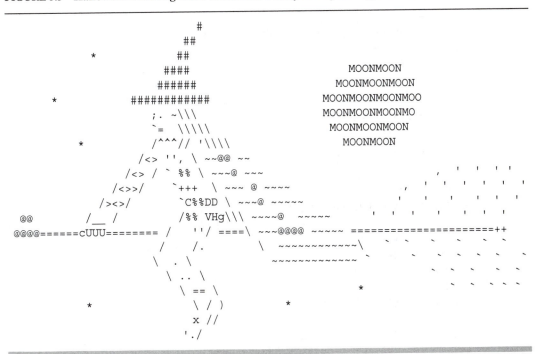

creation of common understanding, solidarity, and group identity. Conversational humor is extremely social and embedded in shared knowledge and cultural codes. For instance, an understanding of the discussion topic and group dynamics is generally required to understand humor in discussion lists. In online conversation, humor is expressed through both language and graphic markers. For instance, the following graphic humor was observed in a discussion group when a writer apologized for transposing the initials of two group participants:

> The PARSE-INTEGER proposal was submitted by Bernie (BSG), not by Glenn (GSB), though Glenn sent a message endorsing the proposal. My apologies to Bernie and Glenn for the confusion.
>
> .Lanimret ym htiw gnorw gnihtemos ro aixelsyd eb tsuM ttocS--(Yates & Orlikowski, 1993, pp. 7–8).

Another type of humor uses typographical errors. Yates and Orlikowski (1993) argue that in organizational settings, CMC's "ability to support informal textual exchanges unmediated by secretaries (who would be more likely to correct the typographical errors and insist on serious subject lines) allowed participants to develop a playful relationship with the text" (p. 10). Besides using humor in e-mail messages, online participants will also write humorous subject and signature lines (sig), which are discussed in the next chapter. The following is a signature line from the r.a.t.s. Newsgroup:

```
!!!!!!!!!!!!!!!!!!!!!!!!!!!!!!!!!!!!!!!!!!!!!!!!!!!
Emily
ajcul947@unix.stateu.edu
...with nothing particularly witty to .sig...
--
s. robinson
---------------------------------------------------
= How the heck do ya get that .sig to work =
= anyway !!!???
---------------------------------------------------
```

(Baym, 2000, p. 151).

FIGURE 5.4 ASCII Theater Masks

```
.,aa###########@a
a#################@a
#####################@a
####OO############OO##@a
OO##########OOO########@a
###;;;;O######O;;;;#####@a
#O;;' ~;######;' ~;;O###@a
#O;;,.,;O####O;,.,;;;O###a############@a
#OOOOOOO#####OOOOOOOO###@a#############@a
####OOOO\????/OOOOOO####@################@a
####OO###????###OOO#####@CO############OO##@a
#####O###(???)##O######@aC######OOO########@
##{{######=*=######}}##ac.,;O####O;,.,;;;O##
#O###Oo"#######"oO#####a' ^;######;' ^;;O###
aOO###aaa      aaa###OoaC;;;;O#####O;;;;#####
 a#O##OOOOoooOO##O#O#a:OOOO######OOOOOOOO##
  a#OO#########OO##a/##OOOO\????/OOOOOO#####
    ::OOO#####OOO:: ####OO###????###OOO#####
      'O#::;;;#O'  #####O###(???)##O######@a
                   ##########%*%###########a
                   a##O##OOOO^^^OO##O#O#####
                   aOO###aa'       'aa####Ooa
                   a#O##Oo"o######"ooO#####
                         #{{###############}}#a
                     :{#OO#########OO##}:
                       ::OOO#####OOO::
                          'O#::;;;#O'
```

Source: © 2001 Sue Barnes.

Humor often occurs as the response to another message. A central aspect of humor in discussion groups is having knowledge about the topic under discussion (Figure 5.5). For instance, experience with soap operas is required to understand the humor expressed in a social newsgroup talking about soap operas. Similarly, knowledge of computers is essential to understand the humor being expressed in a discussion group debating computer standards. Adding humor to online correspondence makes participating in an online group more social, enjoyable, and fun.

FIGURE 5.5 **The Representation of Smoking Marijuana Using Emoticons.** Participants in this IRC session need to have a knowledge of smoking marijuana to understand the humor of the messages being exchanged.

```
Line 416    <Kang> *inhale**hold*. . . . . . . . . . . . . . . . . . .
            >why?
            <Thunder> :-)
            <Kang> :|

Line 420    <Kang> :|
            <Kang> :\
            <Thunder> heheheh . . . .
            <Thunder> hehehehheh
            <Thunder> that was great

Line 425    <Kang> :|
            <Kang> :)
            <Thunder> hehehehehhe
            <Kang> *exhale*
            <Kang> :0

Line 430    <Thunder> :| :| :\ssss :)
            <Kang> hheeeheee
            <Thunder> :-Q :| :| :\sssss :)
            <Kang> ever . . . mmmmmmmm . . . . heard of Gainsville Green?

Line 435    >:-) cute
            <Kang> My hometown!
            >never heard of it
            ***Thunder sets the topic to :\:-Q :-|:-|:\sssss:-)

Line 440    <Thunder> uggg
            ***Thunder sets the topic to :\:-Q :-|:-|:\sssss:-)
            <Thunder> there we go
            <Thunder> the : was a problem I needed a \
```

From "Hmmm ... Where's That Smoke coming From?" Writing, Play and Performance on Internet Relay Chat, Brenda Danet, Lucia Ruedenberg, Yehudit Rosenbaum-Tamari, *Network & Netplay*, pp. 41–76. ©1998 American Association for Artificial Intelligence.

Figurative Language and Metaphor

Shared physical context is missing in CMC. Consequently, online correspondents must create their own contexts. Building contexts through words relies on the use of figurative language and metaphor. **Figurative language** is an expressive use of language in which words are utilized in ways that are nonliteral. This type of language is used to suggest illuminating resemblances and comparisons. According to Gibbs (1994), "Pragmatic accounts suggest that figurative language understanding is separate from 'normal' or 'ordinary' linguistic processing because of its heavy reliance on contextual, real-world knowledge" (p. 5). In contrast, he argues that the use of figurative language occurs as part of ordinary speech.

The lack of visual cues in online discourse tends to make many online correspondents write in ways that are more expressive, figurative, and metaphorical than the way they would traditionally write. Gibbs contends that recent advances in cognitive linguistics, philosophy, and psychology show that a large portion of language is metaphorically structured. Gibbs (1994) states: "People conceptualize their experiences in figurative terms via metaphor, metonymy, irony, oxymoron, and so on, and these principles underlie the way we think, reason, and imagine" (p. 5). Figurative language is often used in online discourse. As a result, people need to realize that electronic messages should not be interpreted literally (Figure 5.6).

As described in Chapters 2 and 3, verbal and visual metaphors are incorporated into CMC experience. Visual metaphors, such as the desktop, are integrated into software design to help make operating a computer easier, and verbal metaphors help users conceptually perceive cyberspace. The use of metaphor and figurative language stimulates imagination and are central to online experience because they compensate for the lack of sensory information. The use of metaphor in chat rooms make people "think" that they are talking to someone, rather than writing. Chat participants frequently say, "I went to the chat room and I was talking to a guy who had a similar problem." The idea of "talking" to other people is a strange way to describe sitting at home alone typing into a computer keyboard. Shirky (1995) explains this as follows:

> Although all of the communications you can currently have on the net are written, they can often be more like a casual phone call than a formal letter. In such a case, the phrase "I was writing back and forth with this guy" sounds odd and doesn't capture the immediacy of the experience—it's more like talking. On the other hand, if someone on the net were writing a document meant more to be read than replied to, such as a list of questions and answers about a particular subject, he or she would still call that writing. On the net, the definition of the word talking has changed from "using spoken words" to communicating in a fluid, reciprocal way (p. 3).

Metaphors such as e-mail and chat describe what people do when they are online. Moreover, linguistic metaphors contribute to the perception of cyberspace created through CMC. Metaphors used in both text-based correspondence and the Web help to establish the context in which communication occurs.

FIGURE 5.6 Figurative Internet Language. Poetry often uses figurative language. The following is a poem that was distributed on the Internet. It describes a feeling, rather than actual events. The word *invalid* in the title can be interpreted in several ways. First, the author of the poem had difficulty walking and was considered an invalid. Second, the dream could be considered invalid because it never really occurred. Internet correspondents will often write messages to evoke a feeling, rather than describe factual events.

```
INVALID DREAMS

I walk a lot when I dream.
I walk across a park in New York that lies oddly,
Between something that looks like Eighth Avenue,
And the Dakota Apartments,
Where an old friend I haven't seen in years,
Is waiting to take me to lunch.
I walk to the railway station,
I have no bags. . . .

I walk the main street in a small town,
Designed by Ray Bradbury.
I walk down the main street and meet old friends,
Whose name I do not remember.
But I love them all.
And I miss them all.
I haven't seen them in years.
We walk together, sometimes.
And have ice cream sodas,
On a marble topped counter in the drug store.

Then I walk alone again.
And up the stairs to the room,
Where my father lies dying,
In a bed next to John Kennedy.
I have things to tell them.
But, I cannot, until I join them.
So I walk on.

I do not want to stay there.
I am late for lunch.
I will miss my train. . .
So I keep walking.
And then I walk with the pain in the center of my chest.
```

Language and Action

The lack of physical cues in CMC can increase the amount of mental resources devoted to message construction. Walther and Tidwell (1996) say, "In CMC there is no need physically to backchannel, hold in one's waist, nod, smile, or remember to 'look interested,' etc. We may shift attention from our need to maintain simultaneous expressive systems and devote it instead to language selection" (pp. 305–306). The shift from fully sensory communication to text-based expression challenges online participants to establish new behavioral norms because the communication environment does not provide the same social cues as face-to-face interaction.

Some Internet genres provide emotional markers. A common MUD practice is **verbverbing**, which is the double repetition of actions, for instance, hughugs, nodnods, and smilesmiles. Language in MUDs becomes a hybrid between written words and textual gestures. Additionally, MUDs and online games provide programming commands that enable players to express emotion. In synchronous genres, language is generally used in the present tense with actions and feeling mixed in.

In social MUDs, interaction generally occurs through the following five commands: "say," "pose," "whisper," "page," and "page-pose." The "say," "pose," and "whisper" commands are used between players in the same virtual room or space. For example, if a player named Jane types "say Hello," everyone in the room will see Jane says, "Hello." The "pose" command enables players to mix actions and words together. For example, if Jane types, "pose smiles warmly," everyone will see Jane smiles warmly. These commands can be combined in the following way. Typing "pose smiles warmly and says, "Hello"" will be seen as Jane smiles warmly and says "Hello" (Figure 5.7). Language on MUDs mimics social practices.

Adventure MUDs generally provide players with several hundred commands divided into verb and adverb categories. Combining words from these categories enables players to express actions and feelings. According to Reid (1994), the most popular verbs are smile, bow, shake, greet, grin, nod, laugh, wave, giggle, sigh, hug, wait, and kiss. The popular adverbs are: happily, demonically, evilly, sadly, smilingly, deeply, passionately, knowingly, insanely, erotically, inanely, and warmly. Beyond conventional language, MUD participants have invented their own ways of using words and language. For example, some MUD worlds use gender-neutral pronouns such as spivak, which is referred to as e, em, eir, eirs, eirself.

In MUDs and other CMC genres, words are used to both define the communication context and exchange messages. Consequently, language moves between *transparency* and *opacity*. Instead of transparently reading text, players are aware of the fact they are looking at a screen to read words. The text-based nature of MUDs constantly reminds players that they are navigating through a textual world. However, players can become so engaged by the communication process that they forget they are interacting with others through text. When this occurs, the exchange becomes transparent. Players are simultaneously drawn in by other players' expressions and stepping back to reflect on their responses, which makes players move back and forth between transparency and opacity. Experiencing a shift between transparency and opacity occurs in both CMC and HCI.

FIGURE 5.7   IRC Commands and How They Appear

/invite command

as seen by the inviter as:

***Inviting PooBear to channel +Winnie

as seen by the invited person as:

***ChrisRob invites you to channel +Winnie

/join command

produces the following:

***ChrisRob has joined channel +Winnie

/kill command

as seen by IRC operators:

*** Notice -- Received KILL message for ChrisRob. Path
school_name.edu! PooBear (You don't know how much this hurts me. .
.)

as seen by the "victim:"

*** You have been killed by PooBear at school_name.edu!PooBear (You
don't know how much this hurts me. . .)

*** Use /SERVER to reconnect to a server

/kick command

as seen by the kicker and other members of the channel:

*** ChrisRob hs been kicked off channel +Winnie by PooBear

as seen by the person kicked

*** You have been kicked off channel +Winnie by PooBear

/nick command

produces the following message:

*** ChrisRob is now known as PoohMe

Source: Adapted from Reid, 1991.

Speech-Act Theory

HCI creates an action-oriented relationship between the computer user and the software program. Users select commands that instruct the machine to perform an action. Software commands control machine actions, and there is an action-oriented relationship between words and/or icons represented on a computer screen and the operations they perform. Language is also the method used to communicate between the programmer and user. As described in Chapter 3, software designers incorporate conversational messages into their designs. As computer technology advances, interfaces are increasingly using natural language as a method of HCI.

Speech Acts and Interface Design

Many interface designers base their design concepts on **speech-act theory** (see Winograd & Flores, 1987; Suchman, 1987). Suchman (1987) says: "Researchers in natural language understanding have embraced Austin's (1962/1975) observation that language is a form of action, as a way of subsuming communication [into an interface] model" (p. 39). Speech-act theory derives its theoretical framework from the philosopher J. L. Austin (1962/1975). Austin argues that sometimes saying something is actually performing an action:

> . . . for instance, the utterance "I do" (take this woman to be my lawful wedded wife), as uttered in the course of a marriage ceremony. Here we should say that in saying these words we are *doing* something—namely, marrying, rather than *reporting* something, namely *that* we are marrying. And the act of marrying, like, say, the act of betting, is at least *preferably* (though still not *accurately*) to be described as *saying certain words*, rather than as performing a different inward and spiritual, action of which these words are merely the outward and audible sign (pp. 12-13).

In software design, speech-act theory is applied to programs that plan meetings and organize schedules. Mundane office tasks have now become software features. These actions are coordinated by electronic calendars that link group members together. When a meeting is scheduled, an e-mail message is sent to all of the participants.

Similarly, agent software is designed to perform actions for the user. For example, agents can search the Internet to collect data on specific topics. Other types of existing agent tasks include handling electronic mail and recommending books, music, and other forms of entertainment. Experiments are also being conducted with buying and selling agents that will negotiate the purchase of a product without the direct control of the user. Price parameters are set by the respective users and the buying and selling agents will search the Internet for a match. Scheduling, managing e-mail, locating information, and recommending entertainment are all actions performed by software, which is a form of action-oriented language.

Speech Acts and CMC

In CMC environments, words perform actions. Although it could be argued that electronic actions are virtual, some actions do have real-world consequences. The "virtual" actions of computer users can arouse real feelings and emotions in other people. For example, a number of online participants have transformed their "virtual" feelings into real-life friendships. Online behavior follows the patterns of real-world behavior, and people can become extremely emotionally involved with others through text-based correspondence. For instance, MUD players often engage in virtual weddings and behave online as romantic couples.

When players become totally immersed in their online interactions, making a distinction between real actions and linguistic ones can become difficult. For example, Chapter 12 describes a virtual rape in cyberspace. Although the actions were all typed and imaginary, the women involved in the incident experienced emotional distress. No physical harm was done; however, emotional pain was felt. Similarly, spouses of people who engage in cybersex argue that these relationships are a form of infidelity. Although no physical encounters take place, partners argue that their spouses have emotionally cheated on them. The words people share in CMC genres can effect relationships both on- and offline.

Language Usage and CMC

In organizational contexts, CMC is often used to support face-to-face situations. For instance, CMC is used in education to augment traditional coursework. Many of the new linguistic conventions previously described can be observed in CMC conversations. A study conducted by Murphy and Collins (1997) revealed that students develop and carry out their own linguistic conventions to help them make meaning out of text-based exchanges (Figure 5.8). Students used acronyms, graphic accents, and paralinguistic cues to more clearly communicate with each other.

Murray (1991) studied office workers to explore how they use CMC. She discovered that CMC provides another communication option. Some people will use e-mail instead of face-to-face meetings or the telephone. For example, a quick, simple request for information is easily done through e-mail, but long, detailed explanations are better given in a face-to-face meeting. CMC is also a preferred method for requests for action because people do not need to spend extra time engaging in social niceties. Additionally, e-mail is more permanent and it keeps a record of the conversation. Finally, e-mail allows people to think before they reply, something that is difficult to do in face-to-face meetings. Although CMC provides another way for people to communicate with each other, communication patterns tend to follow the same gender styles that exist in face-to-face settings.

Gendered Discourse

Internet correspondence has made scholars aware of gender differences in online communication styles. For instance, Herring (1994) observed that 68 percent of the messages posted by men criticized and/or ridiculed other group members and supported the notion that online communication is often male dominated and male oriented. Herring observed that men use strong assertions, self-promotion, and an authoritative orientation that challenges others. In contrast, women use apologies, questions, a personal orientation, and explicit justification in their discourse. Studies conducted by Herring (1999) and Charles Soukup (1999) reveal that a male style of discourse tends to dominate online communication. Men are more likely to represent themselves as experts, and they answer questions or supply information. In contrast, women are often more supportive, and they express appreciation and thanks and try to make other people feel welcome in the group. In fact, Herring (1994) argued that gender styles are so distinct in Internet communication that when a supportive message is signed with a male signature, people will question the actual gender of the person.

In general, online gendered styles of communication often correspond with gendered face-to-face conversational styles. For example, Tannen's (1990) categories of "rapport

---

FIGURE 5.8   Linguistic Conventions Used by Students in Chat. Murphy and Collins (1997) observed the following ways in which students used linguisitc conventions in an educational chat room:

---

1. Use of Keywords

   Using keywords, personal names, or initials as a descriptor at the beginning of a line, indicates the subject of the entry and makes it easier for others to understand the message.

   ```
   BOB: we need to decide on an overall topic heading to use in this discussion
   RE TERMS: Could someone please define the term *frame* for me?
   PCM: Do you want the definition for psychological frames or play frames?
   ```

2. Use of Shorthand Writing

   Shorthand writing, including acronyms, are frequently used in chat discourse.

   ```
   SALLY: Has anyone spoken to Prof M lately?
   HOMEWORK: imho this assign is 2 tough.
   ```

3. Building Social Presence

   A sense of social presence can be established by referring to participants by name and by sharing activities both on- and offline.

   ```
   PCM: Mary that was a very good answer to the ? asked.
   BOB: Is anyone going to happy hour at BJ's pub?
   ```

4. Adding Playfulness and Humor

   Having fun with the text adds to the sociability of the communication exchange.

   ```
   BOB: Quiet Mary is doing a bang-up job here.
   PCM: Shhhh . . . Its getting too noisy in this room.
   ```

5. Adding Nonverbal Cues to the Text

   Nonverbal textual cues, such as underlining, punctuation marks, and capital letters, can be used to expresss nonverbal communication. For example, typing in capital letters indicates shouting. But this style of writing is often understood as being hostile or negative.

   ```
   PCM: Boy was that a tough one!
   MARK: I'LL TELL YOU AGAIN IF YOU *STILL* HAVEN'T GOTTEN IT.
   SALLY: Don't get *snipity* with us!
   ```

6. Continuation Through the Use of Ellipses

   Students used ellipses (. . .) to indicate the continuation of a thought or idea from one line to another. (These are also used to indicate a pause.)

   ```
   SALLY: People should be advised to check the Web Site first . . .
       . . . then we can all discuss the issue together.
   PMG: Well . . . Let me think about that.
   ```

7. Using Graphic Accents

   Students occasionally express themselves by using emoticons and smilies. Emoticons are particularly helpful when expressing sarcasm in a message.

   ```
   PMG: Bob do you mean that there are NO quiet students in this class ;-)
   ```

Source: Based on Murphy & Collins, 1997.

talk" versus "report talk" could be used to describe online interactions. Women engage in rapport talk to establish connections and build relationships. This type of talk emphasizes similarities and sharing experiences. In contrast, when men talk, they try to preserve independence and maintain their status in a hierarchial social order. Tannen (1990) states: "This is done by exhibiting knowledge and skill, and by holding center stage through verbal performance such as storytelling, joking, or imparting information" (p. 77).

Due to the lack of visual information in online correspondence, the gender of correspondents is often based solely on their communication style. Aggressive behavior both on- and offline is expected to be male behavior. When women talk in an assertive way, their behavior is viewed as improper. In American culture, there are expected styles of behavior for men and women when they talk.

> Both women and men pay a price if they do not behave in ways expected of their gender: Men who are not very aggressive are called "wimps," whereas women who are not very aggressive are called "feminine." Men who are aggressive are called "go-getters," though if they go too far, from the point of view of the viewer, they may be called "arrogant." This can hurt them, but not nearly as much as the innumerable labels for women who are thought to be too aggressive—starting with the most hurtful one: bitch (Tannen, 1994, pp. 40–41).

Established gender patterns in face-to-face interactions can influence people's perceptions about how to behave in online communication. For example, Herring (1994) reports that both male and female members of academic discussion lists can feel intimidated by aggressive messages. But men and women have different reactions to feeling intimidated. Herring (1994) observes that "men seemed to accept such behavior as a normal feature of academic life, making comments to the effect that 'Actually, the barbs and arrows were entertaining, because of course they weren't aimed at me.' In contrast, many women responded with profound aversion" (p. 2).

Online correspondence can also break down gender stereotypes and make people aware of gendered styles of communication. For example, in online debates, some women can be aggressive and disagree with men without any problems, but when two women become aggressive in an online argument, the male members of the group can perceive this as improper behavior. For example, an online participant reported that when she and another woman disagreed about a technical issue, she immediately received a private message from a man snickering about her "catfight." Thus, concepts about face-to-face gendered behavior influence online behavior.

In early CMC research, it was observed that men often contributed more to online discussions and wrote longer messages than women. Because men dominated online conversations, some women argued for all-female groups. Female groups, such as Systers, allow women to mentor other women in the discipline of computer science without male interference. Dr. Anita Borg, the founder of Systers, argues that female discussion groups are necessary for women working in male-dominated professions such as computer science because they create a female support system. According to Borg, "Women need female role models and mentors. A primary function of women-only interaction is mentoring. Exposing women to the full range of significant interactions among women, without the perception of help or input from men, serves to bolster self-esteem and independence" (cited in

Camp, 1996, p. 123). Syster members argue that their online group can help to build self-esteem and validate female behavioral norms both on- and offline and that women-only discussion groups can help to counter the effect of cultural stereotyping by enabling women to interact with each other and develop a strong sense of self.

Although gendered styles of behavior have been observed in online correspondence, individuals are noticing that men and women do not always follow stereotypical patterns. For example, a female student made the following observation about a soap opera discussion group:

> What I noticed most about the etiquette of the group was a deep respect each member had for another's opinion, even if it was contrary to his/her own. Violators of this rule were strongly denounced by other members.
>
> By joining this discussion group, I was pleasantly surprised to notice that quite a few men were involved in the discussion, and that the moderator of the group was in fact a man as well. I had always assumed that day-time soap operas were primarily only of interest to women (cited in Barnes, 2001).

Baym (1995) observed that male and female participants in soap opera lists are often friendly and participants dislike rude or flaming behavior. Conversely, men and women flame and aggressively argue with each other in other types of groups. For example, Brail (1996) describes how she and another woman fought back against angry Usenet posts from men who refused to talk about the band Riot Grrls:

> The woman who wrote the original note fought back, posting angry, curt responses to the one or two men, who were leading the charge against the "stupid" Riot Grrls. My blood pressure increasing, my heart pounding and my body aching for justice, I joined the fray. I'm a natural writer—wordy, passionate—and, in a world where you are your words, I am loud. I bellow, I scream, I prognosticate. I was writing and what I thought at the time were noble words, defending the honor of all women (p. 144).

Contrary to gender stereotypes, females use aggressive language and flame other people. As a result, flaming itself is not a gender issue, but a characteristic of online correspondence. The following is an example of a flame written by a woman:

> ```
> Once again Jack you purposely misread in order not to confront a
> conflict within yourself. . . . I am, as usual, saddened that some-
> one who claims as much education as you (uh, credentials) can still
> only reduce arguments to on-off absurd positions and name calling.
> But I realized it is your problem, not mine. GET OVER IT JACK! (cited
> ```
> in Barnes, 2001).

In other instances, gender differences in online conversational styles often follow traditional gender lines. For example, Clerc (1996) observed that in newsgroups discussing television programs "women focus on character issues while men more often discuss hardware and special effects" (p. 85). These two different threads of conversation can coexist. However, when women begin to lust after male actors, the men on the list become a bit hypocritical. "A common, if mild, masculine response is 'How would you ladies like it if us guys started slobbering on about the actresses?'—a remark that blatantly ignores the rampant slobbering in the perennial 'big tits' threads" (p. 86). When stereotypical gender lines are crossed, group behavior becomes the topic of debate and gender wars can erupt. Male list members will argue for current social patterns; in contrast, female members will point out gender inequalities.

Baym (1995a) says that the gender balance in some groups will influence the communication process. In predominantly female groups, the personal topics discussed are ones that particularly affect women. Additionally, there is a social taboo against insulting one another, which is considered to be male behavior. Female-dominated groups try to discourage aggressive messages and flaming. As a result, a more friendly environment is established that encourages female participation and polite behavior, which is often associated with female styles of online discourse. The way in which people use words on the Internet can provide gender cues to other participants. Interpretation of these cues is based on face-to-face experiences.

Rhetoric and the Internet

Both male and female online participants need to develop competent linguistic styles. Rhetoric, an ancient Greek discipline that was applied to public speaking, is the art of using words effectively. With the introduction of electronic media, rhetorical studies have been expanded to include television, films, and the Web. Aristotle's work *The Rhetoric* is one of the most well-know descriptions of the rhetorical process. Aristotle argued that communication is primarily a verbal activity in which a speaker tries to persuade audience members. Persuasion occurs through skillful construction of an argument and delivery of a speech.

As presented in Chapter 1, there are three main aspects of an oral presentation—ethos, pathos, and logos. Ethos is the information source, such as the speaker, author, or Web site creator. Credibility, one of the five basic criteria for evaluating Web sites described in Chapter 4, is a key aspect of persuasion and believability. Our conceptions about the source of information have an impact on whether we believe the message to be true or false. Pathos is the emotion evoked in the audience. In visual media, such as television and the Web, images are often combined with words to evoke an emotional response in the viewer. Finally, logos is the nature of the message being presented by the source to the audience. Speakers use a variety of techniques to support their arguments, such as examples, facts, statistics, and analogies. Online discussions and argumentation can be examined by using these three criteria.

A number of scholars, including Jay David Bolter in *Writing Space: The Computer, Hypertext, and the History of Writing*, Richard Lanham in *The Electronic Word*, and Michael Heim in *Electric Language*, have explored the impact of computers on language usage. Bolter contends that computer icons introduce picture writing into the writing process, and Lanham argues that computer screens destabilize the reading process. Readers of electronic texts no longer transparently read words on the screen; instead, they look at the typefaces. Thus, reading is not transparent because readers are more conscious of the process and will alter type styles and page layouts. Visual elements are now included in electronic rhetoric. All of these authors agree that computers have had an impact on writing and the rhetorical presentation of ideas.

Welch's Rhetorical Approach to the Internet

Welch (1999) defines the study of rhetoric as "the study of ways of presenting oneself in a variety of subjectivities to the world, of reorganizing and deflecting the barbs of hostile rhetoric, and of coming together with other people in a variety of contexts" (p. 73). According to Welch, thought and speech depend on each other. Her work is based on the pre-Aristotelian theory of rhetoric described by Isocrates and Diotima. Isocrates did not engage in public speaking, rather, he wrote pamphlets as written performances for, in his view, the production of written discourse was equally as important as the speaker and audience. The act of writing separates reader and writer, who develops inner speech that cultivates the advanced, complex thinking skills associated with the act of writing. For instance, writers must be able to create an abstract conception of their audience, and they need to be able to simultaneously think about competing concepts. Producing discourse through writing and speaking is central to the construction of both private and public constructions of the world.

Welch contends that Isocratic rhetoric resembles **postmodernism**, an intellectual movement that rejects the modernist values of rationality, progress, and overarching explanations about human nature and culture. Postmodernists celebrate the decline of "grand narratives" and emphasize the fragmentation and dispersed nature of contemporary life. Interactively accessing information from globally distributed databases through the Web is an example of the postmodern experience.

The introduction of electronic media changed the ways in which messages are delivered to audiences and created **electric rhetoric**. Electric rhetoric presents information as fragments that are nonlinear yet juxtaposed; for example, MTV videos are collages of short video images and hypertext links interconnect pieces of information. Audience members and computer users must create meaning from these fragments. Electric rhetoric is repetitive and mixes fragments of mass, high, and modernist culture together. Welch (1999) identifies the following nine oral features of electric rhetoric that can be applied to the Web:

1. *The Web is additive rather than subordinate.* Web surfers can interact with a variety of texts to acquire additional information.
2. *The Web is aggregative instead of analytic.* Information is highly associative and it is not necessarily presented in a logical, linear way with rigid categories.
3. *The Web is redundant.* Web sites often have a surplus of text with numerous links. This use of redundancy helps the user navigate the site.
4. *The Web is conservative.* It replicates the conservatism of the world. However, it can also undermine the status quo. For example, Web information can oppose racist views and provide alternative narratives to ones generally found in Western culture.
5. *The Web is close to the human lifeworld.* People can develop a close relationship with their computers and the Web sites with which they spend time interacting.
6. *The Web is agonistically toned.* Web users are engaged in mutual inquiry and collaboration. Agonism tends to occur when participants have a clash of ideas. This is best illustrated by the use of flaming, further described in Chapter 12.

7. *The Web is participatory instead of objectively distanced.* Users are encouraged to participate and collaborate with each other.
8. *The Web is homeostatic.* Sites are maintained through dynamic equilibrium, and on-line interaction can lead to unpredicted consequences.
9. *The Web is situational rather than abstract.* New forms of personal expression can be found on the Web, such as the sharing of individual stories and Weblogs.

Training in electric rhetoric requires students to develop both visual and verbal abilities. Central to Welch's approach is learning to interpret the ways in which messages are situated, raced, fragmented, self-consciously performed, gendered, and relative to the person. Messages are created within cultural contexts, and ideologies influence message production. For example, the original text-based Internet was primarily an educational system that did not allow advertising. The Web, however, is a commercial system filled with advertising and promotional messages. As discussed in Chapter 4, interpreting the validity of Web messages can be a complex process.

In addition to the five criteria for evaluating Web-based information, rhetorical analysis of Web sites also includes visual evaluation. Visual messages tend to persuade on an emotional level. Understanding the feelings evoked by a Web site is part of a rhetorical analysis. Visual evaluation involves an examination of the visual layout and design of a site and how information is presented. Figure 5.9 provides a series of questions to ask yourself when you are evaluating a Web site. By exploring both the content and visual design, Web users can begin to identify the persuasion techniques used by Web site creators. In contrast to persuasive computing, a topic covered in the opening chapter, electric rhetoric attempts to make receivers of messages aware of the persuasive process.

FIGURE 5.9   Rhetorical Analysis of Web Sites. Welch argues that the rhetorical process also includes an examination of the visual messages being communicated in electronic media. The following questions can be used to visually critique a Web site:

---

1. Are the graphics on the site designed to capture your attention or distract you?
2. Are the pictures or images placed on the site a form of visual persuasion? Are they designed to make you think or feel a certain way?
3. What emotions do you feel when you look at the site?
4. Do the pictures or images on the site complement and support the text? Do they compete with the text for attention? Do they contradict the textual message?
5. Are there any visual metaphors used in the site to help provide a context for the messges being presented?
6. How do the visuals on the site influence your interpretion of the messages being presented?
7. Does the visual arrangement of elements on the site stress different ideas? How does the layout effect your interpretation of the information,? For example, does the site look professional and highly believable?

Summary

Scholars have examined the differences between orality and literacy. Ong argues that electronic media introduce a type of *secondary orality*, which is supported by the use of print technology. To compensate for a full range of visual and verbal information, Internet users play with language usage. Acronyms, graphic accents, and emotional markers are often mixed in with written messages to indicate emotional feelings. Language usage with computers is action oriented. Software languages control machine actions, and software is also used to coordinate human actions. A number of interface designers have incorporated Austin's *speech-act* theory into their design methodologies.

When people communicate with each other through the Internet, it is often through textual exchanges. Gendered styles of online discourse reflect the ways in which men and women speak in face-to-face settings. However, Internet genres are often dominated by male discourse styles. Understanding the ways in which people use electronic language can be explored through traditional rhetorical concepts. Welch argues that electric rhetoric should be included in rhetorical studies. Features of electric rhetoric include adding information, redundancy, association, conservative worldview, dynamic equilibrium, and participation. Electric rhetoric analysis attempts to make Web users aware of the persuasive concepts embedded in messages.

WEB RESOURCES

ASCII Art: http://www.ascii-art.com
IRC Chat: http://www.yahoo.com/Computers_and_Internet/Internet/Chat/IRC/
http://www.cs.utk.edu/~hill/nicecafe/cafe.html

TERMS

Acronym is a word formed from the initial letters or portions of letters belonging to a group of words. Online, acronyms are often made up of the first letters of a series of words to speed up response time.

Electric rhetoric presents information as fragments that are nonlinear yet juxtaposed; for example, MTV videos are collages of short video images and hypertext links interconnect information.

Figurative language is an expressive use of language in which words are utilized in ways that are nonliteral.

Graphic accents (also called **emoticons**) are smiley faces and other ASCII character designs that add clarity, expressiveness, emotions, and aesthetic elements to Internet communication.

Paralanguage applies to both spoken and written forms of linguistic communication. In written language, paralanguage is the visual appearance of written materials, including punctuation, spelling, neatness, and the use of space for margins and between words.

Postmodernism is an intellectual movement that rejects the modernist values of rationality, progress, and overarching explanations about human nature and culture. In contrast, postmodernists celebrate the decline of "grand narratives" and emphasize the fragmentation and dispersed nature of contemporary life.

Secondary orality is more deliberate and self-conscious than primary orality because it is based on the use of writing and print, which are essential for the manufacture, operation, and utilization of the technologies that support it.

Speech-act theory derives its theoretical framework from the philosopher J. L. Austin, who argues that words can perform actions.

Verbverbing is the double repetition of actions in online discourse, for instance, hughugs, nodnods, and smilesmiles.

EXERCISES

1. Select an Internet genre. Identify and examine the paralinguistic cues that occur in the online exchanges. What do these cues tell you about the people participating in the exchange?

2. E-mail can be written in both a formal and an informal style. Look at the following list of situations and identify which style of writing should be applied to each. Select a formal and an informal situation and write an e-mail message for each.

   Sending an e-mail message to your professor
   Sending an e-mail message to inquire about a job
   Sending an e-mail message to one of your parents
   Sending an e-mail message to your best friend at another college
   Sending an e-mail message to a discussion list

3. Observe a discussion list or chat room. Explain how paralanguage is being used and identify different examples. How does the writer use paralanguage to enhance the message being communicated? Could the same message be sent without the use of paralanguage? Why or why not?

4. What do you think? Could words be considered actions? Support your opinion.

5. Divide into small groups. Each group should research different types of software programs that facilitate small group communication, such as MUDs, MOOs, groupware, computer-supported cooperative work, etc. Collaborate on writing a paper using only e-mail correspondence. When the paper is finished, discuss the advantages and disadvantages of e-mail–only correspondence. What suggestions would you make for the use of e-mail in future task-related correspondence?

6. Use the questions in Figure 5.9 to conduct a rhetorical analysis of a Web page.

BIBLIOGRAPHY

Aristotle (1954). *The rhetoric & the poetics of Aristotle* (W. R. Roberts, Trans.). New York: The Modern Library.

Austin, J. L. (1962/1975). *How to do things with words* (2nd ed.) (In J. O. Urmson & M. Sbisa (Eds.) Cambridge, MA: Harvard University Press.

Barnes, S. B. (2001). *Online connections: Internet interpersonal relationships*. Cresskill, NJ: Hampton Press.

Baym, N. K. (1995a). The emergence of community in computer-mediated-communication. In S. G. Jones (Ed.). *Cybersociety: Computer-mediated communication and community* (pp. 138–163). Thousand Oaks, CA: Sage Publications.

Baym, N. K. (1995b). The performance of humor in computer-mediated communication. *Journal of Computer-Mediated Communication, 1* (2). [Online] http://www.ascusc.org/jcmc/vol1/issue2 (June 18, 2002)

Baym, N. K. (2000). *Tune in, Log on: Soaps, fandom, and online community*. Thousand Oaks, CA: Sage Publications.

Bolter, D. J. (1991). *Writing space: The computer, hypertext, and the history of writing*. Hillsdale, NJ: Lawrence Erlbaum Associates.

Bradshaw, J. M. (1997). *Software agents*. Cambridge, MA: The MIT Press.

Brail, S. (1996). The price of admission: Harassment and free speech in the wild, wild, west. In L. Cherny & E. R. Weise (Eds.), *Wired_Women* (pp. 141–157). Seattle: Seal Press.

Camp, L. J. (1996). We are geeks, and we are not guys: The systers mailing list. In L. Cherny & E. R. Weise (Eds.), *Wired_Women* (pp. 114–125). Seattle: Seal Press.

Clerc, S. (1996). Estrogen brigades and "big tits" threads: Media fandom online and off. In L. Cherny & E. R. Weise (Eds.), *Wired_Women* (pp. 73–97). Seattle: Seal Press.

Ferris, S. P. (1996). Women on-line: Cultural and relational aspects of women's communication in on-line discussion groups. *Interpersonal Computing and Technology, 4* (3–4), 29–40.

Gibbs, R.W., Jr. (1994). *The poetics of mind*. New York: Cambridge University Press.

Gozzi, R., Jr. (1999). *The power of metaphor in the age of electronic media*. Cresskill, NJ: Hampton Press.

Havelock, E. A. (1963). *Preface to Plato*. Cambridge, MA: Harvard University Press.

Heim, M. (1987). *Electric language: A philosophical study of word processing*. New Haven: Yale University Press.

Herring, S. (1994, June). *Gender differences in computer-mediated communication: Bringing familiar baggage to the new frontier*. Paper presented at the American Library Association Annual Convention, Miami, Florida. [Online]. Available: http://cpsr.org/cpsr/gender/herring.txt (April 26, 1995).

Herrings, S. C. (1999). The rhetorical dynamices of gender harassment On-line. *The Information Society, 15* (3) 151–167.

Jenkins, H. (1992). *Textual poachers*. New York: Routledge.

Katzman, S. (1994). Quirky rebuses: "Graphic accents" in telecommunication. *The Archnet Electronic Journal on Virtual Culture, 2*, (4) pp. [Online].

Kozar, S. (1996). Enduring traditions, ethereal transmissions: Recreating Chinese New Year celebrations on the Internet, pp. 27. *The Journal of Computer-Mediated Communication* [Online]. Available: http://www.ascusc.org/jcmc/vol1/issue2/kozar.html (April 16, 2000).

Lanham, R. A. (1993). *The electronic word: Democracy, technology, and the arts*. Chicago: The University of Chicago Press.

Lee, J. Y. (1996). Charting the codes of cyberspace: A rhetoric of electronic mail. In L. Strate, R. Jacobson, & S. Gibson (Eds.), *Communication and cyberspace* (pp. 275–296). Cresskill, NJ: Hampton Press.

Loughlin, T. W. (1993, January). Virtual relationships: The solitary world of cmc. *Interpersonal Computing and Technology: An Electronic Journal for the 21st Century 1* (1). [Online].

McLuhan, M. (1964). *Understanding media: The extensions of man*. New York: Signet Books.

Murphy, K. L., & Collins, M.P. (1997). Communication conventions in instructional electronic chats. *First Monday, 2* (11) [Online]. Available: http://www.firstmonday.dk/issues/issue2_11/murphy/index.html (April 15, 2000)

Murray, D. E. (1991). *Conversation for action: The computer terminal as a medium of communication*. Philadelphia: John Benjamins Publishing Company.

Ong, W. J. (1982). *Orality and literacy: The technologizing of the word*. London: Methuen.

Pollack, A. (1996, August 12). Happy in the East (^_^) or Smiling :-) in the West. *The New York Times*, p. D5.

Radford, M. L., Barnes, S. B., & Barr, L. R. (2002) *Web research: Selecting, evaluating, citing*. Boston: Allyn and Bacon/Longman.

Reid, E. M. (1991). *Electropolis: Communication and community on Internet relay chat* [Online], 40 pp. Available: http://www.ee.mu.oz.au/papers/emr/electropolis.html (May 15, 1997).

Reid, E. (1994). Cultural formations in text-based virtual realities, 84 pp. (Online) Available: http://www.ludd.luth.se/mud/aber/articles/cult-form.thesis.html (Downloaded October 11, 2001).

Reid, E. M. (1995). Virtual worlds: Culture and imagination. In S. G. Jones (Ed.), *Cybersociety* (pp. 164–183). Thousand Oaks, CA: Sage Publications, pp. 164-183.

Shirky, C. (1995). *Voices from the net*. Emeryville, CA: Ziff-Davis Press.

Soukup, C. (1999). The gendered interactional patterns of computer-mediated chatrooms: A critical ethnographic study. *Information Society, 15* (3) pp. 169–176.

Suchman, L. A. (1987). *Plans and situated actions: The problem of human-machine communication*. Cambridge, MA: Cambridge University Press.

Sutton, L. A. (1996). Cocktails and thumbtacks in the old west: What would Emily Post say? In L. Cherny & E. R. Weise (Eds.), *Wired_Women* (pp. 169–187). Seattle: Seal Press.

Tannen, D. (1990). *You just don't understand: Women and men in conversation*. New York: Ballantine Books.

Tannen, D. (1994). *Talking from 9 to 5 women and men in the workplace: Language, sex and power*. New York: Avon Books.

Ullman, E. (1996). Come in, CQ: the body on the wire. In L. Cherny & E. R. Weise (Eds.), *Wired_Women* (pp. 3–23). Seattle: Seal Press.

Vorlicky, R. (1995). *Act like a man: Challenging masculinities in American drama*. Ann Arbor: University of Michigan Press.

Walther, J., & Tidwell, L. (1996). When is mediated communication not interpersonal? In K. M. Galvin & P. Cooper (Eds.). *Making connections: Readings in relational communication* (pp. 300–307). Los Angeles: Roxbury Publishing Company.

Welch, K. E. (1999). *Electric rhetoric: Classical rhetoric, oralism and a new literacy*. Cambridge, MA: The MIT Press.

Winograd, T. & Flores, F. (1987). *Understanding computers and cognition*. Reading, MA: Addison-Wesley Publishing Company, Inc.

Witmer, D., & Katzman, S. (1998). Smile when you say that: Graphic accents as gender markers in computer-mediated communication. In F. Sudweeks, M. McLaughlin & S. Rafaeli (Eds.). *Network & netplay* (pp. 3–11). Menlo, CA: AAAI Press/The MIT Press.

Yates, J., & Orlikowski, W. J. (1993). Knee-jerk anti-LOOPism and other e-mail phenomena: Oral, written, and electronic patterns in computer-mediated communication. *Center for Coordination Science Technical Report #150* [Online] pp.10. Available: http://ccs.mit.edu/CCCSWP150.html (June 11, 1998).

6 Presenting Oneself Online

Chapter Overview

CMC separates physical appearance from the communication process, which fosters the use of fantasy to fill in missing information. Additionally, the separation of people from their words allows individuals to present themselves in a variety of ways that may or may not resemble their true selves. For instance, people gender bend, or pretend to be a member of the opposite sex.

Online presentations can be carefully crafted to create a positive impression. The different ways people present themselves to others in CMC include verbal descriptions, visual avatars, and creative screen names. Language and the creative use of programming commands help Internet users establish an online personality. This chapter introduces concepts of identity and the presentation of self in CMC. You will learn about

- Traditional concepts of identity formation
- How the Internet alters concepts of self
- How people present themselves online
- The relationship between online identity and self-disclosure
- A contextualized framework for examining the online presentation of self

People who present themselves on the Internet are not always who and what they seem to be. In contrast to face-to-face experiences, online interactions do not allow us to know if people are who and what they say they are. For instance, it is common in MUDs for men to present themselves as women. In chat rooms, people describe themselves as thin instead of stout and tall instead of short. In electronic text-only social contexts, people have an opportunity to create idealized versions of themselves. However, people participating in work-related or professional discussion lists generally present themselves as their actual identities (Figure 6.1).

Online communication can be an equalizing experience because it enables shy people to be bold and the socially reticent to become gregarious. In *Life on the Screen*, Turkle (1995) describes how a variety of socially reticent individuals are attracted to Internet correspondence to develop their social skills. The Internet is a place for engaging in role-playing games and experimenting with different personae. However, Turkle does not consider online actions to be the same as experiences in the real world. She contends, "Today what disturbs us is when the shifting norms of the virtual world bleed into real life" (p. 230).

FIGURE 6.1 E-mail Addresses and Identity E-mail addresses can provide information about the person sending the message. For example, some computer systems place the name of the user next to the e-mail address:

```
smith@university.edu <Sally Smith>
```

Similarly, the address itself can provide information about the organization the person is associated with. For example, company names and the names of universities are often included in e-mail addresses:

```
john_doe@wired.com
```

```
jones@harvard.edu
```

John Doe works for a commercial company; Jones works at a university.

Engaging in Internet correspondence can have an influence on the actual person behind the computer screen. For example, the introductory issue of *Wired* magazine ran an article about a woman whose real life changed because of her online correspondence. The woman was described in face-to-face encounters as "a rather mousy person—the shy type who favored gray clothing of a conservative cut—and was the paragon of shy and retiring womanhood" (Van der Leun, 1993, p. 74). On the Internet she called herself "The Naked Lady." Her online personality was a sexy, lewd, bawdy, man-eating female. As months of online correspondence with men progressed, a transformation began to occur in the woman's real life. "She got a trendy haircut. Her clothing tastes went from Peck and Peck to tight skirts slit up the thigh. . . . Her speech became bawdier, her jokes naughtier" (p. 74). In essence, she transformed herself into her digital persona.

Traditional Concepts of Identity

During different historical periods, people had different attitudes toward concepts of self and social roles. In premodern societies, an individual's identity was fixed, solid, and stable. Identity was based on predefined social roles and traditional social systems with established beliefs and behavior patterns. A person was born into a family with a particular social status and died as a member of a fixed social group. Identity was not subject to reflection or discussion. According to Kellner (1992), "Individuals did not undergo identity crises, or radically modify their identity. One was a hunter and a member of the tribe and that was that" (p. 141). Tradition was an organizing principle of social life. Individuals could not easily alter their social group or their relationship to the group.

In contrast, modern identity is mobile, multiple, personal, self-reflexive, and subject to change. People are no longer born into a rigid social structure; instead, they can create their own identity. Individuals can decide what social roles they play, whether or not to get married, become parents, and work as a doctor, lawyer, teacher, or engineer. Consequently, modern concepts of identity are socially constructed as people assume different roles throughout their lifetime. Modern identity is established as a result of mutual recognition from others combined with self-validation. Giddens (1991) contends that self-identity is *"reflexively understood by the person in terms of her or his biography"* (p. 53, original emphasis). Individual biographies are constructed from the individual's various social roles, and as roles change a personal narrative incorporates the changes.

Although people in modern society have more flexibility in selecting their social roles, the norms of behavior associated with roles tend to be socially fixed. For example, one is a father, daughter, New Yorker, professor, student, liberal, Christian, or a combination of these roles. Although modern society allows individuals to select different roles, the norms associated with those roles have been socially defined. However, as we move into a postmodern society, technology introduces new roles and changes the ways in which we socially interact. As a result, identity becomes less and less stable.

The Internet and Self-Identity

Scholars have conflicting opinions about the influence of the Internet on the formation of self-identity. Gergen (1991) argues that it is difficult to develop a stable sense of self in today's mass-mediated world because media expose people to so many different cultures and ideas. He states, "Citizens exposed to an ever-expanding array of perspectives may on short notice join in symbolic communities with others from around the globe" (p. 253). Exposure to a variety of points of view can create personal conflict because each subculture claims that its perspective is the right one. If every group claims to be right, how will people establish a value system for shaping their behavioral patterns? Individuals who are constantly exposed to conflicting social messages and value systems will find it difficult to develop a stable value system of their own and a stable sense of self. As a result, Gergen is concerned about the impact of global media, especially Web sites, on identity formation.

In contrast, Wynn and Katz (1997) contend, the "Internet does not radically alter the social bases of identity or conventional constraints on social interaction, although it certainly will provide openings for variations based in the new opportunities made available" (p. 298). These authors consider the ability to experiment with identity a positive aspect of CMC. In opposition to Gergen's concern about global media creating social fragmentation, Wynn and Katz (1997) argue that society is already fragmented and the Internet is a potential cultural force that can organize and help support the construction of social meaning.

Other scholars fear that replacing physical presence with textual and symbolic representations of self will allow people to relate to one another in a fantasy world that is no longer grounded in a shared reality. Fragmentation of social experience could lead to conflict and confusion because the Internet provides individuals with the opportunity to create their own subrealities that may or may not have any relationship to the real world. In social contexts such as MUDs and chat, players can role-play and invent personalities. As a result, Poster (1990) states, on the Internet "the self is decentered, dispersed, and multiplied in continuous instability" (p. 6).

The Internet supports a concept of self-identity that is multifaceted. People can represent themselves as their true identity on a discussion list, as a false identity in a chat room, and as a character when playing in a MUD. There are two basic theories about self-identity. The first theory views the individual as having an integrated or self-actualized identity.

Gardner (1983) describes this self as "a self that is highly developed and fully differentiated from others . . . individuals who appear to have understood much about themselves and about their societies and who have come to terms successfully with the frailties of the human condition" (p. 252). In contrast to the idea of an integrated self is the notion of a set of selves. "Rather than a central 'core self' which organizes one's thoughts, behavior, and goals, the person is better thought of as a collection of relatively diverse masks, none of which takes precedence over the others, and each of which is simply called into service as needed" (p. 252). CMC tends to support the second perspective, or a collection of selves.

Poster (1990) has observed that in computer-mediated contexts the individual is affected in the following ways: (a) new possibilities for playing with identities are possible, (b) gender cues are removed, and (c) the subject is dispersed and dislocated in space and time. New possibilities for playing with identity are described by Turkle (1995), who argues that CMC can be beneficial to the development of self. In online contexts, young people can experiment with roles, relationships, and virtual sex without facing real-world consequences, such as careless sex that can lead to pregnancy. Turkle argues that although MUD experiences are removed from the structured surroundings of one's normal life, they can help the development of a personal sense of self. Thus, game playing can have a positive influence on real life because individuals can use online role-playing to act out and experiment with different aspects of their personality.

The Presentation of Self

Goffman's (1959) research on how people present themselves and validate their identity in face-to-face settings can be applied to CMC. Goffman states, "The expressiveness of the individual (and therefore his capacity to give impressions) appears to involve two radically different kinds of sign activity: the expression that he *gives*, and the expression that he *gives off*" (p. 2). What people "give" relates to verbal symbols or their known substitutes that communicate information. What they "give off" involves a wide range of nonverbal actions that others can treat as symptomatic of the actor. In face-to-face encounters, information about the self is expressed through both intentional information sharing and involuntary actions. An underlying assumption of face-to-face encounters is that there is some special "magic" that occurs in nonverbal presentation. Facial expression, gesture, body movement, and clothing are crucial to the development of how we present ourselves. Presenting oneself to others involves both the narrow use of language and a broad range of nonverbal messages. Nonverbal messages convey relational information rather than thoughts. When visual and verbal messages conflict, people tend to believe the visual rather than the verbal messages. This occurs because nonverbal messages provide information about our intentions and emotional responses. For this reason, many businesspeople prefer face-to-face communication because they can look into each others eyes and observe gestures. Similarly, nonverbal cues can alter the meaning of a linguistic message. For instance, when people use a gesture or tone of voice to show sarcasm, one understands that the nonverbal cues alter the meaning of the linguistic statement.

Despite the emerging visual technologies such as the World Wide Web, many Internet genres remain predominantly text oriented. For example, people primarily use the Internet to exchange e-mail messages or participate in discussion groups. As a result, when people present themselves to others online they tend to use written communication. However, the channel of e-mail communication is so extremely limited that senders must make an effort to describe themselves. Since other people cannot see you or hear your voice, you need to make an effort to clearly represent yourself in CMC.

Terminal Identity

Bukatman (1993) coined the term **terminal identity** to refer to the identity created at the interface between the physical body and the TV or computer screen. Terminal identity speaks to the blurring of the boundaries between technology and humans. In contemporary science fiction, humans often connect to machines through interfaces plugged directly into their nervous systems. The novels of William Gibson, the inventor of the term *cyberspace*, most clearly describe this type of interaction. Virtual reality designers have been inspired by his imaginary technological descriptions and have created new ways of interfacing with the computer, such as virtual reality helmets and data gloves.

A new genre of science fiction called *cyberpunk* has developed that describes how people interact with cyberspatial worlds. Cyberpunk science fiction writers describe the countercultures that emerge around cyberspace and network technology. The term *cyberpunk* refers to the people who inhabit cyberspatial landscapes. According to Sirius (1992), *cyberpunk* is a word that has "escaped from being a literary genre into cultural reality. People started calling themselves cyberpunks, or the media started calling people cyberpunks" (Sirius, 1992, p. 64). For example, *Cyberpunk* is the title of Hafner's and Markoff's (1991) book about the outlaws and hackers on the computer frontier. In popular culture, the term is used to describe hackers and people who engage in illegal Internet activities (see Chapter 12). Instead of interacting with the immersive data landscapes described by science fiction writers, however, actual hackers interact with text and Web-based interfaces.

Screen Names, Nicknames, and Pseudonyms

There are many different ways for people to represent themselves in CMC. An e-mail address is a type of identity marker. It is the name people use to locate you on the network. Another type of personal representation is the use of screen names, nicknames ("nicks"), or pseudonyms. In chat interaction, nicknames are used for many purposes, including establishing a net identity, suggesting a willingness to play, making contact with others, and playing gender-identity games.

Many chat participants consider their nickname to be an extension of the self. Names are carefully selected and often invite certain associations or play with the oral sounds of language. Many hackers use colorful screen names, such as "Phiber Optik." Sometimes, these names could be considered masks or electronic costumes. Besides hiding a person's real identity, they also call attention to an individual's imaginative disguise. Many nicknames draw on fantasy and fictional characters from mythology, comics, literature, science fiction, films, and other themes from popular culture.

There are technical limitations to the creation of nicknames (nicks) in IRC. For example, nicks can consist of only nine letters, not all of the characters on the keyboard can be used, and two people cannot use the same nick simultaneously. When people join an IRC channel, they type the following to say their name: /nick Name. Similarly, people select a name when they enter a chat room. Nicknames appear in brackets, for example: <OldBear>, <Lulu>, and <SportsBoy>. In a study of online nicknames, Bechar-Israeli (1996) says that the emergent IRC culture "is a culture which provides freedom in abundance to engage in identity games through the use of nicknames. In this environment, people can create their own identity 'from scratch.' They can change it, and play around with it, constantly, if they choose" (p. 4). Some people will use a variety of names; for example, they will have names in each chat group in which they participate. Many of these names fall into one of seven basic categories: real names; self-related names; technology-oriented names; names of flora, fauna and objects; play on words; figures in literature, films, and fairy tales; and sexually oriented names (Figure 6.2).

Although it is easy to change an online name, many people often keep the same name for long periods. Chat software, however, does not allow two people with the same nickname to exist simultaneously, so some people can log on and find that someone else is using

FIGURE 6.2   Different Types of CMC Nicknames. In a study of 260 nicknames from four different IRC channels, Bechar-Israeli (1996) placed the names into 16 categories. These 16 categories were further broken down into 7 groups.

Category	Percent
GROUP I-People using their real name	6.9
Example: <bobbi>, <SueB>	
GROUP II- Names relating to self or lack of self	46.2
Examples: <shydude>, <oldbear>, <english>	
Examples: <me>, <justI>, <unknown>	
GROUP III- Technology-oriented names	8.9
Examples: <pentium>, <aixy>	
GROUP IV- Names of objects, flora, and fauna	13.9
Examples: <cheese>, <BMW>, <froggy>, <tulip>	
GROUP V- Word play and sounds	10
Examples: <whathell>, <myTboy>, <uh-uh>, <tototoo>	
GROUP VI- Famous people and media characters	5.4
Examples: <elvis>,<madhatter>, <rainman>	
GROUP VII- Sexually oriented or provocative names	3.4
Examples:<sexpot>, <sexsee>, <bigtoy>,<hamas>	
Nicknames with no category	11.2
Total	105.9%

Source: Adapted from Bechar-Israeli, 1996.

their favorite nickname. When this occurs, people can feel as if another has stolen the name, and the topic of chat conversation will change to the loss of the name. Frequently, when an individual behaves in ways considered inappropriate by other members of an on-line group, behavior becomes the central topic of discussion. This is one way in which electronic groups establish a set of behavioral norms.

Another aspect of nicknames is their ability to enable characters to *gender bend* or engage in **gender swapping**. In chat, players frequently "cross-dress" and impersonate a person of the opposite gender, or occasionally, players select a gender-neutral name. Turkle (1995) describes gender swapping as follows:

> On one level, virtual gender swapping is easier than doing it in real life. For a man to present himself as female in a chat room, or an IRC channel, or in a MUD, only requires writing a description. For a man to play a woman on the streets of an American city, he would have to shave various parts of his body; wear makeup, perhaps a wig, a dress, and high heels; perhaps change his voice, walk and mannerisms. He would have some anxiety about not passing, which would pose a risk of violence and possibly arrest. So more men are willing to give virtual cross-dressing a try. But once they are online as female, they soon find that maintaining this fiction is difficult. To pass as a woman for any length of time requires understanding how gender inflects speech, manner, the interpretation of experience. Women attempting to pass as men face the same kind of challenge (p. 212).

Besides the use of nicks or screen names, some chat environments allow individuals to write a more detailed profile that describes them to others. For example, online service providers, such as America Online, provide places for people to post personal descriptions about themselves. IRC has a `/whois nickname` command that provides more information about the person. These descriptions can be based on reality or be totally fictitious. For instance, people who are interested in making a romantic connection through chat rooms would write an attractive description designed to appeal to the opposite sex. Or people can experiment with gender bending by writing a description for the opposite sex. For instance, while observing chat for a class assignment, one of my students observed that women received more attention than men in chat rooms. As a male, he was harassed and ignored. He decided to change his nickname to a female one and write a female profile describing himself. When he entered the chat room as a woman, he quickly received many instant messages from men. His brief experience in gender swapping revealed a number of cultural gender biases that he had previously been unaware of. When experimenting in chat correspondence, changing one's gender can dramatically reveal cultural and individual aspects of gendered communication.

Personal Profiles

Internet service providers enable people to write their own personal profiles to provide more information about themselves. These can be short descriptions that describe age and sex or they can be more detailed profiles that describe physical features and interests. Profiles can provide others with additional information about the person using a screen name, but they can also be based on fiction. The Internet is filled with tales of people using masks for age, race, gender, and class. Moreover, masks can be worn for almost every aspect of identity.

Although profiles can provide additional information, the information provided may be based on fantasy rather than reality.

Signature Files

Currently, we cannot sign our names to our e-mail messages. However, we can create a **signature file**. According to Anderson (1996), "A signature file automatically includes your contact information, e-mail address, and so on into a posting, saving you the trouble of re-membering to sign a message and preventing you from making embarrassing typos in your e-mail address or other pertinent information. Signature files can be quite useful, and thus the feature is included in most posting programs" (pp. 133–134). In most e-mail programs, the information is automatically added to the end of every e-mail message. Using a signature line can help make you a more effective online communicator and can help readers better understand who you are.

The type of relationship that you have with the recipient of your e-mail message can influence the type of signature line that you use. In formal or businesslike relationships, your signature line should include the type of information that is found on a traditional business letterhead along with your credentials. Frequently, e-mail addresses abbreviate the name of a company, but the signature file will clearly identify the organization that you represent. People can also become creative with their signature lines. In an attempt to personalize signature files, people use famous quotations and incorporate simple graphics (Figure 6.3).

FIGURE 6.3 Signature Lines. Two signature lines from professor Harold Q. Smith. He uses the first one on all of his professional correspondence, and the second one he uses when he sends messages to personal friends.

```
Harold Q.Smith (Professor Emeritus), Speech Communication
Trade and Applied Books Editor, New York Press
Editor, VCI: Virtual Culture Inquiries
ISSN 1069-0426. Send submissions to HQS at BFUVM.BFU.EDU
Buffalo Falls University, Falls City, NY 16802
Manuscripts are being accepted for the 2003 volumes.
```

```
Harold Q.Smith, Ret.        |||||      Oh, don't the day seem lank and long
Dealer in magic & spells.    \;/          When all goes right,
   --J. W. Wells            '0.0'         And nothing goes wrong?
Everybody should get        ( v ) /
exactly what they deserve.   \*/ /     And wouldn't life seem exceedingly
                            / \ /      flat.
REAL HARD!!!              /  |=|       With nothing whatever to grumble at?
                            | |
   --HQS                   _| |_                Princess Ida, Act II
```

Before creating an elaborate signature line, you should ask yourself the following questions: Is the quote or character something you would add to written correspondence to business associates, professors, friends, or clients? Will the signature line add to the information overload that already exists on the Internet? Signature lines should not interfere with your message, and they need to support the tone of messages that you are sending. For this reason, some people use several different signature lines—a serious signature line for business correspondence and a humorous one for friends and personal messages.

When you add signature lines to your messages, you need be careful that your signature does not misrepresent you. This is especially important if the name of a company or university is included. For instance, a member of an academic discussion list who had the name of a university in his signature line was highly critical of a student's research survey distributed to the group. His university affiliation led people to believe that he was a professor and highly qualified to make the critique. When it was revealed that the critic was an undergraduate student, he lost credibility on the list. Whittle (1997) warns e-mail users that many companies have policies that prevent employees from speaking for the company in any capacity that is outside their job. For instance, you cannot post public messages about your company or its products or services. If you claim your company's products are absolutely safe, your company could be legally liable if someone relies on that representation and is then harmed. As a result, it is better to represent yourself as an individual and to clearly articulate or disclaim your role in a company. When participating in public discussions, employees will frequently add a disclaimer stating that the opinions expressed in the message are their own and do not represent the opinions of the company they work for.

Net Presence

A concept described by Agre (1994), **net presence**, is based on observations he made about his own Internet behavior. He first became aware of the phrase "net presence" when several people commented about his presence on the network. Agre then began to explore what this phrase might mean. He observed that people were referring to the frequency with which his contributions to Internet communication would appear on an individual's computer screen. These contributions included messages sent to public network forums, messages distributed on his own mailing list, the Red Rock Eater (RRE), and his writings distributed through the network. Besides the formal channels for distributing Agre's messages, his e-mail messages were frequently forwarded to other people around the Internet.

According to Agre (1994) the word *presence* in the phrase "net presence," "nominalizes the continuing fact of [his] being metonymically 'present' through [his] various net activities" (p. 1). One mechanism for presenting an electronic "self" is metonymy. **Metonymy** is the use of the name of one thing for that of another; for example, substituting the words *White House* for *President* in the following sentence: "The White House has signed the bill." In CMC, metonymy is used to represent people because participants are not physically co-present, instead, they are represented by written words. The use of metonymy enables people to say things like "I went to America Online to talk to Jerry." The "I" and "Jerry" create digital representations of the speaker and Jerry in cyberspace. However, Agre asserts that net presence is not something that an individual can directly create:

Rather, I acquire my presence by evidence of me appearing on their screens in a remark-worthy variety of different connections, so that they can infer that I have a "presence" on the net and not just on their particular screens. In this way, "the net" is constructed (rightly or wrongly) as a single, stable space within which someone can have a coherent, stable "presence" (p. 1).

Another element that contributes to net presence is credibility. Credibility is an important aspect of developing an identity both on- and offline. People reading messages need to have a sense that the writer is a reliable source of information. Mandel and Van der Leun (1996) state, "The primary coin of cyberspace is credibility. If you show over time that you are someone whose opinions, demeanor, and attitude are worth taking seriously, more people will endow you with their attention" (p. 54). For example, Agre established online credibility by providing people with relevant information. After reading his morning newspaper, he would often summarize articles of interest in e-mail messages and distribute them on mailing lists. After reading the messages, people felt that Agre was a reliable source of information.

Case Study: Playing a Lawyer on the Web

People have also developed reputations through their Web interactions. A 15-year-old California teenager presented himself as a hot-shot lawyer on a Web site called AskMe.com. AskMe is a software company that developed a program to enable employees of large corporations to share knowledge through their private networks. Employees would post questions on the program and anyone in the company could answer. Corporate expertise could then be organized and shared.

The AskMe salespeople discovered that potential buyers were concerned about heavy use of the program. For instance, could the program support 200,000 people using it at the same time? To address this concern, AskMe decided to create a Web site and offer a version of its software on the Internet. By February 2000, the AskMe site was a heavily used knowledge-exchange Web site with over 10 million visitors in the first year. The company made no money from the site, and it did not monitor the type of information being exchanged. According to Lewis (2001), "The experts were self-appointed and ranked by the people who sought the advice. Experts with high rankings received small cash prizes from AskMe.com" (p. 35).

Fifteen-year-old Marcus Arnold began to offer legal advice on the site and eventually moved up to the number-one position. People began calling him at home and seeking out his opinions about their legal problems. Eventually, his conscience began to trouble him and he admitted that he was only 15. He changed his online profile from "legal expert" to "15-year-old intern attorney expert." After posting his age on the site, he began to receive hostile messages from actual lawyers who were competing against him for rankings. A flame war broke out on the AskMe discussion boards. The lawyers accused Marcus of not knowing what he was talking about and asked him detailed legal questions, which he could not easily answer. Marcus was publicly humiliated by the real lawyers, but he still kept offering advice. Eventually, the people seeking legal advice spoke out and told the lawyers "to leave the kid alone!" They thought that Marcus must be some type of legal genius, and they continued to seek him out for advice. Two weeks after he disclosed his actual age, he was back in the number-one position.

Marcus had never read a law book; his legal expertise came primarily from watching television. For example, he was an expert on *Court TV* and much of his advice could be found by watching Judge Judy. Marcus's parents had mixed reactions to his Internet identity: His mother was proud of her son, and his father was skeptical about all of the people calling their house asking for Marcus. Because physical features are separated from online identity, people can represent themselves any way they want to. Marcus established credibility by the way he interacted with people and by the simple common-sense answers he provided. After he revealed his true identity, people still believed in him. What does this tell us about the Internet and identity?

Avatars

In addition to text-based correspondence, the Web also enables people to create visual representations of themselves. **Avatars** are iconic or pictorial representations of individuals that are displayed through computer networks. The real body exists behind the computer terminal while the electronic avatar roams the frontiers of cyberspace. Avatars are used in multiuser **graphical virtual realities** (GVRs), Web-based online environments in which individuals represent themselves with a visual icon and communicate through textual exchanges—for instance, the *Palace* software described in Chapter 1. GVRs combine a variety of different modes of communication, including speech, writing, emoting, graphic accents, and gestures. Commercial GVRs, which charge a fee for participation, follow in the tradition of computer games. These environments generally provide default avatars for new members and programming features to enable participants to create their own avatars. For example, *Active Worlds* provides default avatars in the role of tourists. New participants can choose between Mr. or Ms. Tourist, two characters dressed in gray outfits with a camera looped around the neck.

Avatars are a new way for people to virtually present themselves in CMC. Kolko (1999) considers the creation of an avatar to be a rhetorical act "because speaking through an avatar incorporates the realm of gestures and visual representation" (pp. 179–180). Users must make the following decisions: to interact in the first person or third person, to create different types of facial expressions, to automate or randomize gestures, and to determine a range of detailed avatar movement. Avatars attempt to provided a visual channel of interaction that more closely resembles a face-to-face exchange. For example, human avatars will have arms and legs with which to express themselves. Large-motion gestures and facial expressions add subtle meanings to the message exchange. Some GVR programs provide menu bars with emotion options, such as smiling and frowning. However, language usage must be synchronized with visual emotional cues to effectively communicate in GVRs.

Personal Home Pages

Personal home pages on the Web provide a better opportunity for individuals to express themselves, but these pages provide less interaction than other forms of CMC because page creators must also provide a e-mail address or a method for interpersonal interaction. Web surfers find personal home pages in different ways. They can use an orderly route; for example, by going to an educational institution and a particular department, they can access a professor's home page. Some universities also provide access to student home pages. In other instances, personal home pages can be located through links provided on another home page. The creators of personal home pages can never be certain about the ways in which people will find them. By providing an e-mail address on the page, interaction can occur between the page's creator and his or her viewers.

In contrast to textual exchanges, Web pages can present photos of individuals and their families, favorite pets, graphics, sound bites, and links to interests, contacts, and friends. Home pages can become a central point for the presentation of the electronic self (Figure 6.4). Moreover, these pages can be carefully set up to make the proper impression. But like face-to-face encounters, Web sites can also convey unintentional messages. This

---

FIGURE 6.4 Categories for Personal Home Pages. Individuals are now using the Web as a form of personal expression and interpersonal communication. Web creators can communicate with their audiences through e-mail and guest books. Additionally Web creators interact with each other by placing their sites into Web ring communities. Moreover, Weblogs, which change on a regular basis, enable individuals to share their views with others.

Professional Orientation

Some personal Web pages are created as an online resume. This page style uses a professional tone of voice and presents work-related information about an individual.

Creative Approach

A variety of different creative approaches can be applied to personal Web pages. Some authors use the Web as a self-publishing medium to present their creative literary works or hyperfiction novels. Illustrators, cartoonists, and designers often use the Web as a showcase to present their work or as a sample of their Web design skills.

Personal Interests

In contrast to the professional approach, some indivduals create Web pages that present personal information about their lives, activities, family, pets, and interests. This type of page often includes family photography and a statement about one's philosophy of life.

Information Kiosks

Another direction that can be used in the development of personal Web pages is to create an information kiosk or site that provides links to other sites relating to a specific topic or interest; for example, a site with links to Internet information about skateboards, recipes, bicycle riding, etc.

Weblogs

Personal sites that comment on and point to other articles on the Web. Weblogs cover a wide range of topics, including technology news and dating services. Some Weblogs have been described as alternative voices and a form of personal journalism. Individuals take on the role of columnist, reporter, analyst, and publisher. Weblogs also include **blogging**, a running commentary with pointers to other sites.

often is the difference between Web sites created by professional designers and ones done by individuals. Miller (1995) is concerned that a gulf may develop "between those of us who have Web Designers to present our selves on the Web and those who don't, as already exists between those who employ Interior Designers in their homes and those who don't" (p. 5). Moreover, Miller notes that there are gender differences in Personal home pages. Men frequently attach a picture of themselves and women often do not. Women seem to be more reluctant to place personal information on their Web pages because they are afraid that they will be harassed. An exception to this rule is when women create professionally oriented home pages, where they include a professional photograph of themselves.

Self-Disclosure

Studies have shown that the lack of face-to-face interaction in CMC supports increased self-disclosure. For example, Sproull and Kiesler's (1991) research on CMC in organizations discovered that "self-disclosure can be extremely comfortable for people interacting with a computer" (p. 45). For this reason, many organizations have supported the development of computer-administered interviews, such as electronic surveys for doing market research, employment and personnel evaluations, tutoring, career guidance, and medical diagnosis.

Self-disclosure can occur in both social and task-oriented online contexts. For instance, Bennahum (1994) reported that he experienced a certain amount of self-disclosure when interacting with students in an educational MOO. A student explains why this happens: "I have a hard time opening up to people or trusting others, and this lets me learn to communicate in a way that [won't] offend me if someone laughs, I can always leave them behind and talk to someone else. The social pressure is not here as much as in real life" (cited in Bennahum, 1994, p. 24). CMC genres can create a more comfortable environment for individuals to share their feelings and develop interpersonal relationships.

Additionally, CMC can increase self-disclosure because many people find it easier to reveal their innermost feelings in text-only correspondence. One reason this occurs is because CMC enables socially shy individuals to develop interpersonal communication skills. By removing the social pressure of immediate face-to-face reactions from others, some people can better communicate. Furthermore, CMC can speed up the relationship-building process. For example, We's (1993) research on cross-gender communication discovered that couples more quickly disclose personal information through CMC than in person:

> Two fascinating stories came from women who met their (eventual) husbands online. It does seem paradoxical that text-based communication, through a computer screen and telephone lines, can be incredibly intimate, but people can become acquainted faster online than in face to face contacts. As one woman said, 'it is like making a friend in hyper-drive. One advances beyond small talk very quickly. Communication can be when it is convenient for each of you and more often (than say, someone you meet only once in a while)' (p. 6).

People have reported they do not think about the messages they type into the keyboard. Instead of carefully choosing written words, they type whatever pops into their heads. A young man described his spontaneous use of online discourse as follows:

> I found during my involvement in discussion, I would blurt out whatever was my initial re-
> action to what people were saying. It is almost like a race to see who could hold the con-
> versation the longest or whose statement was more witty. There is no time to think about
> what you want to say if you want to carry out a good conversation (cited in Barnes, 2001,
> p. 103).

A stream-of-consciousness writing style combined with accessibility to people, makes the
Internet a perfect place for people who need to communicate their feelings. Any time of day
or night, you can always find someone to talk with. Moreover, disembodied messages can
lead to spontaneous writing that often reveals more personal information than people would
normally reveal in face-to-face contexts. Finally, software design can also encourage people to respond quickly to messages. Ullman (1996) explains:

> I read a message. The prompt then sits there, the cursor blinking. It's all waiting for me to
> type "r" for "reply." The whole system is designed for it, is pressing me, is sitting there puls-
> ing, insisting, *Reply. Reply right now*. Before I know it, I've done it: I've typed "re." Im-
> mediately, the screen clears, a heading appears, "From:" my Internet address, "To:" Karl's
> address, "Re:" Karl's subject. And now I reply. Even though I meant to hold the message a
> while, even though I wanted to treat it as if it were indeed a letter—something to hold in my
> hand, read again, and again, mull over—although my desire is to wait, I find it hard to resist
> that voice of the software urging, *Reply, reply now* (p. 14).

However, spontaneous self-disclosure can have a darker side. People can reveal information about themselves that they would never disclose in a face-to-face setting. An Internet participant reported that the speed of sending messages often makes her forget that
there are a number people on the other side of the computer screen. At times she feels as if
her brain is directly connected to the machine because her thoughts can be immediately
typed into the keyboard. When individuals discover the private information that they have
revealed online, they can become embarrassed or anxious. CMC can create a sense of anxiety for people who send spontaneous messages that reveal their momentary moods or feelings. Reading these messages back later when their mood has changed can be distressing.
A term used to describe this type of behavior is **postcyberdisclosure panic** (PCDP), which
describes a situation in which a person reveals inner thoughts and secrets and later, after
thinking about it, gets frightened by the thought of who *could* read the message. Anxiety
can be easily aroused in cyberspace. Feelings of fear, concern, and uneasiness are felt even
by people who are experienced with the medium. Whittle (1997) states, "I consider myself
an emotionally healthy, stable, self-confident individual; and yet I have faced several periods of rather extreme anxiety online" (p. 191). For example, private e-mail messages that
criticized the company Whittle worked for were forwarded to corporate executives. Similarly, Monica Lewinsky's private e-mail messages were taken off the hard drive of her computer and made public.

Although self-disclosure is an element in relationship building, some people reveal
personal information online without realizing who will read the message. This can cause
anxiety and sometimes impact on real-world activities. Therefore, people should be aware
of what information they are sharing with others through CMC.

Gender and Self-Disclosure

When talking online, people often behave in a more uninhibited fashion than they would in traditional face-to-face situations. It has been suggested that "disinhibition" may occur in on-line discussions because of the lack of social cues and social anonymity. Reid (1991) states:

> The lack of social context cues in computer-mediated-communication obscures the bound-aries that would generally separate acceptable and unacceptable forms of behaviour. Fur-thermore, the essential physical impression of each user that he is alone releases him from the social expectations incurred in group interaction. Computer-mediated communication is less bound by conventions than is face-to-face interaction (p. 10).

Disclosure is an important issue in any relationship. According to Vorlicky (1995), men are often socially conditioned not to reveal personal information because self-disclo-sure does not fit our cultural ideas of masculinity. Americans expect men to be less inclined than women to engage in socioemotional and relational patterns of communication. Con-versely, people expect women to exhibit the need for social interdependence, In e-mail ex-changes, expressions of social interdependence include using emoticons, expressions of support, self-references, and self-disclosure. Researchers have observed that when men use pseudonyms online they express more social interdependence. However, there was no ob-served change in this variable for women. Consequently, it is possible that the need for so-cial interdependence is equally strong for men and women (see Barnes, 2001).

It has been suggested that men and women use the Internet for different reasons. Tra-ditionally, women use a variety of media to stay "in touch" with their friends and family. From this view, the Internet is just one more communication medium. In contrast, Ullman (1996) argues that men develop Internet-only relationships. She states, "For men, their on-line messages *are* their relationships. They seem content in the net's single channeledness, relations wrapped in the envelope of technology: one man, one wire" (p. 10). Unlike women, when men engage in CMC there appears to be a gender-role reversal, because they are using it to develop personal relationships. "Men net-surf the way suburban women of the 1950s and 1960s used the telephone: as a way to break out of isolation" (p. 10). This observation especially applies to male software engineers who work for long hours alone with a machine.

Currently, researchers are observing that the Internet allows men and women to break the traditional gender stereotypes of face-to-face encounters and provides both sexes with an opportunity to reevaluate gendered styles of communication. For example, Soukup (1999) examined gendered interaction patterns in chat rooms. He discovered that in both male and female chat rooms, masculine-dominated patterns of discussion emerged. Further research is needed to explore gendered discourse in CMC and its impact on communica-tion styles and self presentation.

Research on Identity and the Internet

A variety of researchers have explored the ways in which the physical self is manifest in computer-generated space, including Stone (1995) and Turkle (1995). It has been argued that the disappearing or mediated body enables people to freely communicate without the constraints of gender, race, or age markers. Ideas can be shared more openly and freely without physical discrimination. For example, in certain face-to-face contexts, women and minorities feel uncomfortable openly sharing their opinions. Internet communication can counter this because gender and race do not have to be revealed in electronic conversations.

Elements such as geography, economic status, education level, literacy skill, language, and cultural literacy do influence the ways in which individuals present themselves to others through CMC. Language connects people to their physical selves. As a result, online representations of self are not totally disconnected from the physical self. For example, the research of Herring (1994, 1999) and Soukup (1999) explore the ways in which gender influences CMC.

Contextualized Framework

Many scholars argue that the production of identity and reality arise out of communication practices. It is through social participation that the concept of identity is constructed. For example, Mead (1932, 1934) described how the self develops from interactions with others. An individual self is established by organizing the attitudes of other individuals toward the self and toward one another through participation in social interaction. For example, when playing a game of baseball, each team member knows his or her role in the game and also the roles of every other player. Because each player understands the role of the "others," players can socially interact and play the game.

Goffman (1959) utilized a performance metaphor to explore the ways in which people present themselves to others. Individuals deliberately control their expressions and express subtle personality traits during communicative performances. Underlying the theories of Mead and Goffman is the idea that the production and reproduction of identity is established through communication.

Building on this idea, Karetnick (2001) develops a contextualized framework for understanding the construction of self through CMC. A **contextualized framework** is an examination of the interplay of what we do and who we are. Researchers can identify a situation and the behaviors associated with it and then examine the communication strategies used by a particular individual. **Interaction patterns** are deliberate actions initiated by an individual that are influenced by the context in which the actions occur (Figure 6.5). By examining the structure or preexisting influences an individual brings to a situation and the communication strategies used in the situation, researchers can discuss cultural systems. Within the cultural system, identity is viewed as a reflection of the strategies participants use to approach the social situation. Individuals are members of larger groups, which are governed by social rules. In a MUD, the *structure* is the set of rules established by the MUD players and the strategy is the manner in which participants play the game. Software design also influences the structure of the MUD because a number of preprogrammed emotional commands are provided for players to use in their messages.

Karetnick studied the interactions of MUD players by saving a transcript of a MUD meeting for later analysis. Each communicative turn contained in the transcript was coded and placed in a database. A key aspect of her study was to examine the ways in which players modified standard programming commands. For example, the laugh command could be

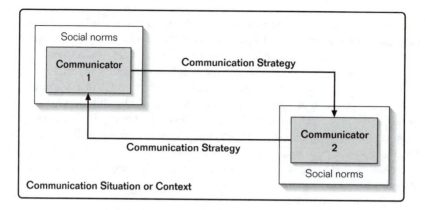

FIGURE 6.5   Contextual Framework. Situations and the behaviors identified with them can influence the communication strategies used by CMC participants.

modified to read "laugh happily" or "laugh softly." She discovered that players used less than 50 percent of the 181 preprogrammed emotional commands available in the MUD. Moreover, manipulation of the programming did not occur very frequently. Strategy in MUDs appears to occur from the choice players make in using universally available conventions. Moreover, the players observed in this study tended to have a preference for conventionally defined behaviors and did not experiment with presenting themselves through modified commands. Following Goffman's theory of self-presentation, players would conduct themselves in socially expected behavior patterns to maintain their own identity and help others maintain theirs. When social bonds were disrupted by negative emotions and comments, offenders would often receive glaring and growling responses in return. Simply stated, when players ridiculed others, they lost face. The social conformity observed by Karetnick is in stark contrast to Turkle's (1995) observations about using Internet genres as a laboratory for experimenting with unexamined aspects of self-identity.

Summary

Concepts about self have changed through the ages. In premodern societies, identity was fixed and stable; during modern times, identity became mobile and subject to change. In postmodern culture, identity can become fragmented because CMC separates physical appearance from the communication exchange. As a result, new possibilities emerge for playing with identity. Goffman's theory about the impressions people "give" and "give off" can be applied to CMC. Screen names, signature lines, personal profiles, and personal Web pages can be carefully designed to present an image of self. However, the representations of self may or may not be based on reality. Gender swapping and idealized self-representations are frequently encountered by online communicators.

Disembodied messages can also lead to increased self-disclosure. People frequently write messages without carefully thinking about what they are writing. This can lead to postcyberdisclosure panic or anxiety about what one has revealed in electronic messages. It has been suggested that disinhibition occurs in CMC because of social anonymity. Moreover, researchers have discovered that men engage in online self-disclosure, which is considered a feminine style of communication. In some cases, CMC appears to be altering traditional styles of gendered communication.

Communication is central to the establishment of behavior patterns. It is argued by Mead and others that the formation of identity occurs through communication practices. Building on this premise, Karetnick proposed a contextualized framework to analyze identity in CMC. A contextualized framework looks at CMC interaction and individual communication strategies.

TERMS

Avatar refers to the icons, pictures, or drawings that players use to represent themselves in online environments, such as the *Palace*.

Blogging is personal running commentary on a Web site that has links to other sites.

Contextualized framework is an approach to studying the behaviors associated with a situation and then examining the communication strategies used by a particular individual within the situation.

Gender swapping is cross-dressing or impersonating a person of the opposite gender in CMC interaction.

Graphical virtual realities (GVRs) are Web-based online environments in which individuals represent themselves with a visual icon and communicate through textual exchanges in, for example, the *Palace* software environment.

Interaction patterns are deliberate actions initiated by an individual that are influenced by the context in which the actions occur.

Metonymy is the use of the name of one thing for that of another; for example, substituting the words *White House* for *President* in the following: "The Whitehouse has signed the bill."

Net presence is the metonymical or electronic presence that a person creates through Internet activities, including the exchange of e-mail messages and participation in a discussion list.

Postcyberdisclosure panic (PCDP) occurs when a person reveals inner thoughts and secrets and later gets frightened by the thought of who will read or *could* read the message.

Signature files are available in many mail programs to automatically include your contact information, e-mail address, and so on in an e-mail message.

Terminal identity refers to the identity created at the interface between the physical body and the TV or computer screen.

EXERCISES

1. Set up a discussion list and write an introductory message that describes and introduces you to the entire group.

2. Locate a number of personal home pages. These can be discovered through searches for other topics and checking university sites. Many university professors and students maintain personal home pages. Write up a description about the person based on the home page. View the same home page with several classmates and compare descriptions with each other to identify similarities and differences.

3. Conduct a more systematic study of personal home pages to decide if the pages fit into the categories identified in Figure 6.4 and to further identify the elements and strategies associated with the personal home page genre.

4. The case study of Marcus Arnold and the AskMe Web site presents a number of discussion questions:

Should a 15-year old be allowed to present himself as a legal advisor online?
How does the Internet alter our concepts of social identity?
What effect could Marcus's behavior have on the legal profession and the way society views lawyers?
Could watching television programs make a person a legal expert?
Could a little knowledge be a dangerous thing? Or should it be respected?

BIBLIOGRAPHY

Agre, P. (1994). Net presence. *Computer-Mediated Communication Magazine, 1* (4) [Online], p. 6. Available: http://www.December.com/cmc/mag/1994/aug/Presence.html (August 9, 2001).

Anderson, J. (1996). Not for the faint of heart: Contemplations on Usenet. In L. Cherny & E. R. Weise (Eds.), *Wired_Women* (pp. 42–55). Seattle: Seal Press.

Barnes, S. B. (1999). Ethical issues for a virtual self. In S. J. Drucker & G. Gumpert (Eds.), *Real law@virtual space* (pp. 371–398). Cresskill, NJ: Hampton Press.

Barnes, S. B. (2001). *Online connections: Internet interpersonal relationships.* Cresskill, NJ: Hampton Press.

Barnes, S., & Greller, L. M. (1994, April). Computer-mediated communication in the organization. *Communication Education, 43* (2), 129–142.

Bechar-Israeli, H. (1996). From <Bonehead> to <cLoNeHEAd>: Nicknames, play, and identity on Internet relay chat. *Journal of Computer-Mediated Communication, 1* (2) [Online], 29 pp. Available: http://www.ascusc.org/jcmc/vol1/issue2/bechar.html (April 16, 2000)

Bennahum, D. (1994, May/June). Fly me to the MOO: Adventures in textual reality. *Lingua Franca*, pp. 1, 22-36.

Bukatman, S. (1993). *Terminal identity.* Durham, NC: Duke University Press.

Dibbell, J. (1996). The prisoner: Phiber Optik goes directly to jail. In P. Ludlow (Ed.), *High noon on the electronic frontier* (pp. 133–136). Cambridge, MA: The MIT Press.

Fowler, R. M. (1994, July). How the secondary orality of the electronic age can awaken us to the primary orality or antiquity or what hypertext can teach us about the Bible. *Interpersonal Computing and Technology: An Electronic Journal for the 21st Century, 2,* (3), 12–46 [Online].

Gardner, H. (1983). *Frames of mind.* New York: Basic Books.

Gergen, K. J. (1991). *The saturated self.* New York: Basic Books.

Gibbs, R. W., Jr. (1994). *The poetics of mind.* New York: Cambridge University Press.

Gibson, W. (1984). *Neuromancer.* New York: Ace Books.

Giddens, A. (1991). *Modernity and self-identity: Self and society in the late modern age.* Stanford, CA: Stanford University Press.

Goffman, E. (1959). *The presentation of self in everyday life.* New York: Doubleday & Company.

Hafner, K., & Markoff, J. (1991). *Cyberpunk: Outlaws and hackers on the computer frontier.* New York: Simon & Schuster.

Herring, S. C. (1994, June). *Gender differences in computer-mediated communication: Bringing familiar baggage to the new frontier.* Paper presented at the American Library Association Annual Convention, Miami, Florida [Online]. Available: http://cpsr.org/cpsr/gender/herring.txt (April 26, 1995).

Herring, S. C. (1999, July–Sept.). The rhetorical dynamics of gender harassment on-line. *The Information Society, 15* (2), 151–168.

Karetnick, R. D. (2001). Constructing the self through modification of convention in computer-mediated environments. *The New Jersey Journal of Communication*, Vol. 9, No. 1, pp. 88–102.

Kellner, D. (1992). "Popular culture and the construction of postmodern identities." In S. Lash & J. Friedman (Eds.), *Modernity & identity* (pp. 141–177). Oxford, UK: Blackwell.

Kolko, B. E. (1999, July–Sept.). Representing bodies in virtual space: The rhetoric of avatar design. *The Information Society, 15* (3), 177–186.

Kraut, R., Scherlis, W., Mukhopadhyay, T., Manning, J., & Keisler, S. (1996, December). The HomeNet field trial of residential Internet services. *Communications of the ACM, 39* (12), 55–63.

Lee, J. Y. (1996). Charting the codes of cyberspace: A rhetoric of electronic mail. In L. Strate, R. Jacobson, & S. Gibson (Eds.), *Communication and cyberspace* (pp. 275–296). Cresskill, NJ: Hampton Press.

Lewis, M. (2001, July 15). Faking it. *The New York Times Magazine*, pp. 32–37, 44, 61–63.

Mandel, T., & Van der Leun, G. (1996). *Rules of the net: Online operating instructions for human beings.* New York: Hyperion.

Mead, G. H. (1932). *The philosophy of the present.* La Salle, IL: The Open Court.

Mead, G. H. (1934). *Mind, self and society.* Chicago: University of Chicago Press.

Miller, H. (1995). *The presentation of self in electronic life: Goffman on the Internet.* Paper presented at the Embodied Knowledge and Virtual Space Conference, Goldsmiths' College, University of London, June 1995 [Online], 7 pp. Available: http://www.ntu.ac.uk/soc/psych/miller/goffman.htm (April 26, 2000)

Mitra, A. (2001). Marginal voices in cyberspace. *New Media & Society, 3* (1), pp. 29–48.

Ong, W. J. (1982). *Orality and literacy.* New York: Methuen.

Phillips, G. M., & Metzger, N. J. (1976). *Intimate communication.* Boston: Allyn & Bacon.

Poster, M. (1990). *The mode of information.* Chicago: University of Chicago Press.

Reid, E. M. (1991). *Electropolis: Communication and community on Internet relay chat.* (Online) 40 pp. Available at http://www.ee.mu.oz.au/papers/emr/electropolis.html (Downloaded May 15, 1997).

Sirius, R. U. (1992). Cyberpunk. In R. Rucker, R.U. Sirius, & Q. Mu (Eds.), *Mondo: A user's guide to the new edge* (pp. 64–67). New York: HarperCollins Publishers.

Soukup, C. (1999, July.). The gendered interactional patterns of computer-mediated chatrooms: A critical ethnographic study. *The Information Society, 15* (2), 169–178.

Sproull, L., & Kiesler, S. (1991). *Connections: New ways of working in the networked organization.* Cambridge, MA: The MIT Press.

Stone, A. R. (1995). *The war of desire and technology at the close of the mechanical age.* Cambridge, MA: The MIT Press.

Turkle, S. (1995). *Life on the screen: Identity in the age of the Internet.* New York: Simon & Schuster.

Ullman, E. (1996). Come in, CQ: the body on the wire. In L. Cherny & E. R. Weise (Eds.), *Wired_Women* (pp. 3–23). Seattle: Seal Press.

Van der Leun, G. (1993). "This is a naked lady." *Wired, Premiere Issue*, pp. 74,109.

Vorlicky, R. (1995). *Act like a man: Challenging masculinities in American drama.* Ann Arbor, MI: University of Michigan Press.

We, G. (1993, April). Cross-gender communication in cyberspace. Unpublished manuscript. Department of Communication, Simon Fraser University, Canada [Online], 8 pp. Available: ftp://cpsr.org/cpsr/gender/we_cross_gender (April 26, 1995).

Werbach, K. (2001, June 18). *Triumph of the weblogs* [Online] 4 pp. Available: http://www.edventure.com/conversation/article.cfm?Counter=7444662 (July 18, 2001).

Whittle, D. B. (1997). Cyberspace: *The human dimension.* New York: W.H. Freeman and Company.

Wynn, E., & Katz, J. E. (1997, Oct.–Dec.). Hyperbole over cyberspace: Self-presentation and social boundaries in Internet home pages and discourse. *The Information Society: An International Journal, 12* (2), 297–328.

Zuboff, S. (1988). *In the age of the smart machine.* New York: Basic Books.

CHAPTER

7 Internet Interpersonal Relationships

Chapter Overview

"Girl meets boy across the Internet and they fall in love." The popular press frequently runs stories about people who make romantic Internet connections, and marry each other. The intimate relationships that develop across the Internet are a stark contrast to early research findings, which argued that CMC would provide low social presence. People get very involved with relationships developed through the exchange of written Internet messages. Due to the lack of physical presence, Internet messages add elements of fantasy to CMC, which can lead to hyperpersonal relationships as discussed in Chapter 1.

Building relationships through the Internet requires people to use different communicative strategies than they would use in face-to-face settings. In contrast to immediate physical first impressions, people can carefully craft messages and manage the impression they communicate to others. Additionally, participants must spend time responding to messages and maintaining correspondence. Chapter 7 explores Internet interpersonal relationships by discussing the following:

- Reasons why people become involved with Internet relationships
- Intimate, social, and professional relationships
- Criteria for examining Internet relationships, which include shared experience, role play, and reciprocity
- Impression management and online relationship building

Building successful relationships using CMC can follow a pattern that is similar to building face-to-face ones. How people meet and the content and the quality of their initial encounter can set the direction of the relationship. Once a relationship is started, the intensity and caliber of the relationship depend on the amount of contact between people (e.g., daily, every few days, weekly, monthly, etc.). In CMC, the pacing of e-mail messages is very important because it reflects what is happening in the relationship. Once a pattern of correspondence is established, psychological reactions can occur when online friends fail to reply to messages at the expected time. Similar to face-to-face friendships, electronic ones are built on regular interaction and reciprocity. According to Chen and Gaines (1998), developing a positive self-image is one motivation for participating in reciprocal CMC relationships. Reciprocity works on the principle of **social exchange** or equity **theory**: An individual attempts to maintain a balance of rewards to costs. Individuals exchanging e-mail messages, participating in discussion lists, and posting personal Web pages must perceive that they receive a benefit from these interactions in order for them to continue.

Motives for Online Interaction

People who use the Internet have motives. Three main reasons why people use CMC are interpersonal communication, information seeking, and entertainment. Despite the numerous new services that have developed around the Internet, e-mail is the most popular reason for Internet use. According to the Pew Internet and American Life Project (2000), 78 percent of the people surveyed sent e-mail. People also look up information, access government databases, find medical data, view clothing catalogs, shop at cybermalls, buy airline tickets, play games, and order books through the Internet. For entertainment purposes, millions of young American use the Internet to download music.

Using the Internet to maintain or establish human relationships is a primary motivation for Internet use. People exchange e-mail messages, access bulletin boards on Usenet, join discussion groups, exchange instant messages, and chat online. Internet service providers understand the need that people have for connection. For instance, America Online promotes its chat rooms and online forums. People need to meet other people and make friends. The Internet can help to meet this need by enabling people to make both professional and social connections through CMC. Walther and Tidwell (1996) state:

> As many of us are aware, CMC is used quite frequently by managers, academic collaborators, friends, and families, those needing emotional or medically-related social support, and by those who spend hours . . . playing games using deliberately selected names, genders, and self-descriptions. In doing so, CMC users report—both anecdotally and through social scientific analysis—that there are aspects of their on-line interaction which are interpersonally and stereotypically comparable, or superior to, parallel off-line activities (pp. 300-301).

For some people, the Internet can begin to replace face-to-face encounters and the telephone as a way to stay "in touch" with friends and family. For others, the Internet is an important way to connect with new people and share experiences, advice, and support. Since the early days of the Internet, CMC has been used for support groups, a variety of types of support groups have emerged on the network to help people share information. Early network users first shared information with each other about how to use and program computers. Today, people share information about medical conditions, family problems, and emotional concerns.

Social Use of the Internet

There are many reasons why people exchange messages over the Internet, including information sharing, engaging in online debate, asking and answering questions, flirting, social contact, playing games, and advocating political positions. For example, the HomeNet study, a field trial at Carnegie Mellon University with the goal of understanding how average people use the Internet, identified the following reasons for Internet use: enjoy myself, get hobby information, learn about local events, read the news, play games, download materials, listen to music, get personal help, meet new people, visit chats and MUDs, influence a group, join a group, get educational information, do schoolwork, get employment information, get product information, buy something, make money, advertise, and sell something. According to Kraut et al. (1997), these reasons fall into four broad categories: entertainment, interpersonal communication, work, and electronic commerce.

One hundred households in the Pittsburgh area participated in the HomeNet study, and extensive study of the participants' Internet usage revealed that people use the Internet primarily for pleasure. Entertainment and personal enjoyment were the major reasons why people logged on to the network. People will regularly exchange e-mail messages with the same people. Often, e-mail correspondence occurs between people who know each other before they begin communicating online. For example, teachers will stay in touch with their students, and recent high school graduates will maintain discussion lists of their friends who have moved away to attend college. People tend to have greater loyalty to e-mail addresses than they do to Web sites because e-mail sustains ongoing exchanges and relationships.

Online Relationships

Similar to face-to-face contexts, CMC enables two people to develop online relationships. Many of us know people who have met their boyfriend, girlfriend, husband, or wife through the Internet. Couples who are separated by distance often stay in touch through e-mail. Similarly, family members who live in different countries and states can easily communicate with each other through the Internet. Teens and adults report using the Internet to stay connected to friends who have moved away, and parents use e-mail to get in touch with their children's teachers. In business, e-mail has become as important as the telephone for coordinating work activities. E-mail, chat, and instant messenger are all CMC tools that people use to develop and maintain interpersonal relationships.

A study conducted in 1996 by Parks and Floyd (1996) examined personal relationships in Internet newsgroups. They discovered that personal relationships were common and that nearly two-thirds of the participants reported meeting people through the Internet. Women were more likely to make friends, and age did not matter. As relationships developed, their breadth and depth increased. A central characteristic of relational development was the creation of personalized language codes and idioms. Moreover, many Internet relationships incorporate other communication channels, such as telephone calls and the exchange of photographs. A common motive for starting Internet relationships is to meet people from the opposite sex.

Intimate Relationships

Online dating has received a tremendous amount of press coverage. Web sites have been set up as dating services and chat rooms use names such as The Flirt's Nook, Romance Connection, and Thirtysomething. These electronic spaces are designed for people to meet and chat. Proponents of online romance argue that the Internet is a good way to know someone before meeting in person. However, transforming an Internet relationship into an actual one can be difficult. The romantic images established through the Internet may be built more on fantasy than reality. As a result, people need to take steps to verify that the other person is who and what they say they are. This is generally done by moving from e-mail to other forms of correspondence, such as exchanging letters and photos, viewing each other's personal Web pages, and talking on the telephone.

Internet dating is considered to be a better way to get to know someone. The elimination of physical appearance and gestures helps people learn more about their partner's inner thoughts and interests. Relationships can start off slowly and build over time. People will talk in detail about themselves and their interests. According to Tamosaitis (1995), "words have the power to connect disparate souls from distant lands minus the weighty significances of physicality" (p. 46). Two advantages of Internet dating are the ability of relationships to build over time and the elimination of disruptive nonverbal information.

A disadvantage of online dating is deception. People can make up screen names and write false descriptions about themselves. False descriptions can set up false expectations and illusions. Moreover, the careful crafting of messages can highlight a person's good attributes and disguise negative traits. Some people argue that Internet relationships do not work because they are built on fantasy more than reality. According to Booth and Jung (1996), in online romance, "Romantic lovers project fanciful images onto the objects of their obsessions and never actually see their partners at all. This sort of affection is completely illusory—much like adoring a movie star or model from afar" (p. 194). People can fall in love with the idea of love and project a fantasy image on others.

Cybersex

The most intimate of all online exchanges is **cybersex**. Cybersex is the exchange of real-time sexually explicit messages through the Internet. Most people who engage in cybersex do it for fun and do not use their real names. However, the innocent sharing of fantasies can lead to more serious relationships. Phlegar (1995) says, "Married people who go online might say that they are neither having real affairs nor short-changing their mates. However, anyone truly addicted to computer sex won't be looking at their behavior rationally and may do serious damage to their marriage without realizing it" (p. 36).

For instance, when a New Jersey man discovered that his wife was exchanging cybersex messages with a man called the Weasel, he sued his wife for divorce. This first case of computer "adultery" made headline news in New York. This "Cybersex Divorce" was called a "groundbreaking suit—an Information Age twist on the most ancient of human foibles (Kennedy, Ben-Ali, & Bertrand, 1996, p. 5). The man claimed that the Weasel had stolen his wife's affections away from him. In contrast to the New Jersey man's reaction to cybersex, Turkle (1995) reported that one wife considered her husband's cybersex experiences to be similar to his reading a sexy novel. For this couple, the husband's cybersex adventures was a way for him to experiment without jeopardizing their marriage. Spouses have different reactions to cybersex encounters.

In addition to cybersexual exchanges, people often disclose sexually explicit information online. Witmer (1997) examined the reasons why people feel safe engaging in sexually explicit online communication. Surveyed individuals did not believe that their Internet activities would affect their careers, and they felt secure about posting risky information on the Internet. Forty-seven percent of the participants believed that the Internet was a private medium. As a result, users perceived a low risk in revealing sexually explicit information. In contrast to the results from this study, additional studies have shown that "private" messages can and do have devastating effects when they are read by other people. Sexually oriented e-mail messages have been sent to employers and people have lost their jobs. For instance, Peter Chung worked in the Seoul office of an investment firm until an e-mail message bragging about his sex life and the degree to which local bankers lavished him with dinners and golf outings was sent to his boss (see Schwartz, 2001). Internet users need to be aware that the messages they exchange with others can be read by third parties, such as systems administrators.

Case Study: Teens on the Internet

Teenagers are now dating on the Internet. A recent study conducted by the Pew Internet & American Life Project revealed that many American teenagers are now doing so. Face-to-face teen romances can also begin and end online. For many teens, intimate conversations and awkward situations are easier to handle online than in person. Teens can think things over before they reply to a message and they do not have to deal with the immediate reactions of others. Moreover, teens do not have to worry about "freezing up," which could happen in a face-to-face conversation.

Both boys and girls have asked people out using instant messenger and have also ended relationships that way. In addition to maintaining or ending existing relationships, some teens develop Internet-only friendships. Chat rooms are places where teens can meet and arrange dates. Participants frequently ask for an age and sex check. People of similar ages will break off into a separate chat room of only two persons, which is what some teens consider to be an "Internet date." Conversation topics mirror what occurs at a face-to-face teen party. Disembodied Internet relationships limit physical contact between most teens. It is difficult for them to meet a net romance in person because of the challenges of distance, lack of transportation, and lack of financial resources. Many teens consider Internet-only relationships to be fun and fleeting rather than serious. Clark (1998) says that "the focus in the Internet date is on individual gratification, teens experience no sense of obligations to the person with whom they are ephemerally committed. . . . If a person fails to show up at the preappointed time, there are no consequences" (p. 181).

Teens reported that the Internet enables them to express themselves more fully and establish meaningful relationships because CMC allows them to focus on personality and intellect rather than attractiveness and style. Several researchers, including Turkle (1995) and Clark (1998), have observed that teens can use CMC to experiment with roles without worrying about physical sex. For instance, Clark reports that the Internet allows teens "to communicate with one another free from the social and peer pressures toward expressed sexuality" (p. 168).

However, the lack of CMC information can lead to misunderstandings that can hurt or destroy a friendship. When instant messages are used for pranks and deception, they can hurt a relationship. For example, one teen made up a screen name and wrote messages to his friend Jim saying that he knew where Jim lived, Jim's phone number, and other personal information about Jim. However, Jim did not think the prank was funny and the trickery hurt the boys' friendship. Some teens are concerned about online deception and they will only communicate with people they already know. Additionally, teens will ignore messages from strangers or people they do not want to talk to.

In the PEW study, 64 percent of the teens reported that they thought the Internet did not help their family relationships. They expressed a concern about Internet use taking time away from spending time with other family members. Similarly, 79 percent of the parents reported that the Internet has not helped to improve their relationship with their children. Although teens are actively using the Internet to maintain their social relationships with friends, the time they spend online could have an impact on their relationships with other family members.

Social Relationships

Beyond sharing e-mail messages with friends and family members, chat rooms, discussion groups, and MUDs create electronic environments in which people can meet and socially interact. Chat rooms are places where people can meet each other and participate in online social events; similarly, MUDs and MOOs tend to be socially oriented. Online services have become aware of the need many people have to make connections, and some online services even try to parallel real communities by creating their digital counterparts. Today, CMC is becoming another way for people to meet people, make friends, and interact socially with others.

In addition to making new friends online, e-mail is often used to maintain friendships. In modern society, people frequently move to different cities and the Internet is a way for friends to stay in touch. Virtual communities enable people to meet others with similar interests, and often, friendships can develop from participation in these communities. Members of online communities often arrange face-to-face meetings (see Chapter 11). An advantage of a virtual community is its ability to keep people connected as they change jobs and move to different cities.

Task-Oriented Relationships

E-mail has become a major method of organizational communication. Task-oriented relationships generally occur in small groups. Problem-solving or task-oriented groups are formed to meet a specific goal or purpose; after the goal is achieved, the group generally disbands. Since the 1970s, CMC has been used to facilitate task-oriented communication between individuals and small groups. The next chapter will describe the types of software and CMC tools that are available to support this type of organizational communication.

As previously stated, early studies on CMC in organizational settings focused on how the narrow bandwidth and lack of nonverbal information would lead to less social presence in the communication exchange. CMC was not considered an appropriate way to get to know someone because it would be more task-oriented and businesslike. However, in the 1980s, researchers (Chesebro, 1985; Hiemstra, 1982) began to notice that a percentage of CMC messages contained socioemotional content. For example, researchers discovered that half of the discussion messages shared on two computer bulletin board services contained jokes, insults, sexual topics, games, stories, and personal information.

Rice and Love (1987) examined the amount and types of CMC content. Specifically they examined socioemotional content, which was defined in Chapter 1, and **task-dimensional content**, which is "interactions that ask for or give information or opinions" (p. 93). They discovered that there is a tendency for active CMC users to add more socio-emotional content. "Even a professionally oriented CMC system involving users who do not otherwise know each other can support a reasonable amount of socioemotional content" (p. 101). Nearly 30 percent of the message content examined in the study contained socioemotional information. Although task-oriented relationships are businesslike, with predetermined goals, individuals can use CMC to develop more personalized relationships.

Online Relationship Development

Unlike face-to-face relationships that develop because of proximity and attraction, Internet relationships often develop from shared interests. For example, there are people participating in thousands of discussion lists. People who engage in group discussions will often privately e-mail other group members. These private exchanges can develop into Internet friendships. On the Internet, interests replace proximity as a primary reason for people meeting and developing friendships.

Human attraction is another reason for establishing relationships. People prefer some people to others. Individuals select and organize information about other people based on the types of behaviors that they think work together. In face-to-face situations, **first impressions** are an important aspect of deciding whether we like or dislike other people. However, first impressions evaluate the personality of an individual with very limited information, primarily physical appearance, and so first impressions are highly susceptible to misperception. For example, studies on first impressions revealed that individuals can jump to quick conclusions about others depending on a variety of factors, including dress, age, and descriptions. Small changes in personal descriptions can alter the ways in which people perceive someone. In a study conducted by Asch (1946), substituting the words *cold, polite,* or *blunt* for the single word *warm* in a list of personality traits altered people's perception of the test subject's personality traits.

Studies conducted on face-to-face versus computer-mediated relationships suggest that people in online relationships are often perceived as more structured or ordered and less spontaneous. According to Wallace (1999), "studies show that what we type is not quite what we would say in person, and others react to this subtle alteration in our behavior. We don't just appear a little cooler, testier, and disagreeable because of the limitations of the medium. Online, we appear to be less inclined to perform those little civilities common to social interactions. Predictably, people react to our cooler, more task-oriented impression and respond in kind" (p. 17). Failure to be civil online can lead to flaming behavior and flame wars. **Flaming** is to speak incessantly and/or negatively about someone or on a relatively uninteresting subject; it is rude behavior by face-to-face standards. One way to prevent flaming is to express more agreement and soften typed disagreements in online conversations. The words people select and their writing style are important communication strategies for presenting themselves online.

Criteria for Examining Computer-Mediated Interpersonal Relationships

Phillips and Metzger (1976) developed a rhetorical framework for understanding interpersonal relationships. The rhetorical position argues that individuals can take action to alter, enhance, or end relationships. Similar to Karetnick's contextualized framework discussed in the previous chapter, individuals use communicative strategies to maintain friendships. In addition to strategies, the rhetorical view argues that people have goals that influence the way in which strategies are used. Phillips and Metzger contend that individuals seek goals in their interpersonal relationships and that they approach their goal seeking in an orderly manner, which can be described and critiqued in ways similar to as public discourse. The rhetorical framework has six standards for identifying interpersonal behavior: sharing common experience, security and satisfaction, understanding the other, role play, reciprocity, and benefit.

A rhetorical approach is being used to discuss online interactions because it is through the effective use of language that online relationships are built. Language in either a spoken or written form enables individuals to take action and learn to enhance or to end relationships with others. Thus, the six criteria of the rhetorical framework can be applied to relationships that develop through different CMC genres. Examining Internet interpersonal relationships can be easier than analyzing face-to-face ones because actual electronic interactions are often recorded and can be analyzed in detail. In contrast, researchers examining face-to-face relationships must record exchanges and make transcripts or rely on secondhand accounts.

Unlike to face-to-face relationships, relationships that form through CMC are built on written rather than spoken words. There are two reasons why written language is an important aspect of online relationship building. First, people who talk over extended periods of time develop a **private language** with their e-mail friends. Private language develops when language is used idiosyncratically by CMC correspondents who share assigned meanings for words and acronyms. Second, e-mail is different from face-to-face interactions because all conversations can be recorded and saved for future reference. Saved messages can indicate milestones in the relationship, for example, a birthday message from an e-mail friend can be printed and saved. Unlike face-to-face conversations, electronic ones can be re-read and can reappear in future messages with comments and reactions. Replying to e-mail, the frequency of contact, and the development of private language all contribute to the building of successful online relationships.

Relationships Build over Time

The elimination of social information in CMC makes participants communicate in a single verbal/linguistic mode. Consequently, it takes more "real time" for participants to exchange the same number of messages in CMC than it does face-to-face. This approach to CMC is called the **social information processing (SIP) theory**. SIP is built on the following ideas. First, communicators' motives for affiliation with others encourage them to develop relationships and will overcome the limitations of a medium. Second, communicators will adapt their communication strategies to the medium in an effort to acquire social information and achieve social goals. Finally, relationship building takes time and CMC relationship development is slower than establishing face-to-face relationships.

Walther's (1994) research revealed that socioemotional expression was greater when interaction between participants occurred over a longer period of time. He states, "Interpersonal impressions did develop over extended time interaction in CMC, and they developed more slowly than in FtF [Face-to-Face] interaction" (477). Additionally, research has revealed that differences between face-to-face and computer-mediated relationships occur in the initial stage of interaction but tend to dissipate over time. However, a factor that influences the development of relational correspondence in CMC is whether participants expect the relationship to be ongoing and possibly lead to future contact. People who believe their relationships are ongoing will work harder to use CMC to maintain the relationship.

When people come together on- and offline, they often form a type of minisociety, complete with legislative, executive, and judicial components. People engaging in relationships must decide on what to do and believe, they must be able to carry out their decisions, and they must have a way of settling disputes. They must also agree on a common definition of what is being exchanged.

Interpersonal relationships can be complementary, symmetrical, or parallel. **Complementary relationships** are based on differences between the partners; for example, one person is dominant and the other is submissive, or one person has knowledge about a subject that the other needs. In contrast, **symmetrical relationships** are based on similarities; for instance, both partners tend to be dominant or both tend to be submissive. In CMC, symmetrical relationships are built around mutual interests. **Parallel relationships** are based on a combination of complementary and symmetrical interactions. For example, one person is dominant and the other is submissive when making decisions about finances, but the roles switch when entertainment decisions are being made. Relationships in which people babble independently without fulfilling some type of complementary, symmetrical, or parallel shared needs are really nothing more than acquaintanceships.

Shared Experience

Relationships must build substantive meanings for the participants sharing the experience. Montgomery (1996) states, "The meanings associated with partners' communicative acts, both verbal and nonverbal, define relationship events like arguments, lovemaking, flirtation, play, discussions, apologies, and so forth" (p. 125). It is through the sharing of experiences and events that people develop a sense of the nature of their relationship. Relationships involve two or more people sharing a common experience for meeting some basic human goal.

Short-term goals are generally defined by the situation in which people encounter each other, and goals are negotiated between the individuals. For example, a student contacts his or her professor to get help understanding a homework assignment, or members of a work group use e-mail to coordinate their meetings and activities. Long-term goals require more time and include building one's self-esteem or developing a friendship. The first step in building a shared experience is understanding the situation or context in which the communication occurs. This is particularly important in CMC because individuals can encounter other people from geographically and culturally diverse backgrounds.

When CMC is a supplement to face-to-face encounters, the participants generally understand the context. For instance, when teachers and students communicate through e-mail, they understand each other's roles and the rules of behavior. However, when people first come together in an Internet discussion list, they may not understand the nature of the communication context because the lack of shared face-to-face experiences can make online conversations difficult to interpret. Quoting portions of an e-mail message can help to establish a shared context for the exchange (Figure 7.1).

Dissimilar external factors, such as linguistic differences, cultural differences, age factors, and gendered discourse can inhibit the building of shared meaning between communicators. However, once participants take the time to understand the different points of view being articulated, group members can share a common experience. Moreover, sharing birthday greetings, births, deaths, and other significant events online can help to create a bond between individuals.

Security and Satisfaction

Another factor in establishing relationships both on- and offline is security and satisfaction. Security develops from the feeling that one fits into society, and satisfaction is ascribed to the awareness that others have verified one's identity. Phillips and Metzger (1976) state, "Security is sought largely through public means, and satisfaction is the product of private and intimate arrangements" (p. 107). Relationship bonding requires a feeling of security because both partners must feel secure in what is going on. For example, for one person to be in charge requires the other to give permission. If one partner gives permission to the other to take charge, who is really in charge? In any relationship, each partner assigns value and the person who assigns the highest value to the relationship will do more to keep it working. In CMC relationships, the person who assigns the highest value to the relationship will write longer messages and spend more time online maintaining the relationship.

In addition to interpersonal correspondence, the medium helps to create feelings of satisfaction. According to Williams and Rice (1983), the interactive characteristic of new media can satisfy interpersonal needs because these media are flexible enough to personalize information. As a result, computer networks can help foster a sense of social presence. **Social presence** is reflected in how participants in a communication exchange would evaluate the medium that is being used on the following criteria: unsociable-sociable, insensitive-sensitive, cold-warm, and impersonal-personal (Figure 7.2). For example, people generally expect a business letter to have less social presence than a face-to-face meeting.

Two factors that relate to social presence are interactivity and the public versus private aspect of the interaction. As previously stated, CMC is interactive and the nature of the interactivity depends on whether the online interaction occurs in synchronous or asynchronous time. Unlike face-to-face encounters, Internet conversations do not obviously occur in a public or private setting. Witmer's study on risky communication, described earlier in this chapter, revealed that people often consider their e-mail messages to be private. But sys-

FIGURE 7.1   Quoting in Message Exchanges

```
Message 1
To:    Sue
From:  Pat
Re:    Meeting
```

Let's get together in June to talk about the book project.

pat

```
Message 2
To:    Pat
From:  Sue
Re:    RE: Meeting
```

>Let's get together in June to talk about the book project.

That's a good idea. But, the early part of June would be better for me because I'm going on vacation in the middle of June.

Sue

```
Message 3
To:    Sue
From:  Pat
Re:    RE: Meeting
```

>>Let's get together in June to talk about the book project.

[Notice the double >> because this line was first sent two messages ago.]

>That's a good idea. But, the early part of June would be >better for me because I'm going on vacation in the middle of >June.

How about June 4th at 10:30 A.M. at my office.

pat

```
Message 4
To:    Pat
From:  Sue
Re:    RE: Meeting
```

>How about June 4th at 10:30 A.M. at my office.

Sounds great! I'll be there.

Pat

Notice how the quoting clarifies the message and creates continutity between messages. People often receive 20–50 messages per day and messages can be forgotten or lost. Requoting eliminates ambiguity and makes it easier to understand messages.

FIGURE 7.2   Message with High Social Presence

From: Wendy

Dear Folks:

"I'd like to know 'What significant artifact you have in your living environment that represents you or something about yourself?'" In my case I would say the yellow paint color of my living room! I call the room my sunshine room. It's a happy place made more so by the bright, cheerful color. I also have painted murals on the exterior of my home (soon to be refreshed) that represent blue skies and summer flowers I would like to enjoy year round. Every time I come into my driveway, I feel transported to an upbeat day no matter what the weather.

Wendy

Source: Wendy Snetsinger. Used by permission.

---

tem administrators at corporations and universities can monitor messages, and e-mail can be forwarded to others without our knowledge. People sitting alone at home typing their inner thoughts into the computer tend to perceive the experience as a private one. However, others can read many computer-mediated exchanges.

Despite confusion over the public-private nature of CMC, it can support feelings of both security and satisfaction. For example, Hauben and Hauben (1997) argue that by electronically interacting with others, individuals can begin to feel more secure. They provide the following example:

> When I started using ForumNet (a chat program similar to irc, but smaller—[Now called icb]) back in January 1990, I was fairly shy and insecure. . . . I had a few close friends but was slow at making new ones. Within a few weeks, on ForumNet, I found myself able to be open, articulate, and well-liked in this virtual environment. Soon, this discovery began to affect my behavior in "real" face-to-face interaction. I met some of my computer friends in person and they made me feel so good about myself, like I really could be myself and converse and be liked and wanted (William Carroll, cited in Hauben & Hauben, 1997, p. 17).

CMC enables socially reticent individuals to develop interpersonal skills because it removes the social pressure of immediate face-to-face reactions from others. Moreover, some people seem to feel more secure about expressing their personal feelings to others online. Individuals who are shy and do not like to speak in front of small groups can use e-mail as a way to express themselves. For instance, shy students will often use e-mail as a way to communicate with their professors. A study by Mazur, Burns, and Emmers-Sommer (2000) examined the effects of communication apprehension and relational interdependence in online relationships. They discovered that people who are communicatively apprehensive perceived higher levels of relational interdependence with online partners. These findings support the idea that socially shy individuals could use CMC to build and develop interpersonal relationships.

Additionally, CMC can help individuals who are experiencing professional or personal problems. Sproull and Faraj (1996) state, "Despite the fact that participants in electronic groups may be surrounded by people at work or school, at least some of them feel alone in facing a problem or a situation" (p. 128). The feeling of facing a problem alone can lead a person to believe that he or she is at fault. Online support groups help to normalize experiences and allow people who share similar problems to meet.

Online groups that share common interests are also likely to share common problems, and members of these groups can provide support for each other. Many different support groups can be accessed through the Internet. Moore (1995) says, "America Online, for instance, has Monday meetings for infertility, chronic fatigue, and 'Marital Blisters.' On Tuesday, there is an AA meeting, a support group for depression, one for eating disorders, a meeting of Adult Children of Alcoholics, and a forum for Panic Support" (pp. 67–68). Electronic support groups exist for every topic from breast feeding to people with cerebral palsy. Today, computer networks have developed into a medium that facilitates the person to person sharing of emotional and informational support.

For some individuals, CMC can be a preferred method of communication. For example, Murray (1991), in her ethnographic study of IBM employees, revealed that employees choose e-mail as a medium of communication to express logical, well-argued statements. E-mail is generally followed by a telephone call or face-to-face conversation. Beginning an interaction through e-mail removes personal and emotional matters from the initial conversation and makes discussions more rationally oriented.

Because e-mail eliminates immediate face-to-face reactions from others, some people find it a superior way to present issues and problems that need solutions. Separating the people from the problems enables individuals to discuss their problems in a less emotional context. Moreover, e-mail provides an opportunity for socially reticent individuals to express themselves in ways that can lead to an improved sense of security and satisfaction.

Understanding the Other

Understanding the other, a basic concept from the writings of George Herbert Mead (1932, 1934), was discussed in the previous chapter. According to Phillips and Metzger (1976), "Each individual in a relationship is able to monitor his [or her] behavior as well as take the position of the other in order to perform an analysis of the situation in which he [or she] finds himself [or herself]. This helps him [or her] find the most effective approach to facilitate goal accomplishment" (p. 182). Unlike face-to-face encounters, CMC can make understanding the other difficult because people can more easily misrepresent themselves. Consider the following e-mail story:

> I started corresponding with a woman I encountered on a discussion network. She had a job at a major university facility and I documented her existence. She lived in the same town as my friend's aged mother, and so I asked her to look in. She did, reported pleasant

encounters with the old woman. Then she reports that her daughter is "hooked on drugs," her ex husband is harassing. She reports tales from her past that pass beyond all that is reasonable and reports she is now doing three therapy sessions a week with her psychiatrist. Shall I take this seriously. She is looking in on my friend's mother. I am, frankly, worried, and I know, I hope, I will be more cautious next time (cited in Barnes, 2001, p. 117).

As in face-to-face encounters, our *first Internet impression* of others may prove to be wrong. Initial impressions both on- and offline are often quick, inaccurate judgements. Therefore, most discussion groups recommend **lurking** and becoming familiar with individuals and the group's dynamics before joining the conversation. Eager new members frequently embarrass themselves. For example, a student who joined an academic discussion list sent a nasty message to the group's leading academic, calling this professor a "cranky old man." This student had not done his homework and did not understand the professor's role in the group as a provocative writer or his professional reputation. As a result, the professor first appeared to the student as "cranky" rather than insightful. After reading more messages posted to the group, the student realized his error and apologized to everyone.

Dual perspective is an aspect of relationship building that can influence how we understand other people. **Dual perspective** is a state of mind that takes into account the realization that the other person may see the world through entirely different eyes. Moreover, it is often important to discover exactly how that other person sees the world in order to adjust your own behavior. Through the understanding that an individual has the capacity to influence others, the individual has a responsibility when he or she does so. Dual perspective enables people to monitor their language and address themselves directly to the needs of the rhetorically sensitive person.

With casual acquaintances, we only have a limited view of the ways in which they perceive the world. This also tends to be true about Internet relationships. When we meet someone through CMC, the conversation is restricted to text and people can control their reactions and opinions. Interactions are not always spontaneous. Individuals can use **negative spontaneity** to carefully craft their messages to create the "right" impression. Therefore, it is important in CMC to observe the behaviors and roles of others. Spending time carefully reading messages will help you better understand the perspectives of Internet friends and members of online groups.

Role Play

Role play both on- and offline is important in the formation of relationships. According to Phillips and Metzger (1976), "Behaviors possible are projected as roles, roles are systematically played and are purposeful. They need to be ratified through the response of the other. Successful ratification enhances self-esteem" (p. 182). People can play a variety of roles in CMC. They can be themselves in discussion lists, create a pseudonym in a chat room, or invent a character to play in an online game.

An online participant's perception of the computer-mediated genre can influence the participant's behavioral roles. Saunders, Robey, and Vaverek (1994) researched status roles in computer conferences and discovered that occupational roles apply to CMC. For instance, in online medical contexts, doctors are viewed as high-status professionals and they "tend to send more sentences to low-status individuals than vice versa" (p. 465). Similarly, in computer-assisted instruction, teachers assume high online centrality. Social roles established in face-to-face contexts are frequently transferred into online encounters. Saunders, Robey, and Vaverek (1994) concluded that "advocates of equalitarian social interaction clearly cannot depend on technology alone to overcome the status differentials inherent in occupations and other social roles" (p. 469).

Unlike roles established in professionally oriented CMC, social roles are more difficult to establish. As in face-to-face situations, social roles emerge as people interact with each other. For example, many discussion groups have a **list guru**, a person who sparks the fires of debate and assumes a leadership position. The leadership role of the list guru will influence the formation of Internet friendships developed through online groups. For instance, a complementary relationship can develop between a list guru and a person who needs information or advice. A well-published academic list guru developed a number of complementary relationships with young scholars who wanted to get published. They exchanged e-mail and instant messages about different book ideas, and the list guru provided advice about dealing with publishers.

A leadership role established in one discussion group does not necessarily transfer to another one. Therefore, some people oppose **cross-posting** messages, or moving e-mail from one online discussion group to a different one. Whittle (1997) contends, "Some participants object to wider distribution of their posts on the grounds that cross-posting of their works might expose them to ridicule or loss of status, or because the original context might easily be lost" (p. 134). Expertise and status on one list do not necessarily transfer to another.

The roles we assume in both professional and social online contexts can influence the nature of relationships that we develop. Therefore, it is important to clearly communicate these roles to others.

Relationships are Built on Reciprocity

Both on- and offline, interpersonal relationships are developed through reciprocal exchanges. Phillips and Metzger (1976) say, "Each person, consciously or unconsciously, conducts a review of his ongoing relationships and, following the pleasure principle, acts to maintain those that satisfy and diminish or extinguish those that do not. Since both parties to a relationship have equivalent opportunity, maintenance of a relationship is a reciprocal process. Something must be exchanged" (p. 182). For successful relationships to occur, people must feel that a beneficial exchange is taking place. For example, people can exchange professional information and provide emotional support for each other. The following are examples of beneficial online relationships from the HomeNet study:

> One professional in the sample gets information from and sends information to a group discussing income tax regulation. . . . A woman has joined an on-line support group dealing with her chronic illness. And many of the teenagers in the sample exchange daily electronic

mail with other kids in their high school, supplementing the endless conversations they have on the telephone and in person (Kraut, 1995, page 2).

Responding to e-mail messages is the first step in building reciprocal online relationships. Whittle (1997) states, "Although net culture is fairly flexible about e-mail turn-around time, the nature of the communication should factor in your decision of when and how to respond, if at all" (p. 53). However, a distinction is generally made between professional and casual use of e-mail. Professional correspondents usually expect a quick reply to their e-mail unless you are out of town. Casual e-mail messages can be read and answered at your convenience.

Responses to online messages can broaden or narrow the exchange depending on whether the response focuses on portions of the original message, offers new ideas, or asks questions to move the conversation in a different direction. Whittle (1997) provides some examples:

- JaneD comments that abortion is wrong and gives three reasons to support her belief. RichM responds by rebutting each of the three reasons and offers four reasons why a woman's right to choose should take precedence over moral judgements about abortion in making law. (Broadening)
- JaneD responds by pointing out that all four of RichM's reasons are based on the assumption that morality cannot be legislated, and she rebuts that assumption by pointing out that ALL legislation is based on morality—i.e., society's concept of right and wrong. (Narrowing)
- Another participant jumps in and comments that the separation of church and state demands that all morality be kept out of all legislation. (Diverting). (1997, p. 71).

When people divert or make outrageous statements to others, many people respond with silence. Ignoring statements is an easy way to deal with inappropriate messages or behavior. Moreover, silence can be used as an avoidance strategy. "A negative use of silence is to drop out of a discussion without comment rather than face up to the weakness of one's position" (Whittle, 1997, p. 71). Rather than reply to criticism, some people will just not respond. Often, no response is perceived as a negative reaction and the person can lose credibility. Additionally, not responding to e-mail can end an online relationship.

In online communication, it is possible to cultivate skill with reciprocity. A small amount of reflected listening can enable an individual to bring the other person's message to the screen so it can be answered line-for-line (Figure 7-3). Quoting sections of previous messages encourages online discussion for two reasons. First, it helps readers contextually understand who and what the writer is replying to. Second, it supports the idea of reciprocity by providing direct feedback to the message sender. Reflected listening is a style of interaction that was used by psychologist Carl Rogers, and it was applied to a computer program called *ELIZA*, one of the first bots ever programmed. Reflected listening is an effective technique for developing reciprocity between online correspondents, and the *ELIZA* program shows that it works well in text-only exchanges (Figure 7.4). Online writers need to learn how to write messages that foster responses. Otherwise,

FIGURE 7.3   A Series of Reciprocal E-mail Exchanges . The following is a series of exchanges between two members of a discussion group. Most of the members had met face-to-face and they were discussing their face-to-face, versus online relationships. The first message, written by Phillip, was responding to a message written by Robert. Notice how Phillip first quotes Robert and then adds his comments.

MESSAGE ONE FROM PHILLIP TO THE GROUP
Date: Wed, 31 Aug 1994 22:17 EDT
From: Phillip M.G.
Subject: Re: real life vs. cyberspace
>Robert B. asks...
> And how does everyone feel now that you met F2F? Did "it"
> live up to expectations? Does whether "it" did or did not
> meet your expectations effect your relationships?
>
> None of my business, really, but Phillip did ask for input.
>
PMG: Well, gee whiz, you don't have to do things just because I
PMG: ask. But it would be interesting to find out. Since I
PMG: was at the epicenter, I confess, I was overwhelmed. Too
PMG: many important people coming all at once and not enough
PMG: time to spend with any of them. Of course, it was not
PMG: enough -- and too much -- at the same time.

PMG: But, a hazard of the internet is that we often do not
PMG: encounter whole people. You do not know who I am off
PMG: list.I can conceal features of my personality I do not
PMG: want you to know about. What if I wore Depends?

MESSAGE 2 ROBERT'S ANSWER TO PHILLIP
Date: Wed, 31 Aug 1994 19:51 EST
From: Robert B.
Subject: Re: real life vs. cyberspace
Phillip:
I thought everyone knew you wore Depends. Whoops. Ah...
ahem. Umm... ah... suspends! I mean... suspend... ers.
Yeah. I thought everyone knew you wore susPENDers. Yeah.
Like Larry King. Harum.
(skitter skitter skitter fade out)

MESSAGE 3 PHILLIP'S ANSWER TO ROBERT
Date: Thur, 1 Sept 1994 20:18 EDT
From: Phillip
Subject: Re: real life vs. cyberspace
You are quite right, you know? I do wear suspenders. How
could you have ever known.
PMG

FIGURE 7.2 *(Continued)*

MESSAGE 4 ROBERT'S ANSWER TO PHILLIP

```
Date:   Fri, 02 Sep 1994 00:15:18 -0600
From:   Robert B.
Subject: Re: real life vs. cyberspace
I occasionally wonder what you look like. If I let myself
ponder the fact that I am talking with people I have never
met and know precious little about in a very informal manner,
I get a bit woozy.
```

Source: Adapted from Barnes, 2001.

FIGURE 7.4 Example of an ELIZA Exchange. An early computer program developed to use reflected listening was called *ELIZA*. *ELIZA* was programmed to emulate the conversational style of a Rogerian psychologist, and the software encouraged people to talk to the program because it gave the illusion of listening and responding. The following is an excerpt from an *ELIZA* exchange. First to speak is a young woman. Her statement is followed by the computer's response in capital letters.

```
Men are all alike
IN WHAT WAY
They're always bugging us about something or other.
CAN YOU THINK OF A SPECIFIC EXAMPLE
Well, my boyfriend made me come here.
YOUR BOYFRIEND MADE YOU COME HERE . . . .
You are like my father in some ways.
WHAT RESEMBLANCE DO YOU SEE
You are not very aggressive but I think you don't want me to notice that.
WHAT MAKE [SIC] YOU THINK I AM NOT VERY AGGRESSIVE
You don't argue with me.
WHY DO YOU THINK I DON'T ARGUE WITH YOU
You are afraid of me.
DOES IT PLEASE YOU TO BELIEVE I AM AFRAID OF YOU
My father is afraid of everybody.
WHAT ELSE COMES TO MIND WHEN YOU THINK OF YOUR FATHER
Bullies.
DOES THAT HAVE ANYTHING TO DO WITH THE FACT THAT YOUR BOYFRIEND MADE YOU COME
HERE
```

Source: Weizenbaum, 1976, pp. 3–4.

their messages will be ignored and the individual will be unable to develop computer-mediated relationships.

CMC Impression Management Model

At times, people prefer mediated communication over face-to-face communication because they can more effectively control the positive impression made on others. A study conducted by Hancock and Dunham (2001) revealed "that impressions formed in the CMC environment were less detailed but more intense than those formed face-to-face" (p. 325). This finding supports the theory that hyperpersonal relationships develop through CMC.

To further examine impression management in CMC, O'Sullivan (2000) developed an **impression management model** for understanding interpersonal mediated communication. The impression management model "views mediated communication channels as a tool for managing self-relevant information in pursuit of self-presentational goals" (p. 403). The model combines both mass media and interpersonal theories, and its focus is on people and the media they use rather than technology characteristics. Uses and gratifications media research, described in Chapter 4, is applied to interpersonal relationships by considering the media tools that people use to pursue communication and relational goals.

The model also incorporates elements of **symbolic interactionism**, a perspective that asserts human interaction is mediated by the use of symbols. According to Wood (1992),"symbolic interaction refers to a process in which humans interact with symbols to construct meanings. Through symbolic interactions we acquire information and ideas, understand our own experiences and those of others, share feelings, and come to know other people" (p. 63).

Impression management focuses on the relational partners' concept of self and how people present themselves to others. Self-presentation theory is based on Goffman's research, discussed in the previous chapter. People can select different media tools to communicate messages and present themselves. According to O'Sullivan (2000), "Individuals are seen as working to regulate what information about oneself is known (and what [is] not known) by others in order to mange the impression that others have of them" (pp. 405–406). People develop communication strategies to manage the ways in which they present themselves to interactional partners. When using CMC tools, such as e-mail, chat, or instant messenger, the missing visual and aural information is seen as an opportunity to regulate information exchanged between two partners. Individuals select communication tools based on the benefit and cost of how each tool can be used to meet communication goals. As stated earlier, teenagers often use CMC in the dating process to control and experiment with their self-identity. The ambiguity of CMC provides more freedom to teens for experimentation and also allow them to regulate the nature, amount, and timing of information shared (Figure 7.5).

Communicative competence and social skills also influence the communication exchange. As described in Chapter 5, the symbolic form of language used in CMC adds new types of communication competence skills that are different from those of face-to-face interaction. In addition to traditional writing skills, online communicators need to know how to use graphic accents and acronyms. Moreover, the medium itself can influence the un-

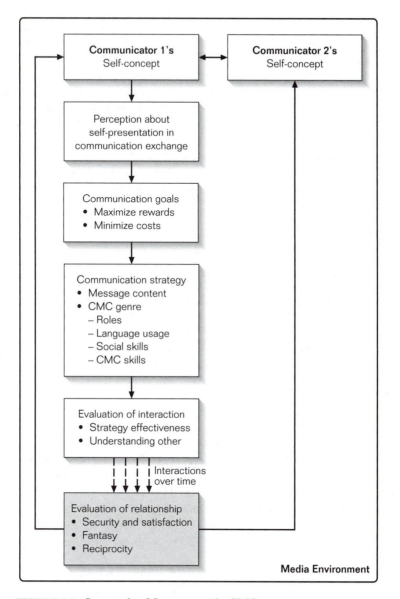

FIGURE 7.5   Impression Management in CMC

Based on O'Sullivan (2000) and adapted to conform to Phillips & Metzger (1976) and terminology used in this text.

derstanding of messages. The lack of visual and aural information can lead to misunderstanding, and therefore, communicators need to add emotional cues to text-only exchanges. In addition to linguistic and computer skills, CMC requires social skills that include the ability to manage interactions.

When O'Sullivan applied this model to a study of individuals involved in romantic relationships, he discovered that people would select different methods of communication depending on the perceived threat or support for self-presentation. A preference for CMC increased when self-presentation was threatened. People realize that CMC can help minimize the effect of embarrassing or unattractive information. Similarly, in business contexts, CMC can be used to present rational arguments and eliminate emotionally charged social cues. The information management model can help us better understand the ways in which people select CMC as a medium for interpersonal communication and relationship development.

Summary

People have reasons for using the Internet, including keeping in touch with friends and family, information seeking, and entertainment. The most popular reason for using the Internet is sending e-mail messages. E-mail can be used to develop intimate, social, and professional relationships. The six standards (sharing experiences, security and satisfaction, understanding the other, role play, reciprocity, and benefit) described in Phillips and Metzger's rhetorical framework for interpersonal behavior can be found in Internet relationships. These standards can be used to help evaluate the quality of relationships that are built through CMC.

A key aspect of Internet relationship building is reciprocity—individuals need to exchange messages for the relationship to continue. Message styles can both encourage and discourage a response. As a result, online friends need to work on establishing communication strategies that will build relationships. Impression management models enable us to better understand why people choose different media to communicate interpersonal messages. The model examines how people present themselves to others, goals of the exchange, the strategies used in the communication exchange, evaluation of the exchange, and evaluation of the relationship.

TERMS

Complementary relationships are based on differences between the partners; for example, one person is dominant and the other is submissive.

Cross-posting messages is forwarding an e-mail message sent to one discussion group to a different group.

Cybersex is the exchange of real-time sexually explicit messages through the Internet.

Dual perspective is a state of mind that takes into account the realization that the other person may see the world through entirely different eyes.

First impressions evaluate the personality of an individual based on very limited information.

Flaming is to speak incessantly and/or negatively about someone or a relatively uninteresting subject; it also is rude behavior by face-to-face standards.

Impression management models view mediated communication channels as tools for managing self-relevant information in pursuit of self-presentational goals.

List gurus are people who spark the fires of debate and assume a leadership position in an online discussion group.

Lurking is reading Internet messages without responding or participating in the group. It is similar to the passive activity of watching television.

Negative spontaneity is delaying the response to an electronic message to enable writers to more carefully express themselves.

Parallel relationships are based on a combination of complementary and symmetrical interactions. For example, one person is dominant and the other is submissive when making decisions about finances, but the roles switch when entertainment decisions are being made.

Private language is language used idiosyncratically by CMC correspondents who share personally assigned meanings of words.

Social exchange theory examines individual attempts to maintain a balance between the perceived costs and rewards of a relationship.

Social information processing (SIP) theory is a view that contends it takes more "real time" to exchange the same number of messages in CMC than it would in face-to-face encounters.

Social presence is reflected in how participants in a communication exchange would evaluate the medium that is being used on the following criteria: unsociable-sociable, insensitive-sensitive, cold-warm, and impersonal-personal. For example, people generally expect a business letter to have less social presence than a face-to-face meeting.

Symbolic interactionism is a perspective that asserts human interaction is mediated by the use of symbols, and it is through symbolic interactions that people acquire information, understand their experiences, and share feelings with others.

Symmetrical relationships are based on similarities; for instance, both partners tend to be dominant or both tend to be submissive.

Task-dimensional content is an interaction that asks for or gives information or opinions.

EXERCISES

1. Interview your friends and family to find out how they use the Internet. How do your interviews compare to the findings of the HomeNet researchers?

2. Examine your own Internet usage. List the friends you stay in touch with through e-mail and how often you exchange messages. Do you have any friends that you met on the Internet? If yes, how did you meet your friend?

3. Observe a discussion list or examine the message logs of a discussion list or Web forum. See if you can identify people who receive responses to their posts and those who are ignored. Can you observe why one message style encourages a response and the others do not?

4. What's your opinion about cybersex and adultery? Should cybersex be considered a form of adultery or is it closer to reading an erotic novel?

5. Is it safe to write sexually explicit e-mail messages? Why, or why not.

6. Impression management exercise: Examine your own use of CMC with your friends and family. When and why do you decide to talk face-to-face, send an e-mail message, call on the phone, or use instant messenger? Discuss how you use different media to manage your own self-presentation.

WEBSITES

E-mail Communication and Relationships: www.rider.edu/users/suler/psycyber
Making Friends in Cyberspace: www.ascusc.org/jcmc/vol1/issue4/parks.html
Pew Internet Project: www.pewinternet.org/

BIBLIOGRAPHY

Asch, S. E. (1946). Forming impressions of personality. *Journal of Abnormal and Social Psychology, 41*, 258–290.

Barnes, S. B. (2001). *Online connections: Internet interpersonal relationships*. Cresskill, NJ: Hampton Press.

Booth, R., & Jung, M. (1996). *Romancing the net*. Rocklin, CA: Prima Publishing.

Chen, L. L., & Gaines, B. R. (1998). Modeling and supporting virtual cooperative interaction through the World Wide Web. In F. Sudweeks, M. McLaughlin, & S. Rafaeli (Eds.), *Network & netplay* (pp. 221–242). Menlo Park, CA: AAAI Press/MIT Press.

Chesebro, J. (1985). Computer-mediated interpersonal communication. In B. Ruben (Ed.), *Information and behavior, 1* (pp. 202–224. New Brunswick, NJ: Transaction.

Clark, L. S. (1998). Dating on the net: Teens and the rise of "pure" relationships." In S. G. Jones (Ed.), *Cybersociety 2.0* (pp. 159–183). Thousand Oaks: Sage Publications.

Hancock, J. T., & Dunham, P. J. (2001). Impression formation in computer-mediated communication revisited. *Communication Research, 28* (3), 325–347.

Hauben, M., & Hauben, R. (1997). *Netizens: On the history and impact of Usenet and the Internet*. Los Alamitos, CA: IEEE Computer Society Press.

Hiemstra, G. (1982). Teleconferencing, concern for face, and organizational culture. In M. Burgoon (Ed.), *Communication yearbook 6* (pp. 874–904). Newbury Park, CA: Sage Publications.

Kennedy, H., Ben-Ali, R. & Bertrand, D. (1996, February 3). Cybersuit to crash: Experts. *The New York Daily News*, p. 5.

Kraut, R. (1995). *The social impact of home computing* [Online] 3 pp. Available: http://homenet.andrew.cmu.edu/progress/ppg.html. [Downloaded April 10, 1996).

Kraut, R., Lundmark, V., Kiesler, S. Mukhopadhyay, T., & Scherlis, W. (1997). *Why people use the Internet*. Available: http://homenet.andrew.cmu.edu/progresspurposes.html

Lea, M., & Spears, R. (1995). Love at first byte? Building personal relationships over computer networks. In J. T. Wood & S. Duck (Eds.), *Understudied relationships: Off the beaten track* (pp. 197–233). Thousand Oaks, CA: Sage, Publications.

Mazur, M. A., Burns, R. J., & Emmers-Sommer, T. M. (2000). Perceptions of relational interdependence in online relationships: The effects of communication apprehension and introversion. *Communication Research Reports, 17* (4), 397–406.

Mead, G. H. (1932). *The philosophy of the present*. La Salle, IL: The Open Court Publishing Company.

Mead, G. H. (1934). *Mind, self and society*. Chicago, IL: University of Chicago Press.

Montgomery, B. M. (1996). Communication standards for close relationships. In K. M. Galvin & P. Cooper (Eds.), *Making connections: Readings in relational communication*. Los Angeles, CA: Roxbury Publishing Company, pp. 124–133.

Moore, D. W. (1995). *The emperor's virtual clothes*. Chapel Hill, NC: Algonquin Books of Chapel Hill.

Murray, D. E. (1991). *Conversation for action: The computer terminal as medium of communication*. Amsterdam/Philadelphia: John Benjamins Publishing Company.

Nie, N. H. (2001). Sociability, interpersonal relations, and the Internet: Reconciling conflicting findings. *American Behavioral Scientist, 45, (3)*, pp. 420–435.

Odzer, C. (1997). *Virtual spaces: Sex and the cyber citizen*. New York: Berkley Books.

O'Sullivan, P. B. (2000). What you don't know won't hurt me: Impression management functions of communication channels in relationships. *Human Communication Research, 26* (3), 403–431.

Parks, M., & Floyd, K. (1996). Making friends in cyberspace. *Journal of Communication, 46* (1), 80–97.

Pew Internet and American Life Project (2000). Daily Internet activities. [Online]. Available: http://www.pewinternet.org (June 9, 2001).

Pew Internet and American Life Project (2001). Teenage life online: The rise of the instant-message generation and the Internet's inpact on friendships and family relationships [Online], 46 pp. Available: http://www.pewinternet.org (August 24, 2001).

Phillips, G. M. (1993, March 28). Re: E-mail survey comments. Electronic message to Interpersonal Computing and Technology Discussion List. IPCT-L@ GUVM.GEORGETOWN.EDU

Phillips, G. M., & Metzger, N. J. (1976). *Intimate communication*. Boston: Allyn & Bacon, Inc.

Phlegar, P. (1995). *Love online: A practical guide to digital dating*. Reading, MA: Addison-Wesley Publishing Company.

Rice, R. E., & Love, G. (1987). Electronic emotion: Socioemotional content in a compuer-mediated communication network. *Communication Research, 14* (1), 85–108.

Sandberg, J. (1996, December 6). What do they do online? *The Wall Street Journal*, p. R8.

Saunders, C. S., Robey, D., & Vaverek, K. A. (1994, June). The persistence of status differentials in computer conferencing. *Human Communication Research, 20* (4), 443–472.

Schwartz, J. (2001, July 8). Loose lips sink more than ships. *The New York Times*, p. 4Wk.

Sproull, L., & Faraj, S. (1996). Some consequences of electronic groups. In M. Stefik (Ed.), *Internet dreams: Archetypes, myths, and metaphors* (pp. 125–134). Cambridge: The MIT Press.

Tamosaitis, N. (1995). *Net.sex*. Emerville, CA: Ziff-Davis Press.

Turkle, S. (1995). *Life on the screen: Identity in the age of the Internet*. New York: Simon & Schuster.

Wallace, P. (1999. *The psychology of the Internet*. New York: Cambridge University Press.

Walther, J. B. (1994) Anticipated ongoing interaction versus channel effects on relational communication in computer-mediated interaction. *Human Communication Research, 20* (4), 473–501.

Walther, J., & Tidwell, L. (1996). When is mediated communication not interpersonal? In K. M. Galvin & P. Cooper (Eds.) *Making connections: Readings in relational communication* (pp. 300–307). Los Angeles: Roxbury Publishing Company.

Weizenbaum, J. (1976). *Human power and human reason: From judgement to calculation*. New York: W. H. Freeman and Company.

Whittle, D. B. (1997). *Cyberspace: The human dimension*. New York: W. H. Freeman and Company.

Williams, R., & Rice, R. E. (1983). Communication research and new media technologies. In R. Bostrom (Ed.), *Communication yearbook, 7* (pp. 200–224). Beverly Hills, CA: Sage Publications.

Witmer, D. F. (1997). Risky business: Why people feel safe in sexually explicit on-line commmunication. *The Journal of Computer-Mediated Communication, 2* (1), [Online], 12pp. Available: http://www.ascusc.org/jcmc/vol2/issue1/witmer.html (August 22, 2001).

Wood, J. T. (1992). *Spinning the symbolic Web: Human communication and symbolic interaction*. Norwood, NJ: Ablex Publishing Corporation.

PART III

CMC and Group Communication

Situational and contextual cues are often lacking in CMC, but the contexts in which CMC occurs do influence the ways in which people communicate and understand messages. The lack of physical co-presence in CMC exchanges makes understanding the communication context an important aspect of CMC message exchange.

CMC is used in a variety of professional and social situations. Early researchers first examined the business use of CMC and concluded that people would not be able to communicate a strong sense of social presence through limited, text-based interactions. However, CMC has turned out to be a medium that creates strong social relationships that are sometimes perceived to be more rewarding than face-to-face ones.

CMC has become a major method of communication for most organizations. In business settings, CMC allows employees of global corporations to easily communicate across vast distances in asynchronous time. Colleges and universities have also embraced CMC as a communication method that facilitates correspondence between students and teachers. CMC is not only used for business and educational purposes, however, it also supports recreational activities and community building. Part III discusses the use of CMC in the following group contexts: organizations, online games, education, and virtual communities. The purposes and practices of using CMC in each context are explored. For example, using CMC in the workplace is very different from playing online games. In work contexts, people generally use their actual identities and follow the roles established in organizational settings. Online games on the other hand, allow people to create characters and engage playfully in conversations.

At present, the most significant CMC context is virtual communities. The idea of using the Internet to both support local communities and build global ones has captured the imagination of people around the world. From the Chilean rain forest to the suburbs of New York, community groups are establishing an identity on the Internet and engaging in local, national, and global conversations. Section III explores group contexts and how group participants use CMC.

8 CMC in Organizations

Chapter Overview

People working in organizations use CMC to correspond with co-workers, keep in touch with clients, communicate with consumers, sell products, and develop relationships with suppliers. CMC is also used to form virtual teams. The asynchronous nature of e-mail and other forms of CMC enables people working in different time zones to more easily communicate with each other. As a result, many businesses have embraced CMC as a major method of communication.

By bridging time and space, computer networks also introduce new patterns of social networks into organizational settings. Traditional top-down hierarchies are flattened because people using e-mail will directly communicate with each other and bypass secretaries and other forms of organizational gatekeeping. The following topics are introduced in this chapter:

- The networked organization, which includes virtual teams and teleworking
- CMC and electronic commerce
- Computer-supported cooperative work (CSCW)
- The Web and organizations
- Organizational CMC research, including the hyperpersonal communication framework and a model of network navigation in hypermedia computer-mediated environments

Cyberspace and cybertime have influenced business and organizational communication. In 1988, Peter G. W. Keen wrote *Competing in Time*, a book that described how e-mail and computer networks could be used to simplify organizational communication. He argued that information systems could increase direct, flexible contact between people, provide simple access to information, and cut layers of management. By removing layers of management in the organizational hierarchy, information would flow faster between people. Computer networks could be used to eliminate travel time and expenses. As a result, decisions could be reached quickly and efficiently. Today, computer networks do increase contact between people and they have flattened the organizational hierarchy.

Easy access to information is achieved through internal and external organizational Web sites. Many different software tools, including groupware, teleconferencing, group decision support systems, electronic data interchange, and just-in-time systems, are used to communicate between employees, management, customers, suppliers, and consumers. Thus, CMC is used to facilitate communication within the corporation and with people outside the organization.

Groups rather than individuals are the basic work unit in the modern organization. Many companies have been moving toward a team approach to management, where team communication is often supported by CMC. **Computer-supported cooperative work** (CSCW) is a category of software programs designed to promote exchanges between and among individuals, small groups, departments, and divisions. CSCW includes e-mail, groupware, group decision support systems (GDSS), and teleconferencing. These software tools are designed to sustain both synchronous and asynchronous exchanges, and they support collaboration between participants who are geographically dispersed.

With the introduction of the Web, the Internet is now being used to allow organizations to directly communicate with consumers. On the original research-based Internet, electronic commerce was discouraged. Using e-mail to advertise a product or service was considered a misuse of network resources. In 1993, the CommerceNet consortium was established to test electronic commerce on the Internet. Today, many people have formed dot-com Internet companies that conduct business solely through electronic commerce. These companies use CMC to correspond directly with their customers. A number of these Internet companies, however, have gone out of business, which raises serious questions about the future of electronic commerce and its effectiveness in replacing traditional methods of face-to-face or direct sales with consumers.

The Networked Organization and CMC

The use of networks and of CMC has been advancing rapidly. Networks that once operated on a local level have connected to the larger Internet. Many companies operate a private **intranet** with connections to the larger Internet. Intranets are computer networks that have been developed for internal organizational use. They have many Internet capabilities, but internal communication is protected by security programs. Corporate intranets enable organizations to connect with offices across the country and around the world.

The networked organization differs from the conventional workplace because it changes concepts of time and space. E-mail can be transmitted globally within minutes. Compared to telephone or postal services, which are often referred to as "snail mail" by electronic converts, networked e-mail is extremely fast. According to Sproull and Kiesler (1991b), "managers are often attracted to [computer] networks by the promise of faster communication and greater efficiency" (p. 116). E-mail also eliminates wasting time tracking down people in their offices. Because e-mail messages are sent and received in asynchronous time at different geographic locations, e-mail creates a communication situation that has no shared physical space or shared sense of time. Finholt and Sproull (1993) remark, "[personnel] can send or read group mail while physically in their office, their secretary's office, a public workstation cluster, a laboratory, home, or (by using portable computers and telephones) in a client's office or on the road" (p. 431).

Employees access their e-mail messages around the clock and from remote locations. Additionally, people can save e-mail messages to be re-read, edited, copied, or forwarded to other individuals and groups of people. E-mail is a useful tool in organizational communication because it can be sent (with the stroke of a key) to one individual or to a group of people. While e-mail messages are primarily in the form of text files, attachments, including charts, graphs, graphics, and photographs, can also be sent through the network. Examples of typical e-mail messages include correspondence, memoranda, legal agreements, and budgets.

The use of computer networks to support organizational communication is altering the way people work. The workplace is no longer limited to a physical office and 9-to-5 office hours. Employees with e-mail accounts and a laptop with modem or wireless portable digital assistants (PDAs) can connect to the office from any location at any time. Studies on the use of e-mail (Sproull & Kiesler, 1991a; Zuboff, 1988) suggest that e-mail changes patterns of attention, social contact, and interdependence within an organization. For instance, when text replaces spoken language during communication, people must now focus their attention on the text of the message because nonverbal cues are missing. As a result, writers must present their thoughts in a clear and articulate manner.

CMC and Management

Davidow and Malone (1992) argue that in the 1990s, "networks of computers have assumed much of the traditional role of management hierarchies"(p. 167). The traditional role of management hierarchies is to provide a structure for the delegation of tasks to different personnel who work together to achieve organizational objectives. To achieve organizational objectives, personnel must communicate with each other and perform coordinated activities. Malone and Rockart (1991) state, "as computers become increasingly connected to one another, people will find many more ways to coordinate their work. In short, computers and computer networks may well be remembered not as technology used primarily to compute but as coordination technology" (p. 128). For example, software agent technology, described in Chapter 3, is incorporated into computer-supported cooperative work (CSCW) programs to help schedule appointments and coordinate activities.

CMC replaces the traditional role of management hierarchies because it uses information previously coordinated by management in the delegation of tasks. As a coordination technology, computers can speed up the rate at which organizations can take in, move, digest, and respond to information. Social contact also changes because messages can be exchanged between any two people with e-mail accounts. In organizational contexts, e-mail addresses are available to employees through the organization's e-mail address directory, which is often online. Access to e-mail addresses enables employees to bypass traditional information gatekeepers, such as secretaries. In a traditional top-down hierarchial method of organizational communication, secretaries act as gatekeepers to buffer telephone calls, mail, and interoffice memos. In the networked organization, this secretarial function no longer filters the flow of incoming messages because e-mail is sent directly to a person's e-mail account and most people read their own mail. Similarly, the secretarial task of typing is also reduced. As more and more executives use e-mail, executives and managers access, type, and send their own messages. For example, executive Ron Compton described his e-mail usage as follows:

> Most of my electronic mail use is with my direct reports and other people I work closely with—accountants, lawyers, planners, and so on. But other people send me messages too. . . . I'll give a speech or talk somewhere, and the next day I'll have three or four messages from people I've never heard of. I always answer them.
>
> Can you imagine somebody sitting down there who gets up the nerve to send a message to the president of this huge company, and then gets one back? I'll bet that every time somebody who doesn't know me gets a message back, a thank-you or something, I'll bet 300 other people will hear about that . . . talk about a machine for changing culture and for communicating! (Boone, 1993, p. 176).

As a method of communication, the ease and efficiency of e-mail is enabling middle managers to transmit and distribute written information to groups rather than to individuals through oral communication. However, when middle managers use e-mail to transmit and distribute information, subordinates must know what to do with the information when they receive it. Subordinates who are doing the actual work are delegated more decision-making power and control concerning the information they acquire. Consequently, proper training is very important because it takes the place of supervision. Training should begin prior to employment. It is increasingly apparent that in order for employees to make decisions and engage in information-based activities, they must have knowledge and skills that enable them to think critically and articulate their thoughts in writing. Employees of networked organizations must be educated workers, that is, workers who understand and use new forms of information technologies, including CMC. According to Davidow and Malone (1992), "This requires the ability not only to read, write, and perform simple arithmetic but to analyze and engineer" (p. 8). At present, colleges and universities are aware of the need for this type of educated worker and many are developing curricula to meet these needs.

Virtual Teams

Corporations use computer networks to bridge time and space and create new spatial configurations for work. Global firms use the Internet as a method of providing services around the clock. Workers located in cities such as New York, London, and Tokyo can service global markets because as one group of workers goes home for the evening another group comes to work. By strategically placing offices around the world, time differences are overcome and a company can operate 24 hours a day.

Employees can also be organized into **virtual teams**. Virtual teams are people who work together as a group from remote locations. Global corporations rely on virtual teams that interact electronically to run the business. For example, top executives will coordinate activities between Europe, Asia, South America, and the United States. Virtual project teams can be formed, reorganized, and dissolved rapidly when the project is completed or the needs of the marketplace change. These flexible teams, created to support the ever-changing requirements of dynamic global business environments, have the potential to be responsive and less expensive, but there are a number of communication issues associated with the use of CMC in this context, including low individual commitment, role overload, role ambiguity, trust, absenteeism, and social loafing. As a result, it is recommended that virtual team members meet face-to-face.

Jarvenpaa and Leidner (1998) examined trust in teams that relied only on CMC interaction. They asked the following question: Could people living in different countries interacting through CMC develop a sense of trust with their other team members? After examining twelve case studies, they concluded that trust is often established through the communication behavior in early CMC exchanges. "Communication that rallies around the project and tasks appears to be necessary to maintain trust" (p. 27). Additionally, complementary comments will strengthen trust, and group members have to explicitly verbalize their commitment, optimism, and excitement about the project.

Teleworking

A major change that CMC has introduced into organizational contexts is the concept of **telecommuting** (Figure 8.1), the ability to conduct office work from a remote location. A number of information professionals provide their services from their homes to their offices through the Internet. In cities such as Telluride in Colorado and Sun Valley in California, information systems have been developed to enable people to telecommute. Larger cities,

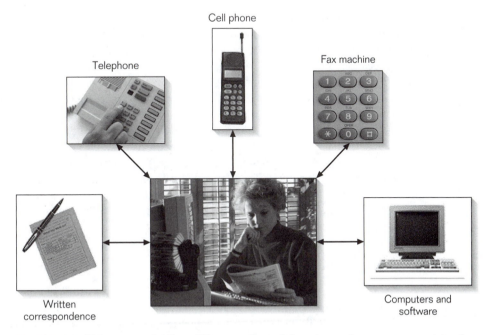

FIGURE 8.1 Telecommunicating. When people work from home, they can use a variety of different media and software tools to communicate with their office, co-workers, and clients.

including Los Angeles, are viewing telecommuting as a way to cut down on traffic, commuting, and environmental problems.

Telecommuting is also called **teleworking**, that is, working from the home or office using information and communication technology. Home teleworkers are both self-employed and employees of major corporations. Many home teleworkers will incorporate regular attendance at the office into their schedules. Research on home teleworking has focused on management issues and the social impact of working at home on family life. For example, some people decide to work at home to be around for their children. However, teleworkers face the challenge of how to maintain a balance between home and work.

Home workers must be able to develop a pattern that allows them to deal with incoming calls that may intrude on family life and the demands of family members, which could interfere with work. They need to develop strategies to cope with these situations—for example, using answering machines and setting up separate phone lines and computers for work and family use. In some cases, telework arrangements provide family homes with computers and fax machines that they would not be able to otherwise afford.

CMC and Electronic Commerce

The widespread adoption of the Web has led to Internet-driven electronic commerce. **Electronic commerce** or **e-commerce** is conducting business transactions and maintaining business relationships through computer networks. According to Dertouzos (1997), there are two types of e-commerce, direct and indirect. **Indirect electronic commerce** involves handling information needed in the process of trading physical goods; for example, selling shoes or buying oil to heat your home. Included in this process is the acquisition of materials to make a product and the shipping expenses involved with sending the finished product to locations such as stores, offices, and homes. **Direct electronic commerce** occurs when the goods themselves can be shipped directly through the network. These goods include e-mail, software, electronic books, medical records, music, movies, travel guides, educational materials, and stock prices.

E-commerce creates opportunities for Internet-based intermediaries to bring buyers and sellers together. For example, Virtual Vineyards is a site that specializes in wine and difficult-to-find specialty food items. The site acts as an intermediary between hundreds of small wineries and customers. The Web can also enable manufactures to sell their products directly without intermediaries. Dell Computers and Gateway Computers sell directly to customers through their Web sites. Web sites provide consumers with the convenience of shopping directly online.

Consumer-Oriented E-Commerce

According to Zwass (2000), E-commerce is used to build three different types of relationships: consumer-oriented, business-to-business, and intraorganizational business. The highly publicized consumer-oriented e-commerce includes home shopping, banking, online stock brokerage firms, and on-demand information and entertainment. An entire range of direct e-commerce companies have been formed that offer everything from virtual university courses to electronic newspapers, music, games, and books. Consumer-oriented e-commerce has become more sophisticated with the incorporation of agent software technology, which has been added to Web browsers to make shopping easier for consumers. IBM's *Browser Intelligence* enables users to keep track of previously visited Web sites and automatically notifies users when sites are updated. Another IBM program, *Personal Shopping Assistant*, can learn consumer preferences and rearrange the merchandise on sites to show users items they like. Products can also be grouped; when one item is purchased, complementary items are displayed to the user. An agent program called *BargainFinder* searches Web sites to find the best price for music CDs. After conducting a search, the agent returns with the name and link of the ten lowest-priced online music stores. The Web also makes it possible for companies to find out about consumer buying preferences and develop direct relationships with consumers. For instance, Gateway Computer configures systems to individual customer preferences.

Business-to-Business E-Commerce

For many years, companies have been using telecommunication systems to develop business-to-business relationships. **Electronic data interchange** (EDI) is defined as "computers talking to computers about standard business transactions" (McGarr, 1993, p. 27). Because EDI systems enable companies to exchange formatted information, customer records and product information can be stored in the networked system and then used in a company's production and/or ordering process. An early EDI system called SABRE was developed by IBM and American Airlines. The system enabled customers to book airline tickets with travel agents without waiting overnight for seat confirmations. Today, an updated version of this software is available on the Web to let customers directly buy their tickets from an airline without a travel agent.

Intraorganizational E-Commerce

Prior to the widespread use of the Internet, many companies had their own proprietary computer networks. For instance, Apple Computer ran its own private network called AppleLink to connect employees and retailers. Today, internal corporate networks are intranets (internal networks). Intranets make organizational databases available to people who work for the company. Many of these intranets use Web pages for the dissemination of information and enable employees to teleconference with one another and collaborate on projects. Proprietary information is maintained behind **firewalls**. Firewalls are keyword-protected layers of security that must be passed through before access to the information is given. Firewall technology enables companies to set up intranets and extranets (external networks). For example, Harley-Davidson's extranet allows dealers to submit financial statements, file warranty claims, and order parts. Similarly, these technologies enable universities to establish online registration systems to allow students to register for classes through the network. Student and administrator access to the system requires the use of special password and keyword numbers and letters.

Computer-Supported Cooperative Work (CSCW) Applications

Organizations are realizing that groups or teams, rather than individuals, are the fundamental unit of work in networked organizations. CSCW provides organizations with software tools that promote exchanges between and among individuals, small groups, departments, divisions, and worldwide personnel. CMC is the most important aspect of CSCW technologies. In addition to e-mail and discussion lists, CSCW applications also include groupware, computer conferencing, and group decision support systems (GDSS). Groupware and GDSS programs are designed to support synchronous collaborative work.

All CSCW applications are capable of supporting participants at different geographic locations. However, each CSCW application is also designed to meet different organizational needs. For example, **groupware** is primarily designed for small groups to collaborate in the writing and editing of documents. **Group decision support systems** (GDSS) are designed to transform small and large groups into productive work teams that resolve issues and reach decisions in an efficient manner.

Groupware

Groupware is a generic term for software programs that enable several people at the same or different geographic locations to work on a single document at the same time. According to Johansen (1988), it is designed for "collaborative work groups [that] are small, project-oriented teams [with] important tasks and tight deadlines" (p. 1). With groupware, each computer screen becomes the participants' blackboard or the flip chart located at the staff conference. Groupware simulates the experience of a group working in the same room. Unlike work recorded on a blackboard or flip chart, collaborative work products created through groupware can be printed, stored, copied, re-read, or forwarded to and from other people.

Because groupware is designed for synchronous collaborative work, individuals must make arrangements to collaborate at a specific time. The person who calls for the conference is generally the conference leader. The conference leader determines the type of work the group will be doing, such as preparing or editing a document. Groupware programs can also retrieve text or drawing files that have been prepared with word processing and graphics software.

Prior to and during a groupware conference, the leader decides whether all participants will be able to actively edit the document. Some participants may need to obtain permission from the conference leader prior to being granted access to the writing or editing capabilities of the software. For example, in educational settings the teacher can deny editing access to students. In a fully interactive groupware session, the leader is the first person to log on to the program. As the other participants log on, they enter their names in a conference box and then choose different cursors to identify who they are and which paragraph they have selected to write or edit.

The conference leader proceeds by either retrieving the document from the word processing program or opening the conference for participants to begin writing a document. In order to avoid "writing congestion," each participant is limited to "entering" his or her cursor in one paragraph at a time. As a result, several participants can work on different paragraphs at the same time. When a participant's cursor is in a paragraph, other members of the group are denied access to the paragraph until the cursor is removed. As the participants write, rewrite, or edit the document, each participant can see the changes that are being made as they are made. Therefore, as each letter of each word is typed, all participants see the letters becoming words on their computer screens.

While the participants are working on a document, they can use chat windows or instant messages to communicate with each other. Chat can help to encourage creativity because if a participant is editing a paragraph, another participant has the use of chat to express a different idea. Unlike face-to-face or telephone communication, where one can develop a good idea and then be unable to repeat or explain it with clarity, chat conversations can be saved and then printed for future reference. Chat conversations can also be stored and reviewed by supervisors.

Groupware is currently being used by attorneys who are in different locations and are negotiating and completing legal contracts or settlements. It is also being used by medical researchers, military personnel, and educators. Teachers use groupware as a hands-on tool to help students develop writing skills and to enhance the process of small group communication. Groupware applications are currently available to support collaborative writing and collaborative drawing processes.

Computer Conferencing and Teleconferencing

Groups of employees can form discussion lists to share information and coordinate projects. **Computer conferencing** is an e-mail discussion group organized by subject or topic. The conference proceedings are automatically distributed to participants by e-mail, and the conference administrator can also archive and record messages. Because computer conferencing is a conference by e-mail, the electronic proceedings can be saved, copied, and forwarded. Participants can also distribute the proceedings to others not in the group. Unlike face-to-face conferences that require a particular date and time, room rentals, etc., computer conferences can be ongoing.

Studies on the use of computer conferencing in organizations have found that electronic conferencing provides employees with a professional learning environment. (Zuboff, 1988; Finholt & Sproull, 1993). According to Finholt and Sproull (1993), a common use of computer conferencing is to ask for help or information: "A requestor can send a message to the group asking, 'Does anybody know . . .?' An answer can reply to the entire group" (p. 433). The ability to question and initiate messages and all of the various responses are available to all participants. As a result of these exchanges, individual expertise and experience becomes shared knowledge. Not all information received from a computer conference is worthwhile, however. Unlike face-to-face proceedings, computer conferences also introduce flaming into the organizational communication process. Opinion-centered messages can spawn heated debates that lead to flame wars. Organizations can guard against flaming by requiring all employees to include their e-mail addresses on every e-mail file.

In addition to text-based conferencing, many hardware and software devices have become available to enable people to transform their computers into a teleconferencing system. Inexpensive Web cameras allow people to send images through the Internet. In working situations, teleconferencing systems allow people to share documents and information along with images of conference participants. Thus, teleconferencing adds some of the visual and verbal cues that are missing in other forms of CMC

Group Decision Support Systems (GDSS)

Group decision support systems (GDSS) create media environments in which members of work groups collaborate on projects. As a tool for synchronous collaborative work, "GDSS is defined as a set of interactive, computerized tools designed to support semi- and unstructured decisions made by groups as well as group work in general" (Beauclair, 1990, p. 153). GDSS technology combines computers, video, audio, and telecommunications systems to support the work process. These systems are designed to help face-to-face synchronous collaboration and communication among geographically dispersed participants. Used as a tool for synchronous collaborative work, GDSS has been specifically developed to support the small group decision-making process and is designed for a variety of group tasks related to reaching a decision. Unlike groupware, which is limited to viewing documents and engaging in chat, GDSS adds video, audio, and telecommunications technology to group communication, which enables groups to work collaboratively in both face-to-face synchronous work situations and across geographic distances.

Using GDSS, groups perform tasks such as "planning, idea generation, problem solving, issue discussion, negotiation, conflict resolution, systems analysis and design, and collaborative group activities such as document preparation and sharing" (Valacich, Dennis & Nunamaker, 1991, pp. 133–134). Although GDSS's primary purpose is to enable small groups or teams to perform tasks in an effective and efficient manner, GDSS programs also help to eliminate some of the problems inherent in group work, including status conflicts and individual roles, which can lead to unequal discussion time and groupthink. **Groupthink** occurs when individual members are pressured into agreeing with other members of the group, usually members that take on leadership roles or have higher status positions in the organization. When groupthink occurs, a group decision is made by pressure and forced consensus. Groupthink not only results in decisions that have not been voluntarily agreed on through knowledge and opinion but also results in inhibiting the thinking and creative processes of individual group members and results in poor group communication. By eliminating groupthink and facilitating more equal participation, GDSS systems can help groups reach higher-quality decisions.

An example of how group members work with a GDSS system is the Meeting Environment or Decision Room developed by the Management Information Systems Department at the University of Arizona. The system divides a large group into a main group and several smaller groups. According to Robinson (1993), the Meeting Environment or Decision Room contains a main conference table that is U-shaped and has sixteen recessed computers that can be used by participants. In addition to the computers located at the main conference table, another computer is connected to a large-screen projection system. All of these computers are connected to a network, and activities done at individual workstations, or groups of workstations, can easily be displayed on the large screen. In addition to the main Decision Room, there are other rooms that "are equipped with microcomputers that are networked to the microcomputers at the main conference table. The output from these small group sessions can be displayed on the large screen . . . [as] small group presentations [or they] can be updated and integrated with planning session results" (p. 37).

Customer Decision Support Systems (CDSS)

GDSS technology has also been applied to Web-based communication between companies and consumers. **Customer decision support systems** (CDSS) connect companies with their customers and present strategic information to help customers make decisions. For example, Turner Broadcasting has developed an online service called *Turner Mania* to enable advertising mangers to plan their campaigns. It is an online decision support system that indicates what type of commercials would work well on which stations, at what times, and in what format. This decision-making tools streamlines the process of media planning and buying.

Electronic Data Interchange (EDI)

A parallel development to CMC is electronic data interchange (EDI) applications, which help computers instead of people exchange sophisticated, formatted, digitalized information. Stated simply, EDI helps computers talk to other computers. Today, EDI applications are being combined with CSCW applications to enable employees to work on computer-aided designs, such as three-dimensional car parts or car designs. The creators of the designs can transmit the digitalized data to other personnel, and when the data arrive, a computerized machine uses the data to develop a clay model.

Ford Motor Company implemented such a system. After six years in development, Ford consolidated its European, Asian, and North American design operations "into a single international network," which Ford calls its "electronic roof." Ford's "electronic roof" is in Dearborn, Michigan. To communicate with the other networked sites that are located in six countries around the world, Ford purchased satellite links, land lines, and cable lines. Using the network, a Ford engineer in England can design three-dimensional drawings and then send the digital data to Michigan. A Michigan designer can bring up the drawings on a workstation and then telephone his English colleague so that they can work together. The colleagues can manipulate the drawings, rotating them and revising them on the screen. Halpert (1993) states, "Later, the data files might be sent pulsing through satellite or fiber-optic circuits in [Italy], where a computerized milling machine can turn out a clay or plastic-foam model in a matter of hours" (p. F7). CSCW combined with EDI enables design teams to work together through the exchange of digital data over computer networks.

In the ordering process, EDI transfers information from a customer's computer to a supplier's computer. Placement of the order will then trigger other computer programs to generate a packing list, shipping order, invoice, inventory charge, or customer profile. EDI eliminates the duplicate keypunching of information and reduces the delay of sending information through the postal service or fax machine. Companies such as Wal-Mart, Levi Strauss, and General Motors have built new types of relationships with their customers and suppliers through EDI technology. According to Davidow and Malone (1992), EDI systems can "ease the manager's burden of interacting with suppliers, customers, and other groups within the same organization" (p. 172). Implementing an EDI system in an organization can also help reduce inventories, promote engineering data exchange, and improve work scheduling and transportation planning and delivery. EDI systems can also be used to improve product marketing and sales by providing market feedback and research information.

EDI influences the social contact and interdependencies between customer and supplier. In EDI systems, orders are programmed to be placed directly by the computer system to the designated supplier. For example, an early EDI system was American Airlines reservation system, which was used by travel agents to book reservations directly. However, in using the system, travel agents became part-time reservation clerks for American Airlines. Today, airline Web sites enable consumers to directly book their airline tickets.

Railroad companies use EDI to track the location of the "rolling stock." Rail cars are marked with machine-readable symbols, and the information is input directly into computer systems. According to Davidow and Malone (1992), "Computers can [also] work out strategies for moving the rail cars to the right locations in order to carry the freight" (p. 167). In addition to tracking railroad cars loaded with stock, EDI can be used to track and prioritize jobs in a factory to indicate the jobs that are most critical to be done.

With the widespread use of the Internet, some EDI applications have now become Web based. Web-based applications can provide information to consumers. For example Federal Express allows individuals to track their packages through its Web site (http://www.federalexpress.com) by using airbill tracking numbers. Senders and receivers of packages can easily find the location of the package by checking the Web site. The Federal Express site also provides up-to-the minute delivery rates.

Just-in-Time (JIT) and Quick Response

Just-in-time (JIT) systems are computer systems that enable companies to produce and deliver finished goods "just in time" to be sold. In other words, JIT is the idea of producing only necessary units in the necessary quantities at the necessary time. Davidow and Malone (1992) believe that "of all the new manufacturing processes, just-in-time is probable the most pervasive" (p. 121).

A type of JIT system used in the fashion industry is called **quick response**. Quick response creates electronic connections that link companies to the production and distribution chains. Quick response is a two-way system: One direction speeds the apparel down through the distribution channels, and the other direction feeds back results to each of the companies on the electronic chain. As a result, all levels of the fashion industry, from suppliers of fibers (such as wool and cotton), to the mills that weave these fibers into fabric, to the factories that sew garments, to the retail stores that sell the garment, to the consumer are connected in the electronic chain.

A variety of different information technologies are used in the quick response communication process. These technologies include the bar code standard, portable computer terminals, scanners for data collection, established data communication formats, and, of course, networked organizations. It is perceived that fully implemented quick response systems will help companies respond quickly to customer demand. For example, when a sweater is purchased at a store in New York City, a scanner reading the bar-coded label could automatically trigger ordering, shipping, and production activities that go all the way through the production chain back to the wool warehouse in Georgia.

By combining all types of electronic and CMC technologies, the fashion industry has developed a new way of doing business and created electronic partnerships among suppliers, producers, distributors, and retailers. As electronic partnerships become more and more prevalent, computer systems are increasingly performing tasks that were delegated to middle managers and semiskilled, and low-level employees. To meet the challenge of employment, today's students must possess computer skills, knowledge, technical expertise, the ability to think and reason critically and articulate thoughts in writing, and work cooperatively in group environments.

Organizational Adoption of the Web

Organizations adopt a new technology for a variety of reasons. Organizational innovation and adoption studies tend to explain the adoption of new technology based on organizational characteristics (size, age, reliance on technology) and the benefits a technology provides (information flow, profit, reputation). Although Web sites promise to provide benefits to organizations, these commercial benefits have yet to be proven on a large scale. The recent demise of many dot-com companies illustrates this point.

Organizations have a number of concerns about establishing Web sites including unproven commercial benefits, ease of access, and security issues. Despite these concerns, the rapid and widespread adoption of the Web quickly reached a **critical mass**. Rogers (1995) defines critical mass as "the point at which enough individuals have adopted an innovation so that the innovation's further rate of adoption becomes self-sustaining" (p. 313). The adoption of the Web technology by organizations suggests that other social factors are involved. A study conducted by Flanagin (2000) revealed that social pressures occurring on the interorganizational level are an important influence on technology adoption. Social pressures include fads and fashions, leadership in the industry, and organizational visibility. For instance, organizations that consider themselves to be leaders in their industry are more likely to adopt a new technology, such as the Web. In addition to these social pressures, Flanagin discovered that interorganizational social pressures also played an important role in an organization's decision to adopt the Web. He states, "If organizations believed that other organizations in similar businesses or fields had a Web site, [organizations] were likely to have adopted one themselves" (p. 637). Additionally, organizations that relied on advanced technology were early adopters of Web sites and a degree of faddishness was also associated with Web adoption. Organizations with Web sites were viewed as avant-garde and cutting edge. According to this study, social pressure factors were a key reason why organizations adopted Web technology.

Approaches to Organizational CMC Research

Organizations were the first contexts in which researchers studied CMC, and social presence theory was one of the first theories to be tested by CMC researchers (Hiltz, Johnson, & Turoff, 1986; Rice, 1984). The fewer cues (visual, verbal, aural, etc.) a medium provides, the lower the social presence. According to this theory, videoconferencing systems would provide a higher level of social presence than e-mail because videoconferencing has more cues. Social presence theory focuses on the quantity rather than quality of information being transmitted by different media.

Other researchers applied Berger and Calabrese's (1975) uncertainty reduction theory to CMC. This theory argues that people have a need to reduce uncertainty about other people, which they do by acquiring information about other people's behavior. Reducing uncertainty is important in the development of interpersonal relationships. For example, sharing photographs can help to increase uncertainty in CMC relationship building.

As more people began to use CMC, research began to conflict with these earlier theories. Walther (1992) proposed the social information processing theory, described in the previous chapter, as another approach to understanding social presence in CMC. This theory was later modified by incorporating social-psychological and cognitive theories to account for the hyperpersonal process that occurs in CMC (see Chapter 1.). Social information processing theory was later transformed into the hyperpersonal communication framework.

Hyperpersonal Communication Framework

Walther, Slovacek, and Tidwell (2001) developed the **hyperpersonal communication framework** (Figure 8.2). As previously stated, the hyperpersonal perspective is an approach that attempts to understand why some CMC users experience stronger levels of affection and interpersonal assessment than they do in face-to-face contexts. The four aspects of the hyperpersonal communication described in Chapter 1 (receivers, senders, channel, and feedback) were used to discover what would happen when photographs of participants were introduced into different types of virtual teams.

The study revealed that seeing photographs prior to and during computer conferencing had a positive effect on affection and attractiveness in short-term teams in which par-

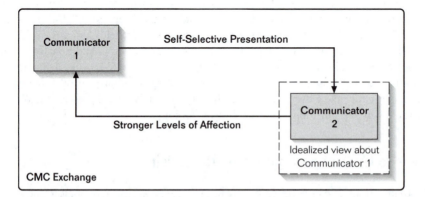

FIGURE 8.2 Hyperpersonal Framework for Virtual Teams. CMC users can experience stronger levels of affection for others with limited cues. Selective self presentation combined with idealized (fantasy) views of others can lead to more friendly online relationships.

ticipants were unacquainted. Conversely, team members who met and spent time together online before the picture was introduced had less affection and social interaction after seeing the pictures. Virtual teams using CMC who never saw each others' pictures had the strongest positive feeling of affection and attractiveness. According to Walther, Slovacek, and Tidwell (2001), "When there was no photograph, greater familiarity was significantly associated with increased intimacy/affection and social attraction" (p. 123). Thus, photographs can hinder hyperpersonal communication in groups that meet only through CMC for extended periods of time.

The presence of photographs also influenced self-presentation. Both idealization and selective self-presentation take place when no photograph is present. Without photographs, perceptions of physical attractiveness are based on the success of an individual's self-presentation. When pictures are introduced into CMC, self-presentation can be negatively correlated with physical attractiveness. Walther, Slovacek, and Tidwell (2001) state, "It appears that when partners' photographs are shown, the less physically attractive they are, the more they engage in successful self-presentation, perhaps in a compensatory manner. Or the more physically attractive partners are, the less successful they believe their impression management efforts are" (p. 123).

What became clear from this study is that CMC participants do work on how they present themselves to others and how they mold other's impressions of them. Long-term, invisible CMC tends to make people more friendly. Virtual teams that have the time to develop relationships through CMC will have a better chance of building interpersonal relationships, and photographs do not necessarily help in the relationship-building process.

Model of Marketing Communication in Hypermedia

Examining CMC from a business approach, Hoffman and Novak (1995) have proposed a model of network navigation in hypermedia computer-mediated environments (Figure 8.3). **Hypermedia computer-mediated environments** (CMEs) are defined "as a distributed computer network used to access and provide hypermedia content (i.e., multimedia content connected across the network with hypertext links)" (p. 3). The first global implementation of a hypermedia CME is the Web. This new technology enables consumers to interactively access content, such as product information, provided by commercial organizations. Used as a marketing medium, the Web incorporates features from broadcast television and static print-based advertising. As Internet bandwidth increases, more commercial Web sites are adding digital video to the multimedia mix of content presented through the Internet.

The network navigation in hypermedia CME model expands flow theory, described in Chapter 2, into a marketing communication model for hypermedia environments. It combines the four flow dimensions of control, attention focus, curiosity, and intrinsic interest with characteristics of interactive media. For example, site navigation, computer skills, and telepresence are incorporated into flow theory. Navigation is a self-directed processes in which consumers move through hypermedia environments. Moving through the environment creates the flow experience.

The flow experience requires consumers to have the appropriate skills and challenges. The following items can prevent flow: distractions, passage of time, control, and self-consciousness. In the first stage of flow, control characteristics (skills and challenges), content

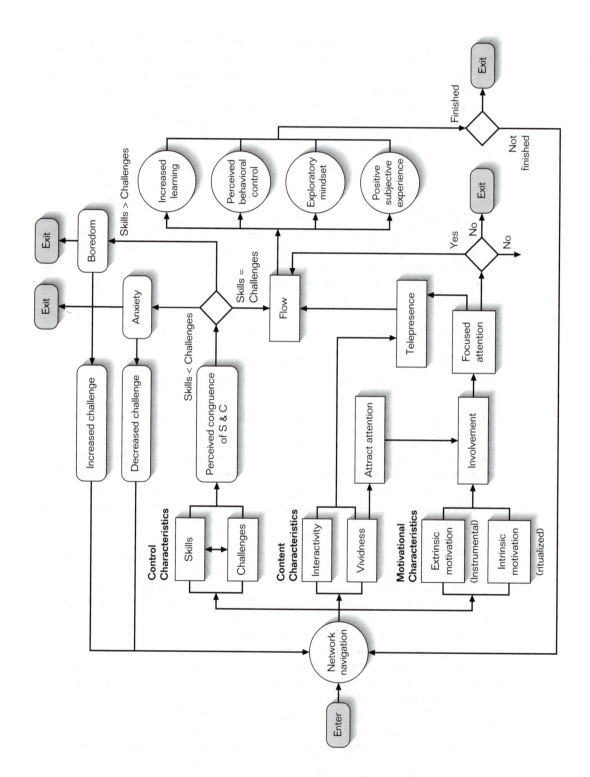

characteristics (interactivity and vividness), and motivational characteristics (extrinsic and intrinsic) influence the experience. Consumers move in and out of flow based on these characteristics. Extrinsic motivations are associated with achieving a goal, such as locating information or buying a product online. Intrinsic motivations are activities performed for no apparent reason other than doing the activity itself. For instance, people will surf the Web as a way to pass time. In addition to motivational factors, hypermedia CMEs must keep the attention and involvement of the consumer for successful site navigation to occur.

Hoffman and Novak argue that the successful flow experience associated with hypermedia environments will provide consumers with greater perceived behavioral control. The interactive nature of hypermedia provides more consumer control than is possible with passive mass media. Additionally, interactivity leads to higher levels of playfulness and experimentation, which result in a more positive subjective experience. Conversely, these same characteristics could have negative consequences. Because flow experience can provide its own reward, for instance Web surfing, consumers may be distracted from purchase-related activities. Playfulness may also require more time to complete a task. However, time could be turned into a positive Web site feature because marketers want consumers to spend time examining and exploring their Web sites. Finally, flow has been connected to overinvolvement, which leads to mental and physical fatigue. Thus, marketers need to test their sites in terms of the flow experience to make sure their target consumers will have positive flow experiences when visiting their Web site.

Summary

The introduction of CMC and CSCW applications, such as electronic mail, computer conferencing, groupware, and group decision support systems, alters the flow of information exchange within an organization and between organizations and creates different channels of and methods for communication. Further, the combination of CSCW and EDI has enabled computer-aided designs to be transmitted worldwide and to be reproduced through computerized machinery. In addition, EDI has enabled the creation of electronic partnerships among suppliers, producers, distributors, retailers, and customers. Accordingly, the introduction of these new organizing and informing technologies have resulted in radical

---

FIGURE 8.3   Model of Network Navigation in Hypermedia Computer-Mediated Environments. The Model of Network Navigation in Hypermedia Computer-Mediated Environments expands flow theory into online organizational communication. Users must be motivated, interested, and feel in control of the communication exchange to access information and navigate online environments, such as the Web. Successful Web-based organizational communication is a complex process that involves creating a sense of telepresence by the organization. For interactive Web exploration to continue, users must experience the following: increased learning, perceived behavioral control, need for further exploration, or a positive experience.

From Donna Hoffman and Thomas Novak, Marketing in Hypermedia Comptuer-Mediated Environments: Conceptual Foundations, *Journal of Marketing*, July 1996, Vol. 60, pp. 50–68 changes in organizational hierarchies, collaborative and cooperative group efforts, and the way in which communication occurs within organizations.

Several different research approaches have been applied to the study of CMC in and between people and organizations. Walther, Slovacek, and Tidwell (2001) developed the hyperpersonal communication framework to understand why some CMC users experience stronger levels of affection and interpersonal assessment than those occurring in face-to-face contexts. From a business perspective, Hoffman and Novak's network navigation in hypermedia CME model expands flow theory into a marketing communication model for hypermedia environments that explores how consumers experience Web sites.

TERMS

Computer conferencing is an e-mail discussion group organized by subject or topic.

Computer-supported cooperative work (CSCW) is a category of software programs designed to promote exchanges between and among individuals, small groups, departments, and divisions.

Critical mass is the point at which enough people or organizations have adopted an innovation to make that innovation's further rate of adoption self-sustaining.

Customer decision support systems (CDSS) connect companies with their customers and present strategic information to help customers make decisions.

Direct electronic commerce occurs when the goods themselves can be shipped directly through the network, including e-mail, software, electronic books, medical records, music, movies, travel guides, educational materials, and stock prices.

Electronic commerce or e-commerce is conducting business transactions and maintaining business relationships through computer networks.

Electronic data interchange (EDI) is computers communicating to other computers about standard business transactions, such as cutomer records and product information.

Firewalls are keyword protected layers of security that must be passed through before access to the information is given.

Group decision support systems (GDSS) create electronic environments in which members of work groups collaborate on projects.

Groupthink occurs when individual members are pressured into agreeing with other members of the group.

Groupware is a generic term for software programs that enable several people at the same or different geographic locations to work on a single document at the same time.

Hypermedia computer-mediated environments (CMEs) are distributed computer networks used to distribute and access hypermedia content, which includes multimedia content connected through hypertext links. An example is the World Wide Web.

Hyperpersonal communication framework is an approach that attempts to understand why some CMC users experience stronger levels of affection and interpersonal assessment than those occurring in face-to-face contexts.

Indirect electronic commerce involves handling information needed in the process of trading physical goods.

Intranets are computer networks that have been developed for internal organizational use.

Just-in-time (JIT) systems are computer systems that enable companies to produce and deliver finished goods "just in time" to be sold.

Quick Response creates electronic connections that link companies to the production and distribution chains. It is a two-way system: one direction speeds the apparel down through the distribution channels and the other direction feeds back results to each of the companies on the electronic chain.

Telecommuting is the ability to conduct office work from a remote location.

Teleworking is working from the home or office using information and communication technology.

Virtual teams are people who work together as a group from remote locations.

WEB SITES

Electronic Commerce: http://www.ascusc.org/jcmc
Marketing in Hypermedia CMEs: http://ecommerce.vanderbilt.edu/research/papers/pdf/manuscripts/ Conceptual Foundations-pdf.pdf
The Quick Response Center: http://jan.ucc.nau.edu/~ipct-j/1995/n4/schorr.txt
Virtual Organizations: http://www.ascusc.org/jcmc/vol3/issue4/

EXERCISES

1. Split into teams. Each team should develop a report on the latest trends in CSCW software programs with examples of how corporations are using these technologies. Team members should delegate tasks to research, write, and present the group report.

2. Interview a person who works for a major corporation and ask him or her how they use CMC in their organization. Try to determine whether or not their company uses any of the systems described in this chapter.

3. Research the topic of telecommuting. What are the advantages and disadvantages of telecommuting for employees?

4. Interview someone who has purchased a product online and have them describe their shopping experience. What are the benefits and disadvantages of electronic shopping versus going to a physical store?

5. Select and critique two different commercial Web sites. Begin your critique by reviewing the criteria described in Chapters 4 and 5.

BIBLIOGRAPHY

Andrews, E. L. (1991, June 23). Plugging the gap between e-mail and video conferencing. *The New York Times*, p. 9.

Baecker, R. M. (1993). *Readings in groupware and computer-supported cooperative work*. San Mateo, CA: Morgan Kaufman Publishers Inc.

Beauclair, R. A. (1990). Group decision support systems and their effect on small group work. In G. M. Phillips (Ed.), *Teaching how to work in groups* (pp. 151–172). Norwood, NJ: Ablex Publishing.

Berger, C. R., & Calabrese, R. J. (1975). Some explorations in initial interaction and beyond: Toward a developmental theory of interpersonal communication. *Human Communication Theory, 1*, 99–112.

Bly, S., Harrison, S. R., & Irwin, S. (1993, January). Media spaces: Bringing people together in a video, audio, and computing environment. *Communications of the ACM*, pp. 28–47.

Boone, M. E. (1993). *Leadership and the computer*. Rocklin, CA: Prima Publishing.

Davidow, W. H., & Malone, M. S. (1992). *The virtual corporation*. New York: HarperCollins Publishers.

Dertouzos, M. (1997). *What will be*. San Francisco: Harper Collins.

Dreyfus, H. L., & Dreyfus, S. E. (1986). *Mind over machine*. New York: The Free Press.

Dutton, W. H. (1999). *Society on the line: Information politics in the digital age*. New York: Oxford University Press.

Engelbart, D., & Lehtman, H. (1988, December). Working together: The 'human system' and the 'tool system' are equally important in computer-supported cooperative work. *Byte Magazine*, pp. 245–252.

Finholt, T., & Sproull, L. S. (1993). Electronic groups at work. In R. M. Baeker (Ed.), *Readings in groupware and computer-supported cooperative work* (pp. 431–442). San Mateo, CA: Morgan Kaufman Publishers Inc.

Flanagin, A. J. (2000). Social pressures on organizational Web site adoption. *Human Communication Research, 26* (4), 618–646.

Forester, T. (1987). *High-tech society*. Cambridge, MA: The MIT Press.

Gaver, W. W. (1992). The affordance of media spaces for collaboration. *ACM 1992 Conference on Computer-Supported Cooperative Work, Sharing Perspectives*, October 31 to November 4, 1992, Toronto, Canada. New York: Association for Computing Machinery.

Halpert, J. E. (1993, August 29). One car, Worldwide, with strings pulled from Michigan, *The New York Times*, p. F7.

Hiltz, S. R., Johnson, K., & Turoff, M. (1986). Experiments in groups decision making: Communication process and outcome in face-to-face versus computerized conferences. *Human Communication Research, 13*, 225–252.

Hoffman, D. L., & Novak, T. P. (1995). *Marketing in hypermedia computer-mediated environments: Conceptual frameworks* [Online], 35 pp. Available: http://ecommerce.vanderbilt.edu/cmepaper.recvision.July11.1995/cmepaper.html (July 2, 2001).

Jarvenpaa, S. L., & Leidner, D. E. (1998). Communication and trust in global virtual teams. *Journal of Computer-Mediated Communication* [Online], 30 pp. Available: http://www.ascusc.org/jcmc/vol3/issue4/jarvenpaa.htm (October 27, 2000).

Johansen, R. (1988). *Groupware: Computer support for business teams*. New York: The Free Press, Division of Macmillan.

Keen, P. G. W. (1988). *Competing in time*. New York: Ballinger Publishing Company.

Kiesler, S., Siegel, J., & McGuire T. W. (1991). Social psychological aspects of computer-mediated communication. In C. Dunlop & R. Kling (Eds.), *Computerization and controversy* (pp. 330–349). Boston: Academic Press.

Malone, T. W., & Rockart, J. F. (1991, September). Computers, networks and the corporation. *Scientific American* [*Special issue*], pp. 128–136.

McGarr, M. S. (1993, July). EDI software survey. *EDI World*, pp. 27–39.

O'Keefe R. M., & McEachern, T. (1998, March). Web-based customer decision support systems. *Communications of the ACM, 41* (3), 71–78

Rice, R. E. (1984). Mediated group communication. In R. E. Rice & Associates, (Eds.), *The new media: Communication, research, and technology* (pp. 129–156). Beverly Hills, CA: Sage Publications.

Robinson, M. (1993). Computer supported co-operative work: Cases and concepts. In R. M. Baecker (Ed.), *Readings in groupware and computer-supported cooperative work* (pp. 29–49). San Mateo, CA: Morgan Kaufman Publishers.

Rogers, E. M. (1995). *Diffusion of innovations* (4th ed.). New York: The Free Press.

Schrage, M. (1991, August 2). Computer tools for thinking in tandem. *Science Magazine*, pp. 505, 507.

Sproull, L., & Kiesler, S. (1991a). *Connections: New ways of working in the networked organization*. Cambridge, MA: The MIT Press.

Sproull, L., & Kiesler, S. (1991b, September). Computers, networks and work. *Scientific American* [*Special issue*], pp. 116–123.

Valacich, J. S., Dennis, A. R., & Nunamaker, J. F., Jr., (1991). Electronic meeting support: The Group-Systems concept. In S. Greenberg, (Ed.), *Computer-supported cooperative work and groupware* (pp. 133–153). London: Harcourt Brace Jovanovich, Publishers.

Walther, J. B. (1992). Interpersonal effects in computer-mediated interaction: A relational perspective. *Communication Research*, Vol. 19, pp. 52–90.

Walther, J. B., Slovacek, C. L., & Tidwell, L. C. (2001). Is a picture worth a thousand words? Photographic images in long-term and short-term computer-mediated communication. *Communication Research, 28* (1), 105–134.

Winograd, T. (1988, December). Where the action is. *Byte Magazine*, pp. 256A–258.

Zuboff, S. (1988). *In the age of the smart machine*. New York: Basic Books.

Zwass, V. (2000). Structure and macro-level impacts of electronic commerce: From technoloigal infrastructure to electronic marketplaces. In K. E. Kendall (Ed.), *Emerging information technologies* (pp. 289–316). Thousand Oaks, CA: Sage Publications.

9 Online Games

Chapter Overview

Entertainment is a key motive for Internet use. Since the early days of computing, games have been a popular form of online entertainment. Interactivity is a key reason why online games are fun to play. In addition to play, Internet games are often social spaces in which people chat and interact with others. Both Internet researchers and journalists have examined online games called MUDs (Multi-User Dungeons or Dimensions). These electronic environments are called text-based virtual realities because players create their own imaginary worlds.

With the development of the Web, many other types of popular games are now available online including the Palace, Cybergate, bingo, and blackjack. The Web's graphical features create visual virtual environments for players to represent themselves and interact. However, a growing social concern is Internet gambling. Because Web sites can be accessed across national boarders, Internet gambling challenges local and national gambling laws. The following Internet game topics are presented in this chapter:

- Short history of computer games
- An overview of MUDs
- MUDs and social behavior
- MUD genres, including adventure, social, and educational
- Gaming and gambling on the Web
- Brenda Laurel's theatre model of computer interaction

The PEW Internet study on teenagers revealed that 66 percent of the teenagers interviewed used the Web to download or play games. Since the early days of computing, games have been a form of computer-based entertainment. Today, high-speed modems enable people to play computer games over the Internet. For example, gaming zones are places where people can log on and play everything from bridge to *Scrabble*. Both individual and group games are available twenty-four hours a day, seven days a week.

Historical Overview of Computer Games

Early computer users invented games. For instance, *Spacewar* was started in the early 1960s at MIT by a programmer named Steve Russell. A simple space ship appeared on the screen and the player shot it down. It was a popular game played on expensive university mainframe computers by engineering students around the United States. Steven Levy (1984) says, "The game *Spacewar*, a computer program itself, helped show how all games—and maybe everything else—worked like computer programs. When you went a bit astray, you modified your parameters and fixed it. You put in new instructions" (p. 61). Writing the instructions for *Spacewar* involved programming graphic representations of rocket ships on a computer display terminal. The game combined new methods of programming with computer-generated visual display screens. Over time, the game grew more varied and complex.

The first electronic video game was developed in 1972 by Nolan Bushnell. Bushnell was an engineering major at the University of Utah and an avid player of *Spacewar*. David Evans, one of the pioneering developers of computer graphics, ran the Utah computer science program and he inspired Bushnell. In addition to attending engineering courses, Bushnell had a part-time job in an amusement park. While working at the park, Bushnell acquired knowledge about the workings of the coin-operated game industry. He studied people's game preferences and their spending habits. But for his own personal amusement, Bushnell played *Spacewar* on the university's mainframe computer.

One night while Bushnell was playing *Spacewar*, he began to wonder if it would be possible to transform this mainframe computer game into a game that would be accessible to consumers. But, he decided that *Spacewar* was too complicated a game for general use. Therefore, he created a simple game called *Pong*, based on the idea of a ping-pong table. *Pong's* computer program was simple enough to fit on a small microprocessor chip.

In 1972, Bushnell found the financial backing to start his new company, called Atari. In its first year of business, Atari managed to sell $13 million worth of video games. *Pong* was Atari's first product and it was extremely successful as a coin-operated arcade computer. *Pong* was also the first electronic game for use with television sets. It was the starting point for future interactive home video games, such as *Nintendo*, *Sega*, and *Playstation*. While the video game market flourished offline, text-based games began to develop online.

Short History of MUDs

In the early 1970s, a number of computer researchers at the Stanford Artificial Intelligence Laboratory were fantasy fans, naming the rooms in the AI Lab after locations described in J. R. R. Tolkien's *Lord of the Rings*. Researcher Donald Woods wrote a program called ADVENT, which became commonly known as *Adventure*. The game was inspired by a program written by Will Crowther at Xerox PARC, who had written a text-based game about an explorer seeking treasure in a network of caverns. In *Adventure*, a player assumed the role of a traveler in a Tokienesque setting who would fight off enemies and overcome obstacles to eventually discover a treasure.

The game describes scenes, for instance being in a forest with a sword beneath a tree. Simple commands, such as "get sword," "look tree," and "go north," allowed players to navigate the virtual forest. New descriptions would appear on the screen based on the actions of the player. Unlike commercial computer games, such as *Pong* and *Pacman*, which had specific goals for winning the game, *Adventure* allowed users to imagine and plot their own actions. *Adventure* became very popular, and many other single-player games began to appear. In the late 1970s, as computer networking began to develop, the first networked, multiuser game, called *Mazewar*, was written by Jim Guyton. Players would wander around a maze and try to shoot one another. Other games, such as *WIZARD* and *Scepter*, followed.

The first MUD was created by Roy Trubshaw and Richard Bartle in England in 1979. Called *DUNGEN*, it was created as a multiuser game that allowed players to communicate with each other. DUNGEN was a fantasy-style game that encouraged players to compete against each other to gain points by going on quests, killing monsters, and finding treasure. Bartle, asked to design a version of his game for CompuServe, came up with *British Legends*. Players became Wizards or expert players by mastering the *British Legends'* universe.

Alan Cox, an original MUD player, decided to create his own game. It was called *AberMUD*, named for the town of Aberystwyth, where Cox lived. In 1989, another MUD fan, Jim Aspnes, from Carnegie-Mellon University wrote *TinyMUD*. *TinyMUD* was created to run on UNIX-based computers and was the first social MUD. Instead of gaining points and killing monsters, players were given access to commands that enabled them to communicate with each other and build worlds. Social MUDs stress cooperation and interaction, rather than competition and mastery.

In the early 1980s, MUDs were accessed through dial-up systems that existed as databases on proprietary networks, and players connected to them with a modem and online service. Since the spread of the Internet, MUDs have evolved into a variety of forms. In 1988, the software releases of *AberMUD* and *Monster* prompted the creation of many imitators. MUD communities emerged based on "families" of MUDs, including the DikuMUD and TinyMUD communities. Other MUDs include COOLMUDs, LP-MUDs, MAGEs, MOOs, MUSEs, MUSHes, TeenyMUDs, and UberMUD. Players often participate in several MUDs at the same time, forming communities that span several different MUDs.

The most common adventure-style MUDs are Tolkienesque fantasy worlds, followed by science fiction worlds, and MUDs based on historical places, such as the Wild West, the prehistoric era, or a medieval village. Over time, the meaning of the acronym MUD changed from its original Multi-User Dungeon to Multi-User Domain and Multi-User Dimension. Most of the MUD systems running on the Internet are for social or entertainment purposes. However, MUDs are also used for academic purposes to explore literature and hold class meetings.

MUDs and Social Behavior

MUDs are software programs that allow multiple users to connect through a computer network. Each user has access to a shared database of information. Users can access "rooms," and "objects," and they can interact with each other. MUDs are textual environments. All commands are typed into a keyboard and the feedback is displayed as text on a computer screen. MUDs were originally *Dungeons and Dragons*-style adventure games, they later developed into means for social and educational interaction. Early adventure MUDs were combat oriented; players gained levels based on their experiences of killing computer-controlled creatures and solving puzzles. In social MUDs, people collaborate to build a new imaginary world, rather than engage in combat. Social MUDs are infinite games that develop as players add new characters, rooms, and objects. MUD software is also used by educators to conduct classes or support CMC discussion because a number of students can interact in a MUD at the same time. For example, students studying Western literature have created Dante's different levels of hell in MUD-space and MUDs have been set up as serious social spaces for the intellectual examination of subjects such as postmodern theory.

MUDs are not for everyone. People need to have good typing skills to engage in this type of interaction because typos and spelling mistakes can create a poor self-representation. Moreover, people who interact in MUD environments must be able to handle three or four conversations at once. Individuals who are accustomed to doing one thing at a time can find MUDs very stressful. In contrast, people who enjoy fantasy and role-playing games often enjoy this type of socializing. As a form of entertainment, Beaubien (1996) identifies three characteristics that make MUDs appealing: (1) synchronous interaction with multiple players, (2) role-playing that promotes freedom and creative expression, and (3) the dynamic nature of CMC.

Both adventure-style and social MUDs have established behavioral norms. Players must follow the rules or they will be disconnected from the MUD. One role of **Wizards** (expert players) is to maintain order on the MUD. When a person is misbehaving, the Wizard will send a warning to the individual. If the behavior continues, the person's connection to the MUD is terminated. Rules include respecting other players, listening to advice and suggestions, using proper channels for messages, and sending a private message to the creator when there is a problem with the MUD.

Player Presentation

When first joining a MUD program, a player must select a name, but the name cannot belong to another character. MUD players create their own characters or virtual identities. Most players do not use their real names; instead, they create an imaginative new one. Names are typically single words, and they become the foundation for the player's virtual disguise. Names can be conventional, such as Bob, Sally, and Joe, or they can be borrowed from characters in books, television, and film. Names can also reflect ideas, emotions, and symbols. Players can be possessive about their names and often resent other people who select similar names. For example, a player named ZigZag would not like another player using the name ZagZig. After selecting a name, players will then write a description of their character (Figure 9.1). Descriptions are both simple and detailed.

Names and character descriptions are completely in control of the user. Other players only know what you tell them. Some players will create several characters. The role-playing nature of MUDs enables players to stand back and observe the action. Like an author of a novel or short story, players often view the narrative world of the MUD as an outside observer. However, they often keep a simultaneous emotional connection to the self-fashioned characters they invent.

MUD players are anonymous. There are no commands to discover the real identity of other players (Figure 9.2). Players' personal privacy is guaranteed and they can only be known by what they specifically tell others. Self-presentation is very important in MUD worlds. Players can be very creative with their personalities and try different behavior patterns. For instance, some players will be rude to others and disrupt MUD interactions.

FIGURE 9.1   MUD Character Description

Her eyes are black, TOTALLY black, no whites or irises showing at all, her teeth and tongue startling flashes of color when she opens her mouth or smiles. She looks human, except for her eyes, her color, and her long, thin fingers (and are there more than 5 fingers there?—it's hard to tell, but you think so). Her hair is snowy white and silken-soft, hanging to her shoulders and blown by any tiny breeze at all. She wears a long gown of deepest black silk, deeply 'vd between her breasts, with a white silken netting (or webbing?) keeping her decent. The gown rests on her shoulder by thin straps, and gathered at her waist is a belt of scarlet silk, showing off her generous curves. Around her neck is a white silk choker. The choker has a black, hourglass-shaped stone set in the front. (Or IS it black? Colors seem to swirl deep within the stone, drawing your eyes, tempting you to "gaze" into it's depths.)

Source: Young, 1994.

MUDs and Behavioral Norms

Every MUD develops its own set of social rules and expectations. Although social rules may not always be apparent to new MUD players, MUDs are highly organized and have methods for maintaining social order and control. Adventure-style MUDs are more structured than social ones. In social MUDs, rules are created by the players as the infinite game progresses. Social MUDs are popular for two reasons: the social aspect of the experience

---

FIGURE 9.2   Basic MUD Commands

@who logged on	Enables players to know the names of other players and their location in the MUD.
@go \<roomname\>	This command teleports players to rooms in the MUD.
@knock\<charactername\>	A command that politely asks other characters if you can join them in their room.
@Join\<charactername\>	Teleports you to the location of a specific character in the MUD.
Page\<character\>\<message\>	Sends a message to another character in the MUD.
n, s, e, w, up, down, out	Commands for moving between connected rooms. The letters stand for directions.
help\<topic\>	Provides help information on specific topics.
look	Provides players with descriptions of the room and players in the room.
look\<objectname\>	Provides a description of an object.
	Enables players to read the notes or written messages on objects.
@quit	Exits the MUD.

and the richness of their verbal descriptions. Players create their own characters, worlds, social structures, and hierarchies. Social MUD characters can be divided into three basic groups: programmers, socialites, and tinysexers. Although sex is a MUD activity, most players primarily socialize and program. Programmers are the people who design and write code for the game. Socialites like to meet and interact with new people. The most skilled programmers have the special title of Wizard and have special powers that are not available to other players. For example, Wizards can use the "@toad" command that destroys someone's character. The **toading** command is used when a player seriously violates the rules of the MUD. Players can become Wizards by proving their programming ability. The administrator or creator of the MUD is sometimes called *god*, and this person has complete control over the entire MUD world.

Adventure-style MUD players can be divided into the following four categories: achievers, explorers, socializers, and killers. Achievers accumulate large quantities of treasure and kill hordes of monsters. Explorers attempt to learn as much as possible about the virtual world and map its topology. Socializers enjoy role-playing and interacting with others. Finally, killers enjoy causing distress to others by getting a weapon and using it on other players. Bartle (1996) compares these categories to a deck of cards: "achievers are Diamonds (they're always seeking treasure); explorers are Spades (they dig around for information); socializers [sic] are Hearts (they empathize with other players); killers are Clubs (they hit people with them)" (pp. 2–3). (See Figure 9.3.)

In both adventure- and social-style MUDs, Wizards are normally treated with a certain amount of respect by other players. Many Wizards often have a virtual room they inhabit that players cannot enter without first getting permission. New players must learn how to use simple software commands to communicate with others, which is done through trial and error. MUDs can be very disorienting for new players because the conversation is chaotic when several people type in messages at the same time and text scrolls by at a fast rate. New players must learn the rules and regulations of the MUD, including being polite to other players, remembering that players are real people with actual feelings, and not wasting computing resources. Players who do not follow these rules are sometimes disconnected and locked out of the MUD.

Central to MUD interaction is the notion that people can experiment with their behavior. For example, it is not unusual for players to approach a complete stranger and start up a conversation in a way that they would never do face-to-face. Some researchers believe that MUD interaction can be beneficial for adolescent identity formation because they allow young people to experiment with their identity without suffering any real-world consequences. However, the real life anonymity of players can also make people behave in socially unacceptable ways. As social laboratories, MUDs are places where people can experiment with both identity formation and developing social structures (Figure 9.4).

Building MUD Relationships

MUD relationships often progress through four stages: introductory, information sharing, physical meeting, and decision making. In the introductory stage, players generally meet at an online social gathering. They begin exploring the idea of building a friendship. In this first stage, interaction is limited to the MUD world. During the second stage, players begin

---

FIGURE 9.3   Conversation Styles of Adventure-MUD Personality Types

---

Achievers

"I'm busy."
"Sure, I'll help you. What do I get?"
"So how do YOU kill the dragon, then?"
"Only 4211 points to go!"

Explorers

"Hmm..."
"You mean you *don't know* the shortest route from <obscure room 1> to <obscure room 2>?"
I haven't tried that one, what's it do?"
"Why is it that if you carry the uranium you get radiation sickness, and if you put it in a bag you still get it, but if you put it in a bag and drop it then wait 20 seconds and pick it up again, you don't?"

Socializers

"Hi!"
"yeah, well, I'm having trouble with my boyfriend."
"What happened? I missed it, I was talking."
"Really? Oh no! Gee, that's terrible! Are you sure? Awful, just awful!"

Killers

"Ha!"
"Coward!"
"Die!"
"Die! Die! Die!"

Source: Bartle, 1996, pp 3–4.

sharing information. The sharing of self by expressing ideas, thoughts, feelings, information, and attitudes is central to relationship formation. At this point, relationships often progress beyond the MUD world and players begin to include telephone contact or share e-mail and snail-mail addresses. At some point in this stage, players must decide if they are going to reveal their true identity to the other player.

Physical meeting takes place in the third stage of relationship building. Many people who meet on the Internet reach a stage in their relationship in which face-to-face meeting is the next logical step. At face-to-face meetings, people discover how honest the other person has been in presenting his- or herself online. In the final stage, players must decide if

---

FIGURE 9.4   Tips for Successful MUDDING

Players should appear approachable.

    1. Do not shout at other players or use unnecessary punctuation.

       Example: Where's *my* piece of pizza!!!!!!

    2. Try not to sound frantic.

       Example: What?!?!?!?!?! Is happening????????????????????

Players should present themselves as being intelligent.

    1. Use correct written English in your messages.

       Example: Hi! What's going on? not Whtz happ'n hear?

    2. Read the Frequently Asked Questions and learn about the MUD world.

Players should try to clearly communicate and prevent misunderstanding.

    1. Let others around you know what you are doing and use the pose command.

       Example: Allen smirks, he says teasingly, "that was dumb." **not** "that was dumb"

    2. Use emoticons to help convey meaning:

       Example: that was dumb :-)

    3. Familiarize yourself with the slang and acronyms used in the MUD.

Respect other players.

    1. Follow the rules and policies established by the Wizards.

    2. Do not engage in spam, typing in messages that repeat or are irrelevant to the conversation.

    3. Respect the role-playing of other characters. Players generally stay in character, unless they indicate that they are switching to their real life identity. IC means In Character and OOC is Out Of Character. Make sure other players know when you are in and out of character.

    4. Be aware of situations of sexual harassment. Female characters flirt in MUD worlds. But, if you believe that someone is threatening you in real life, it should be reported to a Wizard.

    5. Players should behave appropriately in public areas of the MUD.

    6. Players should be courteous toward other players. Behind the MUD character is a real person with feelings.

Source: Based on D. Ciskowski and C. Benedikt, 1995.

they are going to continue the relationship. Relationships can continue online without future face-to-face contact, they can continue both on- and offline, or they can end.

Role-Playing versus Real Life

MUD players are often thousands of miles apart from each other and so it is often difficult for them to meet face-to-face. However, as in other CMC genres, MUD players often become intimately involved with each other. One reason why this occurs in MUD worlds is because MUD players are often college students. They share common college and dating issues, such as course, roommate, career, and relationship problems. Players will discuss movies, music, and current real-world events. Often, MUD players can begin to feel that their online friends are their "best" friends. The following is an example of how MUD players can feel about their online friends:

```
I don't care how much people say they are, muds are not just games,
they are *real*!!!
My mud friends are my best friends, their [sic] the people who like
me most in the entire world.
Maybe the only people who do. . .
They are my family, they are not just some dumb
game . . . . .
```
(Cited in Reid, 1994, p. 26)

Some players will become romantically involved with each other in the MUD world. Reid (1994) says that MUD lovers use MUD commands to transform the virtual stage into a set designed to express and uphold their feelings for each other. MUD players will often exchange tokens and participate in virtual weddings. Players who engage in these relationships take them very seriously. MUD weddings attempt to recreate the trappings of an actual wedding. The entire community of players will be invited to the ceremony, and they will act as witnesses to the event. Upcoming nuptials are publicized in the MUD through the community's newspaper. A member of the community will marry the players by typing the wedding ceremony. Written descriptions of rings are provided along with the wedding vows. Participating in a MUD wedding helps to strengthen the imaginative reality being constructed in the MUD world. Sometimes MUD weddings can evoke real emotions and feelings. Brides have reported bursting into actual tears during the "virtual" ceremony.

Sometimes, MUD weddings are actualized in real life. Players have met in person and decided that their feelings for each other were real. However, meeting a MUD friend face-to-face is fraught with many perils. Two of the largest obstacles to transforming a MUD romance into a real one are physical attractiveness and distance. One young woman reported that when she first met her MUD husband, he did not look like what she had expected. However, she could accept his physical appearance and they became serious about each other. He transferred his job to move close to her and they had a legal wedding. This is not unusual—many people have relocated their jobs to be closer to someone they met on the Internet.

When friendships develop in MUDs, people who live a reasonable distance from each other will often arrange to meet. Players who are geographically distant will try to arrange to meet each other during vacations. Often, occasional visits and online interactions can keep a relationship going. However, in romantic circumstances, one person generally has to make the decision to physically move closer to the other or the relationship will end.

Power and Hierarchies

MUD social structures are controlled by the players. Players who can manipulate elements and control the form of the MUD environment have power. Those who cannot, do not. Power in MUDs is the power to change the virtual world. Wizards have the most power because they can access all of the computer files that create the MUD environment. They also have access to all of the game's commands; players do not have access to *all* commands in most games. The pressure to gain power is more important in adventure-style MUDs because the games are oriented toward the acquisition of greater wealth and power, which helps players survive. In contrast, players of social MUDs do not need to gain higher privileges. Social MUDs often create alternate hierarchies based on social rather than economic factors, such as appreciation and creativity, instead of competition.

In adventure-style MUDs, players only interact with the game and cannot alter the game world. They have no control over game elements and cannot create new ones. In social MUDs, players are provided with commands that enable them to create objects and areas, such as rooms or gardens. Some social MUDs make players behave in certain ways; for instance, players are not allowed to destroy objects created by other players. Additionally, MUD software only gives players a limited amount of disk space to create objects and areas. Players who want to increase their disk quota will either ask a Wizard for additional space or negotiate with other players for some of their disk space.

Characters can kill each other on some adventure MUDs. This is called **playerkilling**, and it adds more danger to the MUD world. The MUD experience feels more real when an uncontrolled element is added. However, some players do not like the practice of playerkilling, which is controlled by technical features and social practices. In some MUDs, players can decide if their character can be attacked by setting a "player killer flag" on the character. Another way to control player killing is by allowing only players on the same level or higher to attack each other. This rule tries to stop experienced players from quickly killing novice players. Novice players need to understand that being killed is often part of learning how to play the game.

Gaining status on a MUD requires players to invest a considerable amount of time learning the specific MUD program on which the game universe is based. It also requires players to get to know other players. Involvement in the game will lead to popularity in the MUD world. Players can become well liked for their willingness to help novice players, chat, and listen to others. People who feel popular in a game environment will play more often.

Gender and MUDs

CMC enables people to play with gender and identity. In social MUDs, players have a chance to escape the assumed boundaries of gender, race, and age and can create a game of interaction in which there are few rules. Initially, players are neuter and the program automatically generates messages that use the pronouns it, its, and so on.

Originally, the majority of MUD players were male and most selected a male gender. However, some male players would assume the identity of females to balance the population. Men and women can express their feminine and masculine sides in MUD worlds. Bruckman (1993) observed that both male and female MUD players enjoy being female characters. "Male players will often log on as female characters and behave suggestively, further encouraging sexual advances" (p. 3). It is generally believed that sexually promiscuous and aggressive female MUD characters are actually men in real life.

Female-presenting players have reported problems in MUDs. Many have been subjected to sexual harassment. As a result, women will assume male MUD identities to avoid being harassed. New female players will also receive special treatment and extra help learning how to navigate the MUD world. To learn a new MUD, men will sometimes describe themselves as a female character to get help understanding the game environment.

Some MUDs have invented their own words for gendered role-playing. Players can experiment both with gender roles and language usage. Rosenberg (1992) lists the following MUD genders and their respective pronouns:

neuter:	it, it, its, its, itself
male:	he, him, his, his, himself
female:	she, her, her hers, herself
either:	s/he, him/her, his/her, his/hers, (him/her)self
Spivak:	e, em, eir, eirs, eirself
splat:	*e, h*, h*, h*s, h*self
plural:	they, them, their, theirs, themselves
egotistical:	I, me, my, mine, myself
royal:	we, us, our, ours, ourselves
2nd:	you, you, your, yours, yourself (pp. 19–20)

By separating physical sexual identity from the communication process, both sexes can play with gender identity and imagine new ones. Additionally, text-oriented MUDs enable players to invent gender-neutral identities and experiment with linguistic descriptions. Reid (1991) says that online interaction provides users with an opportunity to escape from the language of culture and body and return to a more idealized form of text-based communication that she calls the "source code of mind."

MUD Problems

Many problems are associated with MUDs, including unthinking behavior, lag time in correspondence, spoofing, disconnection, and compulsive behavior. The anonymous nature of role-playing games often tempts players to take advantage of the opportunity to do unacceptable things. Abusive and harassing behavior, for instance, sexual harassment, can hurt other players. Some players forget that they are dealing with real people behind the character in the game and consequently hurt the feelings of others.

Lag time is the delay between the entering of a command and its execution by the computer system. According to Marvin (1995), "There is a waiting period between lines, as each participant types a contribution to the emerging exchange" (p. 6). Lag time is measured by the time it takes for a sent message to appear on the screen. When lag time is over five seconds, the realism of the conversation can be lost.

Spoofing is an unattributed communication, or text that appears without the name of a character. MUD worlds are built on the idea that players contribute to the game and that conversations are identified with specific characters. Simply stated, there is a source for every line of text that appears on the MUD. Placing unattributed lines of text in the MUD disrupts the flow of conversation and is considered a breach of good conduct. Many MUD communities do not provide commands for spoofing. To spoof, players must program spoofing commands or copy them from another source and add them to the game. The following is an example of spoofing:

```
Guest says, "what's spoofing?""
Plate says, "this is spoofing""
A can of Spam tromps into the room.
The can of Spam locates it's target.
The can begins making noises like it's gonna hack up a spitwad.
The can of Spam suddenly spews a stream of unwanted text at Guest,
tattoos a knockwurst on its forehead, then floors it out of the room
as fast as it can go.
Plate [to Guest]: Thats spoofing :)
Guest gasps
(Adapted from Marvin, 1995)
```

Players can have trouble logging on to MUDs. Networks are sometimes down and players will not be able to connect. Or worse, players can try to log on and discover that the MUD no longer exists. MUDs can disappear quickly because they lose their host computer, or they can suddenly move to another server without notifying all of the players in the game. This can be distressing for players who have spent a tremendous amount of time exploring the MUD world and building friendships. Unlike discussion lists and other CMC genres, MUD players do not have the e-mail addresses of other players. When a MUD disappears, the people disappear too.

Internet Dependency

A more serious MUD problem is compulsive behavior. Some players engage in excessive game playing or become "addicted" to MUDs. **Internet "addiction"** or **dependency** is a controversial topic. Some researchers do not believe that *addiction* is the proper term to use to describe excessive or compulsive online behavior. But it is a term that is frequently used to refer to people who spend a tremendous amount of time online interacting with others. A typical story about Internet dependency describes a student who enters college and discovers MUDs. The student spends almost all of his or her free time mudding, and the MUD becomes the student's social life. As a result of all the time spent online, the student does poorly in school. It is common for people to lose track of time when they are involved in CMC, and there are stories about students who have spent 24–48 hours nonstop connected to a MUD without properly eating or sleeping. This type of extreme behavior is a concern to mental health professionals.

A recent study conducted by Kubey, Lavin, and Barrows (2001) explored heavy recreational Internet usage and its impact on academic performance. Some schools have become concerned about how heavy Internet use might interfere with academic achievement, social interaction, and face-to-face cultural experiences. Only a small number of college students, approximately 5–10 percent, suffer harmful effects from extensive Internet use. These problems include cravings to go online, sleep disturbance, depression, and withdrawal symptoms from not using the Internet. Spending long, late-night hours on the Internet will also cause students to miss classes, and there was strong evidence that extensive Internet use could create academic problems for some students. However, the study also revealed that synchronous Internet applications can be an important communication outlet for lonely students because they can make new friends any time ot day or night.

MUDs and People with Disabilities

On the one hand, MUDs can disrupt the real lives of people who become compulsive about playing them; on the other, they can provide an opportunity for children and people with disabilities to engage in "normal" activities with others. For example, children hospitalized with terminal illnesses can use computers to enter a world that is not aware of their condition. Since the Internet is active twenty-four hours a day, people can always find someone to talk with, which can be reassuring for people suffering from physical ailments. More important, because their appearance is unknown, children with disabilities can use MUDs as a place to interact with others normally.

For deaf children, the computer can remove barriers to communication. Deaf children can play in MUDs just like everyone else. They can communicate with other children that do not know sign language. MUDs provide a place for people with disabilities to come together on equal terms with people without disabilities. In certain circumstances, CMC can provide communication opportunities for people with physical disabilities and enable them to socialize with others on an equal basis.

MUD Genres

A difference between MUDs and other types of CMC is the fact that MUDs create specific contexts in which users interact with each other. In adventure-style MUDs, the context is created by the game's creator. Players of social MUDs construct the virtual world together. The detailed textual descriptions of MUDs, objects, and characters provide a stronger context for communication exchanges that makes it easier for people to understand messages.

MUDs Object Oriented (MOOs)

MOOs (MUDs Object Oriented) add additional objects and features to the MUD database, including rooms, exits, "things," and notes. MOOs support an embedded programming language that allows players to describe types of behavior for the objects they create. MOO software gives each user access to a shared database of rooms, exits, and objects. Users navigate the database from "inside" the rooms and they see only the objects located in the particular room that they are in. Users move from room to room through the exits that connect them. For example, in LambdaMOO visitors enter through a coat closet and exit into a living room (Figure 9.5). MOOS can be regarded as a form of text-based virtual reality because commands are typed into a keyboard and feedback is displayed as text on the computer screen. These descriptions create an imaginary world with which players interact.

Adventure-Style MUDs

Adventure-style MUDs are organized on a strict hierarchy of privileges. The person who has the most control over the system, commonly called *god* of the MUD, has access to every computer file and can modify them. Gods can control and destroy virtual objects and protect or destroy a player's character. Players have little control over the system and must interact with the environment, kill monsters, collect treasure, solve puzzles, and collect points to gain privileges, such as receiving the rank of Wizard.

In adventure MUDs, players struggle with the internal reality of the game. On some MUDs, characters have to deal with issues, such as hunger, thirst, and sleep. Consequently, they need to protect themselves against the elements and establish safe shelter. If players do not attend to the needs of the character, the character will die. Adventure-style MUDs are not played casually; players need to devote enough time to the MUD to maintain their character. For example, a DikuMUD character can die of starvation. According to Reid (1994), "At the heart of all social structures amongst players of adventure MUDs lies the hard fact that adventure MUD universes are dangerous" (p. 38). Additionally, Bartle (1996)

FIGURE 9.5   Figure Entering Lambda MOO

LambdaMoo is a sprawling house that players enter through a coat closet. Information is available to novice players to orient them to this virtual world. Novices can read the "newspaper" to learn information and can learn basic MOO commands by activating the tutorial. They are also instructed on basic manners with the command "help manner." Novices are encouraged to read all of this information before they open the door to leave the coat closet, which exits into the living room of LambdaMoo. The following is the what players will see when they first enter LambdaMOO:

```
The Coat Closet
    The closet is a dark, craped space. It appears to be very crowded
in here; you keep bumping into what feels like coats, boots, and other
people (apparently sleeping). One useful thing that you've discovered
in your bumbling around is a metal doorknob set at waist level into
what might be a door.
    Don't forget to take a look at the newspaper. Types 'news' to see
it.
    Type '@tutorial' for an introduction to basic MOOing. Please read
and understand 'help manners' before leaving The Coat Closet.
```

---

points out there are four reasons why people enjoy playing in adventure MUDs: (1) achieving game goals, (2) exploring the virtual worlds, (3) socializing with other people, and (4) causing distress to other players.

Social MUDs

Players in social MUDs are encouraged to interact with other players and extend the social environment. Social MUDs allow players to add items and rooms to the game's database. Novice players can even build simple objects. The rank of Wizard does not depend on gaining points; instead, it is a title given at the discretion of the MUD administrator. Several social MUDs are based on the design of a large house or mansion. Some social MUDs are also used as virtual support centers. For instance, Reid (1994) studied JennyMUSH, a MUD for survivors of sexual assault. Other researchers have experimented with online therapy in MUD environments.

Pavel Curtis (1997), the founder of LambdaMOO, identifies three factors that distinguish social MUDs from adventure-style games:

- A MUD is not goal-oriented; it has no beginning or end, no "score," and no notion of "winning" or "success." In short, even though users of MUDs are commonly called *players*, a MUD isn't really a game at all.
- A MUD is extensible from within; a user can add new objects to the database such as rooms, exits, "things," and notes. Certain MUDs, including the one I run, even support an embedded programming language in which a user can describe whole new kinds of behavior for the objects they create.
- A MUD generally has more than one user connected at a time. All of the connected users are browsing and manipulating the same database and can encounter the new objects created by others. The multiple users on a MUD can communicate with each other in real time (p. 144).

Educational or Academic MUDs

The first academic MUD was set up by Amy Bruckman when she was a student at the Massachusetts Institute of Technology (MIT). Called MediaMOO, it was created as a virtual meeting place for students and academics interested in exploring media and communication. Other academic MUDs followed, including PMCMOO for literary and cultural theorists and BioMOO for biologists. Academic MUDs enable scholars and students from around the world to communicate with each other at the same time. Educators use MUD software to hold online meetings.

Web-Based Games

A growing number of action games available on CD-ROM have been adapted for the Internet. Some CD games set up Internet sites that can be accessed through Internet service providers. Connections to the Web site are included on the CD-ROM. Internet games can also be found through online gaming services, such as the Total Entertainment Network, most of which charge an hourly rate. The services match players to participate in multi-player games. Free games, such as blackjack, bridge, poker, backgammon, checkers, and bingo, are also available at sites such as Yahoo!.games or Microsoft's MSN Gaming Zone. Classic games *Space Invaders, PacMan,* and *Donkey Kong*, can be downloaded from the Web. Fantasy sports games are available through the ESPN site (games.espn.go.com), which allows players to compete in various events. Free games help to generate traffic to Web sites, but it is the pay-for-play games that are attracting the gaming industry. Paying for online game entertainment is growing on the Web. Instead of playing against a computer, players compete against each other. Players are attracted to the idea that they can play anytime and find a worthy opponent. Multiplayer games enable players to compete with people from around the world, and these game sites are an emerging area of Web-based interaction.

Multiplayer Games and Game Worlds

The first network interactive computer game with graphics was *Habitat*, which started in the mid-1980s in the United States. It was later introduced in Japan, where it has been con-tinuously operating. Newer games include *Half-Life* (www.sierrastudios.com), a game that combines action and storytelling. Some multiplayer games, such as *Ultima Online*, have built-in language translation software to enable players to carry on conversations with people who speak different languages. In addition to action-oriented games, there are also multiplayer game worlds that are graphical versions of MUD environments, such as the *Palace*.

Schroeder (1997) studied social interaction in two multiplayer game worlds called *Al-phaworld* and *Cybergate*. In these systems, players are represented by avatars. In *Alpha-world*, players select a human body; avatars in *Cybergate* are cartoonlike imaginary creatures. Players talk to each other as they move around a series of interconnected rooms. Both of these systems borrow features from text-based MUDs and computer games. The behavior patterns of players are similar to other types of CMC genres. For instance, play-ers will be verbally rude and aggressive toward each other. Players also establish a rapport by asking where people are from and what they do in the real world. But in contrast to text-based CMC, multiplayer game worlds enable players to have face-to-face interaction be-tween avatars.

Regular game players will entertain each other by inviting people to go places to-gether or to have a party. They will also develop a distinctive online personality. In con-trast, new players act like tourists because they engage in superficial conversations and stay on the periphery of the action. Social bonds develop between regular players, and some companies have exploited this by adding a fee. Players who want to make full use of the world must pay a fee; otherwise, they must remain a tourist, which is represented by a "stan-dard-issue" avatar. The sociological impact of adding a fee creates a two-tier structure of players, regular paid subscribers and visiting tourists. Moreover, players who have made friends in the world can be locked out if they do not pay the fee. Although online gaming worlds are created for entertainment, people who spend time in these online environments do develop relationships. Relationships can be disrupted when the developers of a game world suddenly change the rules.

Internet Reality Games

Majestic, an Internet reality game, blurs the boundaries between reality and fantasy. It uses a variety of different communication devices to surprise and intrigue players. Electronic Arts, the games's developer, charges a subscription rate of $15 per month. The game is played in real time and usually takes two weeks to complete. Snider (2001) describes the game as follows:

> It's a little past midnight when the phone rings, jarring your attention away from the television. Your wife is asleep and the dog lifts its head as you rush to pick up the phone. A voice, cold and menacing, warns you to stop your incessant digging into matters that don't concern you, and—chilling you to the bone—threatens your wife by name. What's happening? Is this for real? Possibly a hoax perpetrated by some callous friend? Not this time: it's the recorded voice of an actor deployed by an online computer game called *Majestic* (p. 46).

Players are contacted by phone, fax, e-mail, and instant messenger programs that provide hints and clues. They receive instructions to visit Web sites and locate clues that uncover secret government and UFO conspiracies. *Majestic's* name comes from an ultrasecret organization that allegedly was formed to cover up UFO landings. To make the game realistic, Electronic Arts has registered hundreds of fax and phone numbers and created dummy corporations with Web sites. As players interact with the game it steadily picks up personal information, which is incorporated into the game and creates a personalized experience. Part of the fun of the game is trying to determine what is real and what is not. Blurring the distinctions between playing on- and offline adds excitement to the game experience.

Gaming and Gambling on the Web

A controversial online gaming topic is Internet gambling. It has been reported that over 700 worldwide Internet casinos are in operation. People living in the United States can sit at home and virtually gamble around the world. Sites are located in Australia, the Caribbean, and the United Kingdom. Most online gambling sites accept credit cards or let people electronically wire cash to set up an account. In addition to traditional casino games, some sites have added live video images of a croupier running a roulette wheel and chat features to simulate an actual casino experience.

An argument against Internet gambling is the fact that it is not regulated and no law enforcement agency monitors it. Other concerns include scams that cause people to lose money and uncertainty about whether laws exist to stop scam artists. Some sites, for example, have not paid customers their winnings. Operators who break state laws are overseas and out of reach of U.S. law enforcement agencies, and the Federal Communications Commission cannot protect people against international wire fraud. Credit card companies, including American Express and Discover Card, have adopted policies that bar the use of their credit cards with companies that run online gambling operations. An association called the Interactive Gaming Council has been established to help build consumer confidence in Internet gambling sites.

USA Today (June, 7, 2000) has reported that colleges are now concerned about students becoming the targets of Internet sports betting sites. The Internet brings a virtual bookie into the classroom and dorm. For instance, the `ncaatournament.com` Web site is a sports gambling site that has no affiliation with the National Collegiate Athletic Association. There have been reports of college students who have spent their tuition money at Internet gambling sites. Fears about compulsive student gambling behavior are growing as Internet gambling sites distribute flyers on campuses and take out advertisements in campus newspapers. A bill has been proposed by the U.S. Senate to stop wagering on amateur sports and to require universities to monitor student Internet use of illegal gambling transactions. The bill, called the *Amateur Sports Integrity Act*, has raised controversy both on and off campuses around the country.

As in other online games, compulsive behavior is a social problem associated with Internet gambling. People will sit for hours at their home computers gambling, where they can lose as much money as if they went to Las Vegas or Atlantic City. There have been reports of people losing $25,000 and $30,000 dollars online. Internet gambling can be intoxicating. Its easy to click the mouse button and forget that you are playing for real money until the credit card bill arrives. From this point of view, monitoring Internet gambling on campuses could help to protect students. However, there are concerns that this type of monitoring would invade a student's personal privacy. As a result, laws that require computer monitoring are controversial.

Brenda Laurel's Theatre Model

Interface and game designer, Brenda Laurel (1993) has developed a theatrical model for understanding how people interact with computer games and software programs. She states that the theatre resembles interface design because both deal with the representation of action. A program can be thought of as giving a performance for its user. The screen is a stage occupied by actors who portray characters performing actions in the context of a scene. The scenery and the objects on the stage support the actions taking place. "In the theatrical view of human–computer activity, the stage is a virtual world: It is populated by agents, both human and computer-generated, and other elements of the representational context (windows, teacups, desktops, or what-have-you)" (p. 17). The hardware and software create the technical backstage magic that supports the performance.

Laurel introduces the metaphor of theatre to models of interface design and CMC. She identifies two reasons why theater is a good way to think about HCI and CMC. First, the objectives of theater and computer interfaces are similar. Each wants to represent actions with multiple actors or software agents. "Second, theatre suggests the basis for a model of human-computer activity that is familiar, comprehensible, and evocative" (p. 21). (See Figure 9.6.)

The fantasy and make-believe aspects of MUDs and other CMC contexts, can be viewed as performances. Online participants develop performance skills to gain attention and create online personas. As in chat, people playing in MUDs are playing a game of "let's

FIGURE 9.6 Brenda Laurel's Theatre Model. Brenda Laurel proposes an alternate view about human-computer interaction, which is based on a theater metaphor. In her approach, everything on the screen (stage) is a representation. Triangles depict humans, software agents, or computer-generated types. The remaining shapes are objects represented in the virtual world. All representations are placed within an oval to suggest the illumination of a spotlight on a stage.

Laurel, COMPUTERS AS THEATRE (paperback), figure 1.8 (pg. 18). ©1991 Addison-Wesley Publishing Company Inc. Reprinted by permission of Pearson Education, Inc.

pretend." MUD players will create characters and perform for each other through the skillful development of characters, use of language, object descriptions, and programming commands.

The dynamic and improvisational nature of MUDs supports a drama metaphor. MUD players can be viewed as actors in an interactive play, where the MUD provides a stage, but not a script. Besides writing their own lines, players must also create the scenery and set the stage for action to occur. All objects, characters, places, and things are given descriptions, which can be simple or complex, by the players. Character and object descriptions can be viewed by other players by using the "look" command. MUD interaction is not created for outside audiences, but is designed for MUD participants. Each player is involved with the evolving drama through MUD interactions.

Summary

Noncommercial games, such as MUDs, existed on the Internet long before the introduction of the Web. MUDs are role-playing games that are primarily adventure-style or social. Players create characters and interact with each other in synchronous time. A key attraction of MUDs is the fact that players are interacting with real people, not a computer program. Playing in a MUD can be compared to an interactive theater experience in which the actors both design the set and write their lines. MUDs have their own rules of social behavior that must be followed. Players who do not follow the rules can lose their connection or, worse, their character could be toaded or eliminated from the MUD.

Since the Web, gaming sites and pay-for-play game sites have developed. These entertainment sites enable players to compete against other people from around the world. In addition to games sites, Internet gambling sites have been established. These globally located casinos do not follow any state or national laws, which has raised concerns about the legality of Internet gambling and how to regulate it. A social concern about online games and gambling is compulsive or addictive behavior. People can spend so much time on the Internet that they neglect their real-world activities.

Interacting with characters and objects on the computer screen can be described as a performance. Interface and game designer Brenda Laurel has proposed a theatrical metaphor for understanding how users interact with software programs. The screen is a stage on which actions occur. The software and hardware provide the backstage technical magic that gives context to the actions, and players collaborate with the program to create a theatrical experience.

TERMS

Internet "addiction" or **dependency** are terms used to describe excessive or compulsive online behavior. They particularly describe people who spend a tremendous amount of time playing games and interacting with other people through CMC.

Lag time is the delay between when a command is entered and when it is executed by the computer system.

Playerkilling in adventure-style MUDs allows players to kill the character of other players.

Spoofing is an unattributed communication or text that appears without the name of a character.

Toading is destroying a MUD player's character. Wizards have the power to toad players, which is generally done only to players who have violated the rules of the MUD.

Wizards are expert players who have extra privileges and often help run the MUD world.

WEB SITES

Clandestine (An Adventure-style MUD): clandestine.mudnet.net/main.html
Classic Computer Games: http://www.classicgaming.com/
http://arcadeathome.com/
Journal of Virtual Environments (formerly Journal of MUD Research): www.brandeis.edu/pubs/jove/
MUDs:
www.circlemud.org
www.fierymud.org
www.rom.org
MUD Resource Collection:
www.godlike.com/muds/
www.mudzine.com

EXERCISES

1. Select a name and create a character description for a character playing in a social MUD and one for a character playing in an adventure MUD. How are these characters similar or different?

2. Break into small groups. Each group should develop its own idea for a MUD game. You will first need to decide if the MUD is going to be social- or adventure-style.

3. Develop your own set of behavioral rules for a MUD. What will happen to players who break the rules? Will they be toaded? Who will enforce the rules?

4. Write a description for the following MUD genders: either, Spivak, splat, plural, egotistical, royal, and 2nd. Use the appropriate pronouns in your description.

5. Conduct a survey in your class to see how many students are playing or downloading games from the Internet. What type of games are being played?

6. Debate the pros and cons of Internet gambling.

BIBLIOGRAPHY

Bartle, R. (1996). Hearts, clubs, diamonds, spades: Players who suit MUDs. *Journal of MUD Research, 1* (1) [Online]. Available: http://www.mud.co.uk/richard/hcds.htm (Oct. 12, 2000).

Beaubien, M. P. (1996). Playing at community: Multi-user dungeons and social interaction in cyberspace. In L. Strate, R. Jacobson, & S. Gibson (Eds.), *Communication and cyberspace* (pp. 179–187). Cresskill, NJ: Hampton Press.

Bennahum, D. (1994, May/June). Fly me to the MOO: Adventures in textual reality. *Lingua Franca*, pp.1, 22–36.

Bruckman, A. S. (1993). Gender swapping on the internet. *Proceedings from INET '93* [Online]. Available: ftp://ftp.cc.gatech.edu/pub/people/asb/papers/gender-swapping.txt (Oct. 11, 2001).

Ciskowski, D., & Benedikt, C. (1995). *Don't be a TinyJerk!* Available: http://www.cwrl.utexas.edu/~claire/texts/netiquette.html

Curtis, P. (1997). Mudding: Social phenomena in text-based virtual realities. In P. E. Agre & D. Schuler (Eds.), *Reinventing technology, rediscovering community* (pp.143–164). Greenwich, CT: Ablex Publishing Corp.

Dibbell, J. (1998). *My tiny life*. New York: Henry Holt and Company, Inc.

Jenkins, C. (2000, June 7). *Net gambling a concern for colleges* [Online], 4pp. Available: http://www.cnn.com (July 2, 2001).

Keegan, M. (1997). A classification of MUDs. *Journal of MUD Research, 2*, (2), 9 pp. [Online] Available: http://journal.tinymush.org/~journal/V2N2/Keegan.html (October 15, 1998).

Kirschner, S. K. (2000, December). Click cliques: Challenges posed by online games generate an added bonus: buddies. *Popular Science, 257* (6), 90.

Kubey, R. W., Lavin, M. J. & Barrows, J. R. (2001, June). Internet use and collegiate academic performance decrements: Early findings. *Journal of Communication, 51*, (2), pp. 366–382.

Laurel, B. (1993). *Computers and theatre*. Reading, MA: Addison-Wesley Publishing Company.

Levy, S. (1984). *Hackers*. New York: Doubleday.

Marvin, L. (1995). Spoof, spam, lurk and lag: The aesthetics of text-based virtual realities. *Journal of Computer Mediated Communication, 1*, (2), [Online], 13 pp. Available: http://www.ascusc.org/jcmc (October 10, 2001)

Perine, K. (2001, May 17). *New bill would force schools to spy on students* [Online], 3pp. Available: http://www.cnn.com (July 2, 2001).

Pew Internet and American Life Project (2001). *Teenage life online: The rise of the instant-message generation and the Internet's impact on friendships and family relationships* [Online], 46 pp. Available: http://www.pewinternet.org. (August 24, 2001).

Reid, E. M. (1991). *Electropolis: Communication and community on Internet relay chat* [Online], 40 pp. Available: http://www.ee.mu.oz.au/papers/emr/electropolis.html (May 15, 1997).

Reid, E. (1994). Cultural formations in text-based virtual realities [Online] 84 pp. Available: http://www.lud.luth.se/mud/aber/articles/cult-form.thesis.html (October 11, 2001).

Rosenberg, M. S. (1992). *Virtual reality: Reflections of life, dreams, and technology* [Online] Available: http://lucien.berkeley.edu/MOO/ethnography.txt (April 15, 1999).

Schroeder, R. (1997). Networked worlds: Social aspects of multi-user virtual reality technology. *Sociological Research Online, 2* (4), [Online], 15 pp. Available: http://www.socresonline.org.uk/socresonline/2/4/5.html. (July 2, 2001)

Shah, R., & Romine, J. (1995). *Playing MUDs on the Internet.* New York: John Wiley & Sons, Inc.

Snider, M. (2001, May 14). Playing with reality: A pioneering online game gets right into user's lives. *Maclean's, 114* (20), 49.

Suchman, L. A. (1987). *Plans and situated actions: The problem of human-machine communication.* Cambridge, UK: Cambridge University Press.

Turkle, S. (1995). *Life on the screen: Identity in the age of the Internet.* New York: Simon & Schuster.

Walther, J., & Tidwell, L. (1996). When is mediated communication not interpersonal? In K. M. Galvin & P. Cooper (Eds.), *Making connections: Readings in relational communication* (pp. 300–307). Los Angeles: Roxbury Publishing Company.

Winograd, T., & Flores, F. (1987). *Understanding computers and cognition.* Reading, MA: Addison-Wesley Publishing Company.

Young, J. R. (1994). Textuality in cyberspace: MUDs and written experience, 22 pp. [Online]. Available: http://eserver.org/cyber/young2.txt (July 27, 1998).

10 Educational Contexts

Chapter Overview

Over the past twenty years, computers have been introduced into education in many ways, including computers in classrooms, distance education, the electronic distribution of course materials, and the Web as a research tool. Although CMC is being integrated into teaching and learning, the educational use of computers raises various issues. These include the changing roles of teachers and students, sloppy research, poor writing, and plagiarism.

E-mail provides a new method for students and teachers to correspond with each other. Discussion lists can be used to support in-class conversations or provide distance education. Students from around the world can come together to talk about academic topics. As an information space, the Web is a resource tool that can supplement course materials and assignments. It can also be used as a virtual classroom to bring together students both locally and globally. This chapter discusses the following subjects:

- The use of informatics in educational settings;
- Education and the Web
- Digital and information literacy
- CMC teaching and learning strategies
- Educational CMC genres
- CMC issues in education, including Web cheating and changing teacher/student roles
- Face-to-face versus computer-mediated classroom discussion

Educational CMC can be placed into three large categories: conferencing, informatics, and computer-assisted instruction. Conferencing (connecting people through CMC) and informatics (using computers as an information manager) are topics introduced in Chapter 1.

Computer-assisted instruction (CAI) is using the computer as a tutor or drill instructor. CAI helps students practice subjects such as writing and math. As a classroom tool, CAI administers tests to students, and the computer can be programmed to keep track of a student's performance. When students mark the wrong answer, the computer can keep score or help students interactively review the material.

In education, the computer is most often used to locate and manage information. For instance, the widespread growth of the Web has transformed the Internet into an educational informatics system. In addition to providing educational information and resources, some Web interfaces are designed to sustain class discussion and conferences. When used as a conferencing system, CMC can support teacher–student interactions and student–student interactions. Educators use both asynchronous and synchronous CMC genres. Asynchronous e-mail supports formal coursework and informal exchanges between teachers and students. Educational MUDs support synchronous group communication across distances.

Using Computers in Educational Contexts

When computers were first being introduced into schools, they were described as a *tutor, tool*, or *tutee*. As a tutor, computers are programmed to be "experts" in a particular subject. Subject material is presented to the student, the student responds, and the computer determines what material to present next. This is a preprogrammed interactive system that shows course material based on how the student interacts with the program. For example, a correct answer will move the program on to the next section and incorrect answers will cause the program to review the subject again. When computers are utilized as tools, students use them to write term papers, calculate math and science assignments, design art projects, locate information on the Web, and create desktop video projects. Used as a tool, computers support traditional classroom work.

In the tutee approach, students learn programming. Computers are basically "dumb" machines that have to be programmed. By writing a program to instruct a computer to perform a specific task, students are learning about concepts and how computers work. For example, the early educational program called *Logo* used the tutee approach to teach math. By programming the computer to perform tasks, such as drawing a square, students learned about mathematical principles.

As computers have become more important in the workplace, pressure has been placed on schools to integrate computers into the curriculum. The development of user-friendly graphical interfaces and the Web has made computers more accessible to students. As a result, many computer-literacy programs abandoned the idea of teaching programming. Instead, students are taught how to operate basic programs, such as word processing, spreadsheet, and Web browser software.

At present, CMC is used in education for a variety of purposes, including sharing information, delivering distance education, developing educational communities, turning in assignments, and interpersonal communication. CMC provides electronic spaces for students enrolled in classes to discuss assignments and work together. It also supports one-to-one communication between students and students and teachers and students.

The Web and College Courses

As discussed in Chapter 4, information on the Web comes from a wide range of sources. In educational contexts, the Web is used to distribute individual course materials, such as outlines, class projects, and reading assignments. A number of Web-based programs also support online class discussion. Additionally, services have developed to post class notes on the Web. Students at major universities are paid a fee to attend classes and make their notes available through the Internet. This is a controversial practice because some educators argue that it encourages students to skip classes. Furthermore, students are recruited for this service through fraternities, and the service is not officially associated with any university. The quality of the notes is thus unclear.

The Web and Writing

Some instructors place student papers on the Web for other class members to read. This collaborative sharing of assignments can help students further develop their writing skills. However, students from other colleges can find these class assignments and do not realize that the papers were written by students, not professionals. For instance, a film professor reported that after posting his student's papers on the Web, his students received e-mail messages from other students who mistakenly thought the papers were written by film experts. Because the Web is a public space, openly published student papers can be accessed by people outside the class.

When students use the Web as a research tool, professors have observed that the quality of written work often declines. Students who rely only on the Web for project information can encounter the following problems: timeliness of sources, meaningless graphics, unattributed quotes, and a hunt-and-peck style of writing. First, the material found on the Web is often limited: bibliography material can be out-of-date or, worse, students will cite a limited number of articles that appear on a single Web site without checking other sites or the library. This can lead to a paper that presents one opinion instead of many. Second, students will insert pictures and graphs into their papers to make them "look" good. On a closer examination, the images will have little to do with the topic of the paper. Moreover, images are often cut and pasted from commercial Web sites, which violates copyright law. Third, quotes are unattributed, and it is difficult to tell who made the statement. A common problem with student writing is failure to make a clear distinction between the student's opinion and the opinions of others. This occurs when citations are not properly credited to authors. Web information can easily be copied without making a note of the citation or source, and it is easy to find pages and pages of corporate sales pitches and commentary on the Web. The credibility of these sources is often suspect. In-depth commentaries, critical reviews, and careful analysis are more often found in printed books. Finally, students will cut and paste sections of articles together and rely on the spelling checker without carefully thinking about the paper or reading it to check for spelling mistakes. There are many grammatical and spelling errors that software programs do not find, for instance, the difference between "their" and "there" or "form" and "from." Rothenberg (1997) says:

> What the Web adds to the shortcuts made possible by word processing is to make research look too easy. You toss a query to the machine, wait a few minutes, and suddenly a lot of possible sources of information appear on your screen. Instead of books that you have to check out of the library, read carefully, understand, synthesize, and then tactfully excerpt, these sources are quips, blips, pictures, and short summaries that may be downloaded magically to the dorm-room computer screen. Fabulous! How simple! The only problem is that a paper consisting of summaries of summaries is bound to be fragmented and superficial, and to demonstrate more of a random montage than an ability to sustain an argument through 10 to 15 double-spaced pages (p. A44).

Thus, a number of issues have arisen about the Web as an educational informatics tool. The Web is not an edited encyclopedia. It is an open information space that allows anyone and everyone to distribute messages. In scholarly work, students need to be *more aware* of whom and what they are referencing because Web references are often cursory descriptions rather than a in-depth analyses . An exception is peer-reviewed scholarly journals, which students often have difficulty finding.

The Web and Academic Publishing

Many academic journals are now available on the Web. Like the editors of printed journals, the editors of electronic journals have control over the material being published. Academic electronic journals are edited and go through a review process to make sure the information is credible. A benefit of electronic journals is their low cost of distribution, individual articles instead of the entire journal can be sent to people who are interested in reading them. Additionally, electronic journals enable academics to distribute articles in a timely fashion. Instead of the months or years it takes for articles to appear in print, they can be published quickly on the Web.

Drafts of articles can also be placed on the Web for feedback and review. Sharing articles in progress helps to build online scholarly communities. CMC enables scholars from around the world to communicate with each other through the exchange of research papers. Often, electronic journals become a collaborative effort shared by geographically distributed scholars because the Internet makes it easier for experts to collaborate. Many journal articles are coauthored through the Internet by exchanging e-mail messages and documents. After the papers are written, reviewed, and published on the Web, they become accessible to scholars and students.

Distance Education

Distance education is another way in which computer networks are influencing education. Distance education programs use both asynchronous and synchronous forms of CMC. For instance, MUDs are used to teach college extension courses. These classes take place at a "virtual campus," where students meet at the same time to discuss course material. The first CMC distance education courses taught subjects like math, writing, and classical literature. Due to current copyright laws, online courses often use materials that are in the public domain. Links are established to public domain texts, such as classical literature, that can be used in coursework. Today, a wide variety of original new courses are being developed for online distance education.

Students who participate in distance education programs need to be highly motivated and self-disciplined because the feedback and excitement of face-to-face interaction are missing. In a study conducted by Haythornthwaite (2001), it was discovered that face-to-face interaction can have a positive impact on distance education students. Additionally, distance education uses CMC genres in different ways. Web-based discussion lists are used for classwide communication, Internet relay chat is used for general communication across the class, and e-mail is primarily used to support communication between teams working together on projects.

Distance education programs oriented toward developing telecommunication skills and cross-cultural interpersonal communication skills are areas that fit well with CMC. However, distance learning can be more time-consuming for both teachers and students. Instructors need to frequently check their e-mail to read and respond to student messages. Students must spend time reading e-mail and participating in online discussions, which can take more time than attending a three-hour-per-week class.

Informatics and Education

The introduction of computers into schools has been optimistically viewed as a way to democratize education in America in that all students will have access to the same database of information. Knowledge will be freely distributed throughout the population, and educational learning communities will form as people of like minds join together through CMC. People can pursue self-directed lifelong learning through Internet resources.

The Internet and Access to Information

Providing access to information is an argument used to connect schools to the Internet. However, access to information is only one small aspect of education. According to Shenk (1997): "Schools are stringent filters, not expansive windows onto the world" (p. 74). Teachers and textbooks edit the vast majority of the world's information, which only allows very small bits of information into the classroom. "When organized well and cogently presented, these parcels of data are metamorphosized into building blocks of knowledge in the brains of students" (p. 75). In contrast, Web information is not well organized. The Web has developed into a system that supports the delivery of enormous amounts of both edited and unedited information. Providing students with increased volumes of data through the Web does not necessarily better educate them, for information needs to be synthesized and critically evaluated.

Moreover, Web information can be limited in perspective and disconnected from meaningful contexts. Disconnected from a context, information has no usefulness. Without a context, we can no longer decide what is relevant and irrelevant to our lives. Context is important for understanding to occur. According to Lakoff and Boal (1995), students need to understand concepts, the historical context of ideas, and the conceptual systems involved. "The same thing is true of 'information' in the computer. In order for anybody to understand 'information,' they have to put an interpretation on what comes out of the machine" (p. 118). Access to information is only one small component of the educational process. Students must also be able to understand ideas and connect them in meaningful ways.

Digital and Information Literacy

Computers add additional skills to the educational process. Students need to know how to operate a computer, access information, use word processing software, and sometimes program Web pages. In today's information society, becoming literate is a complex process.

For example, students working on Web sites need to learn visual communication skills and how to use HTML. Learning additional computer-related skills can be very time-consuming, and many of these skills have not been fully integrated into the curriculum. Moreover, the relationship between technology and literacy has not been carefully examined. According to Harmon (1997), a key issue "is not simply whether schools should be wired but how an educational system built for an industrial age must change to teach the skills required for the age of information" (p. D15).

For example, computers add visual communication to the reading process. Web pages present information in the form of verbal text and nonverbal images. They inevitably include a far higher percentage of nonverbal information than written texts do because Web pages are hypertexts. Hypertexts use icons that are not found in printed texts. These nonverbal devices, such as arrows, buttons, and scrolling bars, are used as navigation tools to guide people through the data space. Levinson (1997) says:

> "Graphics" on computer screens cover a lot of territory. Icons, or stylized little pictures, that help people use their computers—an image-driven command system, in effect, for online and off-line use, usually employed in conjunction with point-and-click, Windows systems— are one kind of graphic. In addition to such hieroglyphics-as-operating-systems, images play an increasing role as content, especially on the Web (p. 165).

Accessing and understanding information on the Web, requires **digital literacy** skills. In his book *Digital Literacy*, Paul Gilster (1997) says that "digital literacy is about mastering ideas, not keystrokes" (p. 15). He defines digital literacy as "the ability to understand and use information in multiple formats from a wide range of sources when it is presented via computers" (p. 33). The multiple formats (text, graphics, sound, video clips) introduced by the Web suggest that literacy now needs to be approached from a perspective of multiple literacies. Since the introduction of television, a number of technology-related literacies have been described. For example, media literacy educator Kathleen Tyner (1998) states, "These multiple literacies have been called *technology literacy, information literacy, visual literacy, media literacy*, and so on" (original emphasis, p. 60). To date, these terms are used in a variety of ways to emphasize the need to develop new skills for using technology and accessing information from the Internet. For example, librarians argue that students need to develop **information literacy** skills. A general definition of information literacy is the ability to become an effective information consumer. It involves learning how to use computer tools and research tools and to develop critical thinking skills (Figure 10.1). Simply stated, the unedited information presented on the Web forces students to become editors.

Many Web pages have been created to help students develop critical thinking skills for evaluating Web-published information (Kirk, 1996; Schrock, 1995–1998; Smith, 1998). These skills involve learning the critical skills necessary to evaluate differing types of content, understanding the use of online graphics, learning to separate form from content, checking the source of information, learning how links can manipulate readers, and learning to make decisions about information choices without depending on a search engine. (See the section on evaluating Web sites in Chapter 4 for a list of Web evaluation criteria.) In terms of visual communication, students need to learn how to distinguish bogus Web sites from real ones, understand the ways in which graphics can distract the reader, and dis-

---

FIGURE 10.1 Information Literacy Curriculum

Educational consultants Shapiro and Hughes (1996) have proposed information literacy as a topic that needs to be integrated into an entire liberal arts curriculum. In addition to computer tools and how to access information, their curriculum adds a critical component. They describe the following seven different aspects of information literacy:

1. **Tool Literacy** is the ability to use current information technology, including software, hardware, and multimedia programs. Tool literacy also includes a basic understanding of computer and network applications, basic programming, data structures, and related terminology. Tool literacy is similar to descriptions of computer literacy.

2. **Resource Literacy** is understanding the form, format, location, and access methods used by information resources. This includes learning the concepts of classification and organization of information and how to use search engines.

3. **Social-Structural Literacy** involves knowing how information is socially positioned and produced and understanding how information relates to universities, research communities, corporations, government agencies, and educational communities.

4. **Research Literacy** is the ability to understand and use information technology tools that are relevant to research and scholarship, for instance, quantitative and qualitative analysis and simulation software programs.

5. **Publishing Literacy** is learning how to format and publish research electronically in both a textual and multimedia format. This would include learning Web publication skills and knowing how to distribute a paper through e-mail and discussion groups.

6. **Emerging Technology Literacy** is developing an ability to understand, evaluate, and make use of continually changing information technologies. It involves knowing when to update software and understanding the human and social context of technology.

7. **Critical Literacy** is the ability to critically evaluate information. This includes developing a philosophical understanding of social issues surrounding technology use, and the political and cultural impact of new technology.

Source: Adapted from Shapiro & Hughes, 1996.

tinguish the differences between educational, corporate, promotional, and media sponsored sites (see the rhetorical analysis of Web sites in Chapter 5).

Information is increasingly being presented in a visual format. Images can be more difficult to interpret than words. Moreover, images have a stronger emotional appeal and can mislead the reader. For instance, it is easy to disguise bogus information with a professional-looking Web design. Students will believe that the information is credible because the site "looks" legitimate. Bringing the Web into the classroom means that educators must introduce a variety of new literacy and critical thinking skills into the educational process to help students evaluate the credibility of information available through the Web.

Developing CMC Skills

CMC can provide several benefits that face-to-face teaching cannot because of its effectiveness and efficiency. After teaching classes through CMC, Santoro and Phillips (1993) discovered that CMC increased "both the quality of student–teacher interaction and the ability of teachers to monitor student progress" (p. 312). When CMC is used properly, students and teachers alike report that the quality of course-related communication can improve.

A study conducted by Kelly, Duran, and Zolten (2001) investigated whether reticent and nonreticent college students used e-mail differently to communicate with faculty. Reticent people avoid communication because they do not want to appear foolish; for instance, reticent students will not participate in class discussions. The study revealed that both reticent and nonreticent students used e-mail the same way to communicate with professors. However, the reticent students preferred e-mail as a method of communication with faculty.

To effectively use CMC, students must become familiar with the technology and comfortable with online interaction. The first step is to learn how to use the computer equipment, and the second is to become a good online communicator. One way to approach developing effective CMC skills is through "rhetoric." As discussed in earlier chapters, rhetoric is the art of effective communication through the sending and receiving of understandable messages. The responsibility of effective CMC starts with the sender of a message. Writers should begin by assuming that no one is required to read what they write and should develop a style that will capture and hold the attention of their audience. Online messages are exchanged for many reasons, including argument, information sharing, and asking or answering questions. Writers should be aware of the purpose of their message. They also need to consider the audience reading the message. Name dropping, using obscure language or terms, techno-jargon, and excessively long contributions can alienate readers. CMC users have complete control over which messages they will read and which they will delete. With the punch of a button, messages are easily discarded.

Internet writers develop a reputation based on their use of language. Bad spelling, improper grammar, excessive punctuation, and illiterate prose make a poor impression. If you observe online discussions, you will see that some writers are responded to and others are ignored. By observing which messages receive responses and the ones that do not, you can learn the basic rhetorical standards for online interaction. For instance, people who talk about themselves and their ideas without paying attention to other online participants are often ignored. In contrast, people who acknowledge the ideas of others, ask questions, and provide useful information will receive positive responses from other group members.

CMC Teaching and Learning Strategies

Teachers using CMC in their courses need to develop strategies to encourage participation. CMC teaching and learning strategies include drawing attention to different perspectives, debates, asking if students are having problems, suggesting brainstorming sessions, online critiques, and using student facilitators. In online discussions, teachers and students should draw attention to opposing points of view, different directions, and conflicting opinions. This is done by reading a series of messages and creating a summary message that identifies different students with specific views on the topic. Identifying different points of view will set the stage for an online debate. Periodically the teacher should ask if anyone is having problems. Rather than ask the question generally, it is best to ask about specific topics relating to the online discussion, for example, whether anyone is having a problem understanding the terms used in the discussion or certain ideas.

Brainstorming sessions can motivate conversation. Brainstorming stresses the concept of generating ideas and is designed not to be critical of people's comments. Opening a discussion to far-out topics or ideas can encourage student participation and lead to new discussion topics. Online discussion could also be developed from students reading an article and posting their review online. Other students can then respond to the reviewer. Each student should be restricted to one or two ideas to allow all students to participate and prevent the critique from becoming repetitive. Conversation can also be encouraged by rotating different students in the role of "facilitator for the week." The student facilitator is responsible for helping to direct the discussion and for posting summaries that encourage student response.

All these strategies can be used in any type of online discussion group, including ones designed for distance education. Two additional teaching strategies for distance education include guest online lecturers and synchronous sessions. Guest lecturers can be invited to present an online paper and respond to student questions. Students can be encouraged to ask questions and engage in discussion with the guest. Baily and Cotler (1994) state, "Bringing in giants in a discipline into direct electronic contact with students has been seen to provide marvelous stimulation of thought and to induce interaction with the method, the guest lecturer, and the content" (p. 191). Setting up synchronous communication sessions are another way to energize a group discussion. Gathering geographically disbursed students together at the same time for an Internet session creates an online environment that is closer to an actual classroom.

CMC Social Strategies

Developing social strategies in CMC helps to create a sense of community. Social information has a way of entering into every type of online discussion. Teachers and students should be aware of this and should develop social strategies to make online interaction enjoyable and friendly. Social strategies include guidelines, welcome messages, chatting, being aware of **lurkers** (people who do not participate), and dealing with rude behavior. Prior to setting up a discussion list, guidelines should be established to outline the purpose of the discussion and the appropriate rules of behavior. All participants should be asked to read the guidelines, which can be referred to if students break the rules.

One way to make a discussion list more social and friendly is to first have people introduce themselves to the group. Starting with the teacher, each participant can send a short, introductory message. An advantage of this requirement is that everyone will be encouraged to participate at the beginning of the electronic discussion. Social chatter also helps to develop a sense of community among students; however, it can also divert the group from serious discussion. Students should not use a course discussion list to share personal e-mail messages with each other, but messages about social and college events should be shared with the group, especially when they relate to the course topic under discussion. If the discussion becomes overly social, the teacher or student facilitator may have to direct the group back to the academic topic by posting a summary of the recent discussion of the topic.

If students ignore the rules or engage in bad behavior, the behavior must be dealt with. For instance, if a student uses improper language or shows rudeness, a private e-mail message should be sent to the individual to remind him or her about the rules of the list. After breaking a rule, students should be encouraged to continue participating in the discussion.

All students should be invited to participate. For this reason, teachers and student facilitators should try to be aware of the people lurking on the list. Lurkers should be encouraged to participate by either sending them a private e-mail message or publicly asking for their opinion. In an attempt to prevent the lurking problem, some professors require students to post a certain number of messages during the course of the semester.

Students who are participating in online discussions should allocate time to read, reflect on, and respond to e-mail messages. This will make participating in online discussions more time-consuming than face-to-face interaction. However, when students take time to reflect on the discussion and their responses, the overall quality of CMC discussions can be higher than face-to-face ones.

Developing Educational Communities

The Internet can be used to connect information and individuals together into a global learning community. According to Shirk (1992), the Web is "a network structure in which any topic can refer to any other topic. Webs can join topics together in vast networks of related information, much like associational thought" (p. 84). The Web's hypertext networking model changes the way in which textual informational is collected and disseminated. The sequential pattern of reading established by printed books is replaced by nonlinear information links connected to computer servers.

Hypertext supports connectivity within and across networked systems. In CMC, the term **network** refers to both a system of computers and the personal connections established between individuals. The technical linking features of hypertext support the development of relationships between people. When academics create links between their Web sites and the Web sites of other scholars, they establish interactive links to others through their sites. Academic sites often create networks of experts and organizations that specialize in a particular subject or topic. Thus, connecting people and sites supports the formation of academic and learning communities. For instance, **learning circle** projects have been formed to bring geographically distant classes together to study a topic of interest. Students collect information, analyze it, and share it with all the other student participants. These exchanges go beyond cultural boundaries. For example, weather is a popular topic for this type of project. Globally dispersed students will collect, share, and analyze weather conditions around the world. Beyond building learning communities, the Internet also connects scholars through e-mail, scholarly discussion lists, and educational MUDs.

Education and CMC Genres

CMC has a variety of uses in educational settings, including simple correspondence between students and teachers, asking research questions, and supporting small-group projects. CMC can extend the boundaries of a campus and bring people together into globally distributed learning communities. The following sections describes how CMC genres are applied to education.

E-mail

Students and teachers often use e-mail as a method of interpersonal communication. Additionally, some schools have started **key pal** exchange programs in which students at different schools exchange e-mail messages. These programs, started by teachers who contact different schools to request partners, have the goal of encouraging the use of computer technology and developing CMC skills. Some teachers establish a particular project with the students of the other school, such as a collaborative writing project or an information exchange.

Discussion Lists

Academic discussion lists can be set up as local or global lists. Discussion lists associated with specific courses are generally set up for class members only. These localized lists consist of students within a single university. An examination of class discussion lists by Phillips and Santoro (1989) revealed that students contacted their instructors more frequently when CMC was introduced into a course and that CMC can be an effective teaching method. Global discussion lists are established to encourage global interaction among students, professors, and experts on a specific topic. These lists are generally open, and students interested in learning more information about a particular subject can join them.

Electronic Forums and Panels

Another way CMC is used in education is assembling a group of remote panelists to address a defined set of topics with an audience of students who share the same discussion list. The faculty member generally acts as a moderator on this type of list. Panelists start by stating their positions and begin discussing the topics. Students then begin directing questions and comments to the panelists. The conversation is stimulated by both the experts and the students. Electric forums can become highly interactive and in-depth discussions. Sometimes these panels are set up to occur during a specific time period, for example, four to six weeks. Selected writings by experts can be distributed to participants prior to the beginning of the discussion. During the designated time period, the expert will answer student questions. Or the discussion can be based on weekly readings assigned to the group. Reading assignments can provide students with background information and a context for discussion and debate.

Educational MUDs

MUDs are used in education to support both classroom instruction and distance education. To add more interest to learning classical literature, one teacher, Leslie Harris has her students re-create Dante's levels of hell in a MUD world. The class is divided into groups with each group developing a different level. The levels include scenery, characters, and dialogue. Building on the theatrical and playful nature of CMC, each group performs for the other groups. Another teacher, Robert Coover, teaches hypertext fiction in the Hypertext Hotel, a MOO based on a hotel metaphor. Students create rooms in the hotel with each room having a story. Different students make contributions to the story and expand it. Coover perceives the MOO to be a playful and experimental writing space and does not expect students to create great literary documents. Other instructors use MUDs to teach English composition. Fanderclai (1995) has observed that students who hesitate to speak in English class are often active MUD participants. Additionally, students develop strategies in MUD communication that they can apply to other forms of writing. Finally, students can mix work and play to create more self-directed learning environments.

Beyond coursework, MUDs can be established to extend the boundaries of the campus. Berkeley's Cafe MOOlano was established as an online meeting space where University of California, Berkeley, instructors and students hold meetings. Instructors also hold "virtual" office hours in the MUD, and students meet to discuss group projects (Figure 10.2).

Virtual Reality Systems

As described in the previous chapter, MUDs are text-based virtual realities. In educational contexts, text-based virtual reality encourages students to be creative and active participants in the learning process. Additionally, MUDs help to develop CMC skills, such as keyboarding, computer, and online interpersonal skills. In addition to MUDs, the term *virtual reality* also describes **graphics-based** and **three-dimensional virtual reality** environments that enable students to build and explore three-dimensional computer models of objects. Software that supports graphics-based virtual reality includes *Virtus WalkThrough*, virtual reality mark-up language (VRML), and *QuickTime VR*.

Graphics-based virtual reality creates a rich experiential environment in which students can explore information. For example, *Virtus WalkThrough* has been used to teach mathematics through the construction of three-dimensional models of a pyramid. The program has also been used to help teach directions to children with dyslexia. When used in educational contexts, graphics-based virtual reality provides motivation, can illustrate fea-

---

FIGURE 10.2   Preparing to Take a MUD Class

Students who are going to take a class in a MUD environment need to prepare themselves for this experience. The following is a suggested list of things to do:

1. Learn the basic MUD or MOO commands and become completely comfortable with them.

2. Understand the way the MUD or MOO works and the rooms or spaces in the MUD.

3. Learn the netiquette of the MUD or MOO to be aware of appropriate behavior.

4. Practice interacting with others in MUDs and MOOs; becoming a skilled CMC communicator requires practice with CMC tools and interaction.

tures of objects, allows students to examine objects, provides learning tools for students with disabilities, and encourages active student participation.

Issues Concerning CMC in Education

There are many issues surrounding the introduction of computers into educational settings, including the changing roles of teachers and students, proper use of network resources, copyright issues, and Web cheating. CMC alters the relationship between students and teachers. The following saying illustrates this change: The sage on the stage become the guide on the side. Students become more actively involved with CMC learning. With the introduction of the Internet into education, every university has an acceptable-use policy to help guide students on the proper and improper use of the university's network resources (Figure 10.3). Every student should be aware of these guidelines. Additionally, each university has a plagiarism policy. Students should become familiar with policies regarding the educational use of computer networks.

FIGURE 10.3   Sample of Acceptable Use Policies

---

1) Acceptable Use—The original purpose of the Internet was to support research and education in and among academic institutions and to provide tools for collaborative work. Your e-mail account must be in support of education and research consistent with the educational objectives of your university. You are prohibited from transmitting any material that is in violation of any U.S. or state regulations, including copyrighted material, threatening or obscene material, or proprietary information. Use of the network for commercial activities, including advertising and political lobbying, is prohibited.

2) Privileges—Using the Internet is a privilege, not a right. Inappropriate use of the Internet will result in the cancellation of your account. The system administrators decide what is inappropriate and their decision is final. University administration, faculty and staff can request the system administrator to deny, revoke or suspend a user's account.

3) Netiquette—Faculty and students are expected to follow the rule of network etiquette. These include:

   a) Being polite to others and not sending abusive messages;

   b) Not using profane or vulgar language;

   c) Do not reveal the personal addresses or phone numbers of faculty or students;

   d) Electronic mail is not guaranteed to be private. System administrators have access to your messages. Messages relating to illegal activities will be reported to the authorities;

   e) All electronic communication and information accessible through the network should be considered to be private property.

Source: Composite from various university acceptable use policies.

As described in Chapter 2, the playful use of CMC can make participating in an on-line group more enjoyable. But too much socializing can interfere with group discussion. When engaging in CMC, students need to maintain a balance between serious discussion and social interactions. Moreover, students need to avoid disruptive behavior, a problem that faces many CMC groups, and education being no exception. This type of behavior will be discussed in more detail in Chapter 12 (Figure 10.4).

Changing Roles of Students and Teachers

Teachers and students using educational CMC have discovered that their roles change in computer-mediated contexts. In the traditional classroom setting, the attention is focused on the teacher. The teacher acts as a gatekeeper by selecting students to speak and monitoring the discussion. In contrast, CMC equalizes control among group participants. Instead of controlling the flow of conversation, the teacher becomes a facilitator and students take charge of the discussion. Similarly, in educational MUDs, the traditional classroom hierarchy is disrupted because teachers cannot dominate the conversation.

With CMC, students must assume more responsibility for their learning. Students must become responsible for their own actions and must develop strategies for accomplishing their educational goals, for the CMC experience provides students with an opportunity to engage in self-directed learning. For instance, Web links enable students to explore topics on their own, without teacher guidance. As CMC democratizes the classroom, this change requires students to become more involved with the course material. Moreover, democratization creates a shift in educational responsibility. The lecture model of education is replaced by a student-directed learning model. For learning to occur students, rather than teachers, must take responsibility.

FIGURE 10.4　CMC and Disruptive Behavior

Flaming and rude behavior can disrupt an academic discussion. Students need to learn acceptable ways to disagree with each other. Your own sense of what is acceptable can guide you in electronic communication, the same way it does in face-to-face interactions. The following rules should be followed to avoid flames in academic discussions:

1. Try to limit the length of your messages to make them easier for other people to read. Scrolling down too many screens of text can lose the reader.

2. When making references to people and ideas provide sources and if you introduce a new concept, it should be explained.

3. Carefully read the messages of other students. Try to respond to what is being said and give other students a fair chance to answer messages.

4. Avoid profanity and personal attacks on others. Arguments and debates should consider and respect other students. A personal confrontation should be done through private e-mail and not in a public group discussion.

Copyright Issues

A new student responsibility is the proper use of copyrighted online materials. Copyright is confusing in CMC because it is unclear whether CMC is written or oral communication. Chat room conversations are highly conversational and informal, and the proper citing of authors is something that we do not generally think about when we listen to conversations. In contrast, scholarly discussion lists consider the written words in e-mail messages to belong to the author. As a result, quotes from these messages should be properly cited. Because e-mail messages belong to their authors, they should not be reposted to other discussion lists without the permission of the author. Some creators of e-mail messages will include a permission statement at the end of their messages that gives others permission to copy and distribute them.

The Internet was originally a research network that made information available to everyone. However, with the widespread commercialization of the Web, much of the information accessible online is copyright protected. For example, the use of articles published in online newspapers and news sites, corporate logos, and cartoon characters on personal Web sites is a copyright violation. Everyone using the Web needs to pay attention to copyright laws and how they protect digital information.

An exception to copyright is **fair use**. Fair use is the reasonable use of a copyrighted work. When following the guidelines of fair use, authors do not need to get permission from the copyright owner, but citations must be included, because this is a legal requirement. Fair use allows academics to make one copy of an article, but not a book, for use by their classes. It does not cover copying articles for sale in course packets or for free dissemination, unless permission is given by the copyright owner. Fair use permits quotation of only brief passages, or a small percentage, of an article, book, or e-mail message.

An important aspect of fair use is the idea that permission for longer excerpts must be granted by the copyright owner. The question of who owns copyrights on electronic information is yet to be resolved. Some people believe that anything posted on the Internet is in the public domain and free for the taking, but this is not true. Most Web pages contain copyright notices, and using pictures or text from these sites is a violation of the copyright law.

Web Cheating and Plagiarism

The Web makes it very easy to copy text and paste it into a paper. Worse, students can take a paper from the Web, place their name on it, and turn it in as their own work. A number of Web sites have been established to enable students to buy term papers. **Plagiarism** is using someone else's words without proper citation or using a paper written by another person. In a university context, plagiarism includes failure to use quotation marks and citations in reports, using a ghostwriter to write a paper, and cutting and pasting paragraphs from articles and piecing them together. Prior to the Web, students could purchase or recycle papers from other students, but the Web makes this practice much easier because many Web-based services have developed to sell papers to students directly through the Internet. Students can search the sites by topic and look for a paper that is close to the theme of their assignment. Conversely, the Web also makes it easier for teachers to locate plagiarized work. Universities can for example, subscribe to services that check student papers for plagiarized material.

Depending on university and faculty guidelines, plagiarized work will earn a student an F on the paper or an F for the entire course. The ability to easily locate papers taken from the Web provides word-for-word evidence of irrefutable plagiarism. In the past, some universities required professors to confront a student with the charge of plagiarism to try to get the student to confess. With the Web, finding a word-for-word document written by another author makes confession unnecessary, and the incident can be reported directly to university administrators. So, although the Web makes it easy to cheat on assignments, it also makes it easier for professors to find cheaters.

Evaluating Face-to-Face Versus Computer-Mediated Classroom Discussions

Educators are interested in examining the effectiveness of CMC in academic settings. Olaniran, Savage, and Sorenson (1996) evaluated the differences between face-to-face and computer-mediated groups in an educational context according to the following criteria: participation, criticism/embarrassment, productivity loss, asynchroneity and record storage/retrieval, training, and timebinding. As previously stated, CMC can facilitate more equal participation among group members because people can communicate concurrently without interference. Constructive criticism can be evaluated more easily in CMC, and students who are communicatively apprehensive can freely participate without calling attention to themselves. In contrast to holding ideas in anticipation of an opportunity to talk, people can write ideas in CMC as they occur. CMC also has the ability to record and store meetings for review at a later time. However, potential disadvantages of CMC are flaming or overly critical and rude comments (see Chapter 12). Thus, participation, criticism, and embarrassment were communication features the researchers examined.

There are several key differences between face-to-face and CMC interaction. First, students must be trained to use the system. Second, students no longer need to be at one physical location at the same time. Asynchronous CMC systems allow people from remote locations to participate at different times in group discussions. Asynchroneity, training, and timebinding distinguish CMC groups from face-to-face ones.

Olaniran et al. compared face-to-face to CMC decision making in classroom groups. They assumed that students in face-to-face groups would be more effective and satisfied. As a result, they would find the decision-making process easier than students participating in the CMC groups. Two stages of the decision-making process were examined, the idea generation stage and the evaluation stage. The study revealed that students had a greater overall satisfaction with face-to-face communication. Students participating in face-to-face meetings were more effective in both the idea-generation and evaluation stages. Even though CMC groups generated more ideas than face-to-face groups, group members perceived themselves to be significantly less effective than the members of face-to-face groups. Students prefer face-to-face communication; they can also, however, productively work together through CMC. Thus, students need to develop a better understanding of how to use CMC.

Summary

In educational settings, computers can be used for both informatics and conferencing. Articles, course outlines, and class notes can be made available through the Internet. More important, e-mail can facilitate communication between instructors and students and among students themselves. Additionally, discussion groups can be set up to discuss course material. Messages can be retrieved and responded to when participants want to reply because everyone does not have to be logged on to the system at the same time. Students can send messages to individuals, post messages for the entire class to read, or send messages to selected class members.

In addition to the use of e-mail and discussion lists, some teachers have set up MOO environments that enable geographically distributed students to converse with each other at the same time. In some universities, CMC is becoming an integral part of courses that meet on campus because students can collaborate on projects and discuss course topics outside the classroom. In other cases, universities are developing distance education programs that enable people who live far away or who have difficult schedules to take classes and earn credit toward a college degree.

The Web brings information directly into the classroom or dorm room. But along with the convenience of CMC, come many new concerns, including developing additional skills to effectively use information and CMC, Web cheating, and the changing roles of students and teachers. CMC fosters a model of education that is student directed, requiring students to take more responsibility for the learning process.

A study comparing face-to-face and CMC decision-making groups revealed that students prefer face-to-face communication. To effectively use CMC, students need to be trained how to productively communicate in educational CMC genres, including e-mail, discussion lists, electronic forums, and educational MUDS.

EXERCISES

1. Set your own learning goals. Pick a topic that you are interested in learning about. Use the Web to research the topic. Evaluate whether or not the Web provided you with the information you were seeking.

2. Divide into small groups, research a topic on the Web, and collaborate in writing a report using CMC. If possible, submit the paper electronically for grading. When the project is completed, discuss the advantages and disadvantages of using the Internet as a research tool and method for developing collaborative writing skills.

3. Research and report on educational MUDs on the Web. What types of skills do you need to learn to be able to talk effectively in MUDs?

4. Create your own definition of information literacy. What skills do you think students need to learn to be literate in an information society?

5. Examine and discuss the acceptable-use policy at your university. Compare it with the acceptable-use policy of a commercial information provider, such as America Online. How are they similar or different?

TERMS

Computer-assisted instruction (CAI) is using the computer as a tutor or drill instructor.

Digital literacy is the ability to understand and use information in a variety of formats from a number of sources when information is presented through computers.

Fair use is the reasonable use of a copyrighted work.

Graphics-based or **three-dimensional virtual reality software**, such as *Virtus WalkThrough*, enables students to build and explore three-dimensional computer models of objects.

Information literacy is the ability to become an effective consumer of information. It involves learning how to use computer tools, and research tools and to develope critical thinking skills.

Key pal exchange programs enable students at different schools to exchange e-mail messages.

Learning circles are the combination of two or more classes through CMC to study a topic of interest.

Lurkers are people who do not participate in online discussion groups

Network refers to both a system of computers connected together and the personal connections established between individuals.

Plagiarism is using someone else's words without proper citation or using a paper written by another person. In a university context, plagiarism includes failure to use proper quotation marks and citations in reports, using a ghostwriter to write a paper, and cutting and pasting paragraphs from articles and piecing them together.

WEB SITES

CMC in Higher Education: www.ascusc.org/jcmc/vol4/issue2/
Communication Studies and Journalism Resources: www.cosmoedu.net/journalismresearch.html
Educational MUD Resources: tecfa.unige.ch/edu-comp/WWW-VL/eduVR-page.html
Electronic Journal of Communication: www.cios.org/www/ejcmain.htm
Human Interface Technology Laboratory/VR in Schools: ftp://ftp.hitl.washington.edu/pub/scivw/pubs/
Interpersonal Computing and Technology:
www.helsinki.fi/science/optek/
jan.ucc.nau.edu/~ipct-j/
Journal of Computer-Mediated Communication: www.ascusc.org/jcmc
Media and Communication Studies: http://www.aber.ac.uk/media/
The Scholarly Electronic Publishing Directory: info.lib.uh.edu/sepb/sepb.html

BIBLIOGRAPHY

Bailey, E. K., & Cotlar, M. (1994). Teaching with the Internet. *Communication Education, 43* (2), 184–193.
Barnes, S. B. (2000). *Online connections: Internet interpersonal relationships*. Cresskill, NJ: Hampton Press.
Barnes, S., & Strate, L. (1996). The educational implications of the computer: A media ecology critique. *The New Jersey Journal of Communication, Vol. 4*, No. 2, pp. 180–208.
Bennahum, D. (1994, May/June). Fly me to the MOO: Adventures in textual reality. *Lingua Franca*, pp. 1, 22–36.

Bromley, H. (1997). Thinking about computers and schools: A skeptical approach. In P. E. Agre & D. Schuler (Eds.), *Reinventing technology, rediscovering community* (pp. 107–126). Greenwich, CT: Ablex Publishing Corporation.

Donovan, D. C. (1995). Computer mediated communication and the basic speech course. *Interpersonal Computing and Technology*, 3 (3), 32–53.

Fanderclai, T. L. (1995). MUDs in education: New environments, new pedagogies. *Computer-Mediated Communication Magazine, 2* (1), 8 [Online]. Available: http://metalab.unc.edu/cmc/mag/1995/jan/fanderclai.html (April 15, 2000)

Furger, R. (1998). *Does Jane computer?* New York: Warner Books.

Gilster, P. (1997). *Digital literacy.* New York: John Wiley & Sons.

Harmon, A. (1997, October 25). Internet's value in U.S. schools still in question. *The New York Times*, pp. A1, D15.

Haythornthwaite, C. (2001). Exploring multiplexity: Social network structures in a computer-supported distance learning class. *The Information Society, 17*, 211–226.

Kelly, L., Duran, R. L., & Zolten, J. J. (2001). The effect of reticence on college students' use of electronic mail to communicate with faculty. *Communication Education, 50* (2), 170–176.

Kirk, E. E. (1996). Evaluating information found on the Internet [Online]. Available: http://milton.mse.jhu.edu:8001/research/education/net.html (August 30, 2001)

Lakoff, G., & Boal, I. A. (1995). Body, brain, and communication. In J. Brook & I. A. Boal (Eds.), *Resisting the virtual life* (pp. 115–130). San Francisco: City Lights.

Levinson, P. (1997). *The soft edge.* New York: Routledge.

Lichtman, J. (1998, December). The Cyber Sisters Club: Using the internet to bridge the technology gap with inner city girls. *T.H.E. Journal*, pp. 47–50.

McComb, M. (1994). Benefits of computer-mediated communication in college courses. *Communication Education, 43* (2), 159–170.

National Telecommunications and Information Administration (1999, July). *Falling through the Net: Defining the digital divide.* Washington, DC: U.S. Department of Commerce.

Olaniran, B. A., Grant, T. S., Sorenson, R. L. (1996, July). Experimental and experiential approaches to teaching face-to-face and computer-mediated group discussion. *Communication Education, 45*, pp. 244–259.

Phillips, G. M., & Santoro, G. M. (1989). Teaching group discussion via computer-mediated communication. *Communication Education, 38* (2), 151–161.

Rothenberg, D. (1997, August 15). How the Web destroys the quality of students' research papers. *The Chronicle of Higher Education*, p. A44.

Santoro, G. M., & Phillips, G. M. (1993). Speech Communication 350—Group Problem Solving. In J. Boettcher (Ed.), *The Joe Wyatt Challenge* (pp. 309–314). New York: McGraw-Hill, Inc. Available: gopher://ivory.educom.edu/00/stories101/Speech-Comm-350.txt

Schrock, K. (1995–1998). Critical evaluation information. [Online]. Available: http://www.capecod.net/schrockguide/eval.htm (April 15, 2000).

Shapiro, J. J., & Hughes, S. K. (1996, March/April). Information literacy as a liberal art. *Educom Review, 31* (2) [Online]. Available: http://www.educom.edu/Web/pubs/review/reviewArticles/31231.html (April 17, 2000).

Shenk, D. (1997). *Data smog: Surviving the information glut.* San Francisco: Harper Edge.

Shirk, H. N. (1992). Cognitive architecture in hypermedia instruction. In Edward Barrett (Ed.), *Sociomedia: Multimedia, hypermedia, and the social construction of knowledge* (pp. 79–93). Cambridge, MA: The MIT Press.

Shneiderman, B., & Kearsley, G. (1989). *Hypertext hands-on!: An introduction to a new way of organizing and accessing information.* Reading, MA: Addison-Wesley Publishing Company.

Smith, A. (1998). Evaluation of information sources [Online]. Available: http://www.vuw.ac.nz/~ag-smith/evaln/evaln.htm (April 17, 2000).

Taylor, R. P. (1980). *The computer in the school: Tutor, tool, tutee.* New York: Teachers College Press.

Tyner, K. (1998). *Literacy in a digital world.* Mahwah, NJ: Lawrence Erlbaum Associates, Publishers.

11 Virtual Communities

Chapter Overview

Through the widespread use of computer networks, people are now able to gather and form small communities that exchange messages through cyberspace. Although members meet in the perceptual space created by computer networks, they behave as if they are meeting in an actual physical space. As a result, the spirit of community can be developed and sustained through CMC.

Virtual communities generally come together through the sharing of mutual interests, instead of geographic proximity, in contrast to community networks, which form around a geographic location and the interests of local citizens. There are a various types of Internet communities, including MUD communities, support communities, audience communities, and Web rings. The concept of community building is a central idea behind Internet communication. This chapter introduces the following community topics:

- Changing concepts of community
- Virtual communities
- Collaborative mass media
- Types of Internet communities
- The social identification/deindividuation (SIDE) model

People engaging in CMC can establish a sense of community that is similar to traditional face-to-face communal behavior. When the same people are repeatedly encountered in chat rooms, MUDs, newsgroups, and discussion lists, long-term relationships can develop in ways similar to in-person friendships. However, keeping an online group together takes more effort and commitment because people can disappear by simply not turning on their computers. Groups that *do* stay together for a long time begin to create their own history, electronic rituals, and customs. Because many of these activities parallel ones found in geographic communities, online groups are considered by many people to be a new type of community. Furthermore, belonging to an online community can provide a stable environment for its members who frequently move around the country or change jobs. Whatever one's physical location, members of online communities can stay connected to each other across time and space.

The Development of Virtual Communities

In 1968, Licklider and Taylor described the computer as a communication device and predicted that computer networks would support the formation of interactive communities. Unlike to traditional communities, interactive ones would bring together individuals from geographically dispersed locations. Following this prediction, computer scientists used the early Internet to form electronic research communities that shared working papers and e-mail messages. This online group sharing of expertise and information greatly contributed to the speedy development of computer technology in the United States.

As the Internet expanded, more scientists and technologists became connected. Over time, an Internet community began to emerge. Valauskas (1996) defines **Internet communities** as "a collection of individuals who use computers, software, and other means to discuss common interests transcendentally, outside of time and space" (p. 2). The original inhabitants of the Internet created their own processes for self-regulation and tolerance to keep life orderly on this new electronic frontier. Rules established by the pioneering members of Internet communities can be found in netiquette statements, frequently asked questions, and the appropriate-use guidelines distributed by universities.

Twenty-five years after the Internet began, Howard Rheingold coined the term *virtual community* to characterize the interpersonal relationships that he had developed on a computer network called the Whole Earth 'Lectronic Link (WELL). Rheingold (1993) stated, "my direct observations of online behavior around the world over the past ten years have led me to conclude that whenever CMC technology becomes available to people anywhere, they inevitably build virtual communities with it, just as microorganisms inevitably create colonies" (p. 6). Virtual communities are defined by Rheingold (1998) as

> . . . a group of people who may or may not meet one another face to face, and who exchange words and ideas through the mediation of computer bulletin boards, and networks. When these exchanges begin to involve interwoven friendships and rivalries and give rise to the real-life marriages, births, and deaths that bond people in any other kind of community, they begin to affect these people's lives in the real world. Like any other community, a virtual community is also a collection of people who adhere to a certain (loose) social contract and who share certain (eclectic) interests. It usually has a geographically local focus and often has a connection to a much wider domain (p. 116).

Simply stated, **virtual communities** can be described as informational and emotional support groups that form the same type of bonds as geographic communities where people share their experiences. However, the webs of personal relationships that develop through the Internet are created across geographic space. Unlike traditional communities, virtual ones do not depend on physical closeness. Members can interact with each other through their "virtual" presence or telepresence in computer-generated space. As described in Chapter 2, **telepresence** is the experience of presence created when using a communication medium, such as a telephone, computer network, or teleconferencing system. The word *presence* refers to the actual natural perception of an environment; in contrast, *telepresence* refers to the mediated understanding of an environment. Because perceiving the social presence of others is mediated, electronic villages have come to be known as "virtual" as opposed to "real" communities. As communities, they act as gathering points for people with common interests, beliefs, and ideas and are supported by a variety of CMC genres; for example, MUDs, bulletin boards, newsgroups, and discussion lists. Electronic communities are generally established because of shared personal, recreational, and professional interests, such as a hobby, role-playing games, providing mutual support for addiction or medical problems, exchanging computer information, and talking about popular television programs or recording artists. For example, Baym (1995, 2000) researched an online fan group called rec.arts.tv.soaps (r.a.t.s.), a recreational discussion list of daytime soap operas and found that after a decade of online communication, the thousands of people who have participated in r.a.t.s. have created a dynamic community filled with social nuance and emotion.

An advantage of virtual communities over face-to-face ones is that race, gender, age, national origin, and physical appearance are not immediately apparent. People have to decide whether they are going to make this information public. As a result, individuals with physical disabilities who have trouble forming new friendships discover that virtual communities treat them as if their disability did not exist. Similarly, people who are housebound or unable to socialize in face-to-face settings can develop online relationships. Often, the bonds of electronic friendship can be just as strong as face-to-face ones. For example, members of one virtual community (VC-L) believe that they have established true friendships through their electronic conversations and the amount of time they have spent together online (see Barnes, 2001). They believe that group members are real friends because they share their daily experiences with each other. Members of virtual communities have observed that they are conducive to friendship for four reasons. First, people can reveal at will; information such as sex, age, and race is not immediately exposed. Second, connection is voluntary; people can turn on and off their involvement at will. Third, people can conceal personality traits through calculated and edited replies, or they can embellish the self presentation by creating new electronic personalities. Finally, people can hide defects, such as physical disabilities and shyness. For these reasons, members of virtual communities believe that the time they spend together and experiences they share create communal bonds.

Changing Concepts of Community

The formation of virtual communities through computer networks is changing our ideas about communities. Traditionally, communities were viewed as groups of people who live in the same geographic area and follow the same set of behavioral rules. They are people who have physical access to each other and who have similar interests—people who can talk to each other and interact in face-to-face meetings. Like members of traditional communities, members of virtual ones also share birth announcements, deaths, and personal triumphs or sorrows. Frequently, members of virtual communities who stay together for long periods of time want to meet each other in person. It is common for virtual communities to arrange face-to-face gatherings.

Jones (1995) used the terms *Gesellschaft* and *Gemeinschaft* to discuss community in the information age. *Gesellschaft*, or "society," refers to people who have economic, political, and social relationships, without any particular psychological relationships. People are brought together into a particular Gesellschaft through their common behavior or concerns.

In contrast, major social groupings emerge from Gemeinschaft, or communities where people live together because of a commitment. For example, families become extended families and families group together to form tribes. In Gemeinschafts, people have a place and fit in somewhere as a son or cousin, hunter or tiller, etc., and this understanding of social roles is an instantaneous confirmation of self. An important aspect of Gemeinschaft is the reinforcement of personal identity.

As culture became more industrialized, Gesellschaft, or social forces, became a more powerful socializing influence than local communities. Today, the changes started in the industrial age are continuing to evolve as we move into the information age. As a technological development, the Internet is part of a larger social transformation in which mass media emerged as a major social influence. The rise of mass media in society led to a communication shift from interpersonal to mass communication as a primary method for communicating social norms. Beniger (1987) argues there has been a dramatic shift in interpersonal control of individual behavior by traditional communal relationships (Gemeinschaft) to impersonal, restricted, and mediated control, or Gesellschaft.

The interactive features of the Internet, which support **many-to-many** and **one-to-one communication**, expands this trend. The Internet adds to the increased use of mediated forms of communication over face-to-face interaction. Many-to-many communication allows groups of individuals such as a discussion list or MUD environment, to share information. E-mail, on the other hand, is a one-to-one method of communication (Figure 11.1). The widespread use of the Internet supports mediated exchanges between individuals and between groups.

Discussion Lists versus Virtual Communities

Currently, there are thousands of discussion groups exchanging daily conversations through the Internet. However, most of these groups would not consider themselves to be "communities." This raises the following question: What is the difference between a discussion group and a virtual community? According to Rheingold, one difference is trust. Frequently, people who participate in discussion lists do not reveal enough personal information about themselves to inspire trust in other members. People that form communities do have a sense of trust because they freely share personal information and gain the confidence of other group members.

Several other answers to this question have been discussed by online communities, such as the media_ecology list. Members of this group have suggested the following two differences. First, participants in virtual communities perceive themselves to be part of a community and group members. Second, as a group they develop socially acceptable rules of online behavior, such as following social behavior patterns that support civil conversation and group sharing. Flaming and rude styles of communication are discouraged and respect for others is encouraged (Figure 11.2).

Building Virtual Communities

According to Doheny-Farina (1996), " a true community is a collective (evolving and dynamic) in which the public and private lives of its members are moving toward interde-

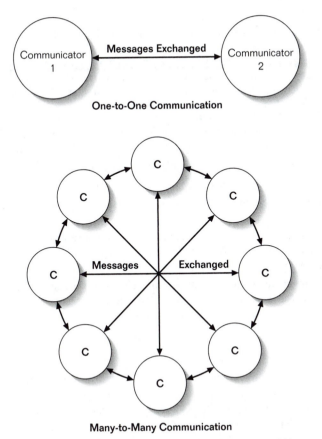

One-to-One Communication

Many-to-Many Communication

C = Communicator

FIGURE 11.1   Model of One-to-One and Many-to-Many Communication

pendency regardless of the significant differences among those members" (p. 50). In today's culture it is more difficult to maintain geographic communities because people move, go to college, change jobs, and generally do not stay in the same physical location their entire lives. As a result, people will join new communities and drop out of others throughout their lifetimes. Stacy Horn (1998), the founder of the online community ECHO, states, "This is what online communities offer: a connection to people. That's all any virtual community has to offer" (p. 20). As a connection point, people can meet online and build relationships. Often, these friendships can move beyond the computer screen and into the real world. Similarly, Dyson (1997) wrote, "as the world seems to get more complex and more overwhelming, and public life ever more scary, people look to communities for fellowship and

---

FIGURE 11.2   Suggestions for Writing Messages That People Will Respond to

---

In CMC, observing the messages of others and identifying points of support and irritability can help the online communicator write purposeful rather than expressive messages. Because expressive talk can be counterproductive to the general group discussion, the following guidelines are suggested for improving online correspondence:

1. Pay attention to what has been going on before you contribute to a conversation. Your own sense of what is acceptable may effectively guide you in electronic communication as in life.

2. Limit your messages so that they are conveniently readable by others.

3. Try to give references and sources when you make a statement of fact.

4. Give other people a fair chance to answer. And be sure to read what they say before you try to answer it.

5. Avoid profanity, blasphemy, and ad hominem out of respect for other readers. If you must confront, it is considerate to do so off the networks. For example, send a direct e-mail message to the person.

6. Norms will transform into rules over time. Meanwhile, good sense and self-protection mandate that you take care with what you say and how, when, and where you say it.

---

security" (pp. 31–32). In a complex and changing world, online communities can remain stable and accessible to people who frequently move or change jobs. Virtual communities stay together as members move around the country because participation is not dependent on geographic location. Phillips (1996) stated, "Community, in this formulation, is not a geographic notion but a symbolic one. Community is created and maintained by people in interaction. It is a process of creating communal ties through which individuality is constructed, interpreted, and contained. It is a relational concept" (p. 40).

Building virtual communities requires four criteria: a name, the use of civil language, growth and continuity, and a group history. One of the first steps in building and sustaining a virtual community is naming the group. Community names function as a prefix and as a way for group members to address each other and identify with the group, for example, Dear VC-Lers, the VC-Lfamily, VC-Lites, and "Hey ho out there in VC-Land." ("VC" stands for virtual community; the acronym of any online group could be substituted here.)

A central component of community building is the establishment of rules of behavior that promote the use of civil language and orderly conduct. Language usage in virtual communities is often playful, humorous, and friendly. Group members will reference each other, express solidarity, and generally share feelings of congeniality that are dimensions of interpersonal relationship building.

Additionally, online groups need to develop techniques to sustain the group and build the community. As people leave the group there must be others to replace them. Moreover, virtual communities need a core group of people to spark discussion, introduce topics for debate, and generally keep conversation going. For example, when the moderator of a popular discussion group passed away, his death bonded the group together into a community, but the remaining members could not sustain the feeling of a community because the moderator was also the person who kept the discussion going. When no one came forward to replace the moderator's role as list guru and provocateur, the group gradually disbanded.

Douglas Schuler (1996), a founder of the Seattle Community Network, stated, "History is an integral part of communities'—and hence its inhabitants'—identity and character" (p. 4). Establishing a group history revolves around the sharing of significant experiences. Many online communities have shared their feelings when a prominent member of their group has passed away. For instance, Rheingold (1993) describes how a member of the San Francisco-based community, the WELL, committed suicide both on and offline. A man named Blair first committed "virtual" suicide by erasing all of his messages stored in the WELL's discussion list archives. According to Rheingold (1993), "The shock of ripping out several years' worth of postings from a very prolific writer made the fabric of recorded conversations, the entire history of the WELL's discourse to that point, look . . . moth-eaten" (p. 36). Shortly afterwards, Blair ended his actual life. "From the moment we heard the news, the population of the WELL went through a period of transformation. Joking around with words on a computer keyboard is one thing. Going to Blair's funeral and talking to his family face-to-face was another" (p. 36). Many WELL members lived in the San Francisco area and could attend the actual funeral. But members who could not attend the funeral in person shared online eulogies together. Births and deaths are significant events that contribute to the history of a virtual community.

Replacing Geographic Proximity with Common Interests

Gradually, geographic commonalities are being replaced by psychological ones, such as religion, common interests, sports, and sexual orientation. Relationships formed on the Internet, at the outset, are part imaginary. The people encountered via e-mail do not have corporeal form and so fantasy must fill the gaps. To turn an online connection into an actual personal friend takes real effort. It is much easier to build relationships face-to-face. So why do people keep spending time online? The most compelling reason is the simplest one: human contact.

The high level of interactive participation required by CMC often gets people involved not only with the medium but also with each other. Some scholars predict that the Internet will bring people together into a large global village. Others believe, in contrast to the image of a single unified community, that the Internet is "an environment in which a profusion of different villages will flourish" that are centered on common interests. (Dyson, 1997, p. 6).

The Internet and Local Communities

Many local communities have also set up community networking systems to support local communication and make government documents available to citizens. Additionally, entrepreneurs have set up community networks to promote local commerce in cities or geographic regions. Although the purpose of these networks is to support local communication, some scholars are concerned about their impact on physical communities. For instance, Doheny-Farina (1996) argues that electronic communication separates us from physical communities and that electronic discourse will have a negative impact on traditional communities. He states, "in reality, electronic communication pushes in exactly the opposite direction—toward the shadow we call virtual community. In immersing ourselves in the electronic net, we are ignoring our real, dying communities" (p. 8). Geographic place and real communities give meaning to the virtual experience. Conversely, virtual correspondence can distract people from the local community experience. Doheny-Farina (1996) argues that traditional communities are tied to place, which includes complex social and environmental rules and requirements. Moreover, people cannot easily subscribe to a physical community in the same way they join a virtual one. People must live in a community because "it is entwined, contradictory, and involves all our senses. . . . The hope that the incredible powers of global computer networks can create new virtual communities, more useful and healthier than the old geographic ones, is thus misplaced" (p. 37). Local community involvement is an important aspect of social life, and should not be replaced with Internet groups.

Collaborative Mass Media and Communities

A large portion of the content generated on the Internet and Web occurs within the context of small group discussions and virtual communities. Rafaeli and LaRose (1993) thus call the Internet a collaborative mass media system. **Collaborative mass media systems** are those in which the audience is the primary source of media content and also the receivers of it. Collaborative mass media expands the model of mass media from a one-to-many information flow to a many-to-many information exchange. For example, Bulletin board systems, discussion lists, and newsgroups are collaborative systems in which users primarily provide the content.

In contrast, organizations and media corporations create a large portion of the content distributed through the Web. For instance, major media corporations that own radio stations, television networks, newspapers, and magazines have established Web sites to make their media content available to Internet audiences. Media industry professionals often make a distinction between what they consider to be media-related content and messages posted to the Web by individuals. Media content includes articles, news reports, video footage, or audio sound tracks edited and distributed through the various media. In other words, media content goes through a process of formal editorial control and gatekeeping. Media content is also created to be consumed by audiences. The media industry's definition of content would not fit the description of collaborative mass media because collaborative mass media content comes from the audience members themselves and often is not subject to any editorial control. Instead of using the term *collaborative mass media*, media industry professionals often refer to the content created by audience members as "virtual communities." In terms of CMC, reader and viewer responses to Web content fit into the category of discussion lists, rather than virtual communities.

Case Study: VC-L

A key feature of a community is the establishment of rules of conduct. The following case study illustrates how members of a virtual community (VC-L) dealt with an individual who wanted to break one of their community rules. A group of about twenty-five people who met originally on a public discussion list started VC-L as a private community. The community is unmoderated and keeps no archives. The group expects participants to keep their own records, if they care to, and to copyright their messages, if they want to. Any topic is acceptable for discussion with the stipulation that members may be asked to drop a topic if it has been previously discussed in detail.

Any group member can nominate a new member to the list. New members are expected to introduce themselves with a short biography and to describe their topics of interest. An informal vote is taken, and most new people are welcomed into the community. Complaints about the operation of the community are directed to the moderator, who makes them a topic of general discussion. Rules and policies are altered at the will of the membership, and nominations for new members are sent to the moderator, who sends out the nomination message to the entire group.

Restricted membership is a behavioral rule in the VC-L community. Additionally, all members must use their real names. New members are generally discovered through interactions on other lists, from personal correspondence, or from face-to-face encounters. The sponsoring VC-L member will describe the new member to the rest of the group and/or forward a writing sample for an informal vote. Here is a sample of a nomination request:

```
Here is the post from someone I think would be a good addition to
VC-L.
I know her from several other lists.
Susan Z.
```

Following this request, Susan posted a sample of the nominee's writing style, and the proposed member wrote about a topic of interest to the VC-L group. It should be noted that Susan says that she "knows" this person from several other discussion lists, which means the nominee has established a credible identity on the Internet.

If personal identity is not established, an individual cannot join VC-L. For example, a person named Thomas Hobbes was nominated to join the group. Two aspects about Hobbes disturbed other VC-L members. First, members objected to the fact that he identified himself as a Mensa member in his introductory message. Members felt that it was inappropriate to brag about one's IQ status to other people. But more important, it was discovered that Thomas Hobbes was not his real name. Through the exchange of private messages between Hobbes and VC-L members, it was revealed that he was a journalist using a false identity. The person calling himself Thomas Hobbes said that he was exploring the computer underworld for book research and that he wanted to protect himself and his family from possible harassment after publication. He made the assumption that his book would receive the same negative attention that Bruce Sterling received after writing *The Hacker Crackdown*. Unlike other lists, VC-L has established online behavioral rules about membership and actual identity. Participating in the group using a false identity was against community standards because a level of trust had been established between the current members. After a group discussion about Hobbes, the moderator wrote the following:

```
Nope on Hobbes!

We have Mensa and no real name, we may have an ax murderer. Do
you want me to write him a rejection letter. e.g.

Dear Mr. Mensa or Whatever:

I am listowner of VC-L a community of friendly conversationalists
who do not talk dirty to one another. I am probably smarter than
you because my IQ is higher than the surface temperature of
planet Venus. I have also published 44 books (and three more
coming this year) and 300 articles, none of which I was ashamed
to sign with my real name.

I hereby declare you unacceptable for membership in our
community.
Yours truly,
Albert Einstein
:)
Seriously folks -- my suspicious glands are triggered.

I find myself wanting references. When a man lies once, I think
there is a presumption. I think there are some people on this
list who disagree with me and some I disagree with. There are
some I am very close to and some I hardly know.

But I have not met a liar. In the time we have been together,
there has not been one time I can recall that anyone did anything
"dirty". I think that is a most remarkable record, given we have
about 45 people more or less brushing up against each other.

I would be wary of Mr. Hobbes under any name and I think I would
be doing more direct conversation and posting less to the list if
he was around. Now you are encountering the real me. In my other
persona, out there, on the other lists I can play games, pose,
strut, brag, and bully. Here, I think I have been civil and when
I slipped a little someone I trusted told me about it.

My own feeling is that in this case, one strike is out and this
journalist should go and journal elsewhere.
```

(July 2, 1994, 18:20 EST)

An essential element of community building both on- and offline is the establishment of rules of social behavior. In the VC-L community, members cannot use false identities. They can use electronic nicknames, but actual names must be known by other group members. Because of this rule, members have developed a sense of trust about the people they are communicating with online, and this trust extends into the world beyond the computer screen.

Types of Online Communities

CMC can bring people together who are geographically scattered and provide a community connection for individuals who move frequently. However, the network can also be used to facilitate local communication among people who live in the same geographic vicinity. For example, Free-Nets and community networks are attempting to make the Internet available to local groups to encourage face-to-face community involvement. Interpersonal relationships and community building already make up a large part of the noncommercial content being distributed through the Internet. Beyond community building, Internet proponents argue that the medium can also be used to encourage local community participation.

Corporations have realized that the community-building feature of the Internet can be used to develop consumer-oriented electronic commerce. Community sites can be used as portals to the Internet; for instance, GeoCities, a community-oriented Internet company, has attracted investors because of its high traffic volume and the fact the site can be used creatively to reinforce a sense of community while pursuing marketing objectives. Community sites enable companies to sell products and services to people with similar demographic profiles and interests. Music companies, for instance, can pitch new albums to music-related discussion lists. The following sections describe the variety of different types of communities on the Internet and Web.

Free-Nets

Free-Nets and "community computing" groups attempt to make computer services accessible to local communities. Free-Nets are run by the community for the community. Individuals contribute their time, effort, and expertise to operating the system. According to Strangelove (1993), "Any individual in the community can access the Free-Net through a computer with a modem. For those who do not own a computer, terminals are provided in schools, universities, libraries, and other community centers" (p. 1). As the name implies, no one is charged for the use of Free-Nets.

The purpose of these networks is to provide the local community with health care, library, education, recreation, law, government, special events, and any other information of interest to the general public. These systems attempt to bring local communities together by providing information, promoting democracy, and facilitating free access to publicly funded research. Moreover, Free-Nets attempt to "increase the frequency and ease of communication between voters and their elected officials and decrease isolation and loneliness that many experience in the midst of sprawling urban areas" (Strangelove, 1993, p. 1).

Supporters of the Free-Net movement, which became popular in the mid-1990s, are optimistic about the influence computer networks will have on democracy and communities because the networks support public discourse. Currently, there are many Free-Net systems under development around the world, but in the United States the movement is on the decline and commercially oriented community networks are gradually replacing the Free-Nets.

Community Networks

Unlike virtual communities formed by individuals communicating together through the Internet, community networks are built around a physical place. Participants share a common neighborhood or city and participants know each other. For example, the Blacksburg Electronic Village is an early community network that was established for residents living in Blacksburg, Virginia. Alice McInnes (1997) researched a community network called the InfoZone based in Telluride Colorado. She discovered that the InfoZone acted as a medium for political discussion by generating more in-depth analysis of issues and enabling more individuals to express their opinions. A concern about community networks is they will further isolate individuals and discourage face-to-face contact. In contrast, McInnes's study revealed that the InfoZone increased community involvement both on and off-line.

Communities of Interest

The Internet brings together individuals who share common lifestyles and interests. For example, gays and lesbians "who are inherently dispersed throughout society, have benefitted tremendously from online forums that provide them with the opportunity to share their intimate thoughts about what it means to be gay, practical considerations about living a healthy, happy life, and ways to band together and force politicians to take them seriously as a group of citizens with important interests" (Shenk, 1997, p. 127). Other groups that have benefitted from online communication include Latinos, teenagers, environmentalists, ethicists, therapists, and freelance writers. Internet communities are often referred to as communities of interest.

MUD Communities

Since the spread of the Internet, many different types of MUDs have developed, including TinyMUD, AberMUD, and Diku MUDs. The release of the MUD software for games, such as AberMUD, prompted the creation of many imitators. Gradually, MUD communities that were based on "families" of MUDs communities began to emerge. Users often play in several MUDs at the same time, and they form communities that span several different MUDs.

Social MUDs allow people to role-play and build virtual communities together. For example, LambdaMOO is a social MUD that parallels the real world. Members get married and celebrate memorable events together. Curtis (1996) says that despite the large turnover of MUD players, "MUDs do become true communities after a time. The participants slowly come to consensus about a common (private) language, about appropriate standards of behavior, and about the social role of various public areas (e.g., where big discussion usually happens, where certain 'crowds' can be found, etc.)" (p. 366).

Support Communities

Online support groups can also develop into virtual communities because participating in support groups is often an emotionally charged experience. Moreover, online support group members act in ways that are similar to face-to-face support groups. Online support communities enable people to share common experiences, create stories to normalize their experiences, and meet people. Additionally, the shift from speech to writing can be beneficial in the support process because asynchronous communication enables people to write thoughtful replies to people in need. As a result, when experiences and personal triumphs are presented in a written form, they may seem more powerful and clearer than similar messages shared at in-person meetings. Sharing emotionally charged written messages can lead to the feeling that one belongs to a community rather than an online group.

Audience Communities

Groups of audience members, often called *fans*, will share their interpretations of media texts with each other. These individuals will generally discuss a particular program, such as *All My Children* or *Star Trek*. Fans establish practices to share information, interpret the show, and discuss it. CMC enables fans to exchange ideas and share interpretations with each other. Baym (2000) contends that traditional audience researchers do not generally use the term *community*. However, fans of programs do form communities through their Internet interactions because people participating in these groups build personal relationships. She states, "Being a member of an audience community is not just about reading a text in a particular way; rather, it is about having a group of friends, a set of activities one does with those friends, and a world of relationships and feelings that grow from those friendships" (p. 207). Many audience communities exist on the Internet, for instance, newsgroups such as rec.arts.tv.soaps.

Media Communities

A difference between audience communities and media communities is whether the community is established by audience members or Web site designers. Many sites that provide content produced by the media industries (newspapers, magazines, radio stations, television stations, etc.) will add areas for audience members to post messages. Web designers make a distinction between edited content and messages written by Web users. Media professionals often consider edited material to be "content" and user comments to be "virtual communities." For example, The *New York Times* Web site contains articles from the newspaper (content) and discussion areas for readers to respond and interact with each other (virtual community). Other sites that are designed to develop media communities include Oxygen.com, MSNBC.com and Oprah.com.

Oprah Winfrey's Web site has an area that is specifically called "community." Her site describes community as: "Find ways to reach people where you live . . . Connect to a larger world of others with interests and passions just like yours" (Oprah.com). Beyond providing information on topics such as health, fitness, and food, the site also contains message boards, online support groups, and fan areas to talk about the *Oprah Winfrey Show*. By encouraging audience members to interact with each other, the Oprah Web site is incorporating many interactive features that encourage audience participation and involvement.

Web Rings

Often, the Web is a one-to-many channel of communication that supports the distribution of information. **Web rings** have emerged to provide a method for linking common Web-based interests. Sites are banded together into linked circles that enable people to find sites more quickly and easily. According to Elmer (1999), Web rings bring together two distinct Internet features: (1) the ease of searching for information on the Web and (2) the sharing of resources between members of specialized online communities.

To interact directly with other people through the Web, individuals must send e-mail messages to Webmasters, submit messages for posting on discussion lists, or enter chat areas. The two-way sharing of information on the Web requires the incorporation of e-mail and chat features into Web pages. At present, more traditional text-based CMC genres are being integrated into Web sites. Similarly, Web-based resources are becoming increasingly integrated into e-mail messages because people place Web links within the body of their messages. Individuals reading e-mail with Web links can click on the link and access the Web site.

These links will often direct people to specialized information that may be difficult to find through major search engines. Search engine technology presents sites in a hierarchical order, and often searches can result in a limitless number of "hits" that makes it difficult to locate specific information. Moreover, many search engines support the new economy of electronic commerce and direct people to commercial sites or services. In contrast to commercial search engines, Web ring guides offer a subject-based index and a function to search for communities of Web sites. The linking together of Web sites into virtual communities started with Britain's EUROPa (Expanding Unidirectional Ring of Pages) and STRANDS (Special Threads Assorted Netter Discussing). Elmer (1999) states there are over 40,000 Web rings containing more than 500,000 individual Web sites already in existence. Topics discussed through Web rings include everything from politics to the weather. Each Web ring is started and maintained by an individual Web site owner who assumes the role of "Ring-Master." Ringmasters can create their own grassroots networks of Web sites (Figure 11.3).

FIGURE 11.3   How to Decide Whether or Not to Create a New Web Ring. The `Webrings.org` Web site warns people about some of the potential problems of becoming a RingMaster.

If you decide to set up a Web ring, there are three things to consider:

1. Starting a Web ring takes time. You need to find sites to join the ring, e-mail the creator of the sites, and convince the sites to join, which can be frustrating because it's time-consuming.

2. Once a ring starts to grow, the responsibility of RingMaster/RingMistress is lots of work.

3. Establishing and maintaining a good Web ring requires a strong ability to use and understand HTML. Web rings are usually started by experienced Web users. If you are new to the Web, it is better to join a ring, rather than start one. Participating in a Web ring will also provide a better understanding about how they work.

For more information on Web rings visit http://www.Webring.org

Social Identification/Deindividuation (SIDE) Theory

A number of different approaches have been used to research online groups, including cues-filtered-out and hyperpersonal communication, described in Chapter 1. Another important theory is the **social identification/deindividuation (SIDE) theory**, which was developed by Postmes, Spears, and Lea (1998, 2000). The theory argues that the elimination of visual cues (anonymity) in CMC genres makes people conform to accepted social norms. "When communicators share a common social identity, they appear to be more susceptible to group influence, social attraction, stereotyping, gender typing, and discrimination in anonymous CMC" (Postmes et al., 1998, pp. 1–2). The SIDE Model is built on several earlier theories, including **social construction theory**, **deindividuation theory**, and **social identity theory**.

Social construction theory examines the reciprocal influence of technology and social contexts. The methods people use to collect, record, and interpret information about social situations will influence the way they define and understand social structures. In the SIDE model, both characteristics of the Internet and social contexts influence the ways in which people behave in CMC genres. For example, the lack of visual and aural cues in CMC allows people to communicate anonymously. In MUDs, people assume roles and develop characters, in business contexts, on the other hand, people generally reveal their true identity. How, when, and why people reveal their actual identity depends upon the social context.

Deindividuation theory was developed by observing crowds. Deindividuation is a decreased awareness of the social environment and self, which leads to reduced adherence to social norms. "It is defined as a psychological state of decreased self-evaluation, causing antinormative and disinhibited behavior" (Postmes, Spears, & Lea 1998, p. 5). Researchers examined the behavior of crowds and what causes them to either run amok or follow leaders. They discovered that being a member of a crowd causes a loss of individual awareness and identity. When individuals are part of a crowd, they become anonymous and no longer accountable for their actions. In contrast to this theory, individuals in CMC groups, even though visually anonymous, tend to be more responsive to the group's norms.

Social identity theory argues that individuals have a range of social identities and that the crowd does not make an individual lose awareness of self. Instead, a shift in social identity occurs and crowd members will see themselves as being part of the group. Consequently, people adhere to the group's norms (Figure 11.4).

Group members establish boundaries for themselves. Social stereotypes and norms are used to define social behavior and differentiate groups from each other. Cues-filtered-out researchers argued that CMC would cause a breakdown in social norms and roles, for example, flaming and rude behavior. SIDE model research reveals the opposite effect: Online participants will assume that other people are similar to themselves and that they share comparable norms and characteristics. As a result, social evaluations of others through text-based CMC are perceived more positively and individuals adhere to group behavioral norms.

Visually anonymous CMC appears to strengthen conformity to group norms and behavior. The absence of individual social cues enhances awareness of group identity and behavioral norms. Although CMC provides an opportunity to erase social boundaries, it can

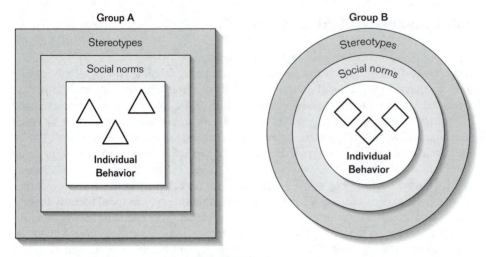

FIGURE 11.4   Visualization of SIDE Theory. Members of groups set boundaries for themselves through stereotypes and social norms. Social behaviors differentiate groups from each other. People participating in Internet groups tend to share comparable norms and characteristics, while adhering to group behavioral patterns.

also reinforce stereotyping, gender typing, and discrimination. People will often follow group patterns of behavior instead of break the rules as individuals.

Summary

The early developers of the Internet realized that people would use this new medium to communicate with one another and form communities that span geographic space. Internet communities are communities of interests. People come together to discuss topics and share information and experiences. Over the twenty-five years that the network has been in existence, a variety of online communities have emerged. The term *virtual community* was coined by Howard Rheingold to describe his experiences on a San Francisco-based network called the WELL.

As the Internet continues to evolve, new types of online communities have begun to appear. These include Free-Nets, community networks, communities of interest, MUD communities, support communities, audience communities, media communities, and Web rings. Web rings present an alternative way to locate information on the Web and bypass commercial search engines by forming communities of interest.

There are four characteristics that differentiate virtual communities from discussion lists. These include trust, social rules, community building, and a group history. Online groups create their own behavioral norms. To be accepted in the group, individuals must behave accordingly. The SIDE model explains how media characteristics combined with social context influence the ways in which group members socially use CMC and establish different group norms.

TERMS

Collaborative mass media systems are systems in which the audience is the primary source of media content and also receivers of it.

Deindividuation theory is a decreased awareness of the social environment and self, can lead to reduced adherence to social norms.

Internet communities are collections of individuals who use computers, software, and other means to discuss common interests through the network. The rules of behavior that were established by the original Internet community of scientists, researchers, and technologists are still being used by many online communities today.

Many-to-many communication allows groups of individuals, such as a discussion list or MUD environment, to share information.

One-to-one communication is exchanging messages, such as e-mail, with another person.

Social construction theory examines the reciprocal influence of technology and social contexts. The methods people use to collect, record, and interpret information about social situations will influence the way they define and understand social structures.

Social identification/deindividuation (SIDE) theory argues that the elimination of visual cues (anonymity) in CMC contexts makes people conform to accepted social norms.

Social identity theory argues that individuals have a range of social identities and the crowd does not make an individual lose awareness of self.

Telepresence is the experience of presence that is created when using a communication medium, such as a telephone, computer network, or teleconferencing system.

Virtual communities are informational and emotional support groups that form the same type of bonds as geographic communities by sharing human experiences.

Web rings have emerged to provide a method for linking together common Web-based interests. Sites are banded together into linked circles that enable people to find them more quickly and easily.

WEB SITES

First Monday Internet Journal: http://www.firstmonday.org
Howard Rheingold's Virtual Community: http://www.rheingold.com
Media Ecology: http://www.media-ecology.org
Web Rings:
http://www.December.com/cmc/mag/1999/jan/elmer.html
http://www.Webring.org

EXERCISES

1. Find out whether or not there is a community network in your local area. What type of communication does the network support? Does it provide local information? Encourage face-to-face events? Support discussion groups?

2. Make a list of the different communities of which you are a member. Do any of these communities use CMC as a method of communication? How is it used? If CMC is not used, how

could it be utilized to facilitate communication in the different communities to which you belong?

3. There are conflicting opinions about whether or not communities can really develop through computer networks. Discuss whether or not online groups of people should be considered a community.

4. Some scholars believe that the formation of virtual communities will be harmful to geographic communities. What do you think? Will virtual communities have a positive or negative impact on real ones? Why?

5. Pick a topic that is of interest to you. It could be your favorite soap opera or a hobby. Search for this topic using a traditional search engine and a Web ring. Report on the results.

BIBLIOGRAPHY

Barnes, S. (2000). Developing concepts of self in cyberspace communities. In S. B. Gibson & O. O. Ovideo (Eds.), *The emerging cyberculture* (pp. 169–201). Cresskill, NJ: Hampton Press.

Barnes, S. (2001). *Online connections: Internet interpersonal relationships*. Cresskill, NJ: Hampton Press.

Baym, N. K. (1995). The emergence of community in computer-mediated-communication. In S. G. Jones (Ed.), *Cybersociety: Computer-mediated communication and community* (pp. 138–163). Thousand Oaks, CA: Sage Publications.

Baym, N. (2000). *Tune in, log on*. Thousand Oaks, CA: Sage Publications.

Beniger, J. R. (1987, June). Personalization of mass media and the growth of pseudo-community. *Communication Research, 14* (3), 352–371.

Boczkowski, P. J. (1999). Mutual shaping of users and technologies in a national virtual community. *Journal of Communication, Spring 1999*, pp. 86–108.

Cohill, A. M., & Kavanaugh, A. L. (2000). *Community networks: Lessons from Blacksburg, Virginia* (2nd ed.). Norwood, MA: Artech House, Inc.

Curtis, P. (1996). MUDing: Social phenomena in text-based virtual realities. In P. Ludlow (Ed.), *High noon on the electronic frontier* (pp. 347–373). Cambridge, MA: The MIT Press.

Dibbell, J. (1998). *My tiny life: Crime and passion in a virtual world*. New York: Henry Holt and Company.

Dohney-Farina, S. (1996). *The wired neighborhood*. New Haven: Yale University Press.

Dyson, E. (1997). *Release 2.0: A design for living in the digital age*. New York: Broadway Books.

Elmer, G. (1999). Web rings as computer-mediated communication. *Computer-Mediated Communication Magazine, January* [Online] 3pp. Available: http://www.december.com/cmc/mag/1999/jan/elmer.html (October 22, 2001).

Horn, S. (1998). *Cyberville*. New York: Warner Books.

Jones, S. (1995). Understanding community in the information age. In S. Jones (Ed.), *Cybersociety* (pp. 10–35). Thousand Oaks, CA: Sage Publications.

Licklider, J. C. R., & Taylor R. (1968, April). The computer as a communication device. *Science and Technology*. (Online) 41 pp. Available: http://gatekeeper.dec.com/pub/DEC/SRC/research-reports/abstracts/scr-rr-061.html (July 10, 2001).

McInnes, A. (1997). The agency of the InfoZone: Exploring the effects of a community network. *First Monday, Issue 2* [Online]. Available: http://www.firstmonday.org (October 17, 2001).

Phillips, D. J. (1996, January–March). Defending the boundaries: Identifying and countering threats in a Usenet Newsgroup. *The Information Society, 12* (1), 39–62.

Phillips, G. M., & Metzger, N. J. (1976). *Intimate communication*. Boston: Allyn & Bacon.

Postmes, T., Spears, R., & Lea, M. (1998, Dec.). Breaching or building social boundaries?: SIDE-effects of computer-mediated communications [Online]. *Communication Research, 25* (6), 689–715 [Online], 20 pp. Available: *ProQuest #339204819* (July 9, 2001).

Postmes, T., Spears, R., & Lea, M. (2000). The formation of group norms in computer-mediated communication. *Human Communication Research, 26* (3), 341–371.

Rafaeli, S., & LaRose, R. J. (1993). Electronic bulletin boards and "public goods" explanations of collaborative mass media. *Communication Research, 20* (2), 277–297.

Rheingold, H. (1993). *The virtual community*. Reading, MA: Addison-Wesley Publishing Company.

Rheingold, H. (1998). *Virtual communities*. In F. Hesselbein, M. Goldsmith, R. Beckhard, & R. F. Schubert (Eds.), *The community of the future* (pp. 115–122). San Francisco: Jossey-Bass Publishers.

Schuler, D. (1994). Community networks: Building a new participatory medium. *Communications of the ACM, 37* (1), 39–51.

Schuler, D. (1996). *New community networks: Wired for change*. Reading, MA: Addison-Wesley Publishing Company.

Shenk, D. (1997). *Data smog*. San Francisco: Harper.

Strangelove, M. (1993). *Free-Nets: Community computing systems and the rise of the electronic citizen* [Online], 2 pp. Available: http://www.vcn.bc.ca/sig/comm-nets/strangelove.txt (June 21, 2000).

Valauskas, E. J. (1996). Lex networkia: Understanding the Internet community. *First Monday, Issue 4* [Online]. Available: http://www.firstmonday.org (October 21, 2001).

PART IV

CMC and Society

In addition to using CMC to build human relationships, the Internet supports political, civic, and global communication. Community is a centralizing concept for both local and global Internet communication. CMC can be used to organize people in new and powerful ways, however, it can also be used for evil purposes. Participating in a global community requires us to learn about the positive and negative uses of the Internet. Part IV describes some of the many cultural issues facing citizens today as the Internet replaces other forms of communication as a primary method for sharing information.

Negative behavior patterns, such as flaming, spamming, and hacking, will be discussed. These behaviors are regulated through both social norms and governmental laws. Other Internet topics currently being hotly debated include copyright, anonymity, and privacy. While the Internet enables us to easily correspond on a global level, it also leaves an electronic record of our correspondence, which can be accessed by others.

On a positive note, the Internet is considered to be a medium that will foster the development of community building and support democratic principles. For example, it has been suggested that the United States use Internet voting systems. Democracy and the Internet will be examined along with globalization issues. Viewed from the global perspective, the Internet introduces many American concepts into nations around the world. For instance, everyone does not share the American concept of freedom of speech. Should freedom of speech be applied to the Internet?

Along with Internet issues, models for discussing and analyzing Internet concerns are also introduced, including Gattiker's cube model for comparing different types of online behavior and Lessig's model for regulating the Internet. Because Internet communication now influences just about every aspect of our social and professional lives, examining the social issues relating to Internet use is critically important. Each chapter in this section presents topics of social concern for citizens living in an Internet age.

12 Disruptive Online Behavior

Chapter Overview

Early CMC researchers believed that the limited cues available through CMC would lead to rude and disruptive behavior and not foster the development of relationships. The first part of the theory was correct. People often behave badly in CMC correspondence. One reason may be that limited cues make people exaggerate their behavior to make a point. Flaming and shouting occur in many different types of online discussions. In some cases, this behavior becomes so extreme that it will disrupt correspondence and Internet communication.

Disruptive online behavior is an aspect of CMC that can affect individuals, online groups, and social order. There are different categories of disruptive behavior, including flaming, provocateurs, gender-bending, and spamming. Disruptive behavior patterns raise a number of social issues, which include hacking, hate speech and the spread of computer viruses. Gattiker has developed a model for examining Internet conduct. Chapter 12 covers the following aspects of disruptive behavior:

- Flaming
- Spamming
- Gender-bending and misrepresentation
- Dealing with disruptive behavior in CMC
- Social concerns, including hackers, cyberterrorism, hate speech, pornography, and the spread of computer viruses
- A model for comparing codes of conduct on the Internet

When communication technologies are introduced into a culture, they are criticized for ushering in new varieties of social ills. According to Katz and Aspden (1997), "When the telegraph, telephone and the automobile were in their infancy, each of these three earlier 'communication' technologies found vitriolic critics who said these 'instruments of the devil' would drastically alter society (which they did) with disastrous consequences for the quality of life and the moral order" (p. 81). Similarly, Internet critics argue that it too will contribute to moral decay. For example, people argue that the Internet is disruptive to social order because it promotes flaming behavior, distributes pornography, supports cyberterrorism, and disseminates hate speech. From the spread of spam to criminal hacking, the Internet introduces a new set of social ills that deserve closer examination.

Disruptive Behavior in CMC

Early participants in Internet culture shared similar backgrounds because many were computer professionals and academics. These Internet pioneers helped each other navigate and learn the new electronic frontier. In addition to sharing software tips, participants would voluntarily modify their behavior to avoid criticism and flames. Troublemakers were quickly embarrassed and were filtered out of discussions by software. Social forces helped groups maintain order, and participants respected each other, even when they disagreed. But as more people connected to the Internet, it became harder for the old-time Internet users to maintain order in cyberspace (Figure 12.1). Individuals became rowdy and commercial interests discovered e-mail as a method for delivering advertising messages. Consequently, newsgroups were disrupted by off-topic posts and advertisements. Groups were bombarded with MAKE MONEY FAST offers and hundreds of junk e-mail messages. Once orderly newsgroups became chaotic spaces filled with flaming and commercial messages.

A common feature of all CMC genres is the uninhibited effect they have on human behavior. Participants often behave more freely than they would in face-to-face situations. For instance, people say things in flaming messages that they would probably never say in a face-to-face conversation. Exaggerated statements are commonly found in most discussion groups. In addition to the anonymous nature of CMC, an influx of new Internet users introduced disruptive behavior patterns into CMC. For example, individuals began to deliberately use aggressive and disrespectful behavior to agitate groups and destroy established virtual communities.

Flaming as Disruptive Behavior

The vast migration of new users to the Internet disrupted bulletin board services, CompuServe forums, and newsgroups. Many online groups have been upset or disbanded because of online misbehavior. For instance, the CommuniTree, a computerized bulletin board community founded in the mid-1970s, was destroyed by an onslaught of obscene messages posted by schoolchildren. The children, mostly boys, had access to Apple II computers with modems. They quickly learned the dial-up phone number of the CommuniTree bulletin board and began logging on to their conferences. However, the intellectual level of the discussion did not appeal to adolescent interests, so the boys began posting messages to express their discontent. CommuniTree's systems operator (sysop) was puzzled, surprised, and annoyed by the crude messages posted by the boys, and she exiled the messages, making them invisible to the community. Although exiled messages become invisible, they still use disk storage space. These invisible messages collected into a garbage heap that eventually filled the entire hard drive of the bulletin board's computer system.

After having their unwanted messages removed from the system, the boys discovered another way to disrupt the community. They hacked into the CommuniTree computer, discovered bugs in the system, and crashed it. Eventually, the bulletin board service had to shut down because the systems operator could not keep up with the boys' pranks. In researching this incident, Stone (1995) reported that the boys' newfound power to destroy things at a distance, the anonymous nature of their correspondence, and the fact their actions were risk free contributed to their online misbehavior.

FIGURE 12.1   Anonymous Message on How to Be Annoying On-Line. This is from an item titled "How To Be Annoying On-Line" by someone named Spy. It was circulated around the Internet.

Here's how to be a pest-by-modem:

*Make up fake acronyms. On-line veterans like to use abbreviations like IMHO (in my humble opinion) and RTFM (read the f...... manual) to show that they're "hep" to the lingo. Make up your own that don't stand for anything (SETO, BARL, CP30), use them liberally, and then refuse to explain what they stand for ("You don't know? RTFM").

*WRITE ALL YOUR MESSAGES IN ALL CAPS AND DON'T USE PERIODS OR RETURNS SO THAT EVERYONE HAS TO SCROLL ACROSS THEIR SCREENS TO READ EVERY LINE ALSO USE A LOT OF !!!!!! AND DDOOUUBBLLEESS TO SHOW THAT YOU'RE EXCITED ABOUT BEING HERE!!!!!!!

*When replying to your mail, correct everyone's grammar and spelling and point out their typos, but don't otherwise respond to the content of their messages. When they respond testily to your "creative criticism," do it again. Continue until they go away.

*Software and files offered on-line are often "compressed" so that it won't take so long to travel over the phone lines. Buy a compression program and compress everything you send, including one-word E-mail responses like "Thanks."

*Upload text files with Bible passages about sin or guilt and give them names like "SexyHouseWives," then see how many people download them. Challenge your friends to come up with the most popular come-on. Take bets and calculate odds on the results of each upload's popularity.

*cc: all your E-mail to Al Gore (vice.president@whitehouse.gov) so that he can keep track of what's happening on the information Superhighway Internet.

*Join a discussion group, and tie whatever's being discussed back to an unrelated central theme of your own. For instance, if you're in a discussion of gun control, respond to every message with the observation that those genetically superior tomatoes seem to have played an important role. Within days, all discussion of gun control will have ceased as people write you threatening messages and instruct all other members to ignore you.

Source: Anonymous humorous message sent to author by Gerald M. Phillips on March 10, 1995.

Flaming is probably the most publicized form of online misbehavior. Groups such as alt.syntax.tactical use flaming as a strategy to stage online battles; they invade online groups where essentially harmless people gather on the Internet. Fiedler (1994) describes the activities of alt.syntax.tactical as follows:

> So how exactly does this work? First they decide which newsgroup to invade (like the cat group), then they send their spies in. The spies pretend to be cat lovers and talk about feeding problems, getting other people to comment. To start the fun off, one of the spies will calmly ask, for instance, for a recipe for roast cat, because his cat died and he does not want it to go to waste. The real cat people get all excited and say nasty things to the spy. That's the signal for the other spies to act: Some defend the first spy, some pick fights with the defenders and so on.
>
> By the time the alt.syntax.tactical people are done, virtually all the conversations on the newsgroup are among the spies—everyone else is so disgusted that they drop out. If you're a member of one of these invaded groups, the feeling is almost exactly as if a bunch of savage horsemen had come riding into your front yard (p. 20).

This is an extreme example of flaming, but it shows how flames can upset established online groups. According to Mabry (1998), people engaging in face-to-face conversations prefer to agree and they keep conversations orderly. In contrast, flaming is a conversation strategy used to compete for group leadership positions, exclude people from the group, and disrupt group activities. All of these actions upset group harmony.

Another type of disruptive behavior is trolling. Baiting people to react to outrageous messages is called a **troll**. **Trolling** is posting a message designed to create a predictable response or flame to a discussion group. The term is adapted from fishing, where it means trailing bait through a spot in the water hoping a fish will bite. Originally, trolls were developed to make new Internet users appear clueless; experienced Usenet users would know not to respond to the outrageous messages posted by pranksters. Today, people troll to get attention, to disrupt online groups, and to simply misbehave.

Experienced trollers will spend time carefully choosing a subject and constructing a message. Messages are directed at two different audiences, the regular group participants and lurkers. For example, an English bricklayer posed as an American student to post a negative comment about American students on all of the college newsgroups. He then left the students alone to handle the flames. This troll ran for a year and generated 3,500 responses. At some point, this trolling incident was blamed on an innocent American student, who lost her Internet account and was expelled from her high school for abusing the computer system. Although some people find trolling to be a game, others have been harmed by this type of misbehavior. Often, innocent bystanders are blamed for the actions of others, which can lead to loss of Internet privileges and personal credibility.

Provocateurs

Another online behavior problem is provocateurs. Discussion groups need people to post provocative messages to generate discussion. Occasionally though, provocative messages can turn into the **provocateur problem**, a problem that occurs when individuals use the technique of provocation to disrupt discussion groups. This strategy was first used on public affairs discussion lists by anarchist groups, who deliberately tried to shut the public groups down. Their technique was then taken over by individuals with a more pointed purpose—to nullify the effectiveness of discussion lists that aim to increase public participation and decision making through the Internet.

There are several characteristic ways in which provocateurs work. First, provocateurs can subscribe to a list under many different identities. While list managers are attempting to nullify the provocateurs they have identified, others or the same person can continue the provocations using different names and strategies. A typical strategy is to accuse the people who blow the whistle on the provocateur to be the source of the problem. For example, when alt.syntax.tactical invaded the cat lover's newsgroup, the provocateurs accused a woman in the cat group of starting the conflict. The woman had reported messages sent by members of alt.syntax.tactical to authorities. This innocent woman's name was then placed on a list of names of provocateurs that was circulated around the Internet. Because of the incident, the woman nearly lost her job.

Second, members of online groups will find it difficult to believe that there are people who are disturbing the discussion simply to provoke or troll the list. If the list managers let the more sophisticated members of the group try to stop the provocateurs, these people will be flamed and the situation will escalate. Moreover, naive list members may unknowingly join forces with the provocateurs in attacking the people who are trying to stop the disruption. Flame wars will replace normal discussion topics and create such disgust among the list's membership that the list will shut down or become moderated to prevent inappropriate messages from being sent to the group.

Some groups are disrupted by a single provocateur who, for whatever reason, insists on sending numerous off-topic messages to the group. These people will frequently post long, irrelevant messages that annoy other people. Experienced Internet users will ignore these messages. However, this does not always stop the provocateur. For instance, after being ignored, one provocateur began answering her own messages. Group members will try to politely tell these people that their behavior is inappropriate, but instead of paying attention to the warnings, provocateurs often ignore the suggestions and continue their bad behavior. With a single provocateur, several things can occur. First, many group members may sign off from the list. Second, if the provocateur is not stopped, the list can eventually cease to be active because no one will participate. Third, the provocateur can be eliminated from the group. When this happens, the list will continue. Removing an individual from a group can be either an individual or group decision. Frequently, group participants will discuss the situation off-list and ask the list manger to remove the person. In other cases, the decision can be made by the list managers themselves.

List managers can take several steps to try to prevent the provocateur problem. First, the purpose of the list should be clearly stated and members should be made aware of the public and open nature of their discussion. Second, the list manager should have the authority to decide when someone is deliberately disrupting the discussion and should be able to remove this person from the list. Third, group members should be informed that it is not permissible for them to post messages telling others to get off the list. If group members feel that someone is being disruptive, they should report this to the list manager and let the manager deal with it. Otherwise, a flame war can erupt between people who want the person kept on the list and those who do not. Finally, list managers should make it clear to members that the provocateur problem does exist and that it can disrupt groups. Frequently, the aim of the provocateur is to ruin the confidence people have in the list by making it impossible for people to disagree without resorting to flames or personal attacks. Group members who are sensitive to flames may escalate the provocateur problem by accusing others of flaming. One basic trick of provocateurs is to accuse someone else of flaming to heat up the situation. List managers should ask members to send accusations of flaming directly to them to avoid an all-out flame war.

Once people understand how provocateurs work, it is fairly easy to identify them. Provoking messages are often irrational, off-topic, and outrageous. They frequently include crude and childish comments. These messages are designed to throw people off-balance and to elicit a somewhat hysterical response to the original message. Savvy Internet users will let outrageous messages die and not respond. Another approach to the provocateur problem is to use e-mail filters. When provocateurs disrupt discussion groups, members can set up a **bozo filter** to bury the provocateurs' posts in a subsidiary folder on their hard drive. For example, one provocateur would send twenty messages a day to a list, disrupting the balance of the conversation. Group members quickly filtered his messages using bozo filters to maintain an orderly discussion. Software is often used to deal with provocateurs because these people are often difficult to reason with. Thus, provocateur disruptions can be dealt with through e-mail filters, moderation, list expulsion, or, in extreme cases, disbanding the group.

Spamming

Some provocateurs will send numerous messages to a list. This type of disruptive behavior is called spamming. A **spam** is a message that is repeated over and over again to numerous e-mail accounts, discussion lists, and newsgroups. Often, these messages do not relate to the topic the group is discussing. According to Moore (1995), the term *spam* comes from "an old Monty Python routine, the one in the restaurant where someone orders, 'Spam, Spam, Spam, Spam, Spam, Spam, Spam, Spam, Spam, Spam, and eggs'" (p. 218). Today, spam has become the junk mail of the Internet because it is often unsolicited promotional messages sent in bulk to thousands of Internet users. Receiving large volumes of irrelevant messages is disruptive to individuals, group interaction, and sometimes the Internet itself.

Spamming first became widely publicized in 1994, when Laurence Canter and Martha Seigel decided that they could make money by advertising their legal services through Usenet newsgroups. The service they promoted was helping alien residents of the United States get green cards to enable them to legally work. This first use of spam later became known as the Green Card Incident. To find potential clients, these lawyers sent the same e-mail message to over 6,000 newsgroups. What they did not realize is that many people subscribe to numerous newsgroups. Consequently, some people encountered hundreds of copies of the "Green Card" notice because of their membership in different groups. At that time, the Internet did not have very much advertising, and network users did not like having their time wasted. Many people became angry over the messages they received. Angry Internet users began responding to Canter and Seigel's message by sending them lots of flaming e-mail. The return traffic generated by the original spam was so large that the network service provider Canter and Seigel subscribed to was knocked off the Internet. Canter and Seigel's account was canceled for misuse of network resources.

Prior to the commercialization of the Internet in the mid-1990s, spam was not a major problem. Unsolicited e-mail consisted of messages from pranksters, chain letters, or individuals who mistakenly sent messages to an entire list instead of an individual. Commercial messages were rare; the Green Card Incident was the first widespread use of e-mail for advertising purposes. As the Internet became more commercial, spam increased. By 1997, spam rates were increasing at a rapid pace, and they continue to be a major problem for many users.

Most spam people receive today is in the form of junk mail. People who receive printed junk mail usually ignore it and throw it away, but computer users who receive spam will try to get back at spammers by flaming them. Spam and antispam messages flowing through the Internet can slow down the network by creating high volumes of traffic. To prevent this problem, Internet network operators are joining together to protect people from unsolicited e-mail, and new regulations have been suggested to deal with unwanted messages. For instance, filtering software is available to help weed out spam. Filtering can work in both directions: Filters refuse unwanted incoming messages and they block reply mail to any filtered address. This prevents the Internet from becoming overloaded with spam and antispam messages.

The increased use of spam has led to legal cases. For example, America Online attempted to block Cyber Promotions from sending spam to AOL subscribers. In the suit, it was decided that Cyber Promotions did not have a First Amendment right to send spam to AOL subscribers. Consequently, AOL had the right to use software tools to block the messages. In other instances, companies that produce spam have been sued because they used the trademarked names of other businesses in their false return e-mail addresses.

Two factors contribute to the use of spam. First, bulk e-mail is inexpensive to send. For example, 100,000 e-mail messages can be sent for under $200 and do-it-yourselfers are able to buy a million e-mail addresses for under $100. Serious bulk e-mailers will purchase software that enables them to send 250,000 messages per hour with forged headers. They can also harvest e-mail addresses from online services, the Web, and newsgroups. Second, it is easy to obtain pseudonyms to bypass filtering software. Filtering software screens messages based on the name or e-mail address of the sender. Bulk e-mailers can frequently change names to avoid filtering efforts. Although spam is inexpensive to send it can be expensive to receive. People waste their valuable work time downloading and deleting unwanted messages. As spam grows, its costs to Internet service providers and consumers increases. In addition to software filters, solutions to the spam problem are being sought through legal means. As a form of misbehavior, spam can be very disruptive to individuals, organizations, and Internet service providers (Figure 12.2).

Gender-Bending and Misrepresentation

Another type of misbehavior reported about the Internet is gender-bending, or presenting oneself online as a different sex. Gender-bending was first described in an article called "The Strange Case of the Electronic Lover" written by Lindsy Van Gelder and published

FIGURE 12.2   Example of Spam

```
To: barnes@email_account.com
From: Online Promotions <opromo@spamnet.com.>

****READ THIS MESSAGE IT WILL CHANGE YOUR LIFE****
You can earn money$$$$$ working at home. Hundreds of people have made
thousands of dollars per week with our program.
E-MAIL US NOW FOR MORE INOFMATION
$$$$$$$$$$$$$$$$$$$$$$$$$$$$$$$$$$$$$$$$$$$$$$$$$$$$$$$$$$$$$$$$$$$$$$$$$$$$
```

in a 1985 issue of *Ms. Magazine*. The article described how a woman named Joan spent over two years becoming a popular member of the CompuServe conference system. Joan joined the women's discussion groups and exchanged e-mail messages with female friends whom she met on the network. However, after a series of complex incidents, it was discovered that Joan was actually a prominent New York male psychiatrist named Alex. Alex had become engaged in a bizarre and all-consuming experiment to experience being female. The women on CompuServe who befriended Joan felt betrayed by Alex's deception. Alex was able to keep up the online persona of Joan for a long period of time because Joan described herself as disabled and unable to talk on the phone or meet in person. The stories Joan told online friends to avoid face-to-face contact eventually led to the discovery that Joan was really Alex.

The idea that a man would impersonate a woman on the network angered and confused the people who became friends with Joan. Alex's misrepresentation of himself to gain trust and friendship was viewed as an act of betrayal. A key factor was the misrepresentation rather than the gender-bending. Today, gender-bending is a more accepted online behavior pattern because people are aware of it. Depending on the motives of the individual, gender-bending occurs as misrepresentation or playful interaction.

Professional writer Jesse Kornbluth (1996) decided to gender-bend on America Online because he found female discussions groups more interesting than male groups. When Kornbluth first experimented with male-oriented chat rooms, he discovered that most of the men were not interested in serious discussions. However, when he joined the women's groups, they would stop talking and give him a hard time because he was a man. To solve this problem, Kornbluth decided to become a virtual woman named MsTerious. The first time he joined a women's chat as MsTerious, the women asked him questions to verify his gender identity. After answering the questions correctly, MsTerious was handed a virtual cup of coffee and welcomed into the group. Kornbluth played the role of a woman to have fun and interact with others. In his case, gender-bending was a way to engage in social conversation. This story illustrates a change in attitude about gender-bending as a type of misbehavior. Today, many people just accept it as part of the online experience.

However, gender-bending can create identity issues for some people. Psychosocially speaking, the impact of creating an online persona and its influence on the actual person are still unknown. Researchers Turkle (1995) and Stone (1995) compare the ability to construct and deconstruct different identities in cyberspace to multiple personality disorder (MPD). Goldenson (1970) describes MPD as "a rare dissociative reaction in which two or more relatively independent personality systems develop in the same individual" (p. 843). Computer networks enable people to project facets of both conscious and unconscious aspects of themselves through both real and invented identities. However, in contrast to MPD, which examines whether multiple selves can inhabit a single body, cyberspace separates the body from the self. As a result, Stone argues that our concepts of *self* and *body* operate differently in virtual space. Separated from physical appearances, people can pretend to be who and whatever they want to be. In online situations, such as MUDs and MOOs, role-playing is fun and a social game, but sometimes role-playing can have a real impact on individuals. For instance, several incidents of role-playing gone awry have disrupted online groups and caused emotional distress for MUD participants.

Disruptive Behavior in MUDs

Researchers and journalists have reported several incidents of misbehavior in MUD environments. For instance, Reid (1994) describes an incident that occurred in a social MUD called JennyMUSH. JennyMUSH was established as a virtual help center for people who had experienced sexual abuse and assault. The administrator of the MUSH was a psychology student who was interested in the treatment of abuse survivors. Members of this MUD community had established strong personal bonds with each other by sharing their common trauma stories. For many members, JennyMUSH was the only place in which these individuals could discuss their experiences. Unfortunately, a single user disrupted the harmony and balance of this special online community.

Two weeks after joining the group, one character used the MUD's commands to change into the virtual manifestation of a character that the other players would fear. This person changed his or her character's name to Daddy and used the "shout" command to send messages to every other member connected to the MUD. Virtual violent and graphic assaults were described. Some members logged off the system, many pleaded with Daddy to stop, and others began threatening the character. But nothing stopped the assaults. At the time this occurred, none of the MUD's administrators or Wizards were online. After half an hour of abuse, one of the Wizards logged on, saw what was happening, and took control of the player's Daddy character and made it impossible for Daddy to communicate. Additionally, the Wizard changed the character's name from Daddy to Vermin and gave it the following description:

```
This is the lowest scum, the most pathetic dismal object which a
human being can become.
```

The terrorized players took their revenge and expressed their hatred and rage. After the incident, JennyMUSH became more security conscious. The shout command was eliminated, and members are now able to stop unwanted messages by using a "gagging" command. All new members must provide the administrator with a working e-mail address and their actual, legal name. All of these changes were the result of the disruptive behavior of one person. Another more widely publicized case of disruptive MUD behavior was committed by a group of young college students.

Case Study: Rape in Cyberspace

The rape in cyberspace was first described in a New York weekly newspaper called the *Village Voice*. The virtual rape was committed by a group of male college students who participated in LambdaMoo, a MOO established by researchers at Xerox PARC to explore the development of social relationships through CMC. The event occurred in the crowded living room, which was described in Chapter 9. The living room is a common room and a central gathering place for LambdaMOOers to party. More important, the room captures the communal spirit of the thousands of players who participate in this MUD environment. Reporter Julian Dibbell (1993) began his article about the rape in cyberspace with the following paragraph:

> They say he raped them that night. They say he did it with a cunning little doll, fashioned in their image and imbued with the power to make them do whatever he desired. They say that by manipulating the doll he forced them to have sex with him, and with each other, and to do horrible, brutal things to their own bodies. And though I wasn't there that night, I think I can assure you that what they say is true, because it all happened right in the living room—right there amid the wellstocked bookcases and the sofas and the fireplace—of a house I've come to think of as my second home (p. 38).

As Dibbell researched the incident, separating the cyberspace experience from the real-world events became difficult. The online events began with a male character named Mr. Bungle, who appeared in the living room about 10 P.M. Pacific Standard Time. He immediately started to use a software tool called a *voodoo doll* to force one of the other characters in the room to unwillingly perform virtual sexual acts. His first victim was a character named Legba, who was described as a Haitian trickster spirit. Mr. Bungle was soon ejected from the living room area, and he went to hide in his private room in the MUD. However, his voodoo doll worked at a distance and he continued to attack other victims. After his first attack on Legba, he began to control another character named Starsinger, who described herself as a rather nondescript female character. Finally, an old-timer named Zippy, who had Wizard status on LambdaMoo, fired a magic gun that thwarted the voodoo doll and silenced Mr. Bungle's evil laughter.

As a reporter, Dibbell explored the event both on- and offline. In real life, Mr. Bungle was the communal character of an entire New York University dorm floor, Legba was a woman living in Seattle, and Starsinger was a woman living in Pennsylvania. According to Dibbell (1998), "The young man at the keyboard on the evening of the rape had acted not alone but surrounded by fellow students calling out suggestions and encouragement" (p. 30). Months after the event, the woman in Seattle confided to Dibbell that she had experienced posttraumatic stress and that the content of the rape scenario had an emotional impact on her. According to Dibbell, the woman's response to the virtual rape only made sense in the dissonant gap between reality and virtual reality that occurs through CMC. Online communication can stir emotional feelings in people. MUDs and MOOs appear to be highly stylized games; however, behind the characters are actual people with real emotional responses. The rape in cyberspace illustrates how people can blur the distinctions between on- and offline experience and exemplifies how the emotional content of cyberspace can bleed into the real world.

The rape in cyberspace forever changed this online community. The night after the incident, Legba sent a public message to the social-issues forum posted in the living room to be read by the entire LambdaMOO community. She argued that Mr. Bungle should be punished for his crime. In the wake of the incident, the group had to face the reality that they needed to set online behavioral norms and standards. LambdaMOO participants began to experiment with developing their own "virtual" legal system.

According to Mnookin (1996), "Just as players may construct themselves in novel and creative ways, they may also imaginatively construct political institutions and social forms" (p. 18). Often, online experiences tend to reflect real life. For instance, LambdaMOO creator Pavel Curtis (1996) observed: "Social behavior on MUDs is in some ways a direct mirror of behavior in real life, with mechanisms being drawn nearly unchanged from real life" (p. 351). The Lambda legal system borrows from the American legal system because players assume that freedom of speech and the right to privacy in the real world apply to their online communities. For example, LambdaLaw does not explicitly establish a free speech right or a privacy right, yet most players presume that these rights exist in LambdaMoo. Because legal issues in MUDs parallel real life, this online environment provides an opportunity for participants to engage in debate, experiment with creating laws, and critique individual and social behavior. Consequently, CMC has the potential to be a utopian space for creating possible worlds and exploring the construction of social meaning.

In addition to members of LambdaMoo, journalists and academics have reflected on the social construction of rape in modern society as a result of the rape in cyberspace. At the center of the feminist debate over rape and pornography is whether or not pornography is a representation of an act or *an act itself.* American courts have upheld decisions to protect pornography under free speech because it is considered to *represent* an action, rather than *be* an action. However, Katherine MacKinnon (1993) argues against this point of view because women's bodies must be used and sometimes destroyed in the process of making pornographic representations. Consequently, an action must occur to make the image. If this broad view of rape were applied to CMC, virtual rape could be treated as an actual rape. In contrast to Katherine MacKinnon, Richard MacKinnon (1998) argues against a broad view of rape that considers representations of rape to be an action. This broad definition would introduce a social construction of rape into CMC genres that would have the same emotional, psychological, and sociological consequences as a physical rape. Richard MacKinnon (1998) asserts, "Feminist theorists seeking social parity for women have fostered a broadening of the concept of rape to include conceptions which do not necessarily involve penetration or even any physical contact" (p. 148).

Mr. Bungle's unwelcome act in LambdaMoo and the reactions of the women involved have raised important questions about the meaning of cybersex and online rape. When writing the article, Dibbell was interested in the oscillation between the virtual and the real and the ambiguity between the two. At present, CMC is raising questions about our social understanding of politics, violence, and representation. Online communities also provide us with an opportunity to reimagine standards for individual and social behavior along with concepts of rape.

Dealing with Disruptive Behavior in CMC Genres

Different types of online groups manage disruptive behavior in various ways. For example, LambdaMOO set up a legal system and discussion group moderators often handle the provocateur problem. In a study of conduct control on Usenet newsgroups, Smith, McLaughlin and Osborne (1998) report that reproaches for different types of behavioral offenses will vary according to group. Flaming and language improprieties are considered negative behavior patterns in the majority of the groups they analyzed. Additionally, group members tend to be less tolerant of people who are frequent behavior offenders. Single offenders are generally left alone. Responses to misbehavior are often made through the exchange of private e-mail messages rather than group discussions. To avoid escalating the problem, individuals are asked to alter their behavior privately.

In MUD and MOO environments, Wizards can eject people who behave badly by toading them. The @toad command instructs the computer system to destroy a person's character. A more democratic approach to dealing with MUD misbehavior is to allow the victims of bad behavior to banish a character. Victims can place a banish mark next to the name of the character who committed the offense. A character with a specified number of banish marks next to his or her name will eventually be toaded. Banishing takes control away from the Wizards and allows players to participate in the removal of an offensive character.

In an analysis of antisocial behavior in CMC, Walther, Anderson, and Park (1994) applied Walther's *social information processing perspective*, described in Chapter 7, to a study of online behavior. Their research suggests there is a relationship between time and social dynamics. For example, Walther (1994) discovered that an expectation of future interaction with an online correspondent often makes people exchange positive relationship-building messages. Although time influences positive social behavior, the study was unable draw the same conclusion about negative behavior. Misbehavior on the Internet is a topic that communication researchers need to examine in further detail.

Disruptive Behavior and Social Concerns

One type of misbehavior on the Internet that has received a tremendous amount of attention is hacking. Stories in the news report on hackers who disrupt the operation of major Web sites and the Internet itself. For example, the *New York Times* Web site has been shut down by hackers and other sites have crashed because of online pranks. In addition to hacking, a number of controversial issues are associated with Web sites. For instance, Holocaust revisionist Web sites argue that the Holocaust never existed, hate speech sites support the White Supremacist movement, anarchist sites provide information on bomb making, and numerous sites offer pornographic images. Controversial Web sites have led to legal attempts to censor Web-based information and have raised public concerns about the medium itself.

Hackers

Protecting the rights of individuals using CMC is a major topic both on- and offline. Attitudes about free speech and sharing information through the Internet have been shaped by "hacker ethics," established in the 1960s (Figure 12.3). Originally, the term **hacker** referred

---

FIGURE 12.3   Hacker Ethics

According to Levy (1984), hacker ethics include the following:

1. Access to computers—and anything which might teach you something about the way the world works—should be unlimited and total. Always yield to the Hands-On Imperative!

2. All information should be free.

3. Mistrust Authority—Promote Decentralization.

4. Hackers should be judged by their hacking, not bogus criteria such as degrees, age, race, or position.

5. You can create art and beauty on a computer.

6. Computers can change your life for the better.

Source: Adapted from Levy, 1984.

to compulsive computer programmers. For instance, Weizenbaum (1976) described a hacker as a compulsive programmer who "spends all the time he can working on one of his big projects. "Working" is not the word he uses; he calls what he does "hacking'" (p. 118). Hackers were skillful technicians who explored computer technology and tried to write programming code in the smallest amount of space possible. Hacking started at MIT, where an entire culture emerged around computer technology. However, as computer technology spread throughout American culture, hacking began to be associated with breaking into government and corporate computer systems. As a result, the image of the hacker has been transformed from harmless computer nerd to dangerous Internet outlaw.

In a study of hackers, Halbert (1997) discovered that the image of the hacker is one of an information deviant: "It is the role of the deviant to mark the boundaries of legitimate behavior" (p. 362). Consequently, deviant hackers help to produce rules for appropriate behavior on the Internet. Sterling's book *The Hacker Crackdown* describes numerous conflicts between hackers and the law. Sterling (1992) asserts: "In 1990 there came a nationwide crackdown on illicit computer hackers, with arrests, criminal charges, one dramatic show trial, several guilty pleas, and huge confiscations of data and equipment all over the United States" (p. xiii).

Starting with Operation Sundevil, the media have played an important role in creating the image of the criminal hacker. Operation Sundevil was a well-publicized clash between legal authorities and hackers. The operation, which involved 150 agents in 12 cities across the United States, was described in a press release distributed on May 9, 1990 by the U.S. Attorney's office in Phoenix, Arizona. Twenty-seven search warrants against hackers were carried out on May 8, resulting in three arrests. The U.S. Secret Service, private telephone security, and state and local law enforcement agencies combined forces to stop hackers from accessing telephone company computer systems. Three hackers using the online names of Acid Phreak, Phiber Optik, and Scorpion were arrested in New York. According to telephone company executives, computer security experts, and law enforcement agents, young hackers are remorseless, malicious invaders who break into other people's computers, hacking is a financial strain on the national telecommunications infrastructure, and hackers are dangerous role models for today's youth. As a result, law enforcement agencies have started to crack down on hacker activities. Viewing the hacker crackdown from the hacker perspective, it is argued that hackers pick the locks on corporate systems as a prank rather than a malicious act. Hackers are young people exploring the new electronic frontier of cyberspace and they really do not harm anything.

Hackers first came to the attention of the FBI in June 1989. At that time, several illicit copies of Apple Computer's *QuickDraw* source code, a closely guarded piece of Apple's intellectual property, had been put into envelopes and mailed to people all over the United States. A group called the "NuPrometheus League" claimed to have committed the crime. When Apple Computer discovered that its property had been copied and distributed, it called the FBI. Almost a year after the crime was committed, one of the recipients of the illegal disks, John Perry Barlow, received a visit from his local Wyoming FBI agent. According to Barlow, the FBI agent was not very computer literate and instead of being interviewed by the agent, Barlow had to explain computer technology and what was actually "stolen." After the FBI visit, Barlow posted an account of the interview on the online service called the WELL. Several days later, Mitch Kapor, a wealthy software entrepreneur, stopped in Pinedale, Wyoming to visit Barlow. They talked for several hours about Operation Sundevil and the hacker crackdown. Afterwards, Kapor decided to get involved, and he contacted a civil libertarian lawyer in New York to discuss the case against the hackers. Kapor and Barlow established the Electronic Frontier Foundation in June 1990. According to Barlow (1996), the purpose of Electronic Frontier Foundation is to "raise and disburse funds for education, lobbying, and litigation in the areas relating to digital speech and the extension of the Constitution into Cyberspace" (p. 486). The Electronic Frontier Foundation supports a libertarian view and was established to protect the rights of individuals on the Internet.

Cyberterrorism

The lack of government censorship and control over information distributed through the Internet contrasts sharply with the situation in traditional mass media. Mass media messages are subject to government regulations and are controlled by the media industries. Critics of the media industries argue that most media (newspapers, magazines, radio and television) are owned by a small number of global corporations whose control of the messages permit only a limited number of points of view to be presented and that many of their perspectives support commercialism rather than the public interest. In contrast, the Internet supports the sharing of public information with few restrictions. All types of views can be freely expressed.

The bidirectional nature of Internet communication enables almost anyone with access to a computer to participate in online discussions and debates. As a result, the Internet fosters interactive mass participation. Traditional mass media are passive, one-directional, and controlled by the media industries, but through the Internet, people can fully participate in a bidirectional uncensored form of communication. Elmer-Dewitt (1995a) describes the Internet as an antidote to commercial mass media: "Rather than catering to the lowest common denominator with programming packaged by a few people in New York, Atlanta and Hollywood and broadcast to the masses in the heartland, the newsgroups allow news, commentary and humor to bubble up from the grass roots" (p. 10).

Mass messages are designed to be broadcast to a large audience. In contrast, **narrowcasting** directs media messages to specific audiences. For example, messages are designed to reach sports fans or cooking enthusiasts. Newsgroups and discussion lists could be considered an extreme form of narrowcasting. Additionally, a percentage of the Internet content is created by users for other users. User-generated content generally focuses on a specific topic of interest. At present, no organization controls the type of content distributed through the Internet.

Discussion about monitoring and censoring Internet communication started after the terrorist bombing of the Oklahoma City federal building. A central issue in the debate is protecting individuals and communities from extreme political points of view. Reports about the Oklahoma bombing suggested, with no evidence, that the bombers used the Internet to communicate their plans. According to Davis (1995), "Long a fertile ground for anarchist and anti-authoritarian thought, Net political culture also includes heaps of right-wing conspiracy theory, racist patriotism, Waco obsession, weapons fetishism, and bitter, seething resentment against the federal government" (p. 28). Conspiracy theories do run rampant on the Internet and theories exist there on just about any topic. Individually these messages appear to be angry rantings, but collectively they reveal a darker side of Internet life.

According to Garfinkel (2000), a radical fringe of Internet privacy advocates engages in online cyberterrorist activities. These people ignore laws and social norms to raise privacy awareness. For instance, in 1992, a northern California group called the cypherpunks started distributing high-level cryptographic software while simultaneously criticizing commercial cryptographic programs. Moreover, they disclosed the security flaws in the commercial programs. Cypherpunks also illegally exported cryptographic software from the United States to other countries. The popular press regularly comes up with news stories about illegal activities that are claimed to be conducted over the Internet. Johnson (1997) wrote, "Right-wing lunatics post recipes for explosives and rouse their members with paranoid visions of immense conspiracies that only they can overthrow" (p. E1). Concerns over the types of messages shared through the Internet have led the United States Parole Commission to restrict federal parolees from using the Internet. Federal parolees can be kept from owning firearms, drinking to excess, consorting with criminals, and using a computer to access the Internet. Johnson goes on to describe the Internet as "the most efficient incubator yet of ideas both ennobling and debased. Each computer terminal is a shiny surface, reflecting not just things in the real world but the simulated reality of the Internet" (p. E6).

After the Oklahoma City bombing, the Net was filled with anarchist rantings and ravings. According to Guisnel (1997), the Internet appeals to militant groups because it is an instant global communication medium. Extremist groups can voice censor-free messages to a worldwide audience. By bringing together people from around the world, the Internet enables people with extreme points of view to find each other and form groups both on- and offline. Moreover, these groups can find information through the Internet that could contribute to terrorists acts. Consequently, law enforcement agencies around the world are monitoring the Internet and exploring possibilities for regulating its content.

Hate Speech

Another Internet issue of major concern in the United States is **hate speech**. Hate speech is making racist or discriminatory comments on the basis of race, gender, origin, disability, or sexual orientation that are designed to intimidate others. Hate speech is protected by First Amendment free speech rights in the United States. Hatemongers use the Internet to spread racial bigotry, Holocaust denial, gay bashing, and other offensive points of view. According to Sharkey (1997), there are estimated to be between 100 and 250 extremist sites on the Internet, including the white supremacist group Aryan Nations, the Ku Klux Klan, and Resistance Records, a white-power record company. In addition to sites sponsored by organizations, individuals can also distribute hate speech. For example, a Northwestern engineering professor named Arthur Butz attempted to convince people that the Holocaust never existed.

Butz was able to use his university's computer system to distribute his message because academic freedom of speech allows professors to voice their personal opinions. Hate speech has become a problem at American universities, and policies are now being written to discourage students and faculty from using university computing resources to distribute it. In addition to setting policies, there are a variety of ways in which individuals can counter hate speech. Guisnel (1997) says one way to stop hate speech online is to send continuous barrages of messages to discussion groups and newsgroups that promote hate speech. The barrage of messages will prevent these groups from spreading their opinions. Others argue that for every site that promotes hate speech, other sites develop to counter the hatemonger's claims. Thus, outrageous claims are countered with facts and arguments. A different approach adopted by the Simon Wiesenthal Center in Los Angeles is to have Internet service providers ban objectionable material from their networks. Many service providers, however, do not want to set standards.

European countries, including France and Germany, do ban some forms of hate speech. In France and Germany, anti-Semitic and Nazi-oriented Web sites are illegal. In Germany, service providers are forbidden to host these sites, and Internet companies cannot ship Nazi materials to German citizens. Amazon.com, for instance, could not sell a copy of Hitler's *Mein Kampf* to its German customers. Similarly, the French government filed a lawsuit against Yahoo! for online racism. Yahoo! was selling Nazi paraphernalia online, which is illegal in France. The French have enacted a law that forbids people to use French computer servers to disseminate racist propaganda or denials of the Holocaust presented as historical fact. Using the logic of the French, some universities have adopted policies to ban Holocaust revisionism on their computer systems because the Holocaust *is* historical fact.

Hate speech promoted by antiabortion groups has raised legal issues about whether hate speech should be protected under the First Amendment. An antiabortion Web site called The Nuremberg Files identified a number of medical professionals who performed abortions. Doctors were placed on a "wanted" list and were identified as "baby butchers" and "child-killers." Although the authors of the site claim they did not want to promote violence, a Buffalo physician was murdered by a sniper shortly after the list was posted on the Web. According to Lipschultz (2000), the "promotion of illegal activities through speech walks the line between speech protected by the First Amendment and action deemed illegal by state and federal laws" (p. 50). Finding a balance between free speech and hate speech is a problem facing many university administrators today, and it is an issue that students need to be aware of.

Pornography

Another type of controversial expression is pornography, which is also protected under the First Amendment. On July 3, 1995, *Time Magazine* ran a cover story called "Cyberporn" written by Elmer-Dewitt. The article described an academic study that was conducted by a college senior named Marty Rimm. According to the study, researchers claimed they had found 917,410 sexually explicit pictures, short stories, and film clips on the Internet. A controversy immediately began both on- and offline about the use of the Internet as a pornographic medium. But as soon as the *Time* article hit the newsstands, Rimm's research was criticized by experts on conceptual, logical, and procedural grounds. According to Wallace and Mangan (1996), "Within weeks after its publication, the Rimm study had been thoroughly discredited" (p. 151). Unfortunately, the flawed report had already been the subject of debate in the U.S. Senate. Senators Grassley and Exon had shown the *Time* article to Congress, and Senator Coates had already cited Rimm's false statistics. At the same time, *Newsweek* published an article titled "No Place for Kids?, " which described stories of sexual predators who used the Internet. In the article, Levy (1995) stated, "Until now parents have believed that no physical harm could possibly result when their progeny were huddled safely in the bedroom or den, tapping on the family computer. But then came news of cases like the 13-year-old Kentucky girl found in Los Angeles after supposedly being lured by a grown-up cyberpal" (p. 47).

Leading the crusade against pornography was Senator James Exon, who proposed the *Communications Decency Act* (CDA). The act was signed by President Clinton in February 1996 as part of the *Telecommunications Reform Bill. New York Times* reporter Lewis (1996b) described the bill as follows:

> Lawmakers said the intent of the act was to halt the flow of pornography and other objectionable material on the Internet . . . . The law makes it a felony, punishable by prison terms and large fines, to make indecent or patently offensive materials available on computer systems where children might see them (p. 1).

On June 12, 1996, however, federal judges in Philadelphia struck down the *Communications Decency Act*. According to Sieger (1996), "The decision represents a landmark victory for individual Internet users, and should preserve the openness and unfettered debate upon which the net was built" (p. 13). He further stated, "The court soundly rejected the arguments offered by the government and the religious right that the Internet should be regulated similar to broadcast mass media" (p. 14). Currently, radio and television stations are prevented from broadcasting pornography and foul language into people's homes. Reversal of the *CDA* is viewed as a victory for freedom of speech in cyberspace.

To counter the criticism of pornography on the Web, a number of pornography sites require credit cards and passwords. However, many sites allow people (even minors) to be "guests" and sample the type of material presented on the site. To deter children from accessing pornography on the Internet, a number of software filtering programs have been developed for parents who want to prevent their children from independently accessing inappropriate Web resources. Developing software solutions for the individual and organizational regulation of Web-based information is an alternative way to regulate offensive material without placing legal restrictions on Internet content.

Such Internet issues as cyberterrorism, hate speech, and pornography are not limited to the United States. According to Lewis (1996a), "All over the world, a growing number of governments, schools, special interest groups and families are struggling to find acceptable ways of tapping into the riches of the Internet without also hitting the darker veins of the global computer network" (p. D1). For example, German officials recently persuaded CompuServe to cut off access to approximately 200 sex-related discussion groups worldwide. However, Internet technologists say that there is no completely effective way to block unacceptable Internet content that is available to tens of millions of people in over 150 countries. Internet pornography and hate speech are worldwide issues, and regulating these types of Web sites is a global concern.

Computer Viruses

An equally important issue is the dissemination of computer viruses through the network. A **computer virus** is a program that does two things: First, it searches for new hosts; second, it makes copies of itself. Many computer viruses attach themselves to another program. If a virus self-replicates without attaching itself to another program it is called a **worm**. Both can quickly spread through computer networks and cause damage. The majority of the viruses attack DOS (disk operating system) and Windows computer systems. Viruses have been deliberately released on the Internet. Robert Morris, a Cornell graduate student, for example wrote a worm program designed to explore the Internet, but a number was wrong in the program and the worm replicated out of control. It caused 6,000 computers to crash. Morris faced legal charges and was fined for his actions.

Not all viruses are harmful. The Hantavirus Pulmonary Syndrome virus, for instance, flips computer graphics to their mirror images every Saturday and antivirus programs protect computer systems from known viruses. When new ones are released, the manufacturers of antivirus programs will distribute updates to their programs through the Internet. At present, there is no international agreement on whether the creation and dissemination of computer viruses is a prank or an illegal activity.

A Model for Comparing Codes of Conduct

Members of different organizations and societies follow different codes of conduct. Gattiker (2001) used cognitive development theory to create a model for comparing different behaviors. Cognitive development theory, originally created and tested by psychologists Jean Piaget and Jerome Bruner, argues that an individual's cognitive abilities develop through a series of stages until they understand language and logic. Language enables people to think about abstract concepts and ideas (Figure 12.4). According to Gattiker (2001), "Progression through the stages of cognitive development depends on an individual's ability to develop a detached, impartial point of view to objectively evaluate a situation as either right or wrong" (p. 123). An aspect of cognitive development is understanding moral values. Cognitive development theorists contend that moral cultural issues involve justice, rights, or harm. However, the moral rules of each culture will vary.

Moral development is placed into three different domains, including personal, moral, and conventional. The personal domain of morality is based on personal preferences and

FIGURE 12.4 A Social and International Approach to the Domain Theory of Moral Development

	Moral Domain	Conventional Knowledge Domain	Personal Knowledge Domain
	Learned through direct observation of harm or injustice caused by a transgression	Learned through exposure to group consensus	Learned through exposure to others (e.g., during childhood) and past behaviors' outcomes
Material Conditions	Objective obligations: Justice, harm, rights, welfare, allocation of resources	Actions that are right or wrong by virtue of social consensus: Social uniformities and regularities, food, clothes, forms of address, sex roles	Psychological states, personal tastes and preferences
Formal Conditions	Rational, universal, unalterable, objective, self-constructed, more serious	Arbitrary, relative, alterable, consensus-based, socialized, less serious	Rational and irrational, arbitrary, relative, alterable, self-constructed
Description	Intrinsically harmful acts perceived directly, or inferred from direct perceptions	Acts are not harmful, have interpersonal consequences, and are meaningful in a specific social context	The domain is outside the realm of societal regulation and moral concern
Infractions	1. Hitting another individual 2. Software piracy	1. Junk mail 2. Loading a computer virus program onto an electronic newsletter/listserver	1. Indescent acts 2. Use of encryption devices
Consequence	1. Social group may castigate 2. Legal or institutional (e.g., school—suspension, work—warning)	1. People may be puzzled or upset about behavior 2. Individual may be encouraged to change or face the consequences (e.g., social outcast)	1. Individual may feel uneasy or good about behavior 2. Based on input from reference group(s) or close friends/family, person may feel uneasy/good about behavior

From Gattiker, *The Internet as a Diverse Community*. © 2001 Lawrence Ealbaum Associates, Inc. Publishers. Used by permission.

tastes. To some people, when an individual disrupts a discussion group by sending trolls or starting a flame war, these types of actions are pranks, but to others they are disruptive and inappropriate behavior. The domain of conventional knowledge encompasses actions that have both interpersonal and social consequences. In this domain, social norms, values, and attitudes influence the meaning of a specific action. For instance, most discussion group members believe that flaming and the use of derogatory language is inappropriate. An individual who flames once or twice will be asked to stop doing it, but individuals who persist in this type of inappropriate behavior will be asked to leave the group. The final domain, the domain of morality, includes violence and harmful social acts. For example, most individuals consider hate speech to be immoral, despite the fact that it is protected in the United States by the First Amendment. However in other cultures, hate speech activities are illegal. Using Gattiker's cube model (Figure 12.5), we can see that activities will be placed in different quadrants depending on cultural views. Gattiker's research revealed that various cultures and organizations have different moral standards. The norms and rules of one group regarding codes of Internet conduct may be different from those of another group. Gattiker's cube model is designed to compare these differences. The cube's x-axis presumes there are two levels of regulation for privacy, safety, security, and confidentiality of infor-

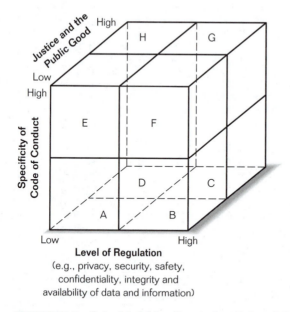

FIGURE 12.5   Cube Model for Comparing Codes of Conduct. This model was developed to compare different codes of conduct that have been established by professional associations, countries, and social good. Individuals should be aware of what they are expected to do and the consequences for violating the codes of conduct.

From Gattiker, *The Internet as a Diverse Community.* © 2001 Lawrence Ealbaum Associates, Inc. Publishers. Used by permission.

mation. The two levels are a high level of regulation and a low level of regulation. The cube's *y*-axis shows the specificity of the code of conduct. For instance, at the top of the cube, social justice is considered and legal actions would be placed in quadrants G and H. Actions requiring social justice include threatening e-mail messages, illegally breaking into a computer system, spreading a computer virus, and stealing software. These actions are legal issues and laws have been passed to stop these activities. In contrast, low specificity means that social justice concerns are not dealt with. Disrupting social norms would fall into the low-specificity level, for instance, sending a flaming e-mail message, which would be placed into quadrant A. Additionally, the model assumes that individuals will follow codes of conduct or else they will face some type of consequence, such as loss of membership in a group.

Codes of conduct for Internet use do already exist. They are described by professional organizations such as the Association for Computing Machinery (ACM). Individual Internet groups also have rules for behavior that are often described in Frequently Asked Questions (FAQ) documents. Because individual personal codes of conduct differ, individual and group reactions to flames, provocateurs, spam, hacking, pornography, and hate speech will vary. Gattiker's cube model for codes of conduct can be used to help visualize the differences between perspectives and the different types of misbehaviors that occur on the Internet.

Summary

Disruptive Internet behavior occurs in both discussion groups and on the Web. Discussion groups and newsgroups encounter problems with flames, spam, and provocateurs. Some individuals engage in the act of trolling, which is sending messages to an online group that are deliberately designed to encourage flames from other people. Online groups have different ways of dealing with misbehavior. Often group moderators or list owners handle the disruptive individual via private e-mail messages. MUDs will toad or expel members. In extreme cases, groups will disband because they cannot regulate provocateurs and stop the disruptive behavior.

The illegal behavior of hackers has become a topic in the popular press. The term *hacking* has taken on a negative connotation from reports about computer break-ins and disrupted Web sites. As the Web becomes more widely used, social concerns over hate speech, cyberterrorism, the spread of computer viruses, and pornography are more widely discussed. Hate speech is a growing issue on the Web as the number of sites that promote extreme points of view increases. It is also a topic that affects college campuses. Gattiker's cube model can help us understand different perspectives on codes of Internet conduct.

TERMS

Bozo filters are software programs that bury the e-mail messages of designated individuals in a subsidiary folder on a computer hard drive.

Computer viruses are programs that search for new hosts and make copies of themselves. The repeated copying of the program can disrupt computer operations.

Hacker is a term originally used to refer to compulsive computer programmers, however, it has recently been used to refer to people who illegally enter or "hack into" computer systems.

Hate speech is racist or discriminatory comments made on the basis of race, gender, origin, disability, or sexual orientation that are designed to intimidate others.

Narrowcasting directs media messages to specific audiences, for example, messages designed to reach sports fans or cooking enthusiasts.

Provocateur problem refers to the use of the technique of provocation to disrupt discussion groups.

Spam is a message repeated over and over again to numerous e-mail accounts, discussion lists, and newsgroups.

Troll or **trolling** is posting a message to a newsgroup that is designed to create a predictable response or flame.

Worms are viruses that self-replicate without attaching themselves to another program.

E X E R C I S E S

1. Research the topic of trolling in newsgroups. Form teams to debate the positive and negative aspects of this type of online behavior. For example, one side could argue that trolling is harmless fun, and the other could take the position that they are harmful.

2. One of the most controversial articles describing interaction in MUDs is Dibbell's article "A Rape in Cyberspace or How an Evil Clown, a Haitian Trickster Spirit, Two Wizards, and a Cast of Dozens Turned a Database into a Society." The article is available online at: ftp://ftp.lambda.moo.mud.org/pub/MOO/papers/VillageVoice.txt A revised version of this article is now located through Dibbell's home page (just type his name into any search engine to find the site and look for the links to his nonfiction articles). This new version is also the first chapter of his book *My Tiny Life*). Please read this article and discuss the following questions:

   a. Do you think the rape in cyberspace should be taken seriously? Why or why not?
   b. Do you think that a computer database should be considered a community? Why or why not?
   c. Do you think that the woman in Seattle overreacted to the Mr. Bungle affair? Does Dibbell present a persuasive argument that "what happens inside a *MUD*-made world is profound, compelling, and emotionally meaningful"? Why or why not?
   d. Do you think that the disembodied act of virtual sex should be considered an action or a representation of an action? Do Mr. Bungle's actions have any relationship to pornography in the real world?
   e. According to Dibbell, to make a decision about "toading" Mr. Bungle, the residents of LambdaMOO first had to define themselves as a community or social organization. What political groups does he suggest were the major forces contending at the meeting in terms of those political forces—who won and who lost?
   f. As a college student, do you think that the university should have been notified about Mr. Bungle? Should any action have been taken in the "real world"? Why or why not?

3. Read Mnookin's article in the *Journal of Computer-Mediated Communication* and discuss how the rape in cyberspace helped to turn LambdaMoo into a virtual community.

4. Discuss the issue of hate speech on college campuses. Should hate speech be regulated? Why or why not?

5. What is your opinion about pornography on the Internet. Should it be regulated? If it is regulated, should it be done by law or through software?

6. Where would you place hate speech on Gattiker's cube for visualizing codes of conduct? Explain why you placed it in a specific quadrant.

WEB SITES

JCMC: Special Issues on Internet and the Law: http://www.ascusc.org/jcmc/vol2/issue1
Moral Panic and Alternative Identity Construction in Usenet: http://www.ascusc.org/jcmc/vol7/issue1/ baker.html
Spam
http://www.cauce.org
http://www.junkemail.org
http://spam.abuse.net/
Computer Professionals for Social Responsibility: http://www.cpsr.org

BIBLIOGRAPHY

Barlow, J. P. (1996). Crime and puzzlement. In P. Ludlow (Ed.), *High noon on the electronic frontier* (pp. 459–486). Cambridge, MA: The MIT Press.

Bennahum, D. (1994, May/June). Fly me to the MOO: Adventures in textual reality. *Lingua Franca*, pp.1, 22–36.

Bunn, A. (1999, March 3). Moltovs and mailing lists. *Salon Magazine* [Online]. Available: http://www.salon.com/21st/feature/1999/03/03feature2.html

Cranor, L. F., & LaMacchia, B. A. (1998, August). Spam! *Communications of the ACM, 41* (8), 74–86.

Curtis, P. (1996). MUDing: Social phenomena in text-based virtual realities. In P. Ludlow (Ed.), *High noon on the electronic frontier* (pp. 347–373). Cambridge, MA: The MIT Press.

Davis, E. (1995, May 2). Barbed wire net: The right wing hunkers down online. *The Village Voice*, p. 28

Dibbell, J. (1993, December 21). Rape in cyberspace: How an evil clown, a Haitian trickster spirit, two wizards, and a cast of dozens turned a database into a society. *The Village Voice*, p. 38. (Also available in P. Ludlow (Ed.). (1996) *High noon on the electronic frontier: Conceptual issues in cyberspace*. Cambridge, MA: The MIT Press.)

Dibbell, J. (1998). *My Tinylife: Crime and passion in a virtual world*. New York: Henry Holt and Company.

Elmer-Dewitt, P. (1995a, Spring). Welcome to Cyberspace. *Time*, pp. 4–10.

Elmer-Dewitt, P. (1995b, July 3). On a screen near you: Cyberporn. *Time*, pp. 38–45.

Fiedler, D. (1994, December). Oh, the places you'll go. *Netguide*, pp. 18–20.

Gaffin, A. (1995, March). Unsenet fish tales. *Everybody's Internet Update, No. 10, An Online Publication of the Electronic Frontier Foundation*. Available: http://www.intersurf.com/~aevinc/aev2trol.htm

Garfinkel, S. (2000). *Database nation*. Sebastopol, CA: O'Reilly.

Gattiker, U. E. (2001). *The Internet as a diverse community: Cultural, organizational, and political issues*. Mahwah, NJ: Lawrence Erlbaum Associates.

Goldenson, R. M. (1970). *The encyclopedia of human behavior: Psychology, psychiatry, and mental health*. Garden City, NY: Doubleday and Company.

Grabosky, P. N., & Smith, R. G. (1998). *Crime in the digital age*. New Brunswick, NJ: Transaction Publishers.

Guisnel, J. (1997). *Cyberwars: Espionage on the Internet*. New York: Plenum Trade.

Halbert, D. (1997). Discourses of danger and the computer hacker. *Information Society, 13* (4), 361–374.

Johnson, G. (1997, March 30). Old view of Internet: Nerds. New view: Nuts. *The New York Times*, pp. E1, E6.

Katz, J. E., & Aspden, P. (1997, December). A nation of strangers? *Communications of the ACM, 40* (12), 81–86.

Kornbluth, J. (1996). You make me feel like a virtual woman. *Virtual City, Winter*, pp. 57–58.

Levy, S. (1984). *Hackers*. New York: Doubleday & Company.

Levy, S. (1995, July 3). No place for kids? *Newsweek*, pp. 47–50.

Lewis, P. H. (1996a, January 15). Limiting a medium without boundaries. *The New York Times*, pp. D1, D4.

Lewis, P. H. (1996b, June 13). Free speech case: Ruling by panel moves the First Amendment into a new era. *The New York Times*, pp. 1, B10.

Lipschultz, J. H. (2000). *Free expression in the age of the Internet*. Boulder: Westview Press.

Ludlow, P. (1996). *High noon on the electronic frontier: Conceptual issues in cyberspace*. Cambridge, MA: The MIT Press.

Mabry, E. (1998). Frames and flames: The structure of argumentative messages on the net. In F. Sudweeks, M. McLaughlin, & S. Rafaeli (Eds.), *Network & netplay*. Menlo Park, CA: pp. 13–26. AAAI Press/MIT Press.

MacKinnon, K. A. (1993). *Only words*. Cambridge, MA: Harvard University Press.

MacKinnon, R. C. (1998). The social construction of rape in virtual reality. In F. Sudweeks, M. McLaughlin, & S. Rafaeli (Eds.), *Network & netplay* (pp. 147–172). Cambridge, MA: The MIT Press.

Mnookin, J. L. (1996). Virtual(ly) law: The emergence of law in LambdaMoo. *Journal of Computer-Mediated Communications, 2* (1), (Online), 30 pp. Available: http://www.ascusc.org/jcmc/vol2/issue1/lambda.html. (October 30, 2001)

Moore, D. W. (1995). *The emperor's virtual clothes*. Chapel Hill, NC: Algonquin Books of Chapel Hill.

Reid, E. (1994). Cultural formations in text-based virtual realities (Online). Available: http://people.we.mediaone.net/elizrs/cutl-form.txt (June 18, 2001)

Rojas, R. (2001). *Encyclopedia of computers and computer history, Vol. 2*. Chicago: Fitzroy Dearborn.

Sharkey, S. A. (1997). The proliferation of hate speech on the Internet: What can be done? (Online). Available: http://wings.buffalo.edu/Complaw/CompLawPapers/Sharkey.htm (June 16, 2001)

Sieger, J. (1996). Communications Decency Act is defeated: Landmark victory for netizens. *Communication of the ACM, 39* (8), pp. 13–15.

Smith, C. B., McLaughlin, M. L. & Osborne, K. K. (1998). From terminal ineptitude to virtual sociopathy: How conduct is regulated on Usenet. In F. Sudweeks, M. McLaughlin & S. Rafaeli, eds., *Network & Netplay*. Menlo Park, CA: AAAI Press/MIT Press, pp. 95–112.

Spinello, R. (2000). *Cyberethics: Morality and law in cyberspace*. Boston: Jones and Bartlett Publishers.

Sterling, B. (1992). *The hacker crackdown*. New York: Bantam Books.

Stone, A. R. (1995). *The war of desire and technology at the close of the mechanical age*. Cambridge, MA: The MIT Press.

Turkle, S. (1995). *Life on the screen: Identity in the age of the Internet*. New York: Simon & Schuster.

Van Gelder, L. (1985/1991). The strange case of the electronic lover. In C. Dunlop & R. Kling (Eds.), *Computerization and controversy* (pp. 364–375). Boston: Academic Press.

Wallace, J., & Mangan, M. (1996). *Sex, laws, and cyberspace*. New York: Henry Holt.

Walther, J. B. (1994). Anticipated ongoing interaction versus channel effects on relational comunication in computer-mediated interaction. *Human Communication Research, 20*, 473–501.

Walther, J. B., Anderson, J. F., & Park, D. W. (1994, August). Interpersonal effects in computer-mediated interaction: A meta-analysis of social and antisocial communication. *Communications Research*, pp. 460–487.

Weizenbaum, J. (1976). *Computer power and human reason*. New York: W.H. Freeman and Company.

13 Anonymity, Privacy, and Copyright

Chapter Overview

Internet characteristics have contributed to a series of new social issues and concerns. For instance, the physical separation of people from their words enables individuals to communicate anonymously through the Internet. People can make comments without taking responsibility for them. In some cases, the digital storage of e-mail messages is used to trace messages back to the source, which raises privacy issues. Internet messages can be copied and read by others. Digitalization makes it easy to duplicate Internet files, which raises additional concerns about copyright abuse.

Anonymous communication, privacy, and copyright are important Internet issues currently being debated. At the center of the debate is the American idea of freedom of expression. People want to freely share information and music files with each other. How do we maintain freedom of expression and simultaneously protect copyrights and community values? This chapter will discuss the following social issues:

- Free speech and the Internet
- Anonymous communication
- Privacy issues, including individual and workplace privacy
- Copyright issues
- Libertarian versus communitarian views of the Internet
- Lessig's model for regulating cyberspace

As a new medium of communication, the Internet expands an individual's ability to exercise the First Amendment right of freedom of expression. As the previous chapter described, hate speech, conspiracy theories, pornography, and individual opinions are freely expressed on the Internet because they are protected in the United States by the First Amendment. According to Constitutional specialist Lawrence Lessig (1999), "the right to free speech in the United States means the right to be free from punishment by the government in retaliation for at least some (probably most) speech" (p. 164). An American citizen cannot be jailed for criticizing a U.S. government official. For instance, at the inauguration of President George W. Bush, people were chanting "hail to the thief" instead of "hail to the chief" and were not arrested because freedom of speech enables American citizens to openly state their political opinions. However, American concepts of free speech are not shared by other countries around the world. Cultural values differ, and this makes regulating Internet content highly controversial because it raises the question: Whose cultural values should regulate the Internet?

Free Speech and the Internet

According to Spinello (2000), speech is central to many Internet issues, including anonymity, privacy, and copyright. Individuals speaking anonymously can cause harm to others by making disparaging remarks without fear of retribution. Freely expressing ideas or engaging in commercial transactions while using a masked or anonymous identity raises issues for Internet users. Commercial Web sites need to make sure that individuals engaging in financial transactions are providing a proper identity.

Information is both disseminated and collected through the Internet. The widespread commercialization of the Internet enables companies to collect consumer information and sell it to third parties. Personal privacy can be at risk when companies distribute this information without the individual's knowledge or consent. If hospitals, for example, were to provide drug companies with the names of individuals who have been diagnosed with specific diseases, they would be revealing private information without the individual's consent. This is an inappropriate use of personal information.

In the United States, free speech is the right to be free from punishment by the government in retaliation for most speech. Besides laws, social norms also regulate spoken behavior. In Internet communities, hacker ethics advanced the concepts of free speech and the open sharing of information. Sharing information was extended to the sharing of software and Internet content. Early hackers freely gave their software programs to each other. Following this behavior pattern, music fans freely share digital recordings with each other. However, the open sharing of music has been challenged by the recording industry as a form of copyright infringement. Anonymity, privacy and copyright issues will be discussed in more detail in the following sections.

Anonymity Issues

As described in the previous chapter, the ability of individuals to remain anonymous on the Internet can lead to misbehavior. The young boys who disrupted the CommuniTree bulletin board could play pranks without risk because it is difficult to associate an individual with an electronic action. CMC introduces new types of identities and social relationships that were previously unimaginable. Under the cloak of anonymity, individuals can engage in socially unacceptable or criminal activities. They can also participate in political activism, receive counseling, and execute commercial transactions.

Many online service providers allow users to create different identities and use online pseudonyms; however, records of the real identities of pseudonym users are kept by the information service provider. But when people use anonymous remailers, they can send totally anonymous messages. The use of pseudonyms on Internet service providers and the use of anonymous remailers have both raised serious ethical questions about how and why people engage in anonymous correspondence. Are people engaging in playful activities (MUDs and cybersex) or are they committing a criminal act (hacking into computers or spreading computer viruses)?

Electronic Identities

Anonymity is viewed by CMC researchers as both positive and negative. A negative aspect is the separation of people from their actions, which can lead to disruptive behavior. On the other, the removal of visual and verbal cues, such as gender, age, race, size, dress, accent, and body language, is viewed as a positive feature. Because personal information is eliminated in CMC exchanges, a diversity of users can interact on a more equal basis. This point has been illustrated by a popular Internet cartoon that shows a dog at a computer keyboard with the caption: "On the Internet, nobody knows you're a dog."

Another piece of Internet folklore goes something like this. A pompous university professor participating in an online discussion group is having a computer problem, the professor sends an e-mail message to the group asking for help. Another member replies with a solution. The solution is so successful that the professor sends a private e-mail message to the respondent to engage him in a private conversation. The professor introduces himself as doctor so-and-so with numerous degrees from prestigious universities, then he thanks the respondent for the help. The respondent replies by introducing himself as Billy Smith, a junior high school student from a suburban community. To the professor's surprise, he was corresponding with a young teenager! By eliminating physical characteristics, people encounter each other only through the words they exchange. The professor has college degrees, but the junior high school student has the technical expertise. On the Internet, technical expertise can carry a higher level of status than diplomas. Moreover, people who would not normally communicate with each other in face-to-fact settings can exchange Internet correspondence because visual cues are eliminated. In reality, we often do not know to whom we are talking on the Internet.

Anonymous Remailers

In 1988, anonymous remailers were created to allow anonymous messages to be sent to certain Usenet newsgroups. **Anonymous remailers** are programs that strip a message header off an e-mail message to make the sender anonymous to the receiver. Headers generally include the user name, the domain name, the time, the date, and the subject of the message. The remailer replaces this information with random headers. Thus, when messages are sent through numerous remailers, the originator of the message can become untraceable.

Anonymous messages can be of benefit in investigative journalism, personal privacy protection, self-help, and whistleblowing. Investigative journalists can use anonymous communication to protect their sources and themselves from harm or legal prosecution. Individuals seeking help for a drug or alcohol problem can anonymously participate in support groups and online counseling. Finally, **whistleblowing**, the making of others outside an organization aware of concerns, neglect, or abuses that could harm the public interest, is facilitated. For example, whistleblowers made the public aware that the Beech-Nut Corporation was using an inexpensive substitute for apple juice concentrate while advertising its product as 100% apple juice. People are often hesitant to use their real names when they are whistleblowing because they are fearful of retaliation from the organization, and so they often send anonymous messages. Anonymous remailer technology enables whistleblowers to expose corruption and dishonesty with a far lower risk of being discovered. According to Rose (1995), anonymous messages also permit persecuted groups to meet online without risk of others discovering their identities and using that information to harass or intimidate individual members" (p. 183). And anonymity encourages speech that otherwise would remain stifled. Members of marginalized social groups, for example, can use anonymity to express their point of view without fear of social ostracism.

Of course, anonymous remailers also make it possible for individuals to anonymously send illegal and injurious materials into public spaces, including copyright infringements, obscenity, stolen credit information, lies, and slander. Anonymous remailers enable people who spread hate speech to hide behind an anonymous wall. Critics of anonymity point out that knowing a speaker's identity is critical to evaluating the truthfulness of information. For instance, knowing whether a statement made about a drug on a medical discussion list is from a doctor or the public relations officer of the drug's manufacturer can help people determine the appropriate amount of consideration to be given to the statement. CMC raises questions about the relationship between anonymity and accountability. Holding people accountable for online activities, such as spam, online deception, hate speech, impersonation, and financial fraud, is difficult because it is not always possible to connect actual people with CMC messages.

Proponents of Internet anonymity compare it to American free speech. Specifically, they reference a 1960 Supreme Court decision that upheld the right to conduct some types of anonymous free speech. In the decision, "the Court invalidated an ordinance requiring all publicly distributed pamphlets to include the name and address of the person who prepared, distributed, or published them" (Cavazos & Morin, 1994, p. 15). American history provides significant examples of anonymous speech. Alexander Hamilton, James Madison, and John Jay, for instance, published the controversial *Federalist Papers* using the pseudonym "Publius." Similarly, authors who publish books and articles using pen names are also writing anonymously.

Case Study: Anonymous Remailers and the Church of Scientology

The use of anonymous remailers came to public attention both on and off the Internet in 1995. On February 1, 1995, "Finnish police presented Johan (Julf) Helsingius with a warrant demanding he provide them with the true name of the person who [had] been using his well-known anonymity server, anon.penet.fi, to conceal his identity when posting to the Usenet newsgroup alt.religion.scientology" (Barlow, 1995, p. 19). The police were trying to identify an individual who had allegedly stolen confidential information from the Church of Scientology. The individual was using Helsingius's anonymous remailer to publish this information. At first, Helsingius refused to comply with the order, but he was told that failure to obey would result in the confiscation of his entire computer system, which contained the actual identities of 200,000 different people from around the world. Many of these individuals were expressing controversial political opinions and would be considered political criminals in their own countries.

Helsingius did not want to endanger the lives of the strangers who used his anonymous remailer. Faced with the decision of having the identity of 200,000 versus one individual revealed, he complied and released the one name. Within an hour, the Finnish police provided the name to both the Los Angeles Police Department and the Church of Scientology. The anonymous user was identified as Dennis Erlich, a former Scientology minister. Erlich had been posting sections of Scientology scriptures to Usenet and criticizing church practices. Several days after his name was revealed, police officials, officials from the Church of Scientology, and lawyers rang the doorbell of Erlich's California home. For over seven hours, they went through his computer system, confiscating all magnetic media and deleting messages from his hard disk.

According to the church, the Scientology scriptures Erlich posted contained proprietary church information, which were considered "trade secrets." Erlich had wrongfully appropriated these secrets for his personal use. In the church's complaint, it described how it protected confidential information and trade secrets, which Erlich had freely distributed on the Internet. If Erlich had simply criticized the Church of Scientology, law enforcement agencies would not have intervened, Helsingius would have been safe, and Erlich's identity would have remained anonymous because libel is difficult to prove. Proving financial damage is a different type of charge. Because the church secrets were made public, the Church of Scientology could calculate actual financial losses. It was this financial aspect of the case that made it possible for the organization to involve international law enforcement agencies. Although unusual, this case demonstrates how an organization can use international legal agencies to silence the voice of a single Internet user.

Central to the Scientology case is the idea of anonymous speech, which combines free speech and the right to privacy. **Anonymous speech** is the right to communicate with other people without revealing your actual identity. The technology of anonymous remailers makes it possible for people to engage in anonymous speech.

Individual versus Community Values on the Internet

On the Internet, there is a social debate over individual rights versus community values. In *Sex, Laws, and Cyberspace* Wallace and Mangan explored the individual versus social issues surrounding many Internet-related incidents. One well-known case is that of a California couple who were tried under the community standards of Memphis. The couple ran a pornography site and the images were legal by California community standards, but illegal in Tennessee. The California couple was tried in Tennessee and found guilty of transportation of obscene materials through the Internet. According to Wallace and Mangan (1996), "The journalistic and legal communities immediately criticized the trial. They generally portrayed Tennessee as the most conservative state in the union and commented on the absurdity of it governing the standards of the on-line world" (p. 27). In this case, individual rights were curtailed in an effort to protect the larger community.

To date, there are various opinions about individual versus community values on the Internet. Free speech proponents often share a **libertarian view** of cyberspace. They believe that individuals rather than governments should establish the norms for online behavior. In contrast, the **communitarian view** argues that community values should set the rules for Internet communication.

Privacy Issues

Another issue of concern to individuals is privacy in CMC exchanges. Privacy is generally defined as the freedom to be left alone. Issues relating to Internet privacy include the collection, accuracy, and use of personal information in databases; the government's accumulation of personal information; privacy violations through corporate monitoring; and privacy in relation to online anonymity.

Collecting information in computer databases is an issue of major concern to the American public. According to Kling (1996), "privacy issues have taken on a new form and a new urgency with the advent of computer matching, a technique involving large databases with unrelated purposes that are cross-checked for consistency" (p. 623). For instance, government-owned state and federal databases are cross-checked to track down parents whose child support payments are in arrears. **Information privacy** deals with the right to control access to one's personal data. For example, individuals should be able to decide when, how, and to whom their personal medical information should be distributed. The ways in which the government has and could use technology to monitor and control individuals also concerns Americans. Government agencies could use database information to regulate aspects of social life. For example, the government checks state automobile registration records against tax records to locate individuals who register expensive cars but report a small income on their tax returns (Figure 13.1).

Individual Privacy

In addition to database privacy, individuals are also troubled about how private information stored on databases is being used. In 1997, America Online (AOL) was criticized for announcing plans to provide lists of its customers' telephone numbers to telemarketers. For many years, AOL had been selling lists of subscriber's names and addresses; now they wanted to sell phone numbers. Customers were afraid that they would start receiving intrusive telephone solicitations and complained.

Currently, there is a tremendous amount of personal information about individuals available on the Web. Names, addresses, phone numbers, and places of employment can be easily found through online searches, and data placed in Web databases are often made available without individual consent. Much of this information comes from publicly available documents, like telephone books and court records. However, another type of personal data collected through the Web is consumer information.

Cookies, Consumer Information, and Web Privacy Issues

Data collected from consumer transactions, such as telephone, mail, and Internet purchases, warranty cards, rebate coupons, and promotional offers, can be placed into databases. **Data**

FIGURE 13.1   Tips for Maintaining Privacy on the Internet

---

1. Become a savvy Internet Shopper. Check out new online shopping services before you register with them.

2. Read the privacy polices of the site. Responsible sites will provide a clear policy to you before you register with the site.

3. Be wary of service providers that supply "start-up" software that will make the first connection for you. Do not provide credit card, checking account, or other types of personal information before you can open an account. Some programs are designed to automatically upload information as soon as the connection is made. The program may be uploading information about your system configuration without your knowledge.

4. Create passwords with nonsensical combinations of upper and lower case letters, numbers, and symbols, for example, x8Ibe33z. Change your password often and don't leave your computer unattended when you are logged on.

5. To avoid leaving digital footprints when you send e-mail messages, use an anonymous remailer or an anonymizer (information is available at http://www.anonymizer.com).

6. It is just about impossible to erase all traces of e-mail because deleting a message will not remove it from the recipient's computer system. You need to be aware that messages you send could be read by others. As a result, personal information such as passwords, credit card numbers, addresses and Social Security numbers should not be sent vial e-mail or discussed in chat rooms.

7. Information published on Web sites can be read by others. It is best not to publish descriptive information about yourself on your site.

8. Privacy protection tools, including anonymous remailers and encryption software, can help Internet users protect their privacy.

Source: Adapted from Gelman, McCandlish, et al., *Protecting Yourself Online: An Electronic Frontier Foundation Guide*, 1998.

brokers are companies who specialize in maintaining consumer databases, which are sold to third parties. New software technologies, including large storage devices and data warehouse software, also enable all types of companies to store large amounts of consumer information, which can, in turn, be sold to other companies for a fee.

The Web has become a major new medium for collecting consumer information. Some sites offer free goods or rewards in exchange for personal data. For example, when people originally signed up for a "free" personal Web page on Geocities, they were required to fill out a detailed form that asked for income and educational information. This information was widely distributed to other companies until the Federal Trade Commission threatened to file a law suit against Geocities. As a result, Geocities had to change its policies. Concerns over how companies use the personal information they collect through the Web have caused many Web sites to post their privacy policies, which state how the information gathered by the site will be used.

Another way that marketers can track Web users and collect information is through the use of cookies. **Cookies** are small data files stored on a user's hard drive when they visit a site. Cookies contain passwords, the user's name, and pages visited on a site. These files are often used to customize Web pages. For example, the Amazon.com Web site can welcome a user by name because it has placed a cookie on the user's machine.

Cookies can be used to keep track of the Web sites a user visits. Text messages can be sent to the cookie's initiator that include pages the user has previously visited. The cookie installed on the user's hard drive can also send periodic updates to the initiator's server. Often, this occurs without the knowledge of the user, which some people believe is a violation of an individual's privacy. Similarly, employers can use cookies to see the names of Web sites that their employees visit when they use company computers. For instance, a company discovered that an employee working the evening and weekend shifts was visiting pornography sites. He was reprimanded for this Web activity.

The Panoptic Sort

Collecting consumer information started in the 1930s when the Spiegel Corporation developed a point system for evaluating credit applications. The system was based on four questions, including the amount of the order, the occupation of the applicant, the applicant's marital status, and the race of the applicant. Over the years, a variety of personal questions have been added to consumer data collection. With the addition of database technology and computers for collecting and sorting consumer data, electronic data is being used, according to Gandy (1993), as a panoptic sort. The **panoptic sort** is a complex of technologies used to collect, process, and share personal information about individuals and groups. After data collection, in a capitalist economy the information is used to coordinate and control access to goods and services.

From Gandy's (1993) view, the panoptic sort is a practice of classification and surveillance. He states that "the panoptic sort is an antidemocratic system of control that cannot be transformed because it can serve no purpose other than that for which it was designed—the rationalization and control of human existence" (p. 227). Gandy considers the technology itself to be strategic rather than communicative. Information collected and sorted with computer technology is used to develop strategic messages designed to influence and persuade consumers. Personal data could be used as a form of social persuasion to influence human behavior. Commercially, personal data is incorporated into advertising messages. Consumers are concerned about data warehouses and what would happen if all the consumer information stored in databases around the world were connected into one large searchable system.

But concerns over the collection and cross-referencing of consumer information have changed dramatically after the terrorist attacks on the World Trade Center. If commercial databases had been linked together, law enforcement agencies might have been able to apprehend the terrorists before the attack. Several terrorists already wanted by the FBI could have been captured through their credit card use. According to France and Green (2001), "The team that attacked the World Trade Center had to buy plane tickets, take flying lessons, communicate with one another, and draw money from bank accounts" (p. 84) All of these activities leave traces in dispersed computer databases. If federal agencies had the ability to data-mine this information, terrorism could be curtailed. **Data-mining** is a type of surveillance that monitors different computer networks.

Linking databases together would allow law-enforcement organizations to detect suspicious behavior patterns. However, databases created for one purpose can be used in other unintended ways. For example, information collected by the state of Massachusetts on health insurance claims was later turned over to the tobacco industry when the state sued cigarette companies. The widespread use of data-mining across computer systems will depend on the creation of effective guidelines for marketers and law enforcers.

E-mail and Privacy in the Workplace

Corporate access to personal e-mail correspondence is another privacy concern. Privacy in the workplace refers to freedom from intrusions by formal institutions and authorities into one's personal life. In the workplace, privacy issues revolve around two key concepts. First, employees should have the ability to keep information about themselves away from others who might use it as a means of control. Second, employees should be able to negotiate privacy issues in the workplace. For example, e-mail has no formalized set of access restrictions. Laws that protect the privacy of contents in paper mail do not apply to e-mail. With e-mail, privacy protection is dependant on an individual's respect for other people's e-mail messages.

Many computer users overestimate the amount of e-mail privacy they have. They mistakenly think that e-mail is similar to a sealed letter or a private telephone conversation. But e-mail messages are stored on corporate computers and companies can monitor these messages. Weisband and Reinig (1995) report that "Rhonda Hall and Bonita Bourke were fired from their jobs at Nissan Motor Corporation in 1990 when management discovered they were receiving sexually suggestive e-mail messages. Nissan's lawyers argued successfully that the company owned the system and had the right to read anything in it" (p. 40). Hall and Bourke were fired because of messages that they received; others have gotten into trouble for messages they have sent. For instance, some companies do not allow employees to use vulgar or sexually oriented language when they use the corporate e-mail system, and student interns have been reprimanded for misusing a company's e-mail system. Employees need to be aware of the e-mail policies of the companies they work for.

Perrolle (1996) argues that Habermas's theory of communicative action can be applied to CMC and CSCW systems to negotiate privacy issues in the workplace. The **theory of communicative action** considers communication the central element of society, and moreover, societies are bound together through their communicative actions. According to Habermas (1990), "The equal rights of individuals and the equal respect for the personal dignity of each depend upon a network of interpersonal relations and a system of mutual recognition" (pp. 202–204). In work environments, mutual recognition can be achieved by establishing an ideal speech situation. In ideal speech situations, all members of a society have an equal opportunity to participate in rational discussion. Perrolle argues that in CMC genres, individuals can participate equally because social status and power cues are eliminated. People who may not speak in face-to-face contexts will have an opportunity to talk in computer-mediated ones.

Creating an ideal speech situation in the workplace has four requirements. First, everyone must be linguistically competent. When using CMC, typing and computer skills would be added to basic language skills to fulfill this first requirement. Second, nondistorted communication needs to be established. Nondistorted communication occurs when people can interrogate each other to determine true versus false claims. In the workplace, truth is often found in formal rules and official knowledge. Often, false claims and rumors occur because people do not know or they misunderstand organizational policies. Two characteristics of CMC that work against nondistorted communication are that all CMC conversations are recorded and employees will often not engage in off-the-record conversations. Although CMC can facilitate interpersonal communication, it can also limit an employee's ability to verify information because there are no opportunities for private and off-the-record discussions. Thus, CMC can reduce opportunities for interpersonal employee privacy.

The third requirement is that people engaged in nondistorted communication must believe each participant intends to have a rational conversation that is not designed to mislead or intimidate. People who engage in online misbehavior will disrupt the ideal speech situation. But it is also true that the visual cues missing in CMC enable lower-status employees to participate more equally. When people focus on factual statements rather than intentions, CMC can facilitate nondistorted communication.

Finally, nondistorted communication needs to be conducted in a way that is socially acceptable to the participants. Group members need to follow the appropriate social norms and behavior established by the online group. Perrolle (1996) says, "In circumstances where opportunities for participation are enhanced and opportunities for one speaker to control another are reduced, [CMC] facilitates privacy negotiations" (p. 57). This occurs because emotionally based arguments are less likely to influence the attitudes of employees, and each employee has an opportunity to voice his or her opinion. Using CMC to create an ideal speech situation thus enables employees to negotiate privacy policies in the workplace.

Privacy and Internet Service Providers

America Online (AOL) has been at the center of privacy disputes. It has been accused of providing private information to third parties. In 1995, AOL was involved in a disagreement between an AOL member and a Caribbean resort. A member called Jenny TRR posted a message on an AOL bulletin board for scuba-diving enthusiasts that was critical of the Carib Inn. In the message, she described a diving instructor at the resort as being "stoned." The owner of the resort was incensed and demanded a retraction from Jenny TRR. When the retraction did not come, he hired lawyers to file a petition for discovery against AOL to find out Jenny TRR's real name. Although subscribers to AOL can use pseudonyms when communicating online, the pseudonyms are connected to real identities stored in AOL's database. In response to the legal action, AOL turned over the subscriber's real name, her address, credit card number, and checking account information to the Carib Inn's attorney.

At that time, AOL members did not expect an Internet service provider to reveal personal information. According to Johnson (1995), "David Phillips, assistant general counsel for America Online, acknowledges that one factor the company considered in weighing the request for information about Jenny TRR was whether it could be sued for defamation" (p. B1). Who was responsible for the comments? Was it AOL or its member? According to AOL, the member was responsible. However, Jenny TRR had violated AOL's policy against "ad hominem attacks" on individuals. As a result, her personal information was released to the resort's attorney. This incident raised questions about an Internet service provider's responsibility to protect personal information.

A second AOL incident became the symbol for online privacy issues. In the fall of 1997, a Naval employee discovered a listing for another member of the U.S. Navy named Timothy McVeigh (no relation to the individual involved with the Oklahoma bombing). In his online profile, McVeigh listed his marital status as "gay." This information was sent to Navy officials, who pressed AOL to reveal McVeigh's true identity. AOL identified the individual and he was discharged from the Navy. As a result of a lawsuit that followed, however, McVeigh, a thirty-six-year-old sailor, was returned to duty. Because personal information and e-mail messages are being saved and stored in databases, it is easy to provide personal information to third parties. As a result, privacy becomes a much more difficult right to maintain in cyberspace.

Encryption and the Internet

One solution to the privacy issue is encryption. **Encryption** is the art of disguising the meaning of a message to enable only the proper recipient to read it. It strengthens privacy by making sure confidential information, such as medical records, financial records, and e-mail, cannot be accessed by others. The term **cryptography** generally refers to data encryption. Cryptography is turning a message into gibberish before it is transmitted over the network. The person receiving the message must have a key to translate the gibberish into intelligible communication. Since the development of writing systems, various encryption techniques have been used. Computer-based encryption algorithms were being developed in the 1960s. The most popular commercial standard is called **Data Encryption Standard** (DES) and was created by IBM researchers and modified by the National Security Agency (NSA). Many e-mail and networking packages currently use the DES standard.

Another simple, secure, and easy-to-use system is **public key encryption**. Using public key encryption, the party receiving the message is given a pair of prime numbers; the product of these two numbers is the public key that decrypts the message. To prevent high-speed computers from breaking the code, the keys are a very long sequence of numbers. Whitfield Diffie, Ralph Merkle, and Martin Hellman developed another method of public key cryptology that splits the scrambling-and-descrambling key into two parts. One part is a widely distributed public key and the other is a private one. Their method enables total strangers to secretly communicate with each other.

Computer-based encryption first became a controversial topic with the development of the **Clipper Chip** encryption device, a microprocessor with an encoded algorithm. Installed in telephones, the Clipper Chip enables individuals to secure their conversations by encoding and decoding the conversation. Each chip has an individual serial number, but the Clipper Chip design also has a universal key that allows the FBI and law enforcement agencies to decode the number. Once the serial number is identified, search warrants and wiretaps can be set up on individual telephone lines. The Clipper Chip has been debated in the United States. Security experts pointed out its technical flaws; for example, the system would be difficult to upgrade because it is hardware rather than software based. Civil libertarians were concerned about the use of the chip violates individual privacy rights. Other groups were concerned that encryption technology could be used by terrorist groups to harm the public and support criminal activities. Thus, the Clipper Chip has raised questions about how to simultaneously maintain personal privacy and protect national security. This is an issue that is still unresolved.

Copyright Issues

Another unresolved Internet issue is copyright protection. Under American copyright laws, people have the right to receive compensation for their creative work. Copyrights laws are established to protect every author's **intellectual property**, which includes written work, photographs, illustrations, music, videos, and computer programs. Intellectual property includes poems, novels, artwork, and inventions. Like owning real estate or a house, people can own intellectual properties by owning the title, that is, the copyright to the work. Works must be in a tangible medium of expression and fulfill three basic requirements to acquire a copyright status. First, the work must be original; second, it must be in a fixed form; and finally, it must be a creative expression, rather than an idea. Once these three requirements are met, the work can be granted a copyright.

Owners of copyrights have the exclusive right to copy, distribute, display, and transmit their intellectual property. For example, corporate trademarks are the intellectual property of corporations. Trademarks are one way in which intellectual property is protected. When people place trademarks, such as the logos of sports teams, on their personal Web sites, they are violating the copyright of the trademark owner. Herbeck and Hunter (2001) found that 43.8 percent of the student Web sites they reviewed contained copyrighted material. Permission can be granted to others to use the work, however, and sometimes works are "licensed." Licensing gives others the right to copy and distribute the work within stipulated guidelines.

Copyright Exceptions

There are exceptions to the American copyright laws, including works in the public domain, copyright-free clip art, government documents, and fair use. Copyright does not last forever, and all works eventually return to the public domain. Works in the public domain are free for anyone to use. For instance, the image of the Mona Lisa is in the public domain. Altering Mona's image is perfectly legal and people have used her face in a variety of ways, including adding a mustache. Works copyrighted before 1978 entered the public domain seventy-five years after their publication. Between 1978 and 1998, copyright lasted the life of the author plus an additional fifty years. Enacted in 1998, the *Sonny Bono Copyright Term Extension Act* lengthened copyright terms by an additional twenty years. Because of this new act, many Disney materials that would now be in the public domain are still the property of the Disney Corporation. Presently, most materials in the public domain are older works or printed editions. Web sites, such as the Gutenberg project, make works in the public domain available to Web users.

Copyright-free clip art and graphics are excepted from copyright law because the creators of these works intended them to be shared, and many Internet ASCII artists freely share their work with others when they distribute it through the Internet. There are a number of professional and amateur clip art services available through the Web. These sites have been linked together into a graphics Web ring to enable people to visit all of the different sites and look for images that will not violate anyone's copyright.

A third exception to copyright law is material that was never copyrighted in the first place. All the publications from the U.S. Government Printing Office, for example, by law cannot be copyrighted because they belong to the American people. Because of this law, documents such as the *Starr Report* on President Clinton and the various versions of the U.S. Census are made freely available in both electronic and printed form. Newspapers and magazines could publish the *Starr Report* without obtaining permission, and students can use U.S. Census data in their research, although it should be properly cited.

The final exception to copyright is called **fair use**. Fair use creates a limited number of conditions under which people can use a copyrighted work without obtaining permission. The central concept behind fair use is that such use of a copyrighted work will not divert any income away from the creator or inhibit the potential for future income. Examples of fair use include quoting a small amount of the copyrighted work and using materials for educational purposes. Newspaper reviewers and authors can site small portions of a work in their reviews and books without obtaining permission from the copyright owner. Usually these passages are under 500 words (Figure 13.2).

Copyright and Digital Media

Protecting digital copyrights is difficult because it is very easy to copy intellectual property available on the Internet. As a result, content providers, such as record companies, book and magazine publishers, movie studios, and software companies, advocate stricter rules and controls over intellectual property. For instance, content providers want to eliminate "fair use" on the Internet and make service providers responsible for policing copyright in-

---

FIGURE 13.2 Copyright Guidelines for Students

Authors can obtain a copyright for creative works, but they cannot copyright ideas. You can write about or describe things that people say. When using direct quotes or portions of a published work, the following are some fair-use guidelines to follow:

1. Only use a small amount of the copyrighted material in your paper or report and make sure that the material is cited properly.

2. The quotations used in your report should be a small portion of an entire work that does not define the essence of the work.

3. Make sure that you are using the work for educational purposes. For instance, placing copyrighted material on your personal Web site would not count as an educational use.

4. Your use of the copyright materials should not affect the copyright holder's ability to receive income from the work. (This is a key reason why the record companies sued Napster. Individuals were making copies of songs without buying CDs, which results in lost income.)

Source: Adapted from Radford, Barnes, & Barr, 2002.

fringement. This is called the **copyright maximalist view**. In contrast, the libertarian approach to copyright supports the hacker concept that "information wants to be free." Libertarians favor a **copyright minimalist view**, the belief that attempting to preserve copyright protection on the Internet is futile. According to this view, the Internet is an open environment and copyright is antidemocratic because it interferes with the free sharing of ideas.

At present, most of the content presented on the Web is copyright protected. However, there is a common misconception that messages posted to public groups can be freely copied and distributed. On the contrary, these messages belong to the individual authors. Additionally, when people copy graphics, sound bites, and text from Web sites, they are often violating the copyright law. For instance, students creating Web pages mistakenly believe that copyright-protected images, such as Disney characters and sports logos, can be cut and pasted into their sites without the creator's permission, but this idea is wrong. In fact, some companies search the Web looking for copyright infringements and will send messages to violators telling them to remove the work from their sites.

The Web is a global medium. Different countries have different copyright laws. The *Digital Millennium Copyright Act of 1998* makes the Unites States copyright laws conform to two treaties adopted by the World Intellectual Property Organization (WIPO). According to the treaties, all countries have to offer copyright protection to foreign works, and the protection must be at least as strong as the protection for works in the native country. Information service providers, such as AOL, Earthlink, and the Microsoft Network must discontinue service to customers that they know engage in copyright infringement. When a service provider receives an infringement complaint, it must remove the material from its computer server. Additionally, copyright owners have the right to be provided with information about the copyright infringer.

Copyright and Napster

The most publicized Internet copyright infringement case involves the music site called Napster. In 1999 and 2000, a number of record companies and the Recording Industry Association of America sued Napster for theft of copyrighted materials. Napster is a popular music-swapping Web site that would freely distribute its proprietary file-sharing software. The company was originally started by a college student who wanted to facilitate music swapping between friends.

The value of the Napster service grew as the quantity and quality of the music increased with each new member bringing his or her collection of music to be swapped. According to CNET news, an estimated 20 million people have used Napster's software to download songs in an MP3 format. **MP3** is a digital compression technology that makes it possible to convert audio recordings into a digital format. Once the recordings are in an MP3 format, they can be uploaded and downloaded through the Internet. In addition, there is **ripping software** that enables users to copy an audio compact disc (CD) directly onto their computer's hard drive by further compressing MP3 into a smaller computer file.

A federal judge ordered Napster to halt the trading of copyright materials. The company could still make available music by artists who had given their permission and could continue to operate its message board services. Napster's attorney's arguing for "fair use," said that the service only made music available for personal use, which was not a violation of copyright. Moreover, Napster collected no revenues and charged no fees. But record industry attorneys' contended that the tens of thousands of people swapping songs online were violating the copyright of major recording labels.

The legal decision essentially put Napster out of business. Planned revenue sources for Napster included targeted e-mail, advertising, commissions from linked online vendors, the direct market of CDs by smaller bands, and sales of Napster products. Although the activity on Napster's site has been curtailed, there are other sites that continue the practice of music swapping. For example, AOL developed an open-source Napster clone call Gnutella, which was available on the Web for about twenty-four hours before AOL shut it down because they were in negotiation with several record companies. During that period, several thousand downloads took place. Quickly, Gnutella-compatible applications grew and the Gnutella Network was formed. The Gnutella Network is a file-sharing community. Members use *LimeWire* v1.0, *ToadNode*, and *BearShare* software to enable them to share certain directories on their hard drives with the Gnutella community (Figure 13.3). Swapping content files (sound, movie, music, and text) through the Internet is an example of establishing a high-tech gift economy.

High-Tech Gift Economy

In contrast to the view that copyrighted material on the Internet should be legally regulated, Barbrook (1998) argues that the Internet functions as a **high-tech gift economy**. A gift economy is based on the circulation of gifts and cooperation between different groups. It is a tribal concept used in Polynesia. The gift economy demonstrates that people can successfully live together without the state or the consumer-oriented marketplace. According to Barbrook, scientific and academic communities are based on a gift economy. Scientific research is funded by the state and/or donations, and scientists do not have to turn their

---

FIGURE 13.3   Tips on Being a Good File-Sharing Citizen

---

1. Keep your computer connected to the network for as long as possible. This allows you to send query results to people who are searching for the files you share.

2. Use software that blocks out Web-based search engines. This will help to prevent traffic jams that are created by Web-based search site users and improve download success rates.

3. Utilize software servants that include features to promote good citizenship. For instance, use programs that do not waste valuable bandwidth by broadcasting unnecessary traffic on the network.

4. Do not overload searches. Searches that use commands, such as "*.txt." create excess traffic on the network. Conserve the network's resources.

Source: Adapted from http://www.limewire.com/

intellectual work into marketable commodities. In both science and academia, contributing an article to professional journals, presenting papers, and freely distributing information enable individuals to gain personal recognition.

The early days of the Internet operated as a gift economy because the Internet was primarily developed by the scientific and academic communities. Researchers freely shared information with each other. For instance, Tim Berners-Lee gave away the original World Wide Web software. In a gift economy, the concept of intellectual property is technically and socially obsolete because people freely share their intellectual works with each other. Every Internet user adds to the collective knowledge on the network, and he or she can access the information from all of the other users. In the end, everyone receives more than they individually contribute.

Commercial interests are placing pressure on governments to regulate information, protect copyrights, and generally bring formal law and order to the Internet. Information that was once freely distributed through the Internet, such as newspaper articles, now costs money to access. Ideas for regulating the Internet will be discussed in the following model.

A Model for Regulating Cyberspace

Harvard law professor Lawrence Lessig developed a model for understanding how to regulate the Internet. A key factor in the model is software code. According to Lessig (1999), code is law. He states, "In real space we recognize how laws regulate—through constitutions, states, and other legal codes. In cyberspace we must understand how code regulates—how software and hardware that make cyberspace what it is *regulate* cyberspace as it is" (p. 6). The restrictions and limitations designed into software code can be used to regulate Internet behavior. For example, filtering software can be used to block Web sites, spam, and annoying e-mail messages.

Software Code

One key software issue under debate is the use of **open-source software**. Open-source software is software for which the **source code** or programming code is available to everyone. For example, when Tim Berners-Lee first developed the World Wide Web, he made the hypertext markup language (HTML) freely available through the Internet to anyone who wanted it. Because the HTML code is open-source software, anyone with access to a computer can create a Web page. In the early days of the Internet, the open sharing of software led to the development of the Internet and the Web. In contrast to open-source software, commercial software vendors produce "closed" programs, and their source code is a highly guarded piece of corporate intellectual property. Individuals do not have access to most software code, which means that software programs cannot be modified or improved by their users. Control of the software code remains in the hands of software companies.

The nature of the code and its software architecture determines how behavior can be controlled in cyberspace. For instance, filtering software attempts to prevent children from accessing pornographic Web sites. Some software architectures provide governments with the power to monitor Internet communication, whereas others do not. The Clipper Chip technology, for example, enables government agencies to identify people who are sending Internet messages. According to Lessig (1999), "the code is a regulator, and the government has a greater interest in the code that regulates better than others" (p. 21). The government's ability to regulate open code has important implications for the future of privacy on the Internet. Some encryption software programs are banned in the United States because the senders and receivers of messages cannot be identified. Law enforcement agencies are concerned that criminals and terrorists will use the encryption software to plan illegal actions. But encryption software that is illegal in the United States is freely available through servers located in other countries.

With the current open architecture of the Internet, it is difficult for governments to regulate online behavior. Although governments can enact laws, the regulation of the Internet involves other factors, including software code, social norms, and economic markets.

Laws, Code, Norms, and Markets

Lessig's model recognizes four constraints that regulate behavior in cyberspace. They are laws, norms, the market, and software architecture. For instance, laws providing copyright protection regulate behavior by forbidding particular activities and imposing sanctions on people who violate the laws. Software can also be designed to copy protect intellectual property. For example, commercial software programs often require users to type in special access code numbers, and some programs use software keys to limit the number of software copies. These copyright management schemes are designed to prevent software piracy.

Market pressures contributed to the passing of the 1998 *Digital Millennium Copyright Act* in the United States, which makes it a felony to write and sell software that circumvents copyright management schemes. However, enforcing the law also requires the support of users. Educating the public and teaching people the proper and improper use of software is another way to enforce copyright laws and prevent illegal software activities.

A combination of factors will be necessary to regulate behavior on the Internet. One increasingly important factor is the growing commercialization of the Internet. Market forces are encouraging the development of software architectures that can protect individual identities and enable secure communication for commercial transactions. Additionally, they support the collection of consumer data with programs such as cookies. Some of these developments are being made outside of the political process, which causes consumers to be concerned about their Internet privacy (Figure 13.4).

The government is addressing privacy issues, and a number of consumer privacy bills have been proposed in the United States. As software architecture, market forces, laws, and social norms attempt to regulate behavior on the Internet, Lessig urges that we first step back and think about what we want the Internet to be. Should the Internet be an open public space that supports free speech, a commercial space for engaging in financial transactions, or should online communities be allowed to set their own norms behavior?

FIGURE 13.4   Four Constraints on the Regulation of Cyberspace

---

1. Market Forces
   (Economic)

---

2. Software Architecture
   (Technological)

---

3. Laws and regulations
   (Political)

---

4. Social behavior and norms
   (Cultural)

Based on Lessig, 1999

Summary

It is fairly easy to use the Internet to correspond anonymously. A benefit of anonymity is the fact that people can make others aware of social problems without risking any personal harm. A disadvantage of anonymous communication is the disconnect between people and their words. False statements can be made without any accountability. But legal authorities can force anonymous remailer services to provide the names of individuals making anonymous statements.

Privacy on the Internet is now an important social issue. Unlike a face-to-face conversation, e-mail exchanges are stored on computer servers that can be accessed by others. Web sites can collect personal consumer information and sell it to marketing companies. Companies can read personal e-mail messages and fire employees if the content of the message is inappropriate. Presently, e-mail has no privacy standards and individuals need to learn the e-mail policies of their companies and Internet service providers.

A larger corporate Internet issue is the protection of copyrighted material. It is fairly easy to copy and transmit documents, music, and movies through the Internet, without the consent of the original author. This has led companies to support legislation to protect copyrights in cyberspace. Lessig has developed a model for understanding regulation of the Internet that contains four elements, including laws, software code, social norms, and economic markets. These four factors together influence the regulation of human behavior on the Internet.

TERMS

Anonymous remailers are programs that strip a message header from an e-mail message to make the sender anonymous to the receiver.

Anonymous speech is the right to communicate with other people without revealing your actual identity.

Clipper Chip is an encryption device that has a microprocessor with an encoded algorithm. It was developed for use by law enforcement agencies.

The communitarian view argues that community values should set the norms for Internet behavior.

Cookies are small data files stored on a user's hard drive when visiting a site. These files collect and store user information.

The copyright maximalist view is a perspective that supports stronger enforcement of copyright protection for digital media.

The copyright minimalist view advocates the free sharing of information.

Cryptography is turning a message into gibberish before it is transmitted. The person receiving the message has to have a key to translate the gibberish into intelligible communication.

Data brokers are companies that specialize in maintaining consumer databases, which they sell to other organizations.

Data Encryption Standard (DES), created by IBM researchers and modified by the National Security Agency, is a common standard used to encrypt e-mail messages.

Data-mining is a type of surveillance that monitors different computer networks.

Encryption is the art of disguising the meaning of a message to make sure only the proper recipient can read it.

Fair use creates a limited number of conditions under which people can use a coyrighted work without obtaining permission.

The High-tech gift economy is a concept of the Internet based on the circulation of gifts and cooperation between different groups.

Information privacy deals with the right to control access to one's personal data.

Intellectual property includes poems, novels, artwork, and inventions. Like owning real estate properties or a house, people can own intellectual properties by owning the title, that is, the copyright to the work.

The Libertarian view of cyberspace believes that individuals, rather than governments, should establish the norms for online behavior.

MP3 is a digital compression technology that makes it possible to convert audio recordings into a digital format for transfer through the Internet.

Open-source software is software for which the source code is available to everyone, such as HTML.

Panoptic sort is a complex of technologies used to collect, process, and share personal information about individuals and groups in order to coordinate and control access to goods and services in a capitalist economy.

Public key encryption uses a pair of prime numbers the product of which is the public key that decrypts the message.

Ripping software enables users to copy an audio compact disc (CD) directly onto their computer's hard drive by further compressing MP3 into a smaller file.

Source code is the code written by programmers. A program is written in source code and then converted into a language that the machine can read.

The theory of communicative action considers communication to be the central element of society and that societies are bound together through their communicative actions.

Whistleblowing is making others outside of an organization aware of concerns, neglect, or abuses that could harm the public interest.

EXERCISES

1. Discuss whether or not restrictions should be placed on Internet speech. Should people be allowed to say whatever they want? If restrictions were placed on Internet correspondence, what should they be?

2. When is it appropriate and inappropriate to use an anonymous remailer? Should restrictions be placed on using this type of technology? Why or why not?

3. How private is your e-mail? Compare the privacy statements from your university and/or information service provider to your own notions of privacy and e-mail.

4. What is your position on collecting and distributing consumer information collected through the Internet? Should companies be allowed to collect this data and sell it to third parties? Why or why not?

5. What personal data should be available through the Internet? Should all electronic data, including credit card information, Social Security numbers, traffic tickets, etc., be openly available to everyone? Why or why not?

WEB SITES

Copyright Office: http://lcWeb.loc.gov/copyright
Copyright Overview: http://www.law.cornell.edu/topics/copyright.html
Cyberethics: http://www.jbpub.com/cyberethics
Electronic Privacy Information Center: http://www.epic.org
File-Sharing Communities: http://www.limewire.com/
Harvard's Berkman Center: http://www.cyber.law.harvard.edu
People for Internet Responsibility: http://www.pfir.org
Privacy Times: http://www.privacytimes.com
Public Domain—Bartlett's Familiar Quotations: http://www.columbia.edu/acis/bartleby/bartlett
Public Domain—Roget's Thesaurus: http://www.thesaurus.com
UCLA Online Institute for Cyberspace Law and Policy: http://www.gseis.ucla.edu/iclp/hp.html
World Intellectual Property Organization Copyright Treaties: http://www.vonerlach.ch/articles/wipo.htm

BIBLIOGRAPHY

Barbrook, R. (1998). The high-tech gift economy. *First Monday, Issue 3* [Online] Available: http://www.firstmonday.org/issues/issue3_12/barbrook/index.html (Nov. 20, 2001).

Barlow, J. P. (1995, December). Property and speech: Who owns what you say in cyberspace? *Communications of the ACM, 38* (12), 19–22.

Bays, H., & Mowbray, M. (1999). Cookies, gift-giving, and the Internet. *First Monday, Issue 4* [Online]. Available: http://www.firstmonday.org/issues/issue4_11/bays/index.html (Nov. 20, 2001)

Borland, J., & Barnes, C. (2000, July 26). Judge issues injunction against Napster. *CNET News.com* [Online]. (July 26, 2000)

Cavazos E. A., & Morin, G. (1994). *Cyberspace and the law.* Cambridge, MA: The MIT Press.

Champ, L. J. (1999). *Web security and privacy: An American perspective. The Information Society, 15* (4), 249–256.

Drucker, S. J., & Gumpert, G. (1999). Real law @ virtual space. Cresskill, NJ: Hampton Press.

France, M., & Green, H. (2001, November 5). Privacy in the age of terrorism. *BusinessWeek,* pp. 82–91.

Gandy, O. H. (1993). *The panoptic sort: A political economy of personal information.* Boulder, CO: Westview Press.

Garfinkel, S. (2000). *Database nation.* Sebastopol, CA: O'Reilly.

Gelman, R. B., McCandlish, S., & members of the Electronic Frontier Foundation (1998). *Protecting yourself online: An Electronic Frontier Foundation Guide.* San Francisco: HarperEdge.

Habermas, J. (1979). *Communication and the evolution of society.* Boston: Beacon Press.

Habermas, J. (1984). *The theory of communicative action* (T. McCarthy, Trans.). Boston: Beacon Press.

Habermas, J. (1990). *Moral consciousness and communicative action* (C. Lenhardt & S. W. Nicholsen, Trans.). Boston: The MIT Press.

Herbeck, D. A., & Hunter, C. D. (2001). Intellectual property in cyberspace: The use of protected images on the World Wide Web. *Communication Research Reports, 15* (1), 57–63.

Johnson, C. (1995, November 24). Anonymity on-line? It depends who's asking. *The Wall Street Journal,* pp. B1, B7.

Kling, R. (1996). Information technologies and the shifting balance between privacy and social control. In R. Kling, ed., *Computerization and controversy: Value conflicts and social choices* (2nd ed., pp. 614–636). San Diego: Academic Press.

Kling, R., Lee, Y., Teich, A., & Frankel, M. S. (1999). Assessing anonymous communication on the Internet: Policy deliberations. *The Information Society, 15* (2), 79–90.

Lee, G. B. (1996). Addressing anonymous messages in cyberspace. *Journal of Computer-Mediated Communications, 2* (1) [Online]. Available: http://www.ascusc.org/jucmc/vol2/issue1 (November 6, 2001).

Lessig, Lawrence. (1999). *Code and other laws of cyberspace.* New York: Basic Books.

Mill, J. S. (1989). *On liberty and other writings.* New York: Cambridge University Press.

Perrolle, J. A. (1996). Privacy and surveillance in computer-supported cooperative work. In D. Lyon & E. Zureik (Eds.), *Computers, surveillance, and privacy* (pp. 47–65). Minneapolis: University of Minnesota Press.

Radford, M. L., Barnes, S. B., & Barr, L. R. (2002). *Web research: Selecting, evaluating, and citing.* Boston: Allyn & Bacon.

Rose, L. (1995). *Netlaw: Your rights in the online world.* Berkeley, CA: Osborne McGraw-Hill.

Spinello, R. (2000). *Cyberethics: Morality and law in cyberspace.* Boston: Jones and Bartlett Publishers.

Teich, A., Frankel, M. S., Kling, R., & Lee, Y. (1999) Anonymous communication policies for the Internet: Results and recommendations. *The Information Society, 15* (2), 71–77.

Wallace, J., & Mangan, M. (1996). *Sex, laws, and cyberspace.* New York: Henry Holt.

Weisband, S. P., & Reinig, B. A. (1995, December). Managing user perception of email privacy. *Communications of the ACM, 38* (12), 40–47.

CHAPTER

14 Democracy and the Internet

Chapter Overview

The interactive nature of the Internet allows citizens to engage in debate. Additionally, the elimination of visual social status cues in CMC allows people to participate on a more equal basis. For these reasons, many writers have described the Internet as a medium that could revitalize democracy. The Internet makes it easier for people to communicate with their government representatives, politically organize, debate topics, and educate each other about political issues.

But this optimistic view of the Internet is countered by the skeptics who do not believe the Internet will promote democratic principles because universal Internet service is not available to all citizens. American use of the Internet to support democratic principles will be discussed in this chapter; global issues are introduced in the next chapter. The following topics will be examined:

- Digital cities and community networks
- The digital divide
- American politics and the Internet
- Internet campaigning and voting
- Citizen activism and the Internet
- Democracy in cyberspace
- A resource model of digitally mediated political life

According to Graham (1999), Internet proponents argue "that the public and interactive nature of the Internet presents us with the means by which, for the first time, true democracy (and hence real consensus) is possible" (p. 60). Used as a communication medium, the Internet will increase the power of ordinary citizens by enabling them to more actively participate in the democratic process. Consequently, the Internet has been described as a truly democratic medium and a forum for the free flow of information and ideas. On the Internet, citizens and their representatives can communicate more openly with little worry about the high costs of political advertising and the editing of media gatekeepers.

But some scholars are concerned about the **digital divide**, those people who have access to the Internet and those who do not. As the Internet becomes increasingly commercialized, it has become difficult for local community groups to maintain public access spaces on the network. **Public access networking** is establishing easy-to-use, affordable, and physical connections to the Internet. Lack of digital literacy skills combined with the fact that no provisions have been made for public networking by Internet providers is keeping many individuals and grassroots community groups from being able to utilize the medium effectively. Presently, broadband Internet providers, especially cable companies, are creating Internet connections without allocating any "bandwidth" or "space" for public access or local community services.

Although the Internet has been popularized as a means of invigorating democracy and community-based communication, some people are not as optimistic about the Internet's impact on democracy. Wilhelm (2000) says that computers can provide us with the illusion of progress, "yet increased computer processor speed and greater telecommunications bandwidth does not automatically advance the human condition" (p. 6). Doheny-Farina (1996) is concerned about people spending so much time in virtual communities that they will neglect their geographic ones. As a result, he advocates the development of community networks based on physical locations.

Digital Cities

Many geographically based community networks have developed on the Internet. Santa Monica's Public Electronic Network (PEN) was an early community network that successfully contributed to local community decision making. Through online discussions, the citizens of Santa Monica were able to deal more effectively with the issue of homelessness in their local community. Homeless citizens could participate in electronic discussion by using public access terminals, often located in libraries. A current example of a successful community network is the Seattle Community Network (SCN), located at www.scn.org. Public Internet connections are provided by the Seattle Public Library, and the network is maintained by a nonprofit organization. SCN is committed to providing access to the system for the citizens of Seattle, providing access to community information, promoting government participation and public dialogue, and serving as a model for other communities. Like the citizens of Santa Monica and Seattle, people around the world are now establishing the digital counterparts of geographic cities on the Internet.

Mitchell (1995) calls a digital city a "city of bits." He contends that the introduction of digital cities alters the character of public discourse, cultural activities, and daily experiences. Traditionally, people had to go some place to discuss topics, chitchat, gossip, joke, and debate political issues, but the formation of digital cities redefines our ideas of gathering places and community. Mitchell describes the city of bits as "a city unrooted to any definite spot on the surface of the earth, shaped by connectivity and bandwidth constraints rather than by accessibility and land values, largely asynchronous in its operation, and inhabited by disembodied and fragmented subjects who exist as collections of aliases and agents" (1995, p. 24). This new city is constructed by software instead of bricks and mortars. Moreover, it is a social structure built on digital words rather than face-to-face interactions.

A number of experimental digital cities and community networks have been established. Often, these electronic counterparts enable citizens to access government and local information directly from the Internet instead of by visiting a physical public building. The Web has also become a way for citizens to create digital representations of their local communities. For instance, through the combined efforts of government, education, and telecommunication services, an electronic version of the city of Amsterdam was created. This new, Web-based city called Amsterdam's Digital City (DDS), is described on the Web site as "an electronic medium providing access to public and administrative information, from government and community organisations" (http://www.dds.nl). The city averages more than 4,000 visitors a day and is creating new channels of communication. Besides providing government and community information, Amsterdam's Digital City also provides chat rooms and spaces for people to socialize. Marleen Stikker, the original "mayor" of Amsterdam's Digital City, describes it as follows:

> Everybody is equal on the Net. People who never left their houses because they were afraid of crowds now regularly gather on bulletin-boards. You encounter people on the Net you would never meet in real life. That need to communicate is very human. What people love most is endless chitchat with each other (cited in Tan, 1995, p. 35).

The government offices of many major American cities have a Web presence. The City of New York's Web site (www.ci.nyc.ny.us) provides the following: press releases, information from the mayor's office, access to city services and agencies, business resources, and information about attractions and events. In smaller cities, such as Telluride, Colorado, community networks can help to promote political discussions and citizen involvement. McInnes (1997) discovered, however, that many Telluride residents were reluctant to become involved with networking technology. As a result, not everyone in Telluride had equal access to the technology to voice their opinions. Although digital cities provide easy access to government documents and information, people are concerned that many individuals will be unable to participate in online political discussions and debates because some citizens are not interested in learning about or using technology (Figure 14.1).

Community Networks

In the early 1980s, community networks and Free-Nets, were established to provide public Internet access points and help those who did not have the funds or technical ability to access the Internet on their own. This is an **end-to-end model** in which transmission mechanisms stay simple and end users develop the many different ways people use the network. Two user developments are text-based community networks and Free-nets. Community networks, locally driven communication and information systems, and Free-nets, which provide free telecommunication services, attempt to give citizens public points of Internet access. Public access sites are often located in community centers and public libraries. Currently, points of access outside the home furnish Internet connections to American Indians, African Americans, and Hispanics who cannot afford in-home services.

Besides providing telecommunication access, community networks also aim to provide services that support community involvement, education, economic development, government and democracy, health and human services, quality-of-life information, and technology training. The role of community networks has been compared to public televi-

---

FIGURE 14.1 Saying No to Technology

A goal of government officials in the United States and elsewhere is to make Internet access available to all citizens. However, there is always a percentage of the population that does not want to get involved with technology, and some people disconnect from it. In July 2001, Stephen Talbott, the editor of the *NetFuture Newsletter*, announced that he was disconnected from e-mail. This was a strange announcement because Talbott is the editor of an online newsletter, which is distributed through e-mail and the Web. Although newsletter business would still be conducted electronically, personal correspondence with Talbott would have to be conducted via telephone or traditional mail services. His decision to discontinue personal e-mail correspondence was influenced by two factors. First, Talbott has a spine problem that is exacerbated by working on the computer. Second, answering e-mail adds stress to his work life. One way of easing the stress is to go off of e-mail. Talbott describes technology in today's society as follows:

> But there is no denying it: in our society today, the centrifugal, interrupting, distracting tendencies have gotten out of control, jerking us around with almost demonic violence. The way television's intrusion has re-shaped household schedules around programs, fragments of programs, and advertisements; the way we are tempted to click through the endless and chaotic doorways presented to us on the Web; the vastly greater ease with which one person can approach another though email—an approach we can initiate with less weight of significance or personal presence than before—in these and many other symptoms you will recognize the contemporary forces that would throw us off our own foundations. What chance do we have to breathe harmoniously between a centered, reflective devotion to our own ever-deepening work (upon which society depends), and thoughtful response to the needs approaching us from the outside (without which we as individuals wither and become selfish)?

Source: Talbott, S. L. (2001, July 27). *NetFuture Issue #121*. Available: http://www.netfuture.org

---

sion and radio, and many public access groups are attempting to integrate the Internet into their media programs. These grassroots community groups understand the importance of public media in all its various forms. Public media are vital to democracy because they often represent the voices of groups and individuals who are critical of corporate ownership and media control.

With passage of the *Telecommunications Act of 1996*, many hoped that Internet access would become more universally available. **Universal service** is a provision that would make telephone services available to most households in the United States. Initially, the 1996 legislation included a provision calling for the telecommunications companies to use a fraction of their profits to help give schools and libraries affordable access to the Internet. Designed to help break the digital divide for children, schools, and libraries around the country, an E-Rate provision was adopted with strong bipartisan support from private and public education and library organizations. But shortly after the legislation was signed and the Federal Communications Commission approved the rules guiding the implementation of the E-Rate, the telecommunications industry launched an attack on the program charging that it was too costly. Three local phone companies filed a lawsuit against the E-Rate, and lobbyists worked behind the scenes to eliminate the program. Using the Internet, a campaign to save the E-Rate was launched by a coalition of nonprofit organizations. More than 22,000 e-mail messages were sent to members of Congress, the Federal Communications Commission, the telecommunications industry, and coalition members urging them to save the program. Despite these efforts, funding for the program was cut in half. However, the online campaign prevented the telecommunications industry from entirely eliminating the E-Rate program. The E-rate program is an attempt to bridge the digital divide by providing Internet services to communities that are not connected to the network.

Digital Divide

Central to concerns about the Internet as a democratic medium is the digital divide, the gap between information haves and have-nots. The 1999 U.S. Department of Commerce's study *Falling Through the Net: Defining the Digital Divide* reported that more Americans than ever have access to telephones, computers, and the Internet. Over 40 percent of American households own computers, and 25 percent of all households have Internet access. Although more Americans have access to the Net, the gap between people who have access to Internet information and those who do not is widening. Two major factors influence this gap, education and income levels. In addition, people living in rural areas are lagging behind urban areas in Internet access.

Access to the Internet occurs on several levels. First, individuals must have access to computers and Internet connections. Second, they must have the proper technology skills to be able to access information from the network. Third, to fully participate in public discourse on the Internet, they must have CMC skills and Web programming skills. The original, easy-to-operate, text-based Internet has now been transformed into the multimedia Web. This change introduced a graphical interface into the process of accessing Internet information. Although graphical interfaces appear to be an easy way to locate information, they add the complexity of visual communication to the distribution and retrieval of information. As a result, graphical interfaces can make it more difficult for some individuals and civic organizations to effectively disseminate information through the Internet.

Today, it is fairly easy to click on an icon and access a Web page. In contrast, designing and programming a Web site is very complex. It requires traditional literacy, visual literacy, HTML programming, and computer literacy skills. The skills required to create a multimedia Web site are so complex that many sites are developed by software teams rather than by individuals. Thus, Web site creation is often similar to the production of television shows or Hollywood movies.

The multimedia capabilities introduced with broadband Internet services are contributing to the transformation of the Internet from a simple, text-based system to one that can support full-motion video. **Broadband services** have a greater capacity for carrying information and can quickly transmit multimedia documents. However, many broadband Internet providers are designing their systems as **walled gardens**. The walled garden strategy, first introduced by America Online, is a media environment designed to keep customers within the confines of the service and sometimes constrains the customer from making choices. Walled garden strategies foster a limited one-to-many model of commercialized interaction rather than an open end-to-end model. Instead of allowing end users to shape the applications developed on the Internet, Internet providers produce the content. Many-to-many discussion groups are also set up and orchestrated by the Internet provider to appeal to members. By providing content and discussion groups, members are encouraged to stay within the "walls" of the provider's Web site. One-to-many models of Internet communication are further supported by broadband services. Broadband Internet services are primarily designed to push information or services into the home or organization and receive back only limited amounts of consumer data. But limitations on bandwidth in any direction compromise the Internet's potential to be a truly democratic medium.

Jung, Qiu, and Kim (2001) have developed an **Internet Connectedness Index** (ICI) to research the digital divide. The index involves nine factors, which include personal computer history, number of tasks, number of Web sites visited, goals pursued, Internet activities, time spent online, influence on lifestyle, computer-dependent relations, and Internet dependency. The purpose of this index is to capture the multidimensional nature of the relationship between individuals and the Internet. The index proposes the concept of connectedness to describe different Internet goals, activities, and communication uses in people's everyday lives. The model goes beyond Internet access issues to include CMC and interpersonal communication as contributing factors toward feelings of Internet connectedness.

Rural American Communities and the Internet

The term *information highway* implies that the Internet will bring information to all areas of the United States, including rural sections. Like the national highway system, which facilitated the shipping of products, the new **information highway** would enable people to access information anywhere in the country and eventually the world.

But to make the Internet truly available to all Americans, many factors in the development of the telecommunications system need to be considered. These include computers with modems, enhanced telephone service, videoconferencing systems, teletext services, and local connections. Additionally, rural communities need physical, financial, human, and social capital resources to be included on the information highway. Developing rural telecommunication systems requires a physical infrastructure of enhanced telephone services that support computer-based communication. Financial backing is required to update continually changing communication technologies. More important, knowledgeable people must be available to help other members of the community learn to use the technology. Community organizations and local groups in rural areas often play an important role in shaping public decisions and the development of telecommunications networks in rural areas. At present, people living in rural communities are not adopting Internet services as quickly as people living in urban centers.

Innovation Adoption and Diffusion

Efforts to encourage innovation adoption and diffusion have targeted rural communities. The **adoption of innovation** is described as the introduction of a new idea that will change the existing order of things. Everett M. Rogers (1995), a pioneer in diffusion of innovations research, describes diffusion as "the process by which an innovation is communicated through certain channels over time among the members of a social system" (p. 5). He identifies four steps in the innovation–diffusion process, including knowledge, persuasion, decision, and confirmation. Knowledge is individual awareness of the innovation and learning about its use. Persuasion occurs when an individual forms a positive attitude toward the innovation. At some point, the individual must decide to adopt or reject the innovation. Finally, the individual seeks reinforcement for the decision made about adoption or rejection.

Innovations are constantly being adapted to changing situations during the process of adoption and diffusion. As a result, the diffusion of a new technology goes through three main stages: *antecedents, process*, and *consequences*. Antecedents refer to the characteristics of individuals; for instance, people are more likely to adopt an innovation if they like change in their life. During the process stage, the four steps of knowledge, persuasion, decision, and confirmation generally occur. The process stage also involves different communication sources, such as mass media, advertising, promotional material, official agencies, informal social sources, and personal influences. Moreover, social and cultural attitudes can influence the adoption or rejection of an innovation. Occasionally, technologies are morally or culturally unacceptable because they could disrupt the values of a social system. The final, consequence stage refers to the later use of an innovation, if it has been adopted. Unequal adoption combined with rejection of the Internet could inhibit its use as a primary democratic medium in the United States because all citizens would then not have equal access to it.

American Politics and the Internet

Participating in the political process is a privilege of American citizenship. Moreover, citizen participation is vital to maintaining a healthy democratic society. Central to political participation is political communication, and the Internet provides a new communication channel for sending political messages and receiving citizen feedback.

Political Discourse and the Media

Politics in a democratic country depends on some form of communication. **Political communication** involves the public, mass media, the government, and interest groups. Because most citizens do not encounter political representatives on a one-to-one basis, politicians depend on mass media to communicate their messages to the public. According to Postman (1985), since the introduction of television, political discourse has gone from day-long heated debates to seconds of sound bites. Kern (1997) states that television has had a negative impact on social trust and voter turnout. In the age of television, presidential debates have become staged events rather than informed debates. In Grossman's (1995) opinion,

> With the prospect that the entire election might well ride on the outcome, most presidential debates have been carefully choreographed pseudo-events, staged appearances rather than spontaneous and revealing discussions. They reveal too little and disguise too much to be of substantive use to voters in the audience (p. 233).

FIGURE 14.2   Citizen and Voter Information and Services

Traditional broadcast TV coverage of campaigns and public affairs, including:

- paid political advertising
- free press coverage

Voting and polling systems include:

- electronic town meetings
- election polling through mail, telephone, or e-mail

TV, cable, and satellite coverage of public affairs, such as:

- cablecasts of local government and public meetings
- US Cable-Satellite Public Affairs Network (C-SPAN) coverage of the House of Representatives and US Senate
- Coverage of the House of Commons debates in the UK

Nonprofit and public-interest group Internet groups and sites, which include:

- Usenet newsgroups discussing public issues
- Internet voter guides such as the Democracy Network

Adapted from Dutton, 1999

The Internet could counterbalance the influence of television on political discourse, people argue, and even could surpass its value because the Internet is an interactive medium that facilitates the development of connections between people and information (Figure 14.2). Better than street corners and public meetings, electronically based discussion groups and chat rooms are places where citizens can engage in political discourse. Citizens can also locate information about candidates and issues on the Internet.

Cyber-politics is a new type of political communication. Whillock (1997) says "cyber-politics involve information dissemination, communication exchange, and the formation of electronic political coalitions across the Internet" (p. 1208). A variety of Internet genres are used for cyber-politics, including e-mail, discussion groups, Web pages, and on-line news. In 1992, a number of political campaigns began to use e-mail to connect campaign strategists, and candidate Ross Perot suggested using electronic town hall meetings in the election process. Both of these techniques have become part of political campaigns.

Case Study: Political Discussion Lists

For the 1992 presidential election, Lee Sakkas (1993) set up three different political discussion groups called BUSH, CLINTON, and PEROT on a computer server at Marist College. The purpose of these lists was to encourage public debate through the Internet. Only one list was a real success, however, the CLINTON list. Within three days of the announcement of the discussion lists, the CLINTON list had almost 200 subscribers engaged in active discussion. Sakkas (1993) explains why the CLINTON group succeeded:

Several things happened with CLINTON right away which proved to be quite fortunate and gave the list its own "personality." One of the first was that a Clinton delegate to the Democratic National Convention from Pennsylvania, Jon Darling, saw the announcement of the creation of the campaign discussion lists, and sent me private e-mail volunteering to provide CLINTON with full text of some of the position papers and speeches that the list subscribers might enjoy reading (p. 4).

Others began to make Clinton speeches and position papers available through the Internet, as well, and Clinton's campaign managers also began distributing complete texts of his important campaign speeches electronically. Making a direct connection between the Clinton campaign and the discussion list created an electronic space for public debate. Lacking these connections, the other lists did not work as well. Moreover, debates on the CLINTON list generated a type of involvement that did not occur in the other two groups. Members of the CLINTON list followed the actual campaign trail, and some participated in the election process. After Clinton won the election, the CLINTON discussion group continued to discuss Clinton politics.

Clinton and his staff understood the potential power of the Internet as a new medium of political communication. In January 1993, the Clinton administration began to use the Internet to distribute White House documents to enhance the flow of political information. According to Whillock (1997), an estimated 40,000 or more people received Clinton White House documents daily through mailing lists or several times a week from servers, newsgroups, and bulletin boards. Clinton and Gore themselves became accessible through the Internet by setting up e-mail addresses for the White House. Since then, many other political representatives have become "wired," and so the Internet is being used increasingly for American political communication.

The Internet and American Politics

In his book *The Hill on the Net*, Chris Casey (1996) presents an insider's perspective on how the Internet is influencing politics. For example, "Vice President Al Gore tested [the Internet] waters from the White House in January 1994 when he participated in a town hall forum on CompuServe" (p. 87). The Senate has experimented with adding online chat sessions to congressional hearings. Today, many representatives have Web sites and can be reached through e-mail. In this way, the Internet is becoming a medium that facilitates direct communication and therefore powerful links between citizens and their government representatives.

Since the introduction of electronic media, we have been witnessing a democratic political transformation. According to Grossman (1995), two developments are propelling this change: "the two-hundred-year-long march toward political equality for all citizens and the explosive growth of new telecommunications media, the remarkable convergence of television, satellites, cable, and personal computers" (p. 4). Today, citizens can see, hear, and judge their own political leaders instantaneously and simultaneously. Whittle (1997) states, "Never before have we been able to reach so many others for such stimulating interactive discussion. We can choose for ourselves what to believe—with more and better information available to us than ever before" (p. 94).

Electronic communication is not as intimate as face-to-face discussions and public town meetings, but according to Grossman (1995), it will extend government decision making by involving more people in the political process and moving politics away from centralized representation. Back in 1964, McLuhan predicted this development: "As the speed of information increases, the tendency is for politics to move away from representation and delegation of constituents toward immediate involvement of the entire community in the central acts of decision" (p. 182). Ralph Nader has described how the Internet is engaging citizens in political discussion:

> In recent years a number of citizen groups have experimented with the use of computer networks as a tool for monitoring government agencies and organizing citizens. Today, using the Internet, it is possible to obtain information on a wide range of important topics and share it among literally millions of people, at a very low cost. The communications are often interactive, allowing citizens to talk to each other, exchange feedback, offer pointers, and debate facts, strategies and values. (cited in Long, 1994, p. 64)

An example of citizens using new technology to influence government agencies occurred in New Mexico when recreational trout fishers stopped plans for a reduction in the flow of the Colorado River by sending e-mail messages to government officials. A spokesperson for the Federal Bureau of Reclamation said, "They mounted a quite effective e-mail campaign, one of the more effective uses of new technology I have ever seen" (Graham, 1997, p. B4). Although e-mail was a key element, the Web also played an important role in spreading information. The campaign to stop the reduction in river flow was started by a recreational fisherman who placed an alert on his business Web site. It instructed trout fishing lovers to e-mail their protests to a list of officials, including the governor of New Mexico.

The Web is a tool that can also be used for advocacy. For instance, Web sites can be used to make citizens aware of impending congressional votes and to ask people to phone, fax, and e-mail their representatives. Advocacy sites use the Web for a variety of reasons, including providing information, lobbying for legal action, fund raising, and identifying potential members.

Internet Campaigning

Political candidates now use the Internet to communicate with reporters, campaign workers, Internet users, and voters. In the Al Gore and George W. Bush presidential election, both candidates used e-mail and the Web in their campaign efforts. E-mail is a very easy and effective way for candidates to issue press releases to reporters. From the reporter's perspective, e-mail makes it easier to get a story into print or on the air. E-mail can be used to distribute information also to campaign workers and political supporters. For instance, campaign schedules and news can be easily circulated. In the Bush–Gore campaign, e-mail was also used to send humorous messages. The Democratic National Committee created a series of e-mail installments called "Bush Lite," which made fun of Mr. Bush's communication failures and his semantic mistakes. These humorous messages were written to capture the attention of Internet users.

Presidential hopefuls establish Web sites to enable voters to read speeches, view advertisements, sign up to work on the campaign, buy campaign products, and solicit campaign contributions. Political Web sites are designed to provide more information about a candidate than a thirty-second television commercial. Additionally, Web sites are used to distribute campaign materials. For instance, during Bill Bradley's campaign for president, his campaign kits could be downloaded from the Internet. The campaign could afford to print only 500 kits and an additional 6,000 kits were downloaded from the site. The Bradley site also collected a list of 23,000 names of Bradley supporters. An Internet campaign consultant reported that Bradley's decision to use the Internet was a large factor in his overall strategy of running an underdog campaign. His approach to the Internet illustrates the idea that the Internet is a powerful tool for building grassroots campaign efforts. Similarly, Governor Jesse Ventura of Minnesota credits the Internet as a significant factor in his campaign victory.

Computer scientist Hal Berghel (2000) is not as optimistic as others are about the impact of the Internet on political campaigns and voting. He is concerned that the Web will be used as a propaganda vehicle. Although more information can be placed on the Web, the quality of the information is, he says, the same old political rhetoric used in other media, which will not improve political discourse. As the Web becomes more commercialized, it may indeed begin to resemble traditional mass media, because the media industries will dominate and control the majority of the Internet's content.

In addition to providing political content, the interactive nature of the Internet makes it possible for citizens to register to vote. The Internet makes it easier for citizens to fill out voter registration forms. Although at present voter registration is a hybrid system because electronic registration is combined with traditional "snail mail," some systems allow people to fill out electronic forms, which are then printed and mailed to them for their signature. Other systems print out forms that can be filled out and mailed directly by the individual voter. Although the Internet makes it easier for voters to register, the future impact of the Internet on political campaigns is still unclear. One development is the movement to create Internet voting in the United States.

Internet Voting

The delayed presidential election results of George W. Bush raised serious concerns about American voting technologies. Consequently, people began to advocate using the Internet as a way to vote. Prior to the election, an Internet Voting Technology Alliance had been formed by an international group of companies and experts. The goal of the Alliance is to review the standards to be used in voting over the Internet. The Alliance is also dedicated to serving the public by providing information and a discussion forum.

The first legally binding Internet election was held in Arizona on March 7–11, 2000. Voters were able to cast their votes in a primary election from home, work, a public library, or a traditional polling place. Several other states have also explored Internet voting. For example, New York State attempted to purchase a secure, accurate, reliable Internet voting system. However, the system they ordered had numerous flaws and the contract was canceled.

Two types of Internet voting systems are currently under development, **remote Internet voting** and **on-site Internet voting** or **polling place systems**. Remote Internet voting systems allow people to cast votes from any computer with an Internet connection. Remote systems raise questions about how to verify the identity of the voter and how to prevent coercion. On-site Internet voting systems require citizens to go to a specific location to vote, where they can cast ballots on Internet-connected machines located at the polling place. On-site systems eliminate many of the risks surrounding remote voting, especially the issue of voter identification.

A benefit of remote Internet voting is that it can provide individuals living in remote areas an opportunity to participate more directly in the voting process. For instance, citizens living in remote parts of Alaska need dog sleds to get to the polls to vote. Remote Internet voting systems would enable these citizens to participate more fully in primary elections and could increase voter participation. However, some states are concerned that Internet voting will discriminate against minority voters who do not have easy access to the technology. There are numerous obstacles to be overcome before Americans can cast their votes through the Internet (Figure 14.3).

Government Documents and the Internet

An underlying democratic principle is the idea that citizens play an active role in monitoring the government. Consequently, people should have a right to access governmental documents and meetings. The free flow of information is essential to a self-governing democracy. In 1966, the *Freedom of Information Act* provided access to the records of federal agencies, except for documents exempt from disclosure. Many government documents have already been computerized and are available through the Internet. Computerized public records are easier to locate, retrieve, and search than paper records.

The Web has also made it easier to access public documents. Web sites that contain government information include THOMAS, the House of Representatives information service, and the CIA Web site. Access to electronic documents by allowing individuals direct access to pending legislation and to their government representatives, could change the relationship between citizens and government.

FIGURE 14.3 Pros and Cons of Internet Voting

Pros	Cons
Increasing access and participation	Technological threat to security
Ability to monitor election	Remote Internet voting is unmonitored
Cost savings	Unequal access to technology
Efficiency	Fraud

Source: *Communications of the ACM*, January 2001.

The Internet and Democracy

The Internet has been described as a democratic medium. Schuler (2001) states, "many people contend the Internet is inherently democratic and its continued penetration worldwide virtually guarantees the triumph of freedom over tyranny" (p. 53). Herring (1993) has identified four characteristics of the Internet and CMC that researchers claim make the Internet a democratic medium. First, the Internet is accessible—increasing numbers of people are gaining access to the technology through the home, school, library, or work. Second, a democratizing characteristic of CMC is its ability to socially decontextualize people. By eliminating social status cues, including dress, accent, voice, race, sex, and appearance, individuals can communicate with each other on a more equal basis. Third, CMC does not have established, agreed-on social conventions. People are less inhibited in their communication behavior, which can lead to a breakdown of traditional hierarchial patterns of correspondence and greater freedom of expression. Furthermore, censorship is rare in electronic communication. Discussion lists often post all messages that people send to the list, and people can place all types of information and opinions on Web sites. As a result, everyone who has access to the Internet can, theoretically, voice an opinion. The lack of censorship on the Internet as a criterion for equal participation is a mistaken assumption, however, Schuler contends. To be a truly democratic medium the following criteria must be met: universal access, support for deliberation, and equal participation in decision making. Now and in the future, powerful economic, political, and social factors influence the Internet's development.

The establishing of democratic communications will not be automatic. It will require ongoing discussion and critical reflection about the dynamic social and economic nature of the Internet itself. Different social groups and nations will react differently to the Internet and its use for political communication. Consequently, people must evaluate technology access and group needs to make certain that all voices are heard in democratic discussions.

Citizen Activism and the Internet

By eliminating censorship, the Internet empowers individuals by providing them with a vast array of different perspectives. Moreover, newsgroups and mailing lists supply research and organizational material for media activists around the world. Today, it is possible for citizens outside the media industries to disseminate information and influence public opinion. Burstein and Kline (1995) point out: "No longer does mainstream media have a sole monopoly on public discourse" (p. 111). On the Net, ordinary people can engage in public discussion and debate.

Hill and Hughes (1998) define **Internet activists** as people who post political e-mail messages on a discussion list or who chat about politics online. Internet activists use the Internet to seek more detailed and specialized information about political events (Figure 14.4). They often seek information from Web sites that are extensions of popular mass media, such as the major broadcast networks, CNN, *The Washington Post*, and The *New York Times*. In addition to seeking information, Internet activists also talk about politics in discussion groups.

FIGURE 14.4   Internet Information Seeking among Internet Users and Activists

	Internet Users	**Internet Activists**
1. Get political news on-line?	35%	73.9%
2. Sources of political news:		
ABC, NBC, or CBS sites	31.4%	46.7%
CNN, C-Span, or MSNBC sites	44.7%	62.5%
National Newspaper sites	54.8%	66.9%
Specialized political sites	14.1%	31.5%
Candidate Websites	24.9%	42.3%
Government Websites	27.8%	49.2%

Source: Hill & Hughes, *Cyberpolitics: Citizen Activism in the Age of the Internet*, ©1998, Rowan & Littlefield Publishers. p. 38. Used by permission.

Hill and Hughes's research revealed that discussion groups often provide a better format for the discussion of political topics than chat rooms. Discussion list comments are more thoughtful, informative, and provide more potential for deliberation. Chat rooms are a difficult format for thoughtful political discussion because the line space is short and the pace is fast. As a result, people often make snap judgements and focus on the actions of others rather than the topic under debate. During past presidential elections, critics complained that the level of political discourse in chat rooms was lower than expected.

Often, young people do not become Internet activists. CNET News.com reported that a study of the Internet generation revealed that young people were getting most of their political information from traditional television rather than the Internet. In a study commissioned by American Express, 400 young people interviewed said that they received political information from television. Only 4 percent cited the Internet as a primary source of election news. This study counters the notion that young people who grow up with computers will automatically use the Internet as a primary news source and become more politically involved.

Democracy and the Web

The convenience and inexpensive nature of the Web, allows ordinary people to express their opinions in ways that are not possible with traditional mass media. However, the idea that the Internet will enhance the democratic process through the influence of average citizens, may be too optimistic. The recent *Falling through the Net* study revealed that a certain percentage of the American population does not have Internet access. As a result, significant voices are excluded from Web participation.

A second Web issue is the politics of search engines or the ways in which search engines locate information. Introna and Nissenbaum (2000) argue that search engines systematically grant importance to some sites at the expense of others. For example, a study by Lawrence and Giles (1999) revealed that search engines indexed only around 16 percent of the total indexable Web. The Web is so vast that search engines cover less than 50 percent of the available sites. Both Web designers and information seekers must pay particular attention to the keywords used to identify a page because it is through keywords that search engines locate data. Information seekers using search engines are most likely to find popular, large sites whose designers have enough technical savvy to understand how to succeed in being recognized by search engines. Moreover, some site owners pay to have their sites recognized. Consequently, there is a concern that search engines will highlight popular, wealthy, and powerful sites at the expense of more meaningful and less popular ones. Thus, search engines could also contribute to an unequal representation of ideas.

The Internet and Deliberative Democracy

Internet proponents view it as a new tool for community building. The Internet is a resource for citizens to share ideas because it enables hundreds, thousands, or even hundreds of thousands of persons to organize themselves in public forums. Moreover, people can access specialized expertise and information from sophisticated database programs. Thus, computer networks are viewed as a way to bring people together to renew a sense of democracy. Rheingold (1993) asserts, "The great power of the idea of electronic democracy is that technical trends in communications technologies can help citizens break the monopoly on their attention that has been enjoyed by the powers behind the broadcast paradigm—the owners of television networks, newspaper syndicates, and publishing conglomerates" (p. 289).

Online advocates hope to see CMC revitalize the open and widespread discussion among citizens that feeds the roots of democratic societies. According to Rheingold (1993), for the Internet to be a democratic medium it must include "open access, voluntary participation, participation outside institutional roles, the generation of public opinion through assemblies of citizens who engage in rational argument, the freedom to express opinions, and the freedom to discuss matters of the state and criticize the way state power is organized" (p. 284).

The Internet is a global medium that exposes people from a variety of nationalities to different cultural norms, a topic that will be discussed in the next chapter. On the Internet, individual national customs, beliefs, and laws are called into question and national perspectives become destabilized because this multivocal medium represents diverse social, ethnic, and religious perspectives. To create an orderly Internet society, people sharing different points of view must agree on common social norms of behavior. Much of the discussion about the future of the Internet will take place within the Internet itself.

Ess (1996) proposes the application of Habermasian discourse ethics as a framework to CMC to help people with diverse perspectives reach democratic consensus. He writes, "The discourse ethic, as it circumscribes the form and character of discourse intended to sustain democratic communities, in fact provides powerful theoretical support for current conceptions of democratizing communication via CMC. In particular, the discourse ethic issues in the call for open and equitable communication and the pluralism of currently existing discourse communities" (p. 216). Using Habermasian principles, people could facilitate understanding between diverse individuals and groups.

To resolve difficulties, Habermasian deliberative democracy would attempt to find a middle ground between polar positions. Deliberative democracy "reflects a concern that citizens' participation in the democratic process have a rational character—that voting, for example, should not simply aggregate given preferences but rather follow on a process of 'thoughtful interaction and opinion formation' in which citizens become informed of the better arguments and more general interests" (Rehg, 1996, p. ix). Majority rule is not simply a statistical effort to tally votes, but instead a larger social process by which people discuss issues, attempt to understand one another, try to persuade each other, and modify their views to counter arguments.

The deliberative conception of democracy argues that democracy is ideally conceived as a process by which people do not implement their preferred point of view. Instead, they consult and deliberate about what values and options are best for the community. Habermas views law and democracy as being mutually supportive. Law establishes the preconditions for democracy. It guarantees voting rights, freedom of speech, and political equality. Laws provide a framework to regulate conflicts and encourage collective goals.

In the Habermasian approach, everyone should be given the right to state his or her position and to criticize others. Through the rational discussion of all ideas and views, group consensus can be achieved. Using this method, individuals with diverse positions could reach agreement. Internet proponents, such as Rheingold and Ess, argue that CMC could be used as a communication medium to facilitate the process of deliberative democracy described by Habermas. At present, many diverse points of view are expressed on the Internet without any means of building consensus.

Governing the Internet

Civil libertarians argue that the Internet thrives because it has no central governing authority. Libertarians support self-regulation and argue that Internet users can develop their own unique structure, standards, and methods for settling disputes. Commercial interests, however, recognize the need for some type of rule-making and rule-enforcing authority to maintain order on the electronic frontier. For example, many disputes over Internet names have already occurred. Two different Blue Note Jazz Clubs are arguing over the same Internet name. One club is located in New York and the other in Missouri. Both have obtained the legal right to use the name locally. The question is: Who should use it globally?

Spinello (2000) describes three different models for governing the Internet: **direct state intervention, coordinated international intervention**, and **self-governance**. Direct state intervention refers to the idea that each nation should govern the Internet in a way that is similar to regulating any other form of mass media. Current national laws should be extended into the realm of cyberspace. This view does not perceive the Internet as a separate space that is different from geographic space; it is simply another communication medium, and individual nation states should regulate it. A problem with this model is digital data are difficult to regulate because information can so easily flow across borders. For example, the French government filed a lawsuit against Yahoo because French citizens could purchase Nazi items from Yahoo Web sites located in the United States. Selling Nazi paraphernalia is illegal in France, but the French are having difficulty enforcing this law within their own national boundaries. Governments that have tried to regulate Internet activities, such as hate speech and pornography, have had varying degrees of success.

Coordinated international intervention calls for the establishment of a cooperative international organization, analogous to the United Nations, to regulate the Internet. This view is based on the premise that the Internet is a separate entity existing outside the geographic boundaries of nation states. However, for the coordinated international intervention model to work, individual nations would have to agree to follow international rather than national regulations. Besides enforcing domain name disputes, this organization would have the power to enforce international regulations on forbidden forms of free speech. For example, pornography sites are against the law in Saudi Arabia, so a question raised by this model is what standards would be used to determine the laws? A larger issue is how would a non-governmental organization be able to dictate and enforce Internet rules?

In the third model, self-regulation, the Internet would be regulated by its own political and social structure. Nonprofit international groups would be chosen to loosely control the coordination of Internet activities. These groups would need to set up guidelines for e-commerce, intellectual property rights, and trademark disputes. The assignment of Internet protocol numbers and domain names has already been turned over to a private, nonprofit group called the Internet Corporation of Assigned Names and Numbers (ICANN), whose charter is to protect the interests of the Internet community. The United States government is leaning toward a self-regulation model but there are some risks associated with it. Internet nonprofit organizations would not be accountable because no one would be able to enforce the policies set by the organizations. Additionally, political forces could come to dominate these organizations for their own national interests.

Anonymous correspondence, discussed in the previous chapter, also makes it difficult for governments and organizations to enforce rules on the Internet. The anonymous nature of Internet correspondence makes it difficult for law enforcement agencies to hold individuals accountable for their online actions. In general, the Internet tends to shift control away from the state and place it in the hands of individuals. Some governments are deeply concerned about this characteristic of the Internet, which is why they want to regulate it.

A Resource Model for Digitally Mediated Political Life

The ability to access the Internet is a major issue in arguments for and against electronic democracy. According to Wilhelm (2000), there are four features of democracy in the digital age. First, citizens need to have the resources and literacy skills to be able to participate in online interactions. These resources include civic and communication skills, such as writing letters, giving speeches, and organizing meetings. In face-to-face situations, people need to be able to participate in everyday speech, understanding, and social actions. Transferred to the online world, an individual additionally must be technologically literate and motivated to participate in online discussion. Second, citizens need to have access and the opportunity to participate in political discussion. Economic considerations contribute to an individual's ability to participate in Internet activities. Third, citizens need to deliberate about topics and subject their ideas to public scrutiny. The system must support interactive dialog, not only the distribution of information. Finally, the design of the networking system needs to support universal, deliberate, and lively political discussion.

All these features create the topography of the online political sphere. The system must be inclusive and accessible to all citizens. Individuals must be provided with educational resources that enable them to become both technologically literate and critical thinkers. Additionally, the system must support deliberation and debate. The **Resource Model of Digitally Mediated Political Life** attempts to connect an individual's socioeconomic status with their ability to participate in online political discourse through an analysis of an individual's technological capabilities (computer literacy skills) and resources (financial and technological) (Figure 14.5). A goal of the model is to establish a causal relationship between an individual's resources and their potential to politically participate on the Internet. After applying this model to an analysis of U.S. Census data, Wilhelm came to the conclusion that resource disparities between those who have access to the Internet and those who do not could widen the digital divide. But fostering learning and critical thinking in the home and school along with the cultivation of lifelong learning skills could help to prepare individuals for political engagement on the Internet.

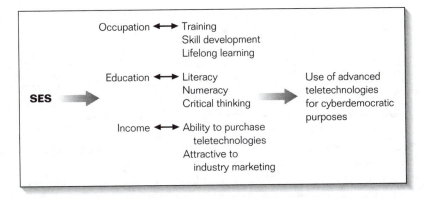

FIGURE 14.5   An Economic Model of Digitally Mediated Political Life

© 2000 Routledge. From *Democracy in the Digital Age* by Anthony G. Wilhelm. Reproduced by permission of Routledge, Inc. Part of The Taylor & Francis Group.

Summary

Internet proponents claim that it is a medium that will revitalize democracy. Internet critics are concerned about the growing digital divide that separates the people who have access to the Internet from the people who do not. The gap in the digital divide is influenced by social, educational, and economic factors.

Since the 1992 presidential election, the Internet has become a major medium for political communication. Candidates distribute campaign materials, press releases, position statements, and speeches through the Internet. Additionally, citizens can join discussion lists and newsgroups to debate political topics. Internet activists are people who exchange political e-mail messages and seek political information from the Web.

The Internet itself has been described as a democratic medium because it eliminates social cues, which makes it possible for people to participate more equally. The Internet can also disrupt social hierarchies because there are no established social rules, and there is no censorship in cyberspace. Moreover, the Internet can be used as a community building tool to bring people together into a new electronic democracy.

Although the Internet is described as a democratic medium, it currently has no governing body. Spinello presents three different models for governing the Internet, including direct state intervention, coordinated international intervention, and self-governance. Wilhelm's resource model for digitally mediated life attempts to make causal relationships between an individual's technology capabilities and resources and their ability to politically participate on the Internet.

TERMS

Adoption of innovation is described as the introduction of a new idea that will change the existing order of things.

Broadband services have a greater capacity for carrying information because the increased bandwidth of these systems enables them to carry multimedia documents.

Coordinated international intervention is a model that would establish a cooperative international organization, similar to the United Nations, to regulate the Internet.

Cyber-politics involves information dissemination, communication exchange, and the formation of electronic political coalitions across the Internet.

The digital divide describes the gap between people who have access to the Internet and those who do not.

Direct state intervention is a model in which each nation would govern the Internet in a way that is similar to its regulation of any other form of mass media.

The end-to-end model is a network model in which the transmission mechanisms remain simple and the end users develop the many different uses of the network.

Information highway is a term, invented by Al Gore, that describes the Internet. The development of a national computer networking system will facilitate the shipping of information and provide people with access to information anywhere in the United States.

Internet activists are people who post political e-mail messages on discussion lists or chat about politics online.

The Internet Connectedness Index (ICI) includes nine factors that index the multidimensional nature of the relationship between individuals and the Internet. It proposes the concept of connectedness to describe different Internet goals, activities, and communication uses in people's everyday lives.

On-site Internet voting systems require citizens to go to a specific location to vote. Voters can cast ballots on Internet-connected machines located at polling places.

Political communication involves the public, the mass media, the government, and interest groups.

Public access networking is establishing easy-to-use, affordable, and physical connections to the Internet.

Remote Internet voting systems allow people to cast votes from any computer with an Internet connection.

The Resource Model of Digitally Mediated Political Life attempts to connect individuals' socioeconomic status with their ability to participate in online political discourse through an analysis of individuals' technological capabilities and resources.

Self-governance is a model that proposes the Internet should be regulated by its own political and social structure.

Universal service is the concept of providing telephone services to almost every household in the United States. The concept is being applied to the Internet.

The **walled garden** strategy, first introduced by American Online, is a media environment shaped to keep customers within the confines of the service and sometimes constrains the customer from making choices.

EXERCISES

1. What is your position on Internet voting? Are you for or against it and why?

2. Should the Internet be regulated? Why or why not?

3. If the Internet is regulated, how should it be regulated—direct state intervention, international intervention, or self-governance?

4. Is the Internet inherently a democratic medium that will create a new electronic democracy? Why or why not?

5. Create your own definition of electronic democracy. What role would the Internet play in your definition?

WEB SITES

Center for Democracy and Technology: http://www.cdt.org
Computer Professionals for Social Responsibility: http://www.cpsr.org

Berkman Center for the Internet and Society: http://cyber.law.harvard.edu
Internet Voting Technology Alliance: http://www.ivta.org
Netfuture: http://www.netfuture.org
Seattle Community Network: http://www.scn.org
Voting Integrity: http://www.voting-integrity.org
White House: http://www.whitehouse.gov

BIBLIOGRAPHY

Berghel, H. (2000). Digital politics 2000. *Communications of the ACM, 43* (11), 17–22.

Burstein, D., & Kline, D. (1995). *Road warriors: Dreams and nightmares along the information highway.* New York: Penguin Books.

Casey, C. (1996). *The hill on the net: Congress enters the information age.* Boston: AP Professional.

Davis, C. N., & Splichal, S. L. (2000). *Access denied: Freedom of information in the information age.* Ames, IA: Iowa State University Press.

Davis, R. (1999). *The web of politics.* New York: Oxford University Press.

Doheny-Farina, S. (1996). *The wired neighborhood.* New Haven, CT: Yale University Press.

Dutton, W. H. (1999). *Society on the line.* New York: Oxford University Press.

Ess, C. (1996). *Philosophical perspective on computer-mediated communication.* Albany, NY: State University of New York.

Graham, G. (1999). *The Internet: A philosophical inquiry.* London: Routledge.

Graham, P. (1997, February 16). E-mail campaign nixes planned river flow reduction. *Albuquerque Journal*, p. B4.

Grossman, L. K. (1995). *The electronic republic.* New York: Penguin Books.

Habermas, J. (1996). *Between facts and norms.* Cambridge, MA: The MIT Press.

Herring, S. C. (1993). Gender and democracy in computer-mediated communication. *Electronic Journal of Communication, 3* (2) [Online], 16 pp. Available: http://dc.smu.edu/dc/classroom/Gender.txt (February 14, 2000).

Hill, K. A. & Hughes, J. E. (1998). *Cyberpolitics: Citizen activism in the age of the Internet.* Lanham, MD: Rowman & Littlefield.

Introna, L. D., & Nissenbaum, H. (2000). Shaping the Web: Why the politics of search engines matters. *The Information Society, 16* (3), 169–185.

Jacobus, P. (2000, Oct. 10). *Young voters glued to the set for politics.* CNET news.com. [Online], 2 pp. Available: http://dailynews.yahoo.com/h/cn/200010 . . . /young_voters_glued_to_the_set_for_politics_1.htm (November 7, 2000).

Jung, J. Y., Qui, J. L., & Kim Y.C. (2001). Internet connectedness and inequality: Beyond the divide. *Communication Research, 28* (4), 507–535.

Kahin, B., & Keller, J. (1995). *Public access to the Internet.* Cambridge, MA: The MIT Press.

Kern, M. (1997). Social capital and citizen interpretation of political ads, news, and web site information in the 1996 presidential election. *American Behavioral Scientist, 40* (8), 1238–1257.

Korsching, P. F., Hipple, P. C., & Abbott, E. A. (2000). *Having all the right connections: Telecommunications and rural viability.* Westport, CT: Praeger.

Laudon, K. C. (1995, December). Ethical concepts and information technology. *Communications of the ACM, 38* (12), 33–39.

Lawrence, S., and Giles, C. L. (1999). Accessibility and distribution of information on the Web. *Nature,* Issue 400, pp. 107–109.

Long, M. (1994, December). We are the world. *Netguide*, pp. 55–66.

Marks, P. (2000, June 1). In Bush-Gore race, 3 words for media: "You've got mail." *The New York Times, Technology Section* [Online], 7 pp. Available: http://www10.nytimes.com/library/tech/00/06/biztech/articles/01email.html (November 7, 2000).

McInnes, A. (1997). The agency of the InfoZone: Exploring the effects of a community network. *First Monday* [Online], 8 pp. Available: http://www.firstmonday.org (January 4, 2000).

McLuhan, M. (1964). *Understanding media*. New York: Signet Books.

Mitchell, W. J. (1995). *City of bits: Space, place, and the infobahn*. Cambridge, MA: The MIT Press.

Mohen, J., & Glidden, J. (2001). The case for Internet voting. *Communications of the ACM, 44* (1), 72–85.

Phillips, D. M., & Von Spakovsky, H. A. (2001). Gauging the risk of internet elections. *Communications of the ACM, 44* (1), 73–85.

Postman, N. (1985). *Amusing ourselves to death*. New York: Penguin Books.

Raney, R. F. (1999, August 3). From experts to novices, candidates try campaigning online. *The New York Times*, p. B10.

Rehg, W. (1996). Translator's Introduction. In J. Habermas, *Between facts and norms*, pp. x–xxxvii. Cambridge, MA: The MIT Press.

Rheingold, H. (1993). *The virtual community*. Reading, MA: Addison-Wesley Publishing Company.

Rogers, E. M. (1995). *Diffusion of innovations* (4th ed.). New York: The Free Press.

Rogers, E. M., & Shoemaker, F. (1973). *Communication of innovations*. New York: The Free Press.

Sakkas, L. (1993). Politics on the net. *Interpersonal Computing and Technology, 1* (2) [Online], 11 pp. Available: http://www.helsinki.fi/science/optek (January 8, 2001).

Schmitz, J. (1997). Structural relations, electronic media, and social change: The public electronic network and the homeless. In S. Jones, (Ed.), *Virtual culture* (pp. 80–81). Thousand Oaks, CA: Sage Publications.

Schuler, D. (2001). Computer professionals and the next culture of democracy. *Communications of the ACM, 44* (1), 52–57.

Spinello, R. (2000). *Cyberethics: Morality and law in cyberspace*. Boston: Jones and Bartlett Publishers.

Sunstein, C. R. (1996, August 18). Democracy isn't what you think. *The New York Times Book Review*, p. 29.

Tan, S. (1995). City on-line. *21•C scanning the Future, 4•1995*, pp. 32–35.

U.S. Department of Commerce. (1999). *Falling through the net* [Online]. Available: www.ntia.doc.gov/ntiahome/fttn99/contents.html (January 5, 2001).

Wayne, L. (2000, Auguat 19). Online coverage fell short of the hype. *The New York Times* [Online], 3 pp. Available: http://www10.nytimes.com/library/politics/camp/081900wh-dot.html (November 7, 2000).

Whillock, R. K. (1997). Cyber-politics: The online strategies of '96. *American Behavioral Scientist, 40* (8), 1208–1225.

Whittle, D. B. (1997). *Cyberspace: The human dimension*. New York: W.H. Freeman & Company.

Wilhelm, A. B. (2000). *Democracy in the digital age*. New York: Routledge.

15 Communicating in the Global Village

Chapter Overview

Writers have offered both utopian and dystopian views of the Internet's future. Utopian writers predict that the Internet will bring about a new era of human cooperation. Because the Internet bridges time and space, people will come together in a large global village. Dystopian writers are concerned about the increasing tribalization and social disconnectedness that could occur as a result of CMC. Due to the lack of face-to-face contact with others, people will become disconnected.

In business and professional contexts, computer technology is connecting people, information, and office automation systems into a new global information society. This global society could have both positive and negative implications for individual nations. The relationship between the Internet and society is explored in this chapter through the following global topics:

- The global village and globalization
- Medium theory
- The global marketplace
- English and the Internet
- The globalization of mass media
- Technophiles versus neo-Luddites
- Theories about the relationship between technology and society

Technological utopianism is the belief that technology makes possible the creation of an ideal world with improved lifestyles and workplaces. In this optimistic view, the Internet will help to bring people together into a new global harmony. Dystopian writers believe, on the other hand, that the Internet will separate individuals and disrupt geographic communities. Predictions and observations about technology attempt to explain the present and future impact it will have on individuals, society, and culture.

The Global Village

An early observer of the new technology, Marshall McLuhan, commented in *The Gutenberg Galaxy* (1962) that electronic mass media were collapsing space and time barriers to human communication enabling people to communicate on a global scale. He coined the term **global village** to describe this change. Today, the global village is used as a metaphor to describe the Internet and the Web. By allowing users from around the world to connect with each other, the Internet has globalized communication. Similarly, Web-connected computers enable people to link their Web sites together, even if the Web sites are located around the world.

In the previous chapter, the Internet was described as a democratic medium that brings people together. However, flaming and the other disruptive behaviors described in Chapter 13 can just as easily tear online groups apart. As a result, there are conflicting utopian and dystopian predictions for the future of the Internet.

Globalization

Global communication networks collapse time and space enabling people and organizations around the world to interact and work together. McLuhan speculated that global media would foster the development of a tribalized society in which individuals would interact within a larger group consciousness. McLuhan and Zingrone (1995) say, "Individual talents and perspectives don't have to shrivel within a retribalized society; they merely interact within a group consciousness that has the potential for releasing far more creativity than the old atomized culture" (p. 259). Similarly, Lévy (1997) contends that digital networks will support the emergence of a "collective intelligence," which he describes as a "universally distributed intelligence, constantly enhanced, coordinated in real time, and resulting in the effective mobilization of skills" (p. 13). Computer networking is the centralizing technology that will cause the development of this global intelligence because people use communication technologies to interact on a global scale.

Both Lévy and McLuhan suggest that by bridging time and space global communication networks could ultimately join people into a large collective. Underlying this concept is the idea that print media separated people into nation states and print technology helped to create the idea of individualism. Through the printing press, the different European languages were standardized, facilitating the establishment of nation states. Books printed in different languages caused people to begin to associate with language groups. Over time, people who would read and write in one language, such as French, began to realize that they were different from people who would read and write in a different language, such as German or English. Linguistic separation eventually led to the creation of national identity. In addition, reading could be done alone, and so reading became a singular rather than a group activity, thus reinforcing the notion of individualism. The printing press's influence on the formation of nation states and individualism is described in detail by Eisenstein (1980).

Electric and electronic media, in contrast, tend to bring people together into a larger group consciousness that is reminiscent of preliterate tribalized oral culture. In oral culture, human communication primarily depends on face-to-face interaction, and people living in oral cultures are interdependent because they have access to each other. According to McLuhan and Zingrone (1995): "Literate man is alienated, impoverished man; retribalized man can lead a far richer and more fulfilling life—not the life of a mindless drone but of the participant in a seamless Web of interdependence and harmony" (p 259). Interdependence can develop through CMC and global communication media as people work together and build relationships.

McLuhan (1964) used the metaphor of the human body to explain different types of media. For example, the book is an extension of the eye and clothing is an extension of the skin. Similarly, he argued that electric technology is an extension of the human nervous system. In 1964, he predicted that rapidly humans would

> approach the final phase of the extension of man—technological simulation of consciousness, when the creative process of knowing will be collectively and corporately extended to the whole of human society, much as we have already extended our senses and our nerves by the various media (p. 19).

By spanning time and space, the Internet and Web extend our nervous system through a global electronic network that connects people in a global embrace. **Globalization** is defined as the interdependence of countries on a worldwide level through the increasing volume of cross-border transactions in goods and services and through the widespread diffusion of technology. As international trade in goods and services grows, global financial transactions increase and a global marketplace emerges. Central to the formation of a global marketplace are mass media.

Mass media have been criticized for homogenizing global culture by disrupting national traditions. Mass media create global mass audiences that are targets for globalized consumer products, such as Pepsi, McDonald's, and the Gap. Around the world, people wear Gap jeans and eat McDonald's hamburgers as they sip Pepsi. Instead of homogenizing culture, the Web has been criticized for fragmenting it. The Web creates a chaotic marketplace of cultures that allows a greater degree of individualization across cultures. Rather than uniting the world into one large, homogeneous global village, the Internet exposes people to cultural diversity. Thus, globalization simultaneously brings people together into a large consumer culture and potentially exposes individuals to different cultures.

Internet Retribalization

Currently, there is concern that large numbers of Internet users will self-select into groups that share their own interests, attitudes, and beliefs. Individuals will choose their own digital neighborhoods and ignore the diversity offered by the Internet. Instead of a unified global village, Thimbleby (1998) argues that the Internet will create a "glocal" environment. A place in which "the local is global, and the global is local" (p. 9). Although the Internet allows people with similar interests to find each other, individuals can form their own segregated homogeneous group that is not exposed to diverse ideas.

Retribalization is a term used to describe the formation of separate Internet groups. For example, Mandel and Van der Leun (1996) argue that the Net is a tribal society. They state:

> In the Net, as in the world, people tend to gravitate to groups and associations that, as individuals, they perceive will be comfortable or in their interests. One can join and be a 'member' of very large organizations—the corporation, the ACLU, the NRA—but one becomes a 'part' of a group (p. 34).

Over time, online groups develop their own rituals and customs out of their shared history. The tribal nature of the Internet described by Mandel and Van der Leun depicts a situation in which people break apart into small tribes rather than unite into a larger, interdependent global village.

Moreover, Shenk (1997) has asserted that Internet society could become fragmented and result on increasing political polarization: "In 1994, the first major political survey of Internet politics revealed, not surprisingly, a virtual world in a state of hyper-fragmentation" (p. 75). Instead of meeting other people to discuss and debate issues of common social concern, members of online groups would gather to promote their own interests and reinforce their own points of view. People who disagree with the group would be excluded from the discussion. Thus, people will only hear one side of an argument and ignore or flame people who do not agree with them. As a result, online groups would reinforce the fragmentation of modern society instead of nurturing convergence. Instead of providing a democratic atmosphere in which citizens could discuss diverse perspectives, the Internet could highlight social differences. On a more personal level, Stoll (1995) is concerned that computer networks will isolate people from each another, rather than bring them together.

As previously discussed, flaming behavior and heated debates often promote intolerance and conflict. For example, Steinberg (1994) states:

> Because a newsgroup is a public space—inexpensively accessible by many people and controlled by no one—it takes only a few prolific users to pollute it with garbage. When adding your two cents costs nothing, neither ignorance of the subject nor lack of relevance seems to keep people from contributing. (p. 24)

Finding a balance between freedom of expression and disruptive discourse is difficult. If people only participate in groups and discussions that support their views, they may not hear all perspectives. People expressing diverse opinions contribute to interesting discussions on the Internet, and the openness of Internet communication has been an important aspect of the formation of Internet culture. But, as described in Chapter 13, if total freedom is allowed on the network, discussion groups can degenerate into uselessness. When this happens, important messages are buried beneath misleading and irrelevant ones.

Styles of online discourse, including flaming and writing skills, can also separate people. For example, substandard rhetorical abilities and social affiliations can prevent people from contributing to discussion groups, even though such groups are considered equal and democratic. According to Hert (1997), the Internet allows anyone to participate in a discussion, however; this is not what really happens. For instance, rhetorical skills and the prestige of publishing can influence online interactions in academic discussion groups. People who are published and have excellent written communication skills have a higher status in groups, and they sometimes discourage participation from others.

In contrast to the idea that the Internet will nurture democratic principles and greater tolerance toward others, messages distributed through the Internet often support the formation of small ideological groups that separate off from others. Technologically, the Internet is a decentralized method of communication, and it could be used to revitalize the democratic process. However, ideological differences, flaming behavior, and rhetorical skills can discourage equal online participation. Although the technology enables us to equally participate, human behavior often leads people to form small tribes rather than a large village.

The Internet as a Paradox

The Internet brings people together, but the way people use the Internet could tear them apart, a paradoxical idea. Individuals tend to gravitate toward others who share similar interests and ideologies. As they bridge time and space through global communications media, individuals could isolate themselves within smaller Internet communities. Logan (2000) observes a similar paradox in terms of physical workplaces and CMC. Telecommuting potentially promotes social isolation. People who telecommute have less social contact with other people, and so the Internet could increase social isolation. On the one hand, the Internet makes it easier for people to communicate on a global level and increases business correspondence. On the other, the Internet could decrease face-to-face encounters in the workplace and cause social isolation.

Will the Internet bring us together or separate us? That depends on how the technology develops and how people use it. Depending on the social context, technology can influence society in different ways. For example, the commercial forces behind the development of the Web are very different from the grassroots movement of Free-Nets. In the future, one of theses approaches could come to dominate the Internet, or they could find a way to coexist.

An Ecological View of the Internet

Viewing the Internet as an ecological system is one way to think about its possible utopian or dystopian future and how this could influence individuals, communities, societies, and culture. Because the Internet is still evolving, both academics and media critics have argued the need for critical examination. Based on his business experience, Davenport (1997) believes we need to understand the ecology of information. **Information ecology** examines how people create, distribute, understand, and use information. Currently, individuals live in an environment in which they encounter external, organizational, and personal information. Examining how people use information is one ecological approach to better understanding the Internet. A different ecological approach is to examine the Internet as a media environment. McLuhan was the first person to conceptualize media (books, radio, and television) as environments. The study of media environments examines a medium's structure, content, and impact on people. **Media environments** are complex message systems that can influence humans to engage in certain ways of thinking, feeling, and behaving because media can structure what we see and say. For instance, the textual nature of e-mail does not include visual and aural information. Consequently, the way people communicate through e-mail is different from the way they do in face-to-communication. In e-mail, people must focus on words rather than people. To compensate for the lack of visual and verbal information, emoticons were developed and oral characteristics were incorporated into writing styles. But people still behave differently in computer-mediated environments than they do in face-to-face ones. Frequently, messages are rude or they express extreme opinions, and e-mail messages are written in a different way than a traditional letters—they are often informal and conversational.

McLuhan's ideas about media environments were later expanded by Postman (1979) into the concept of media ecology. According to Postman (1970), "Media ecology tries to find out what roles media force us to play, how media structure what we are seeing, why media make us feel and act as we do" (p. 161) Every society has its own patterns of communication and information systems, and this media environment can influence social attitudes and concepts of knowledge. For instance, the introduction of computers influenced our attitudes about technology and its role in society and education: today, people often seek technological solutions to social problems and many schools have integrated computer skills into their curricula.

Medium Theory

Similar to an ecological approach to the analysis of media is **medium theory**, which Gladney (1996) describes as "a historical, cross-cultural approach that examines the particular characteristics of each medium, instead of the information that is conveyed in its content" (p. 111). For example, medium theorists would examine the Internet's characteristic of instantaneous global communication, which eliminates space and time constraints in the communication process. Medium theorists are interested in the ways in which information is stored, channeled, and displayed. For example, Meyrowitz (1985) argues that television's presence in the home offers the illusion of a face-to-face relationship. As a result, television creates a new type of intimacy between viewers and performers. Expanding this concept to the Internet, through CMC people can now develop intimate friendships with people they have never met in person. Consequently, CMC can influence social relationships and our attitudes about them. More important, Internet characteristics influence attitudes about global communication and the formation of a global society.

The Global Information Society

Two striking features of the Internet are internationalism and populism. The Internet's internationalism connects people across nations, it is indifferent to national boundaries. People are linked by common interests rather than nationality. As a result, the Internet contrasts sharply with civil societies united by political rule. For this reason, the Internet could potentially be politically subversive. Populism, the second Internet feature, refers to the fact that people have access to the Internet and want to connect to it. People from countries around the globe are becoming Internet users (Figure 15.1).

Global Marketplace

According to Goldsmith (1998), today's computer networks can create global connectedness, or "the opportunity to interact in a way that leads to the rapid and positive evolution of our species" (p. 102). Computer technology has been diffused all over the world through factory and office automation systems. These computerized infrastructures support the development of global corporations that no longer depend on a specific geographic location

FIGURE 15.1 Estimated Number of People Online

World Total	407.1 million
Africa	3.11 million
Asia/Pacific	104.88 million
Europe	113.14 million
Middle East	2.40 million
Canada & USA	167.12 million
Latin America	16.45 million

Source: Nua Internet Surveys.

to conduct business. In contrast to the concept of geographic nations, these corporations embrace virtual mobility and *transnationality*.

Computer networks have fostered the global dispersion of economic power and influence across nations. Schiller (1999) has pointed out that "by the mid 1990s, transnational companies generated some two-thirds of total world exports of goods and services" (p. 38). Transnational corporations have factories, production plants, and offices in several different countries around the world, both developed and undeveloped. Many of these companies reorganized their cross-border production activities with the aid of computer networks. To meet the needs of these global corporations, an improved transnational computer communications system developed with worldwide capabilities. Software development, database management, billing, accounting services, and subscription processing were moved from high-wage to low-wage countries. For instance, animation factories located in South Korea, Taiwan, and the Philippines create many cartoon programs such as *The Simpsons*, broadcast in the United States. To coordinate global business activities, English has been used as an international business language.

Is English a World Language?

English is the predominant language on the Internet and has gained some type of global business status. However, English is not the native language that most people in the world speak. There are three times as many native speakers of Chinese as native speakers of English. According to Wallraff (2000), "about 1,113 million people speak Chinese as their mother tongue, whereas about 372 million speak English" (p. 55). Many people using English on the Internet are second-language or foreign-language speakers, and although many people claim to speak English, there is a question about how well they actually know and understand the language. Often, people who speak English speak another language at least as well, if not better.

The Internet has been cited as an instrument for circulating English around the world; it is estimated that 80 percent of the information available on the Internet is written in English. However, as more non-English speakers gain access to the network, the use of other languages is growing. Spanish, Chinese, German, Portuguese, and many other languages are now thriving on the Web. As a result, search engines, such as Yahoo!, Excite, and Google are now offering their services in multiple languages. For example, Google (2000) says it offers the largest collection of Asian-language Web pages on the Internet. It has approximately 40 million Japanese Web pages, 24 million Chinese pages, and 10 million Korean pages. Google also supports Danish, Dutch, Finnish, French, German, Italian, Norwegian, Portuguese, Spanish, and Swedish.

Another factor influencing a shift away from using English as the dominant language for Internet communication is the development of translation programs. Translation programs, such as Alta Vista's *Babel Fish*, are available on the Internet. Information written in English can be cut and pasted into *Babel Fish* to be translated into a different language, or text written in French, Portuguese, Spanish, Italian, German, or Russian can be translated into English.

The introduction of a variety of languages to the Internet has led to predictions that the Web may soon resemble international television, where audiences expect to view sites in their own language. As the Web becomes more of a mass medium, its audience is changing. Originally, Internet users were highly educated and from English-speaking or multilingual upper-middle-class families. As a diversity of people are becoming connected to the network, more sites are using languages other than English because people prefer sites in their own language. For instance, language has been a deterrent to Internet growth in China because many Chinese are not adept at writing English. Consequently, the Chinese want to develop their own, indigenous Internet culture with Chinese-language sites.

In sum, the globalization of English does not mean that eventually everyone will be able to converse in English. Computers may help with basic translation problems, but people will still need to be able to cope with understanding other languages. Moreover, the introduction of a variety of languages on the Internet could end America's hegemony over Internet culture. Instead of becoming a homogeneous English-speaking mass media system, the Internet could become a series of glocal villages that use different languages. Consequently, native English speakers will still need to learn other languages.

Globalization and National Cultures

Although the Internet connects people on a global level, people can also use it to form small groups with diverse political agendas. For this reason, the Internet's lack of centralized control makes some governments reluctant to let their citizens have Internet access. Nations such as Singapore, China, and Saudi Arabia attempt to censor sites for political and religious reasons. Governmental concern about how people will use the Internet is well founded. Ralph Nader reported that, in the United States, "rather than be the passive subjects of surveillance, citizens are using the Internet and other networks to place the government and corporations under greater scrutiny and to organize on a wide range of issues" (cited in Long, 1994, p. 66). A key factor in Internet activism is the ability of citizens to easily communicate with each other; the decentralized structure of the Internet facilitates this process.

The Internet has been used by people in many nations to facilitate political communication. Long (1994) described how people in the war-torn city of Sarajevo, who where isolated without telephone or mail services, were able to send e-mail through a single phone line. "The makeshift e-mail system had been set up with the help of the Soros Foundation, whose founder, philanthropist and financier George Soros, believes fervently in making the world safe for open discussion and the free flow of information" (p. 55). Access to the Internet is instrumental to achieving Soros's goal, and by setting up the e-mail system, the Soros Foundation enabled the citizens of Sarajevo to communicate with the outside world.

In another project, the Soros Foundation has linked schools in Romania with high schools in California. According to the program's director, the Romanian students send their English homework to the Americans to be checked, and the Americans ask for help with math assignments. Programs such as this one suggest that the Internet could be a valuable tool for enabling people from diverse cultures to interact. By bringing people together from diverse cultures, it is argued, the Internet will teach people tolerance toward one another.

Although people can connect with others around the world, cultural differences can influence communication in cyberspace. Gattiker (2001) has made suggestions to help facilitate successful Internet communication (Figure 15.2). At present, English is the predominant language of the Internet. Sites written in other languages will often have a mirror site in English. However, many Internet participants are not native English speakers. Therefore, careful writing is key and humor should be used with caution. In the future, smaller Internet cultures may emerge that are influenced by different languages and national cultures.

FIGURE 15.2   Suggestions for Successful Global Communication on the Internet

---

To assure that one's message can be read with ease, and that messages are properly interpreted by global audiences, Gattiker reccommends considering the following:

(1) In addition to using a local language, all Internet information should also be available in English*;

(2) To avoid misunderstandings due to cultural, religious, or other differences, Internet communication should be carefully crafted. Colloquial writing is inappropriate. Humor and jokes should be avoided because what is humorous in one country may be negatively perceived in another;

(3) One must realize that English is not the first language for many people. Therefore, careful crafting of one's communication (e.g., words and expressions used) is necessary to enable people with a limited knowledge of English to understand the message;

(4) To maintain speedy communication, keep graphics and colors at a minimum. This will allow individuals with slow-speed modems and limited bandwidth Internet connections to easily access the information.

---

*Note: Not all experts in interface design agree with the idea that English should be the dominant language on the Internet. For example, Thimbleby (1998) states that English speakers are in the minority in the world. China outnumbers all English-speaking nations by 3 to 1. However, English is being used today as an international scientific and business language. For these reasons, having English versions of a site is useful.

Source: Adapted from Gattiker, 2001, p. 94.

Case Study: China and the Internet

As the information age comes to China, the government wants the country to become more technologically advanced and it wants to increase global commerce. At the same time, the Chinese government wants to carefully control the flow of information coming into the country through the Internet. For instance, the Chinese government has used firewall technology to prevent access to hundreds of Web sites that the government considers to be objectionable. Objectionable content includes pornographic sites, international news sources (CNN and The *New York Times*), and sites maintained by human rights groups. Although sites are blocked, Chinese citizens can still acquire censored information through foreign news services. For example, Chinese Internet users can send e-mail requests to receive a daily electronic summary of world news. Additionally, the Web enables Amnesty International to get information into China about Chinese human rights violations.

The number of Chinese Internet users is growing. According to Eckholm (1999), the official count of Internet users in China was 620,000 in 1997 and that number rose to 2.1 million by the end of 1998. This is a small number considering that China has a population of 1.2 billion people. As college students and young professionals become connected to the network, Internet usage is growing. Additionally, as Chinese-made PC clones and Internet services become available, more people can access the Internet from their homes. Currently, most Chinese Internet users go online at work or school, and a number of Internet cafes have opened in major cities, such as Beijing, to offer people access to e-mail and the Web.

Dissident Chinese exiles have flooded the country's e-mail addresses with newsletters that include items suppressed by the Chinese media. Many are stories about prodemocracy campaigns, worker dissatisfaction, and dissident arrests. One newsletter called *VIP Reference* distributes its messages to numerous Chinese e-mail accounts. To prevent the Chinese government from accusing recipients of the messages of subscribing to the newsletter, hundreds of thousands of Americans are also sent the messages. Moreover, the *VIP Reference* newsletter is sent from a different American address every day to make sure the Chinese government does not stop its distribution. Chinese authorities, however, sentenced a computer executive in Shanghai to a two-year prison sentence for providing *VIP Reference* with 30,000 Chinese e-mail addresses. When Chinese security agents suspect someone of distributing inappropriate messages, they will monitor the individual's e-mail, but although they can monitor certain individuals, they cannot monitor all of the hundreds of thousands of e-mail messages circulating through the Internet. Chinese Web designers must also strictly abide by the government's restrictions on Internet content and must avoid creating links to potentially objectionable Web sites. China is becoming a more open society, however, and the introduction of the Internet into Chinese culture could accelerate this process. Despite the attempts to censor information coming into the country, the decentralized nature of the network makes it next to impossible to stop the flow of unwanted messages in China.

Globalization and Mass Media

The decentralized nature of the Internet makes it very different from more traditional mass media, which distribute content created by the media industries. Global messages developed by the media industries are distributed through global media systems, such as CNN. CNN can distribute the same message throughout its worldwide television system. Prior to the 1990s, media systems were primarily national systems, but during the 1990s a global commercial media market emerged. According to McChesney (1999), "the rise of a global media market is encouraged by new digital and satellite technologies that make global markets both cost-effective and lucrative" (p. 78). Contributing to the trend toward media globalization was the formation of transnational corporations, the World Trade Organization (WTO), and the World Bank. All of these organizations helped to create a new form of global capitalism that uses global media to disseminate messages to global consumers.

In addition to financial interests, global media have an impact on media content, politics, and culture. Like the Internet, global media are influenced by the culture and interests of the United States. In some ways, global media could be considered an extension of the American system. At present, the United States exports more entertainment products than any other nation. McChesney (1999) reports that American media companies "have aggressively established numerous global editions of their channels to accommodate the new market" (pp. 80–81). Three of the most important transnational media corporations are Time Warner (now AOL Time Warner), Disney, and News Corporation. In terms of globalization, American cable companies have been called **cable colonialists** because they control the worldwide export of media content and attempt to establish digital satellite TV systems in regional and national markets around the world.

As the Internet becomes a broadband medium, it is increasingly taking on the characteristics of a mass medium rather than an interpersonal one. In the future, mass media trends could be extended to the Internet. For instance, a recent study of Dutch children's Internet usage revealed that they primarily used the Internet as a leisure medium to play games, watch video clips, and visit entertainment sites. Research on Americans however, shows people primarily use the Internet to maintain social relationships through e-mail. The Dutch study was conducted by Valkenburg and Soeters (2001), who examined children's home Internet usage. They found three primary motives for children's Internet use: affinity with computers, information seeking, and entertainment. Children must first of all enjoy sitting in front of a computer, the researchers found. Second, children use the Internet to find information about hobbies and homework assignments. Finally, they visit entertainment Web sites. The use of the Internet as an entertainment and leisure medium is similar to television usage.

Although transnational media corporations are attempting to establish operations in nations around the world, some countries want to protect their domestic media and culture industries. Some nations, including Norway, Denmark, Spain, Mexico, and South Korea, have established government subsidies to maintain their own domestic film industries. The British government proposed a voluntary levy on the revenues from domestic film theaters, which show predominantly Hollywood movies. These theater revenues could then be used to subsidize the British commercial film industry. However, the proposal was not passed by Parliament. Culture ministers from a variety of nations have been discussing how they can protect their own cultural identities in an increasingly American-influenced global media environment. Some nations, such as Singapore, edit and censor for broadcast media content created in the United States. Language usage, for instance, in the Singapore version of the *Sopranos* is vastly different from the American version because curse words have been edited out of the sound track. In such ways, individual nations can establish barriers that make it more difficult for global companies to broadcast their American-produced content.

Global media systems have been considered a form of **cultural imperialism**. Cultural imperialism takes place when a country dominates others through its media exports, including advertising messages, films, and television and radio programming. America's dominance in the entertainment industries made it difficult for other cultures to produce and distribute their own cultural products. Supporters of American popular culture argue that the universal popularity of American media products promotes a global media system that allows communication to cross national boundaries. American popular culture in addition challenges authority and outmoded traditions. Critics of American culture contend that cultural imperialism prevents the development of native cultures and has a negative impact on teenagers. Teenagers in other nations have rejected their own cultural music and dress. Instead, they want to wear American jeans and listen to American recording artists. Rock groups from other countries will even sing in English rather than use their native tongue.

A larger concern in the emerging global information economy is the fact that most of the world's population cannot afford the types of products advertised on global media. People who are constantly exposed to these media messages may want to own products that they can never afford, which could cause social unrest. Mass media portray a lifestyle of consumption that is very different from the lifestyles of people living in many other cultures.

Unequal Access in the Global Information Society

Media and information technologies are increasingly important social elements in the global information economy. A significant portion of our daily activities involves the use of media, including television, movies, cell phones, computers, and the Internet. In the workplace, computer technology plays a central role in personal and organizational communication. Today, most of the economic activity in the United States involves the production, processing, or distribution of information. As a result, information workers make up the majority of the workforce. The impact of a shift in the workplace from industrial workers to information workers has led to the formation of an **information society**.

The spread of the Internet and global communications media has expanded our information society into a *global information society*, a central feature of which is the use of computer networks. The United States was the first country to make the transition from an industrial to an information society. Other nations, including Singapore, France, and Japan, have also made the transition. Working in the new information economy requires people to develop effective communication skills. Estabrooks (1988) points out, "A computer-mediated society draws on the highest levels of human intellect, intelligence, and skills" (p. 180). New types of information products made available through the network require effective communication, reasoning, and analytical skills.

As described in the previous chapter, there is unequal access to the Internet in the United States, but the United States is only one of many nations facing the issue of unequal access to information technology. In his book *Disconnected: Haves and Have-nots in the Information Age* (1996), Wresch vividly illustrates the inequality of access to information around the world. He refers to some groups as "information exiles," people who are totally removed from the information infrastructure. "For example, no one expects Bushmen of the Kalahari to walk around with cellular phones" (p. 12). Wresch argues that access to new technology generally breaks down along traditional class lines. Upper-middle-class and wealthy American families form the bulk of the population that owns computers. Similarly, wealthier school districts tend to have more computers than poorer ones. According to Ratan (1995), "All this disparity comes to a head in this statistic: a working person who is able to use a computer earns 15% more than someone in a similar job who cannot." (p. 25). Thus, the widespread use of computers in an information society further paves the way for the growth of social stratification. Kroker (1993) describes these emerging social groups as the dispossessed, or the homeless on the information highway; the traditional working class who are forced to retrain; the technical specialists who are the "theorists of digital reality"; and the Commanders or presidents of corporations that lead the digital revolution. Unequal access to technology can lead to social stratification in the new global information society and technology skills are used to define these new social groupings.

Technophiles versus Neo-Luddities

Many academics, computer professionals, and social scientists have become increasingly critical of technology and its influence on individuals and culture. People who criticize computer-based technology are often called **neo-Luddites**. The term comes from the followers of Ned Ludlum, who were called Luddites. In the early nineteenth century, Ludlum and his group smashed machinery in England because they thought the machines would destroy their jobs and livelihoods. The Luddites were attempting to stop the use of new technology in textile manufacturing. Although the Luddites were unable to prevent industrial progress, they did give a name to people who resist and oppose technological innovation.

The rapid growth of computer technology and the Internet has led to an increase in resistance to technology and computers. Brook and Boal's *Resisting the Virtual Life* (1995) is a series of essays that are critical of the ways in which people use computers. Similarly, Stoll's *Silicon Snake Oil* (1995) describes some of the ways advanced technology is used for trivial purposes that seem absurd when thought about in depth.

Technophiles is a term coined by Postman (1993) to describe people who are in love with technology. Technophiles are so enthusiastic about the use of new technology that they often fail to weigh its pros and cons and costs and benefits. For technophiles, the search for a technological solution to a problem becomes more important than practical considerations. Technological problem solving becomes an end in itself, and larger social implications are often not examined. Graham (1999) refers to this as the **ideology of technology**, that is, the assumption that the most technologically advanced solutions are the best ones. This belief would lead to a world ruled by technological innovation, which Postman calls a **technopoly**.

There are two assumptions associated with a technopoly. First, that everything that came before a new technology is redundant and obsolete and therefore should be discarded. Consider this idea in terms of software upgrades. Built into the software upgrade cycle is the concept of obsolescence and the constant replacement of old versions of programs with newer ones. Second, individuals and countries that want to prosper must invest in high technology. This second assumption explains why governments, such as those of the United States and China, want to provide Internet access and establish computer literacy programs.

However, technology does not always fulfill optimistic predictions of success. A classic example of an unrealized prediction for computer technology is the paperless office. In the late 1960s, people began to predict that the computer would create an office environment in which paper was no longer used. Making paper copies of documents would become a primitive use of technology. In fact, the copy giant Xerox was so concerned about this idea that it set up a research and development site called the Xerox Palo Alto Research Center (PARC) to create computer-based office technologies. PARC scientists developed graphical interfaces, computer networks, and the laser printer. Thirty years later, our office recycling bins are overflowing with copies of memos, letters, and reports made on laser printers. Instead of eliminating paper, network computer systems have actually increased its use. Often, technology will have the opposite effect to what people predict.

Theories about Technology and Society Relationships

Scholars, social scientists, and journalists try to understand and predict the impact that a new technology will have on individuals and culture. Over the years, several theories have been proposed to explain the relationship between technological development and social change. Williams (1974) placed these theories into two large categories: **technological determinism** and **social determinism**. Chandler (1995) describes four main positions on the relationship between technology and society: extreme technological determinism, weak or soft determinism, sociocultural determinism, and **voluntarism**. Thus, Chandler breaks technological determinism into two categories and adds a third, called voluntarism, which argues that people voluntarily use technology (Figure 15.3). Recently, several new theories have emerged to explain technology and society relationships, including technological realism and social constructionism.

Technological Determinism

Technological determinism is a theory that argues the characteristics inherent in a new technology govern the direction of its development and set the conditions for social change. Scholars associated with the technological determinism perspective include Marshall McLuhan (1962; 1964) and Elizabeth Eisenstein (1980). For example, McLuhan's notion of a global village is based on characteristics inherent to electric media, including the elimination of time and space barriers in the communication process. The ability to eliminate space in the communication process will create a new global sense of communication that is reminiscent of older oral traditions because people will become more dependent on and involved with each other. Thus, the characteristic of eliminating space constraints will cause social change.

Technological determinism is a popular and widely accepted view of the relationship between technology and society. According to this view, as new technologies are discovered they set the conditions for social change and progress. A cause-and-effect relationship

---

FIGURE 15.3   Four Main Viewpoints Toward Technological Determinism

---

1. *Extreme* (also called "strong" or "hard") *technological determinists* present technology as the primary condition for widespread societal or behavioral changes. Hard determinists insist that communication technology will radically transform society and the ways people think. Jacques Ellul (1964) is an example of an extreme determinist.

2. *Weak* (or "soft") *technological determinists* argue that technology is a key factor (that may facilitate such changes in society or behavior. Soft determinists acknowledge that social factors also influence the use and adoption of a new technology. Neil Postman (1985) is an example of a soft determinist.

Views in opposition to Technological Determinism

3. *Sociocultural determinists* contend that technology development is entirely subordinate to its use in particular sociopolitical, historical, and culturally specific contexts. This is is a view shared by many modern sociologists.

4. *Voluntarists* emphasize the idea that individuals have control over the tools that they choose to use. This stance is often taken by technology journalists and computer industry leaders.

Source: Adapted from Chandler, 1996.

is established between the technology and the effect it has on society. Chandler (1995) states:

> Technological determinists interpret technology in general and communications technologies in particular as the basis of society in the past, present and even the future. They say that technologies such as writing or print or television or the computer "changed society." In its most extreme form, the entire form of society is seen as being determined by technology: new technologies transform society at every level, including institutions, social interaction and individuals. At the least a wide range of social and cultural phenomena are seen as shaped by technology. "Human factors" and social arrangements are seen as secondary (p. 4).

A major criticism of technological determinism is the fact that it reduces an entire complex social system to the effects of technology without considering other social factors. Technological determinists often see technology as the major cause of social change, which can be considered technocentrism. **Technocentrism** is a perspective that accounts for almost every social change in terms of technology. The idea is associated with the notion that humans are first and foremost tool makers and tool users.

Some scholars associated with the technological deterministic perspective incorporate social conditions into their analysis. These scholars are referred to as soft or weak determinists. For example, Postman's critique of television in American culture examines both the characteristics of the medium and the capitalist environment of American society. Both the medium and the culture contribute to the use of television primarily as a form of entertainment in the United States. **Soft determinists** argue that the presence of a communication technology is an enabling or facilitating factor contributing to potential opportunities that may or may not be adopted by a particular culture. Instead of focusing on technological characteristics, social determinists see causal relationships between social needs and technological invention.

Social Determinism

Social determinists view technological developments as *symptoms* of some type of other social change. According to Williams (1974), this perspective considers technological development to be "a by-product of a social process that is otherwise determined" (p. 13). For example, Tim Berners-Lee originally developed the World Wide Web technology to solve a social problem. Physicists and other academics were having a problem sharing files and information through the Internet. In order to share a file, computer users had to have the same software programs and information had to be stored in compatible file formats. These conditions made it difficult for academics to easily share resources. To solve this problem, Berners-Lee developed a universal system that would enable computer users to read files on any type of computer; he called it the World Wide Web.

The creation of a universal system that solved the social problem of incompatible files and documents is an example of how technology was used to meet a social need. In contrast to technological determinists who view technology as being the cause of social change, social determinists identify social problems that technology was developed to solve. Both social and technological determinists view the relationship between technology and society as a linear one of cause and effect.

Technological Realism

Many sociological approaches to technology fall into the extreme categories of technological or social determinism. Technological determinists generally overlook the social contexts in which technology is introduced. Conversely, social determinists claim technological advancement is the result of social or cultural forces. To avoid these extreme positions, Schroeder (1997) argues for "a realistic viewpoint which takes into account both the growth of scientific knowledge and the material make-up of technological artifacts, on the one hand, and the social settings in which these become embedded, on the other" (p. 98). The realistic perspective asks questions such as: Where do the advances in technology come from? What are the changing relationships between technological artifacts and social life? Realists examine the changing relationships between technology and social life and how they influence each other.

Technological realism is a philosophy that argues technology is a powerful agent for social change and progress. Unlike technological determinists, realists believe that people can control and direct the ways in which technology is used. Technological realists have a utopian view about the human spirit; they argue that social values will encourage people to use technology wisely. **Technological neutralism** similarly supports a utopian view of technology and society relationships, but in contrast to technological realists, neutralists consider technology to be neutral and free of bias. They argue that technology does not promote one type of behavior over another. Both technological realists and neutralists place human agency at the center of technological change. Instead of a cause-and-effect relationship between technology and social change, the ways in which technology is adopted by a society are directed by people.

Social Constructionism

Society and technology studies conducted by historians, anthropologists, sociologists, and communication scholars suggest that social change is too complex and subtle to be explained solely in terms of technology. Chandler (1995) says, "Technology is one of a number of mediating factors in human behaviour and social change, which both acts on and is acted on by other phenomena" (p. 36).

To counter the technocentrism associated with deterministic theories, a new approach to understanding the relationship between technology and society is emerging, called social constructionism. Edwards's (1996) research on the relationship between the Cold War and the development of computers in the United States used a constructionist model. He maintained that the history of computers needs to be examined in terms of their relationship to the metaphors utilized in Cold War science, politics, and culture. It is only through an examination of the relationship between technological development and culture that the historical development of computers could be fully understood.

Although some authors group social constructionism into the same category as social determinism, there is a difference between them. Similar to technological determinism, social determinism views technology and society as having a linear cause-and-effect relationship. In contrast, social constructionism views technology and its development as a dynamic system rather than a linear process. Tonkiss (1998) points out, "social constructionist perspectives argue that the forms in which we gather, record and interpret knowledge about social life have important consequences for the ways that we define and understand social structures, social groups and social problems" (p. 59). Applying a constructionist approach to their research, Berg and Lie (1995) state; "Several of our studies concluded that changing technologies initiate a period of instability and provide *possibilities* for social change, but we also saw that desirable changes had to be initiated by human action" (p. 337). In addition to studying the interactions between technology and culture, social constructionism also gives human agency a central role in understanding the relationship between technology and society.

Social constructionism examines technology from historical, intellectual, contextual and cultural perspectives and it interacts with these perspectives. Technological change is viewed as a matter of politically significant choices, and the technological metaphor is a fundamental element of culture and politics. Social constructionists ask the following questions: How do people know things about technology? How is knowledge about technology influenced by social contexts? What business, organizational, and political arrangements are formed by technology? What procedures become associated with different technological ideas and artifacts? How do individuals and groups assign meaning to technology? By exploring these types of questions, social constructionists attempt to more fully understand the relationship between technology and society.

Summary

Utopian and dystopian views about the future of the Internet describe two very different future scenarios. Utopians view the Internet as a medium that will create a new global village and a technology that will bring people together. In contrast, dystopians argue that the Internet will separate people into their own small tribes and physically isolate people in the workplace.

At present, the widespread use of computer networks is helping to create a new global information society using global media systems. Global media have been criticized for imposing American media products on other nations. Moreover, the widespread use of English on the Internet has led some people to believe that it is now an international language. However, as nations such as China connect to the Internet, Internet communication is becoming increasingly multilingual. The widespread impact of computer-based technologies on society and culture has caused some people, often referred to as neo-Luddites, to become critical of new technology.

A number of theories have been proposed to explain the relationship between technology and society. These theories were originally categorized as technological determinism and social determinism. However, the widespread changes brought about by the use of computer technology have caused scholars to propose new theories about technology and society relationships. These new theories include technological realism and social constructionism.

TERMS

Cable colonialists are global cable companies that attempt to control the worldwide export of media content and establish digital satellite TV systems in regional and national markets around the world.

Cultural imperialism occurs when a country dominates another nation through their media exports, including advertising messages, films, and television and radio programming.

Global village is a term coined in the 1960s by Marshall McLuhan, today it is used as a metaphor to describe the Internet and World Wide Web.

Globalization is defined as the interdependence of countries on a worldwide level through the exchange of cross-border transactions in goods and services and the use of global media networks.

The ideology of technology assumes that the most technologically advanced solutions to social problems are the best ones.

Information ecology examines how people create, distribute, understand, and use information.

An information society is a society in which the majority of the workers produces, processes, or distributes information.

Media environments are complex message systems that can influence humans to engage in certain ways of thinking, feeling, and behaving because media can structure what we see and say. The study of media as environments is called media ecology.

Medium theory is an historical, cross-cultural approach that examines the particular characteristics of each medium, instead of the information that is conveyed in its content.

Neo-Luddite is a term used to refer to people who do not like to use technology and who criticize it.

Retribalization is a term used to describe the formation of separate Internet groups.

Social constructionism examines technology from historical, intellectual, contextual, and cultural perspectives and how it interacts with these perspectives.

Social determinism is a theory that views technological developments as being caused by some type of social change or social need.

Soft determinists argue that the presence of a communication technology is an enabling factor that contributes to potential opportunities that may or may not be adopted by a particular culture.

Technocentrism is a perspective that accounts for almost every social change in terms of technology.

Technological determinism is a theory that argues the characteristics inherent in a new technology govern the direction of its development and set the conditions for the social change that ensues.

Technological neutralism considers technology to be neutral and free of bias. Technology does not promote one type of behavior over another.

Technological realism is a philosophy that argues technology is a powerful agent for change and progress.

Technophiles is a term coined by Neil Postman to describe people who are in love with technology.

Technopoly is a society ruled by technological innovation.

Voluntarism is a view that argues people voluntarily use technology, and technology itself is neutral.

WEB SITES

Daniel Chandler: http://users.aber.ac.uk/media/Documents/techdet.hml
Marshall McLuhan
http://www.digitallantern.net/mcluhan/
http://www.mcluhan.utoronto.ca/
Technological Determinism: http://www.december.com/cmc/mag/1996/feb/chandler.html
Global English: http://www.theatlantic.com/globalenglish
The Once and Future Web
http://www.nlm.nih.gov/onceandfutureweb

EXERCISES

1. There is a debate over whether the Internet will bring people together only to tear them apart. What do you think? Which side of the debate are you on and why?

2. Describe the media environment in which you live.

3. Examine how the introduction of computers into American society have influenced our attitudes about technology. Try to imagine the United States before and after computers. How did things change?

4. Discuss what role you think the English language should play on the Internet. Should it be the primary language of the network? Why or why not?

5. Using examples from this book and your own research about the Internet, construct an argument for the view of the relationship between technology and society you think is the most accurate.

BIBLIOGRAPHY

Barnes, S. B. (2000, December). Bridging the Differences between Social Theory and Technological Invention. *New Media & Society, Vol. 2 No. 3*, pp. 353–372.

Barnes, S., & Strate, L. (1996). The educational implications of the computer: A media ecology critique. *The New Jersey Journal of Communication, 4* (2), 180–208.

Berg, A. J., & Lie, M. (1995). Feminism and constructivism: Do artifacts have a gender? *Science, Technology & Human Values, 20* (3), 331–51.

Bijker, W. E., Hughes, T. P., & Pinch, T. (1987). *The social construction of technological systems*. Cambridge, MA: The MIT Press.

Brook, J., & Boals, I. (1995). *Resisting the virtual life*. San Francisco: City Lights.

Chandler, D. (1995). Technological or media determinism [Online], 41 pp. Available: http://www.aber .ac.uk/~dgc/tecdet.html (January 24, 2000).

Chandler, D. (1996, February 1). Engagement with media: Shaping and being shaped. *CMC Magazine* [Online], 4 pp. (January 24, 2000).

Davenport, T. H. (1997). *Information ecology: Mastering the information and knowledge environment*. New York: Oxford University Press.

Eastabrook, S. M. (1988). *Programmed capitalism: A computer-mediated global society*. Armonk, NY: M.E. Sharpe, Inc.

Eckholm, E. (1999, February 10). In China, the Internet is double-edged. *The New York Times* [Online] 4 pp. Available: http://www.nytimes.com (archived) (Sept. 25, 2000).

Edwards, P. N. (1996). *The closed world: Computers and the politics of discourse in cold war America*. Cambridge, MA: The MIT Press.

Eisenstein, E. L. (1980). *The printing press as an agent of change*. Cambridge, UK: Cambridge University Press.

Ellul, J. (1964). *The technological society*. New York: Vintage.

Gattiker, U. E. (2001). *The Internet as a diverse community*. Mahwah, NJ: Lawrence Erlbaum Associates.

Gladney, G. A. (1996). Some enduring issues of cyberspace technology: A medium theory. *The New Jersey Journal of Communication, 4* (2), 110–126.

Goldsmith, M. (1998). Global communications and communities of choice. In F. Google Inc. (2000). *Google launches new Japanese, Chinese, and Korean search services* [Online], 1 p. Available: http://www.google.com/newslink.html (September 25, 2000).

Graham, G. (1999). *The Internet: A philosophical inquiry*. London: Routledge.

Hert, P. (1997). Social dynamics of an on-line scholarly debate. *The Information Society, Vol. 13, No. 4.*, pp. 329–360.

Hesselbein, M., Goldsmith, R., Beckhard, R. F., B. Schubert (Eds.) (1998) *The community of the future* (pp. 101–114). San Francisco: Jossey-Bass Publishers.

Kroker, A. (1993). Codes of privilege. *Mondo 2000, Issue # 11*, pp. 60–67.

Lévy, P. (1997). *Collective intelligence: Mankind's emerging world in cyberspace* (R. Bononno, Trans.). New York: Plenum Press.

Logan, R. K. (2000). *The sixth language*. Toronto: Stoddart.

Lohr, S. (2000, Jan. 9). Welcome to the Internet, the first global colony. *The New York Times*, p. WK 1, 4.

Long, M. (1994, December). We are the world. *Netguide*, pp. 55–65.

Mandel, T., & Van der Luen, G. (1996). *Rules of the net: Online operating instructions for human beings*. New York: Hyperion.

Marriott, M. (1998, June 18). As more non-English speakers log on, many languages thrive. *The New York Times* [Online], 6 pp. Available: http://www.nytimes.com (archived) (Sept. 25, 2000).

McChesney, R. W. (1999). *Rich media poor democracy: Communication politics in dubious times*. Chicago, IL: University of Illinois Press.

McLuhan, E., & Zingrone, F. (1995). *Essential McLuhan*. New York: Basic Books.

McLuhan, M. (1962). *The Gutenberg Galaxy*. New York: Mentor.

Meyrowitz, J. (1985). *No sense of place*. New York: Oxford University Press.

Nua Internet Surveys (2000). How many online? [Online], 1 p. Available: http://www.nau.ie/surveys/how_many_online/index.html (January 4, 2001).

Postman, N. (1970). The reformed English curriculum. In A. C. Eurich (Ed.), *High school 1980: The shape of the future in American secondary education* (pp. 160–168). New York: Pitman.

Postman, N. (1979). *Teaching as a conserving activity*. New York: Dell Publishing.

Postman, N. (1985). *Amusing ourselves to death*. New York: Penguin Books.

Postman, N. (1993). *Technopoly: The surrender of culture to technology*. New York: Vintage Books.

Ratan, S. (1995, Spring). A new digital divide between haves and have nots? *Time*, special edition pp. 25–26.

Schiller, D. (1999). *Digital capitalism: Networking the global market system*. Cambridge, MA: The MIT Press.

Schroeder, R. (1997). Virtual worlds and the social realities of cyberspace. In B. D. Loader, ed., *The governance of cyberspace*, pp. 97–107. London: Routledge.

Shenk, D. (1997). *Data smog: Surviving the information glut*. San Francisco: Harper Edge.

Steinberg, S. (1999, July). Travels on the net. *Technology Review*, pp. 21–31.

Stoll, C. (1995). *Silicon snake oil*. New York: Doubleday.

Thimbleby, H. (1998). Personal boundaries/global stage. *First Monday, Issue 3, 3* [Online], 23 pp. Available: http://www.firstmonday.dk/issues/issue3_3/timb (Nov. 22, 2001).

Tonkiss, F. (1998). The history of the social survey. In C. Seale (Ed.), *Researching society and culture* (pp. 58–71). London: Sage Publications.

Vacker, B. (2000). Global village or world bazaar? In A. B. Albarran & D. H. Goff (Eds.), *Understanding the Web: Social, political, and economic dimentions of the Internet*. Ames, IA: Iowa State University Press.

Valkenburg, P. M., & Soeters, K. E. (2001). Children's positive and negative experiences with the Internet. *Communication Research, 28* (5), 652–675.

Wallraff, B. (2000, November). What global language? *The Atlantic Monthly*, pp. 52–66.

Williams, R. (1974). *Television: Technology and cultural form*. New York: Schocken Books.

Wresch, W. (1996). *Disconnected: Haves and have-nots in the information age*. New Brunswick, NJ: Rutgers University Press.

INDEX